AF573796

NORMAN PARKINSON
LIFEWORK

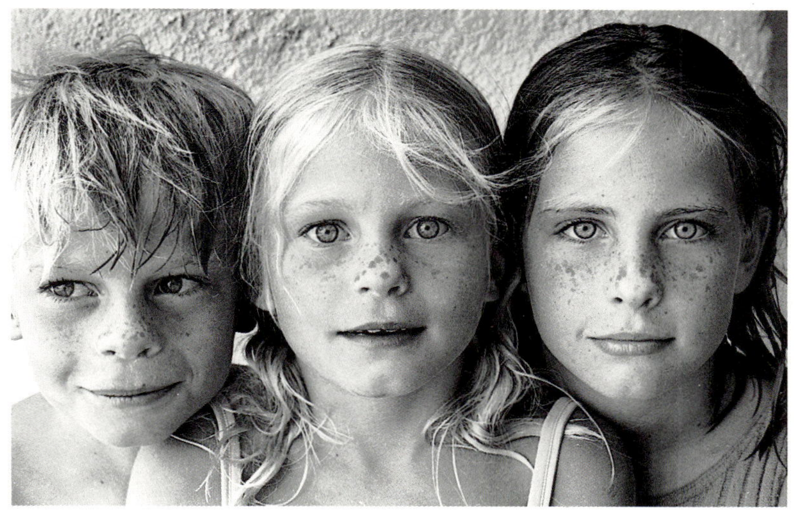

ABOVE *Loel, Victoria and Alex, children of Mrs Patrick Guinness, 1967*
FRONTISPIECE *Tribute to William Henry Fox Talbot: Ingrid Boulting at Lacock Abbey, 1970*

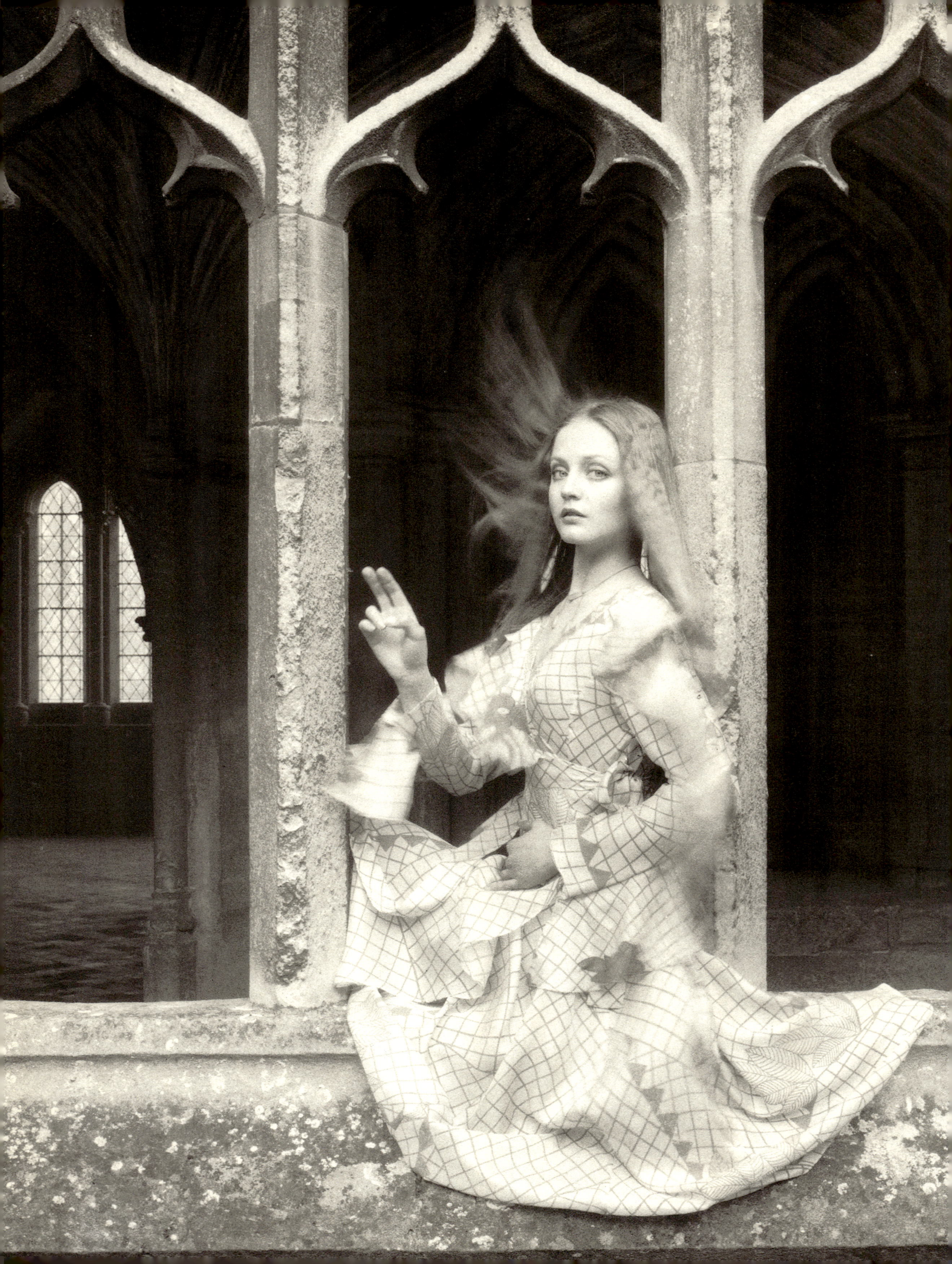

NORMAN PARKINSON

LIFEWORK

WEIDENFELD AND NICOLSON
LONDON

It is customary for each and every book to be dedicated to some person or persons that the reader would seldom have the chance to meet – 'To Mary and Henry', 'To Joan and Ned', etc. etc. – rather like the signatures upon those puzzling Christmas cards that carry no surname which promote hours of bewildering conjecture far into the New Year. My dedication and thanks go to living and breathing people who are easy to identify.

To the proprietors of all the *Vogues*. My thanks to them for hiring me once upon a time and guiding me in the direction of memorable photographs and agreeing to have some included here, and to Diana Edkins, Curator of their archives for her kind co-operation.

To Frank Zachary, Editor of *Town and Country*. Though neither of us is chicken in the ruffled world of the stylish magazine, with his warm unerring taste and my patient camera, we have together hatched some colourful eggs that may be remembered well after we are forgotten.

To Robert Pascall, Chuck Zuretti, Steve MacMillan, Martin Seymour and Nick Read who have separately and together helped me with most of the pictures in this book, sharing understanding and tolerance of my obsession for work.

To Gene Nocon, best black and white printer anywhere, who has invented a brilliant darkroom timer with which I hope he makes his fortune. To Ken Pratt, his apprentice printer who did all the black and white prints for this book. To Nick Paulo, colour processor *nulli secundus*. And to 3M who printed the colour photographs for my 1981 show.

To Terence Pepper of the National Portrait Gallery photographic unit who can sniff out a negative and date it like a truffle hound. If ever my archives are in order, it will be Pepper who has done it.

To Joan Hafey of Young Rubicam in New York who managed to track down the early Hunt's Catsup advertisement.

To Mark Boxer who has put this book together with consummate patience. It has been a most pleasurable revisitation of his talents upon my images, for we first met during the golden years of Jocelyn Stevens' *Queen* magazine when, I believe, we put the glossy magazine trade on its ear. To Tristram Holland who pruned and clarified my halting anecdotes, giving them the respect that I am not convinced they deserved.

To Brooke Astor, my new-found New York friend, with whom I have spent so little time that we have only started the long walk backwards through many friends and unforgettable occasions. But we will get there in the end at the beginning.

And of course, to my wife Wenda, so well included here, for accepting days and weeks alone while I chased the elusive negative.

Finally to the positive, to two inseparable long remembered friends, Zuggie and Crump, who were together before the tick of time.

N.P.

First published in Great Britain by
George Weidenfeld and Nicolson Limited
91 Clapham High Street
London SW4 7TA

Art Director: Mark Boxer
Designer: Behram Kapadia

ISBN 0 297 78212 6

Filmset by Keyspools Ltd
Colour separations by Newsele Litho Ltd
Printed and bound in Italy by L.E.G.O., Vicenza

CONTENTS

CHRONOLOGY

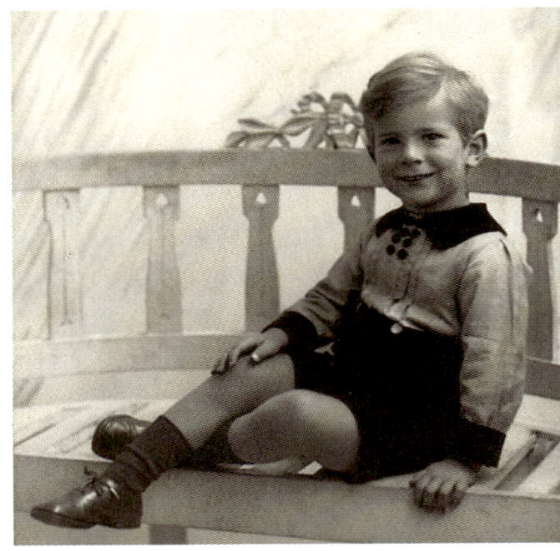

ABOVE *The author aged six. Photograph by a Putney High Street studio photographer*

BELOW *Photographing model Pamela Minchin in his Dover Street studio, 1935. Photograph by Nancy Sandys-Walker, his secretary*

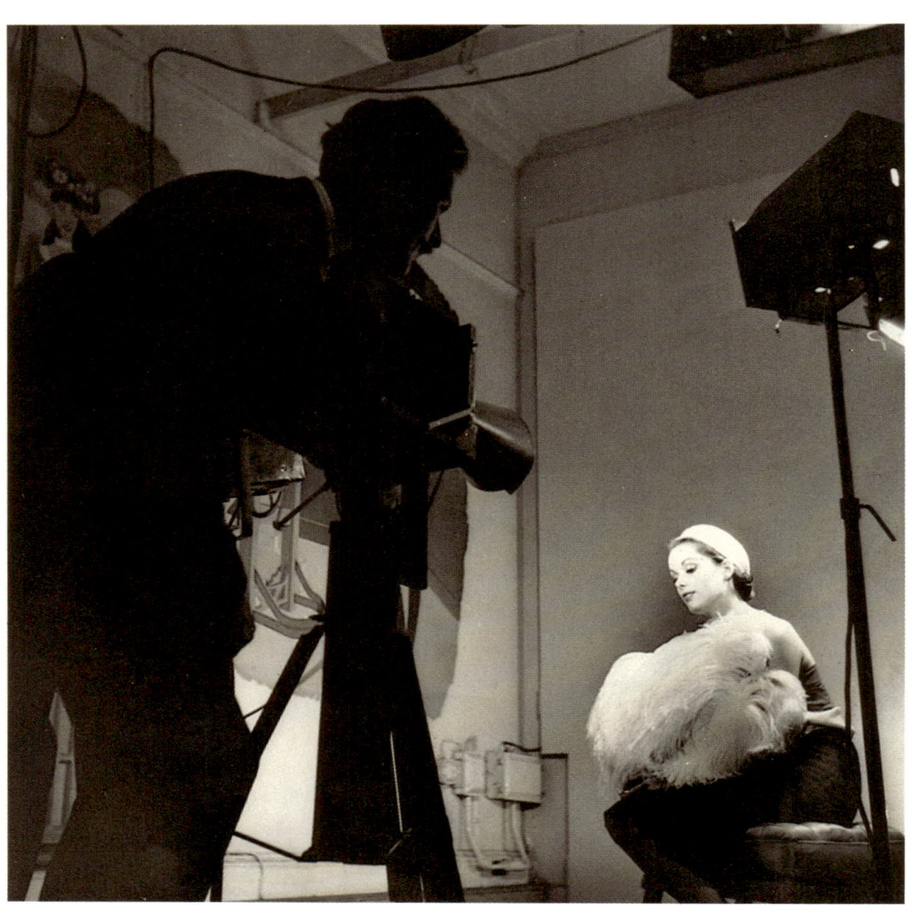

1913 Ronald William Parkinson Smith born on 21 April in Roehampton, the second of three children to William James Parkinson Smith, a barrister, and Louie (née Cobley) who was half-Italian and a direct descendant of Luigi Lablache, the famous basso profundo and music teacher to Queen Victoria.

Evacuated to countryside during the war and spent later childhood in Putney, London.

1927–31 Educated at Westminster School where his strongest subject was art. Encouraged by school art master, H.S. Williamson, who was well known as a painter and a poster artist. Won Henry Luce school art prize. Awarded his pink (colours) for rowing.

1931–3 Apprenticed to a firm of Court photographers, Speaight & Son of Bond Street, run by Richard Neville Speaight whose autobiography, *Memoirs of a Court Photographer*, had been published in 1926. Though somewhat past its heyday, this well-established firm still attracted a cross-section of members of the upper reaches of British Society and minor European royalty. In 1931 Speaights were honoured to take the first official photographs of the second daughter of the Duke and Duchess of York, Princess Margaret Rose. Parkinson focussed the cumbersome studio camera for Richard Speaight to operate through the cable pressure release, and assisted Mr Smart in the darkroom.

1934 After two years of his three-year apprenticeship, Ronald Parkinson with Norman Kibblewhite, another ex-pupil of Speaight's, set up the Norman Parkinson portrait studio at 1, Dover Street, off Piccadilly and near the Ritz. At first the studio specialized in portraits, staying open until 2 am on court nights to photograph a succession of debutantes and their mothers.

1935 15–23 October. First one-man exhibition, opened by the American-born Duchess of Leinster, included portraits of Noël Coward, Vivien Leigh and the Paget twins.

Recruited by P. Joyce Reynolds, Editor of British *Harper's Bazaar*, to take editorial photographs each month for the magazine, working on location and out of doors. Close collaboration with Alan Y. McPeake, the Art Editor whose creative layouts emphasized Parkinson's avowed aim of 'taking moving pictures with a still camera'. Fashion features taken on location in Edinburgh, in the Isle of Wight and in Le Touquet. Commissions included portraits of Joseph Kennedy and his family, then resident in London, and Charles James, the dress designer, photo essays on the Sitwells in their Chelsea home, and surrealist photographs of Edward James, patron of Magritte and Dali.

First magazine cover photograph, a combination with Erté artwork, appears on October *Harper's Bazaar*.

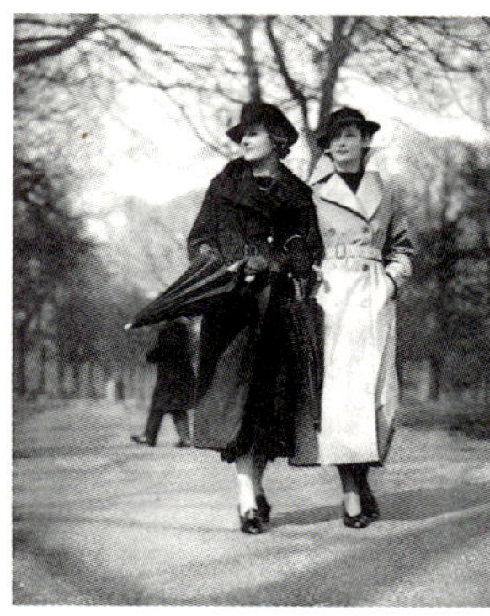

First outdoor fashion photograph, April 1935

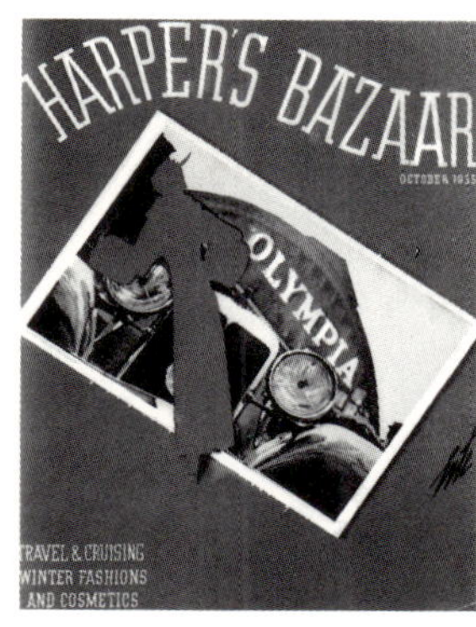

First magazine cover, art work by Erté, 1935

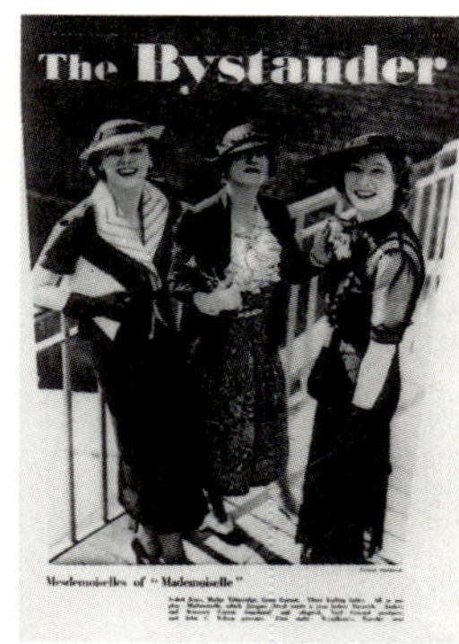

Actresses Isabel Jeans, Madge Titheradge and Greer Garson, 1936

BELOW *Reportage montage for The Sketch, 1936*

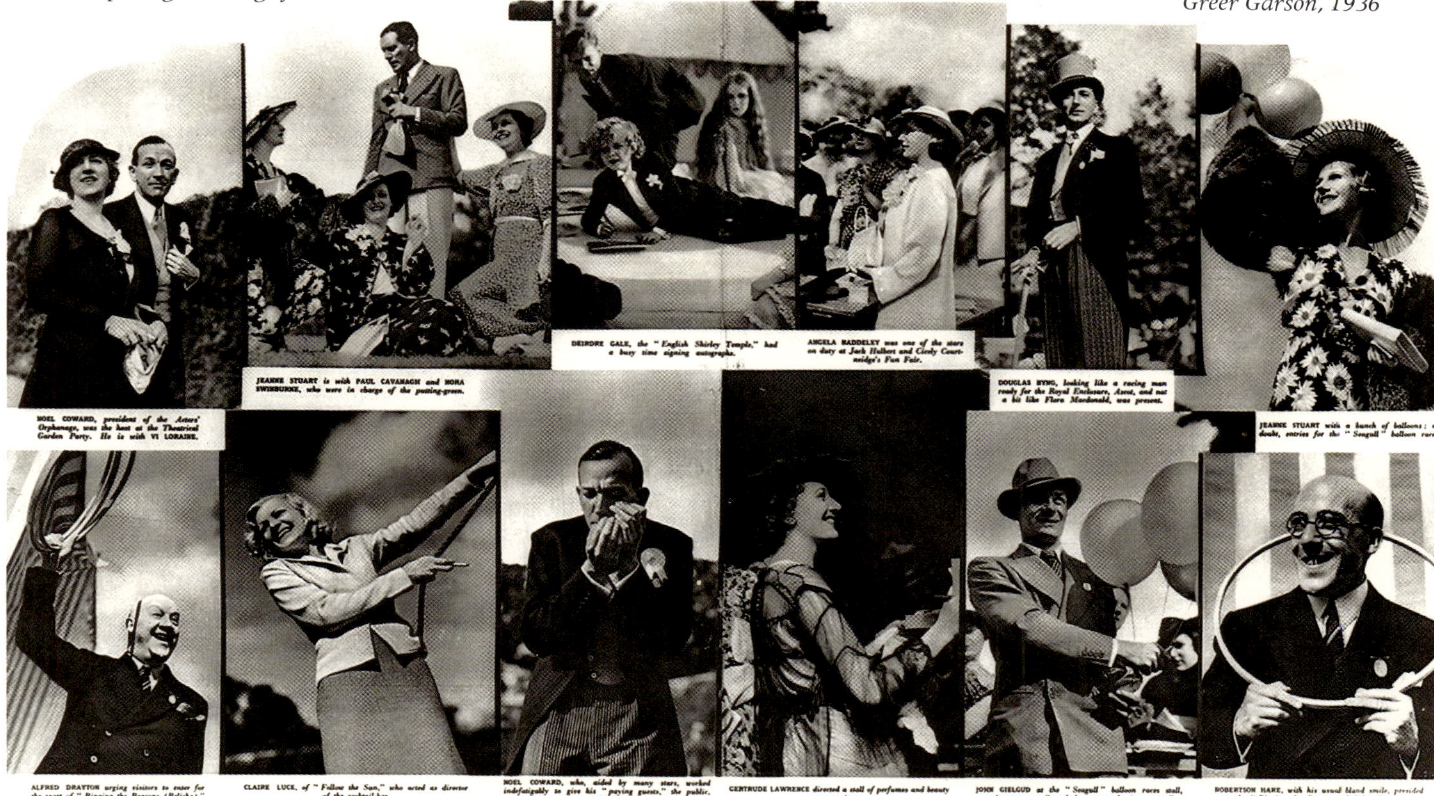

NOEL COWARD, *president of the Actors' Orphanage, was the host at the Theatrical Garden Party. He is with* VI LORAINE.

JEANNE STUART *is with* PAUL CAVANAGH *and* NORA SWINBURNE, *who were in charge of the putting-green.*

DEIRDRE GALE, *the "English Shirley Temple," had a busy time signing autographs.*

ANGELA BADDELEY *was one of the stars on duty at Jack Hulbert and Cicely Courtneidge's Fun Fair.*

DOUGLAS BYNG, *looking like a racing man ready for the Royal Enclosure, Ascot, and not a bit like Flora Macdonald, was present.*

JEANNE STUART *with a bunch of balloons; n... doubt, entries for the "Seagull" balloon rac...*

ALFRED DRAYTON *urging visitors to enter for the sport of "Ringing the Beacons (Belisha)."*

CLAIRE LUCE, *of "Follow the Sun," who acted as director of the cocktail-bar.*

NOEL COWARD, *who, aided by many stars, worked indefatigably to give his "paying guests," the public, a grand time, was snapped lighting a well-earned "fag."*

GERTRUDE LAWRENCE *directed a stall of perfumes and beauty preparations.*

JOHN GIELGUD *at the "Seagull" balloon races stall, urging guests to "send them up and win a prize."*

ROBERTSON HARE, *with his usual bland smile, presided at the "Ringing the Beacons (Belisha)" sports.*

1935–40 As well as monthly commissions for *Harper's Bazaar*, Parkinson contributes a large number of portraits and reportage work to the *Bystander*, a society weekly with a high current affairs bias. Assignments include coverage of tennis tournaments, theatrical garden parties and a two-season coverage of Swiss ski resorts.

1937 Follows Edward, Prince of Wales, to the depressed Welsh mining areas, taking a compassionate series of portraits of the unemployed miners and their families.

Collaborates with Francis Brugière, the avant-garde photographer who was designing a photo-mural for the British Pavilion at the Paris Exposition Universelle, by travelling around Britain taking photographs of traditional

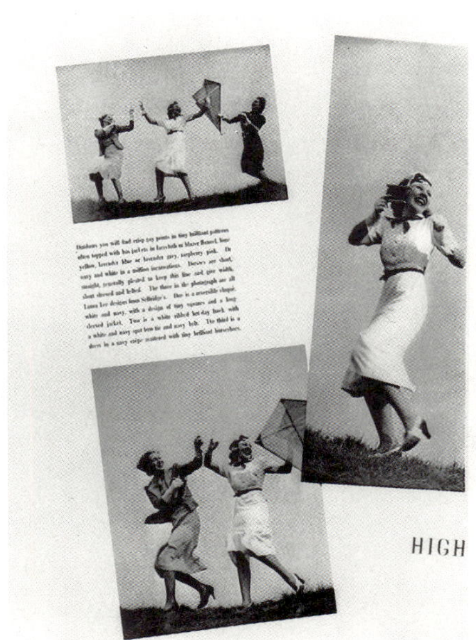

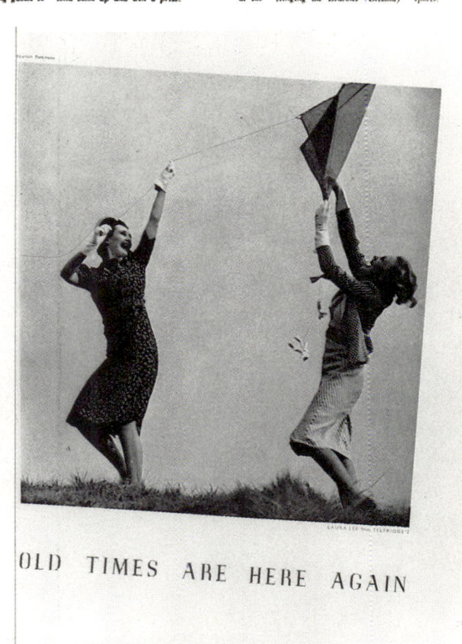

Early fashion photographs used in an Alan McPeake layout for Harper's Bazaar, 1936

RIGHT *Unemployed miner's family, Merthyr Tydfil, South Wales, 1937*

FAR RIGHT *The Trilon, New York World's Fair, 1939*

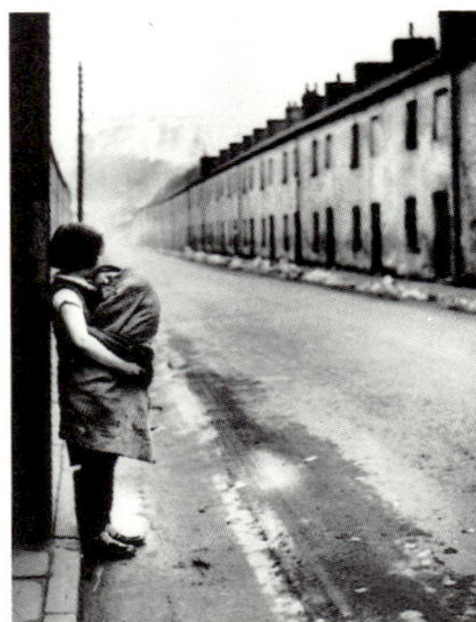

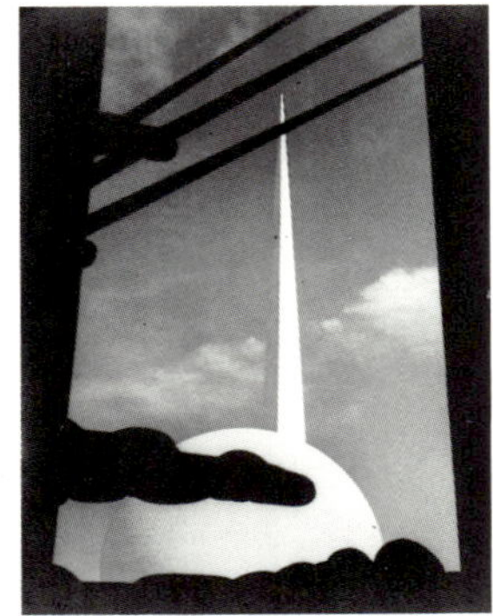

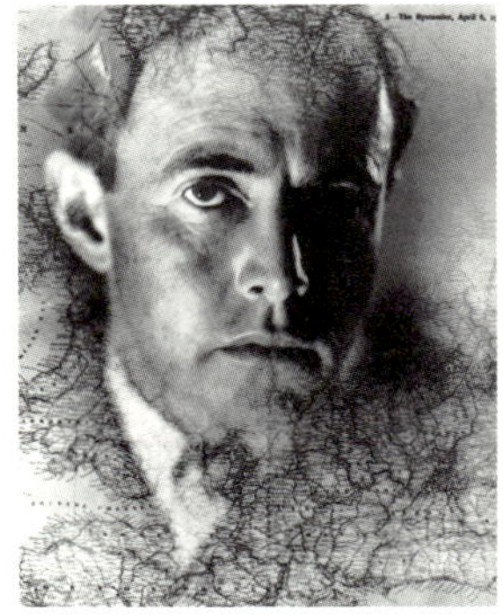

Beverley Nichols, 1938 (Double exposure, taken for publication of Nichols' book, 'News of England')

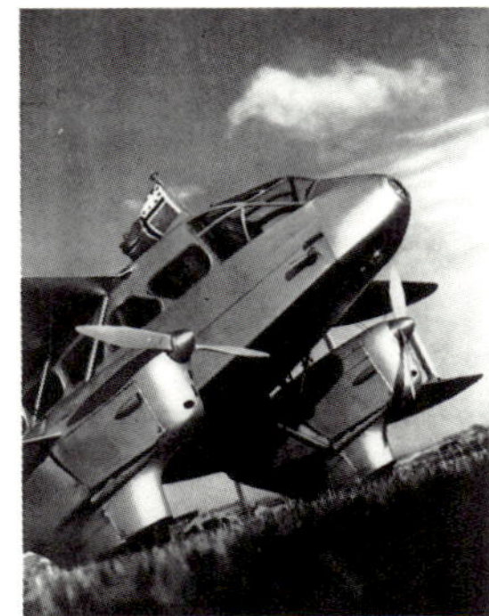

'Winged Leviathan' from the Bystander, 1936

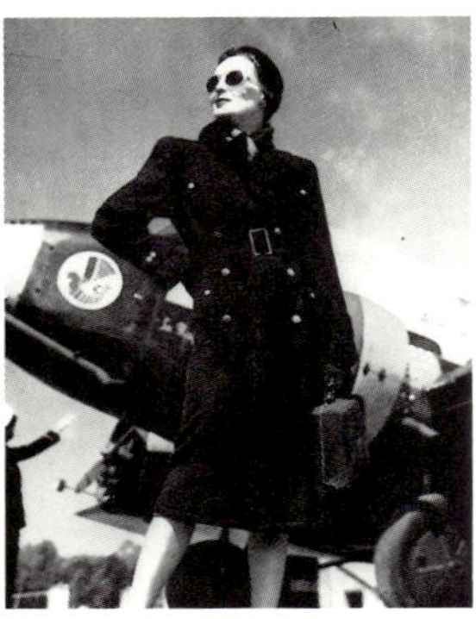

'Bound for Le Touquet in under the hour' fashion shot for Harper's Bazaar, 1939

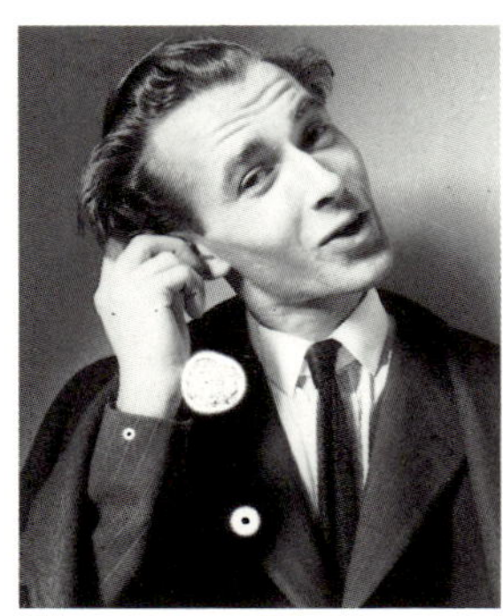

ABOVE *Tom Hawkyard, Assistant Art Editor of British Vogue from 1948–51*

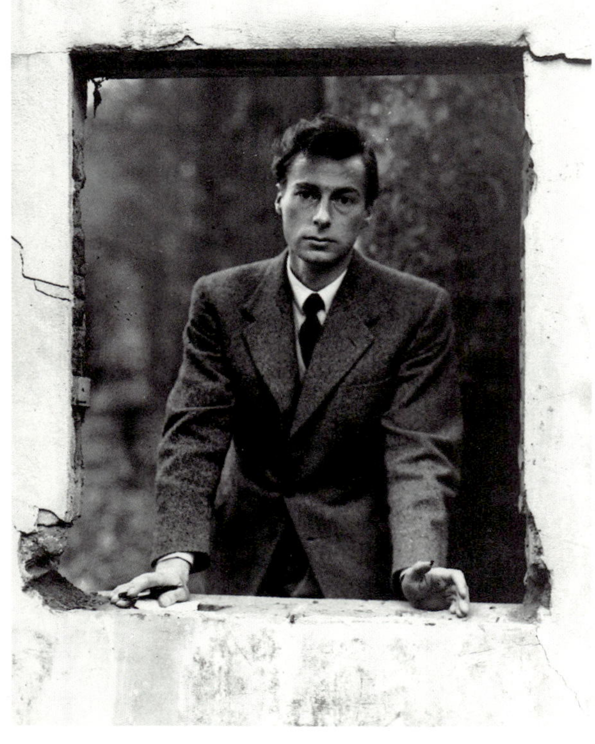

RIGHT *John Parsons, Art Editor of British Vogue from 1940–65*

British 'types'. Also photographs all the other British artists taking part in the exhibition at work, including Eric Ravilious, John Skeaping, John Nash and Charles Wheeler.

1937–39 Extended weekly series entitled 'With the Services' of photographs of the armed forces preparing for war taken for the *Bystander* for recruiting and propaganda purposes.

1938 First colour photographs taken for *Harper's Bazaar*.

Feature on Bath commissioned by Carmel Snow, Editor of American *Harper's Bazaar*.

1939 Travels to New York by sea for a weekend to photograph the World's Fair for the *Bystander*.

Before the outbreak of war, closes studio and returns to his farm at Bushley, Gloucestershire, to contribute to the war effort in the countryside. Does covert work for the Air Ministry, taking photographs for leaflets dropped over occupied Europe.

1942 Begins long association with British *Vogue* under the Editorship of Audrey Withers and Art Editorship of John Parsons.

1947 Meets, photographs and marries Wenda Rogerson.

1949 Photographs London Spring Collections on location near London landmarks, including the 'New Look' in Trafalgar Square.

First of what were to become annual trips to New York to spend six months of each year working for American *Vogue* with Art Director, Alexander Liberman.

Begins long collaboration with Siriol Hugh-Jones, Features Editor of British *Vogue*, who arranges a series of portrait commissions of artists, writers, intellectuals, theatre and musical personalities throughout the 1950s.

1950 Photographs the Paris Collections in colour for the British and American editions of *Vogue*.

First visit to Jamaica.

1951 Travels with Wenda to the Victoria Falls and southern Africa for a special issue of *Vogue* with commentary by Alan Paton. Photographs Wenda posed perilously above the Falls, and on the back of an ostrich (which promptly moved off at considerable speed – as she disappeared into the distance Parkinson was heard to shout, 'More profile, Wenda. More profile.').

Publication of *The Art and Technique of Colour Photography*, edited by Alexander Liberman, which contains a 12-page portfolio of Parkinson's work.
1953 Photographs ten young British actresses epitomizing the 'Young Look in the Theatre' on a gymnasium climbing frame as a humorous tribute to Irving Penn's earlier 'Vogue's Ten Most Famous Models'.

12-page portfolio appears in March *Vogue* of all the leading British couturiers including Norman Hartnell, Michael of Lachasse, Mattli, Elspeth Champcommunal at Worth, Peter Russell, Victor Stiebel at Jacqmar, Michael Sherard, John Cavanagh, Digby Morton, Charles Creed and Hardy Amies.
1954 Advertising photograph for Aquascutum dinner jackets (showing Archie Campbell and Jo Robertson) published in the *Evening Standard* which dramatically increases their sales.
1955 Travels to Haiti with Wenda and John Gielgud to take photographs for January 1956 issue of *Vogue*.
1956 Tours round India taking photographs of models Anne Gunning (now Lady Anthony Nutting) and Barbara Mullen for *Vogue*.

First photographic session in Tobago.
1957 Work included in first Bienalle Photographic Exhibition, Venice.
1958 July *Vogue* features Italian trip with model Nena von Schlebrugge.
1958–59 Photographs series of British aristocrats at home for Pond's cream advertisements.
1959 Bahamas issue of *Vogue* includes his photographs of Carmen under water.
1960–64 With expiry of his contract with *Vogue*, Parkinson is recruited by Jocelyn Stevens to become an Associate Editor of *Queen* magazine. Having been purchased in 1957 by Stevens the long-established title was rethought and redesigned. With its strong team of contributors, including Robin Douglas-Home, Beatrix Miller, Drusilla Beyfus, and Mark Boxer, it became the leading and most influential fashion and features magazine of the early 1960s.
1960 13–23 July Exhibition at Jaeger House, Regent Street, of over 120 photographs including recent *Queen* assignments to Tahiti and Bangkok as well as earlier *Vogue* editorial work and general advertising work. Exhibition includes huge eleven-foot high enlargements, and live fashion models

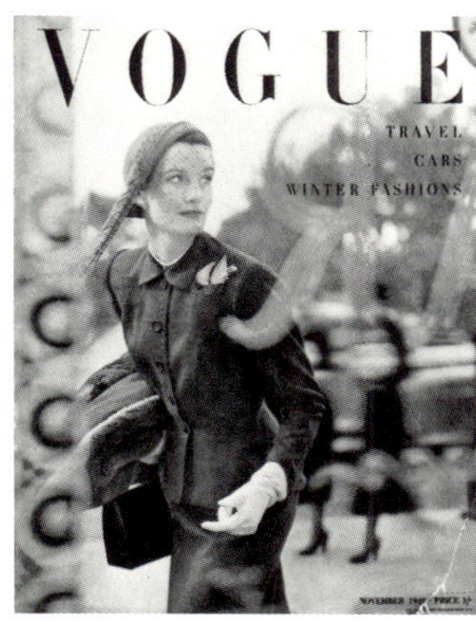

LEFT *Wenda in New York, 1949. Parkinson's first cover for American Vogue*

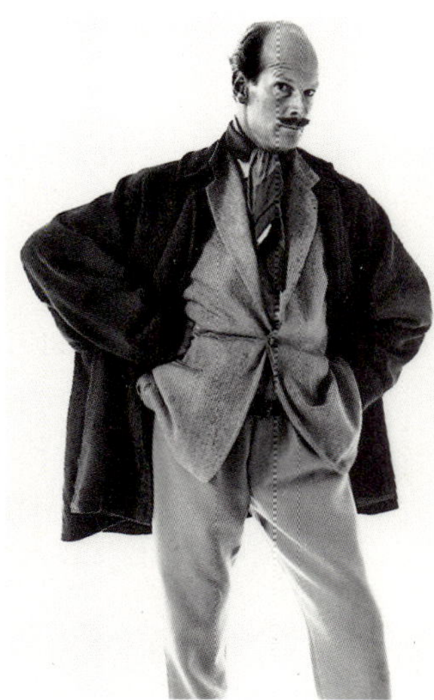

ABOVE *The author photographed by Irving Penn to illustrate a typical Englishman for American Vogue, 1958*

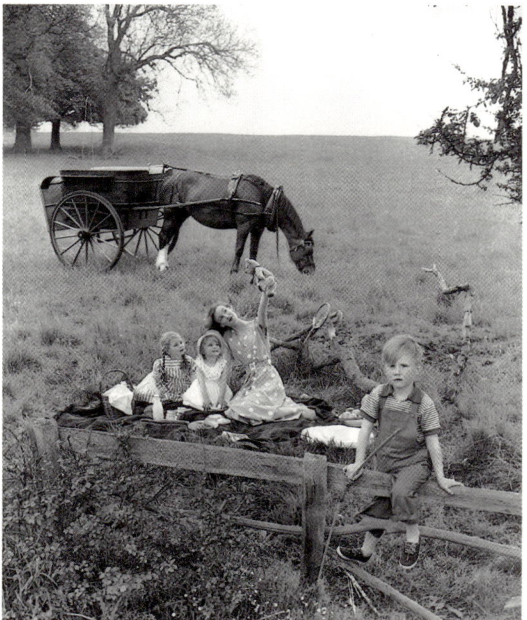

LEFT *Simon Parkinson and Wenda with her niece, Caroline Owen, and Mary Robertson, a fashion shot for Vogue, 1951*

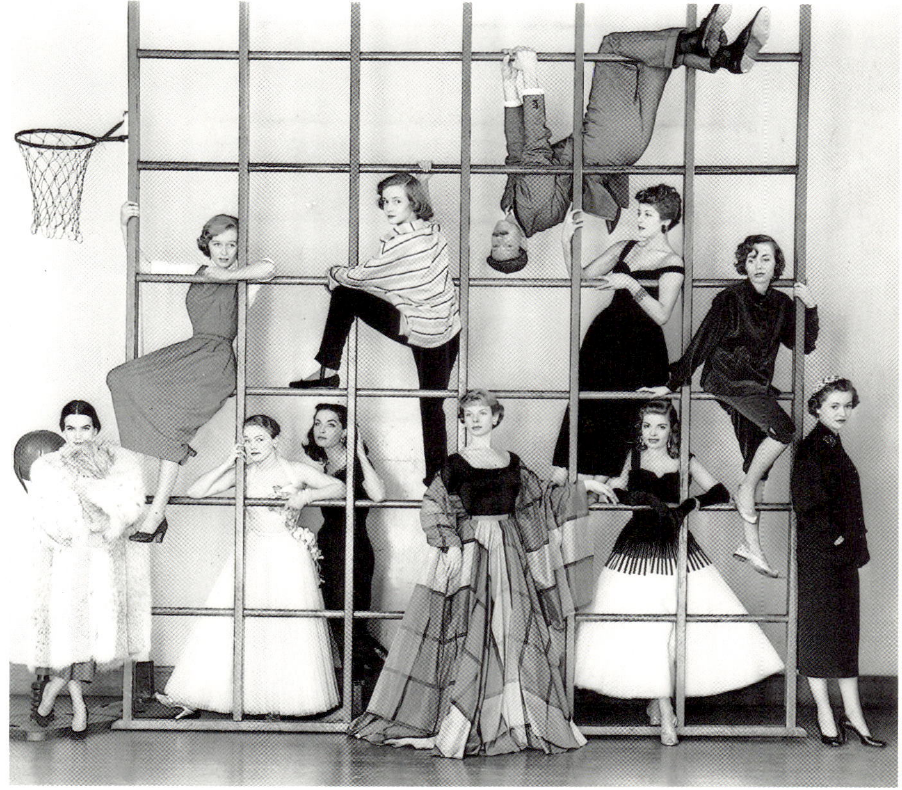

BELOW *'The Young Look in the Theatre', 1953 (Ten British actresses with a self-portrait)*

RIGHT *Vogue cover, Anne Gunning in India, 1956*
FAR RIGHT *Maidenform bra advertisement, c. 1955*
BELOW *On board the Liberté set for New York with Simon and Wenda. Photograph by Slim Aarons, early 1950s*

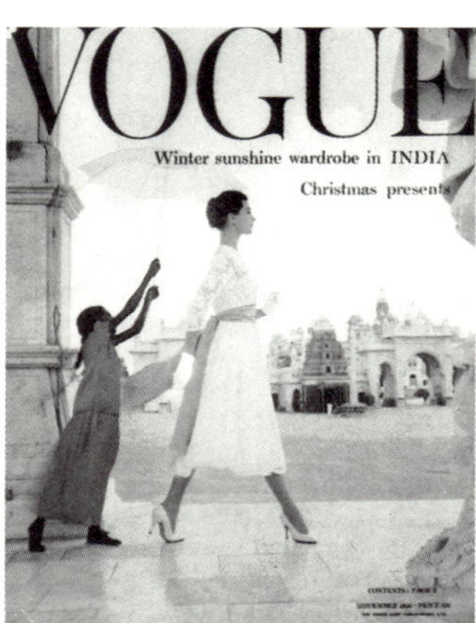

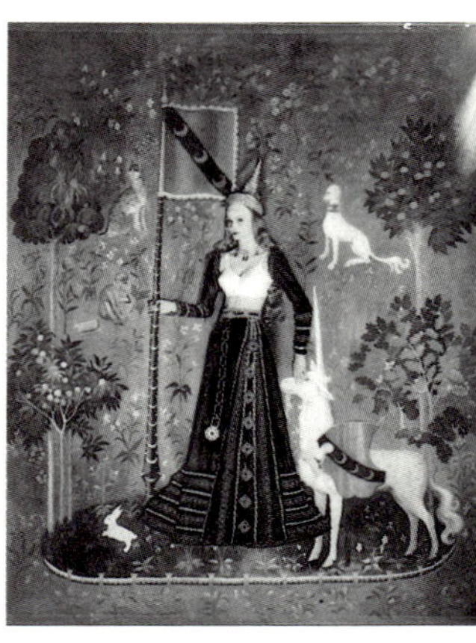

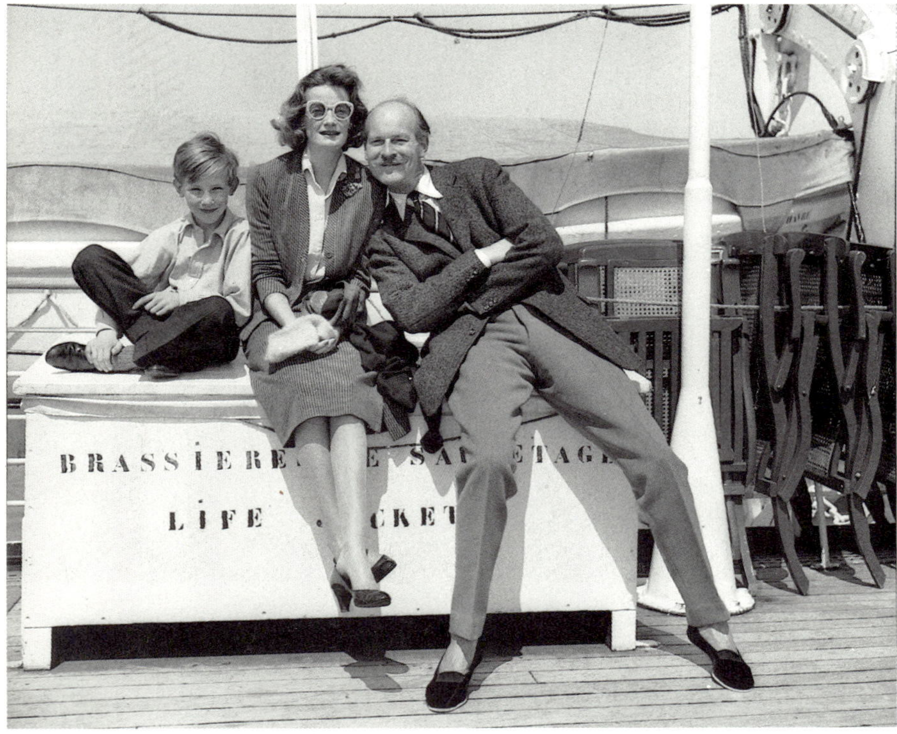

LEFT *Carmen and Chip, a fashion shot, Bahamas, 1959*
BELOW *Underwater with Carmen, Bahamas, 1959. Photograph by Bronson Hartley*

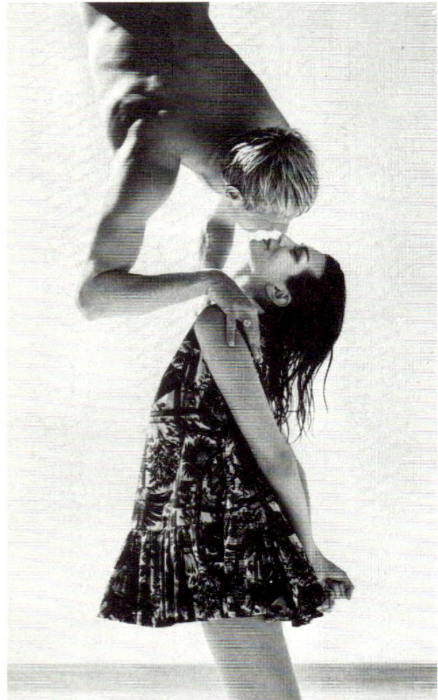

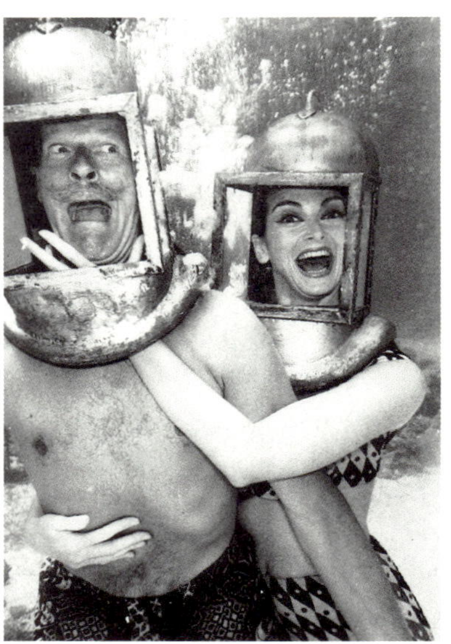

dance in the shop windows to music audible inside and outside the store. All exhibition proceeds go to World Refugees Central Appeal Fund.
1961–64 Continues world-wide assignments for *Queen* up Greek mountains, in the Giza desert, in South America and Blackpool using, as models, Celia Hammond, Jean Shrimpton, Melanie Hampshire, Carmen, Pat Booth and Tania Mallett.
1963 Moves from Twickenham to Tobago, West Indies, to build a dream house from the proceeds of advertising work (which had included campaigns for beer and petrol).
1964 24 February issue of *Queen* features the American Dee triplets modelling the Paris Spring Collection for special issue 'Queen has triplets in Paris' two weeks before Queen Elizabeth II gives birth to her third son, Prince Edward, on 10 March.

Photographs Beatles in their hotel room on visit to London and later in the recording studio. Pictures collected and published as book for American market where Beatlemania is beginning.

Contract with *Queen* expires. Returns to Condé Nast to work until mid-1970s on British and American editions of *Vogue* as well as free-lancing for *Life*, and other international magazines.
1965 Assignment to Peru for American *Vogue* photographing Dolores Wettach at Cuzco.
1966 Photographs Prince Philip, the Duke of Edinburgh, on a royal visit to Tobago while the Queen films the proceedings.

January *Vogue* feature on Mexico.
1967 Makes television documentary for BBC in *One Pair of Eyes* series entitled 'Stay, baby, stay' which includes location work in Rome photographing Marisa Mell as well as interviews and photographic sessions with Twiggy, Raquel Welch, Celia Hammond and Wenda.
1968 Elected Honorary Fellow of the Royal Photographic Society .
1969 January *Vogue* special issue on Ethiopia.

Takes first official photographs of Prince Charles to mark his investiture as Prince of Wales at Caernarvon Castle. Official portraits distributed widely to British schools. Also photographs Princess Anne riding her horse High Jinks in Windsor Great Park and other

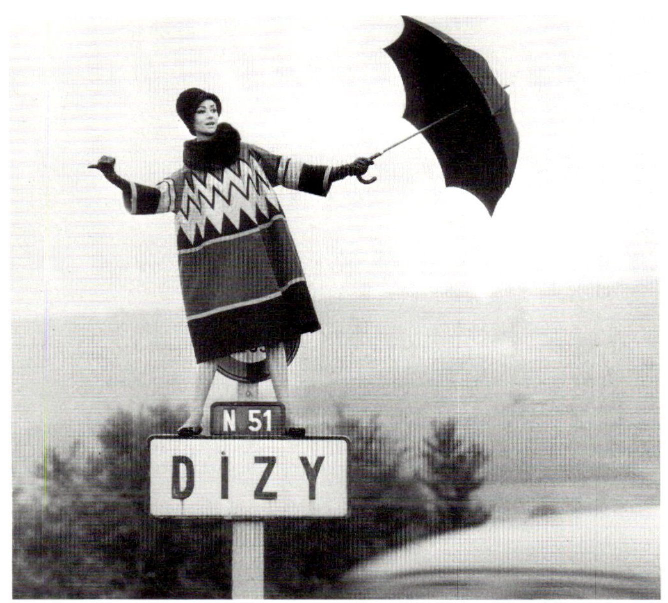

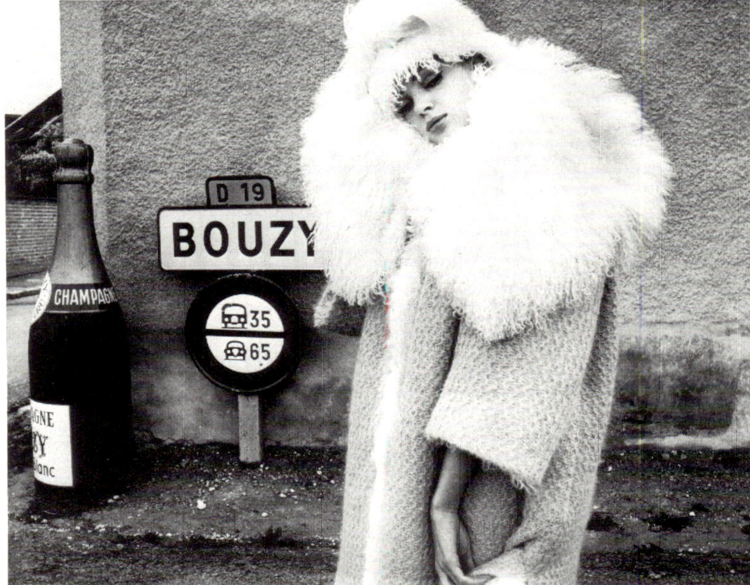

official photographs for her 19th birthday which break new ground as informal official royal photographs.

Photographs Vanessa Redgrave rehearsing the role of Isadora Duncan for Karel Reitz's film.

1970 *Vogue* expedition to San Francisco, Las Vegas and Monument Valley, Utah, to photograph Zandra Rhodes and Mr Freedom and Jean Muir clothes modelled by Jan Ward for publication in January 1971 British *Vogue* and later *Realities* July 1971.

1971 Trip to Seychelles with Fashion Editor Grace Coddington and model Apollonnia van Ravenstein for Robinson Crusoe scenario on Praslin Island and bird sanctuary on Bird Island.

20 August *Life* magazine and all other leading magazines feature official 21st birthday photographs of Princess Anne portrayed as a girl of the times relaxing on the royal estates and driving about town.

1972 Chronicles Elizabeth Taylor at 40 for *Life*, taking her birthday photographs and later wearing a specially-designed wig to match her pet terrier dog.

1973 January *Vogue* features trip to the Algarve and July issue trip to Barbados.

Takes official engagement, and then wedding, photographs of Princess Anne and Captain Mark Phillips.

1974 Takes official 91st birthday photographs of Princess Alice, Countess of Athlone.

For September *Vogue* produces portraits of the leading French couturiers and designers Yves St Laurent, Ungaro, Givenchy, Marc

ABOVE LEFT *Katherine Pastrie in a Nina Ricci coat topped by a black mink collar, 1960*
ABOVE RIGHT *Nena von Schlebrugge in a Balmain fleecy blonde wool coat and hat, 1960*

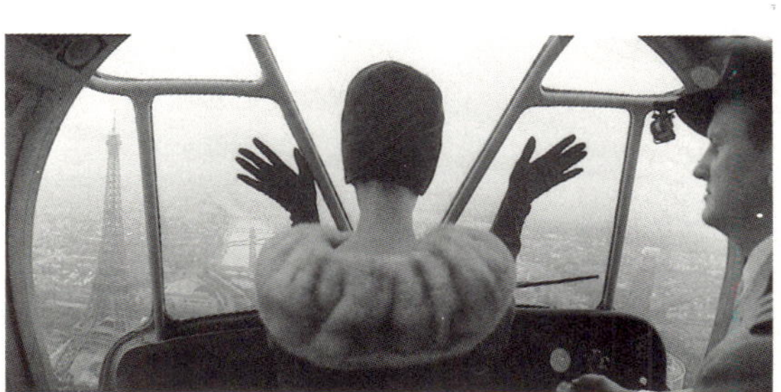
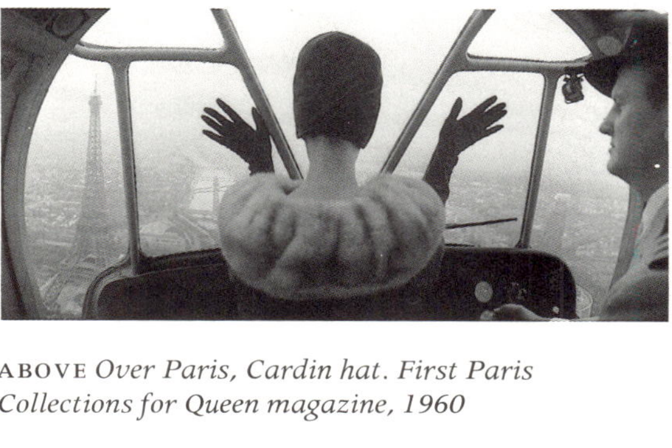

ABOVE *Over Paris, Cardin hat. First Paris Collections for Queen magazine, 1960*

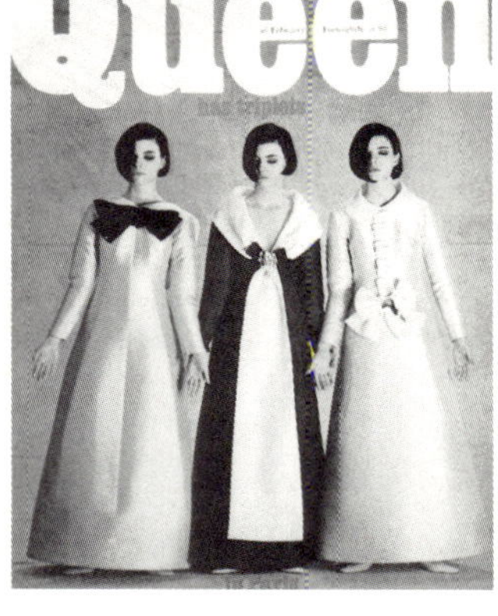

ABOVE *The Dee triplets, Paris Spring Collections, 1964*

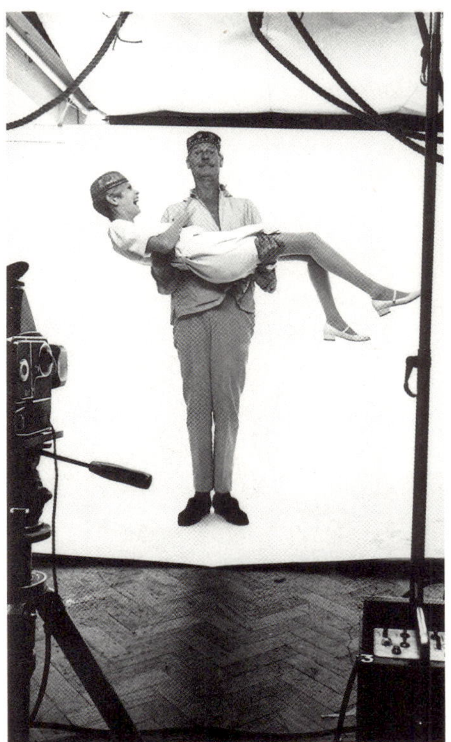

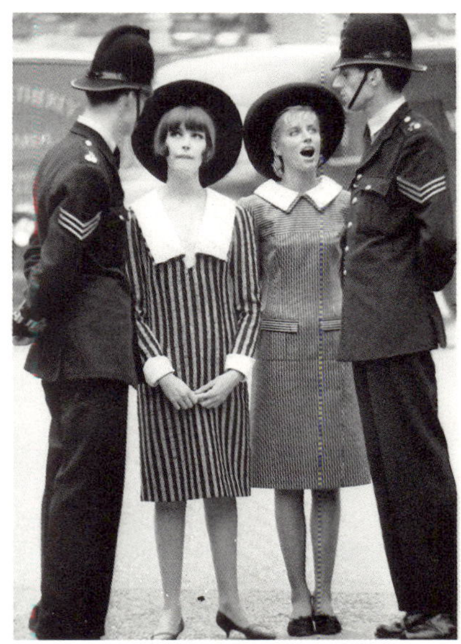

ABOVE *Jill Kennington and Melanie Hampshire in Mary Quant dresses for a Life magazine feature on London fashion, 1963*
LEFT *In Vogue Studio Three with Twiggy (Leslie Hornby), 1960s*

FAR RIGHT *Princess Anne at 21, cover of the Sunday Times Magazine, 1971*

RIGHT *Prince Charles, official investiture photograph as Prince of Wales, 1969*

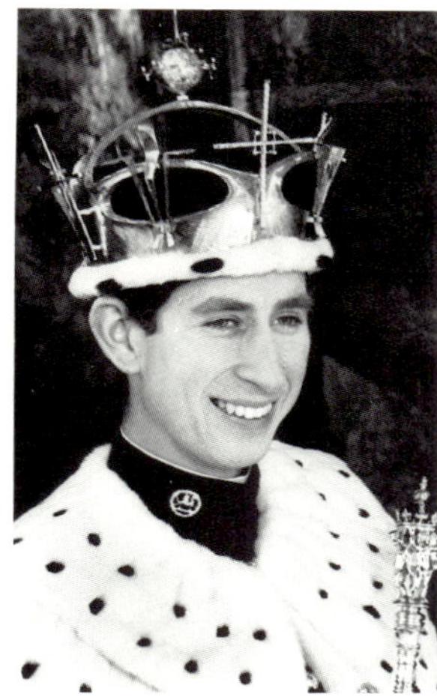

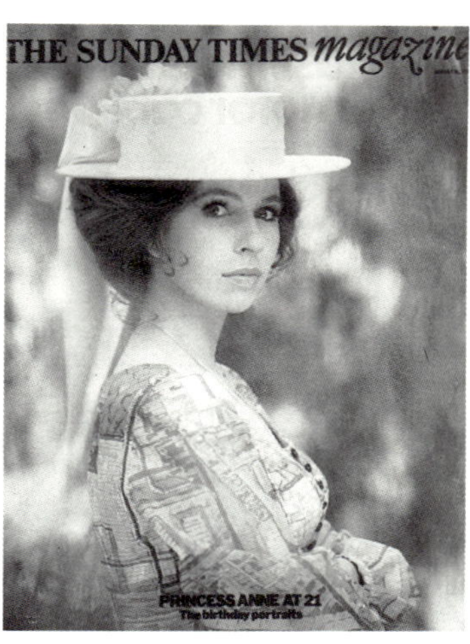

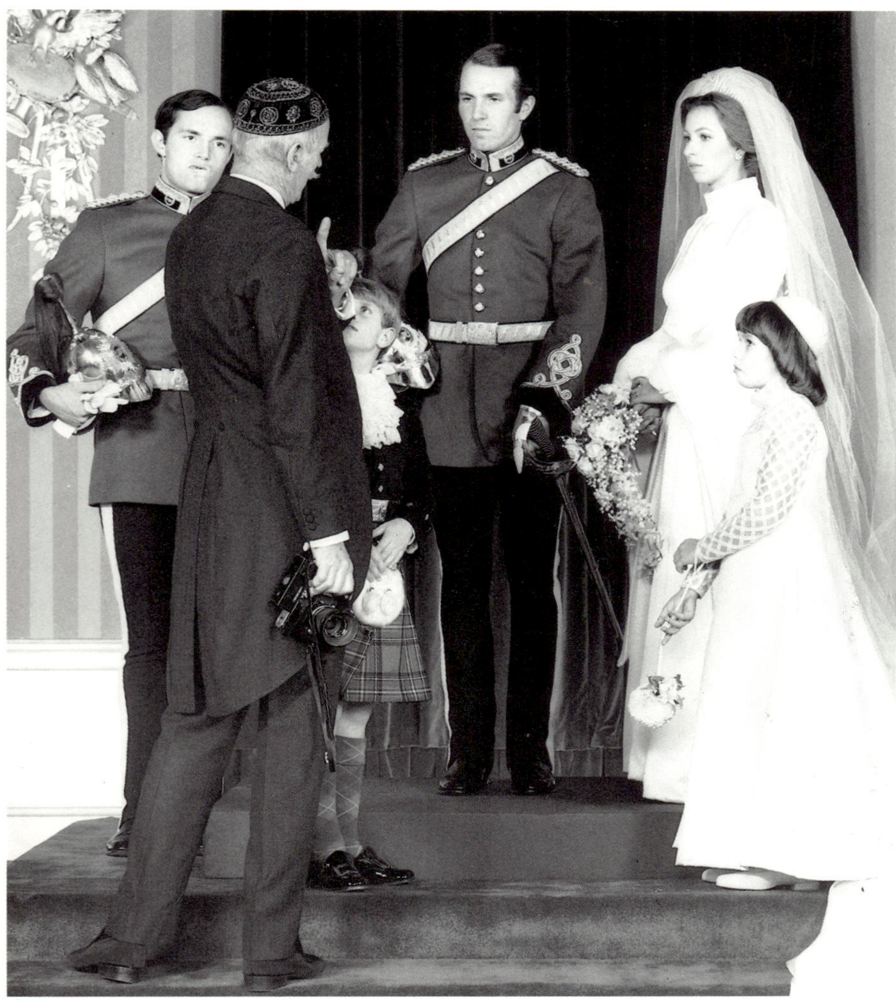

ABOVE *Photographing Princess Anne's wedding, 1973. Photograph by Tim Jenkins*

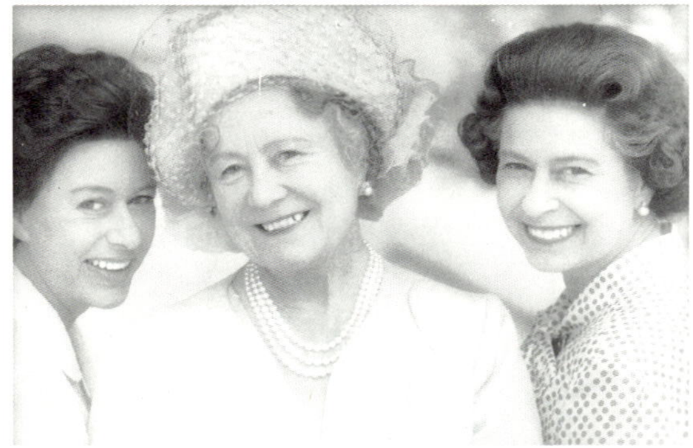

RIGHT *Princess Margaret, Queen Elizabeth The Queen Mother and Her Majesty The Queen. Official 80th birthday photograph for the Queen Mother*

Bohan, Jean Louis Scherrer, and Cardin.
1975 Takes official photographs for Queen Mother's 75th birthday.

Elected Fellow of the Institute of Incorporated Photographers.

Portraits taken include ones of Paul McCartney's daughter, Stella, in Jamaica and Princess Caroline of Monaco.

7,000-mile journey across Russia with model Jerry Hall using locations including a hydro-electric works and the fire temple at Baku.
1976 Autumn issue of French *Vogue* features portrait of Parkinson on its cover.
1978 Publication by Quartet Books of first book, *Sisters under the Skin*, with controversial cover of the McCandless twins which restricts outlets. September issue with feature on dress designer Jean Muir marks last editorial work for British *Vogue*.

Begins regular assignments for Hearst Corporation's *Town and Country* magazine working closely with Features Editor Nancy Tuck Gardiner and Director Frank Zachary. April edition features extended portfolio on 'Lordly London' and the beauties of London.
1979 April *Town and Country* issue features Queen Silvia and the beautiful women of Sweden.

BBC TV documentary, in collaboration with Fyfe Robertson, features location photography in Tobago shooting cover and fashion shots for *Harper's* and *Queen* and preparation and hanging of exhibition at London's Photographers' Gallery.
1980 March *Town and Country* features Pilar Crespi in Sri Lanka on the sands of Trincomalee and at the elephant orphanage; November issue features 'Faces of Modern Mexico'.

Takes official photographs for Queen Mother's 80th birthday, including 'Blue Trinity' portrait of the Queen Mother and her two daughters Queen Elizabeth II and Princess Margaret. (Limited edition signed print marketed, limited to 1,000 copies.)
1981 New Year's Honours elevate Parkinson to Commander of the British Empire.

Takes official 50th birthday photographs of Princess Margaret, and also with her children, Viscount Linley and Sarah Armstrong-Jones, prior to her tour of Canada.

7 August–25 October First major museum retrospective held at London's

National Portrait Gallery breaks gallery attendance records and is visited by Princess Margaret and Princess Alexandra. Entitled '50 Years of Portraits and Fashion' to mark photographic jubilee, the exhibition with over 240 exhibits includes new portraits of Margaret Thatcher, Michael Foot, David Steel, the four joint leaders of the Social Democratic Party, Harold Evans, the three granddaughters of Bramwell Booth, Zandra Rhodes, and Mick Jagger and Jerry Hall in bed, specially taken for the exhibition.

February *Town and Country* profiles portraits of 'New York's Treasures': Brooke Astor, Lisa Taylor, Estée Lauder, Beverley Sills and Suzy Knickerbocker. April issue features 'Queen Sofia and the beautiful women of Spain'. May issue features Carmen Dell 'Orefice at the Hearst mansion in San Simeon.

1982 Lifetime achievement in photography award for contribution to American magazines in May by American Society of Magazine Photographers.

Photographs Elizabeth Taylor at 50 for *Life* magazine.

1983 First retrospective in America opens at International Center of Photography, New York, in April.

Weidenfeld and Nicolson in Britain and The Vendome Press in America publish Parkinson's collected work.

T.P.

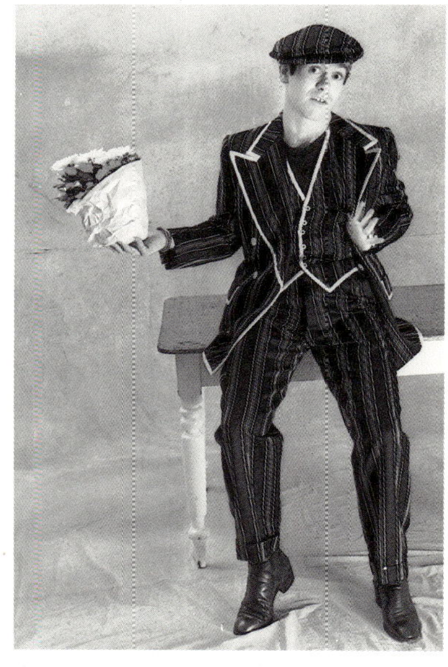

ABOVE *Elton John in a Tommy Nutter suit, 1977*
LEFT *Fashion shot for Italian Vogue, 1974*

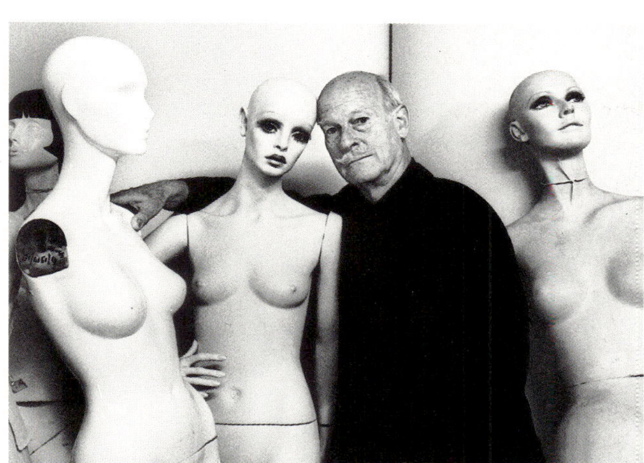

LEFT *In the cellars of the Museum of London with some mannequins. Photograph by Sue Adler, 1981*

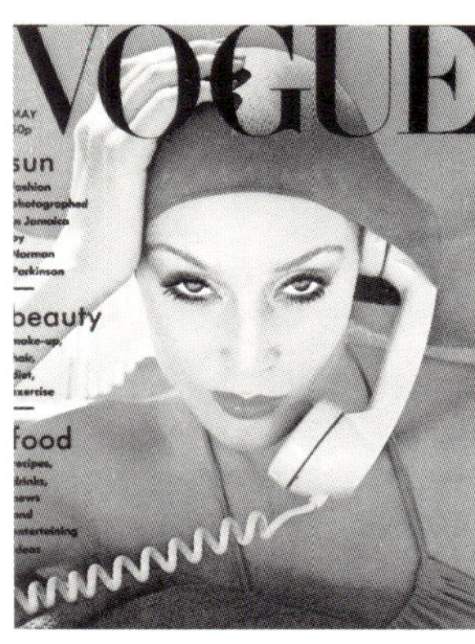

Vogue cover, Jerry Hall in Jamaica, 1975

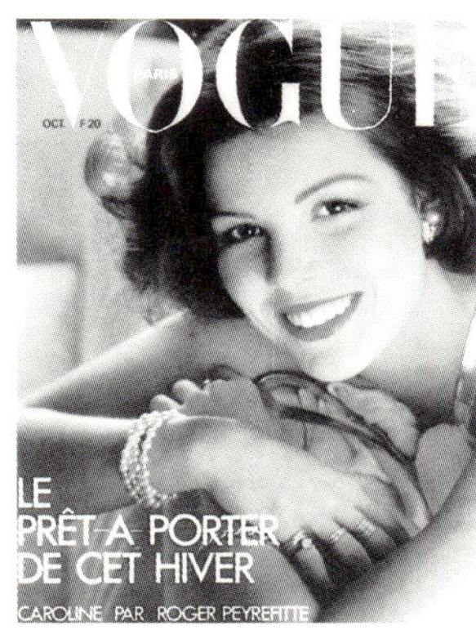

French Vogue cover, Princess Caroline of Monaco, 1977

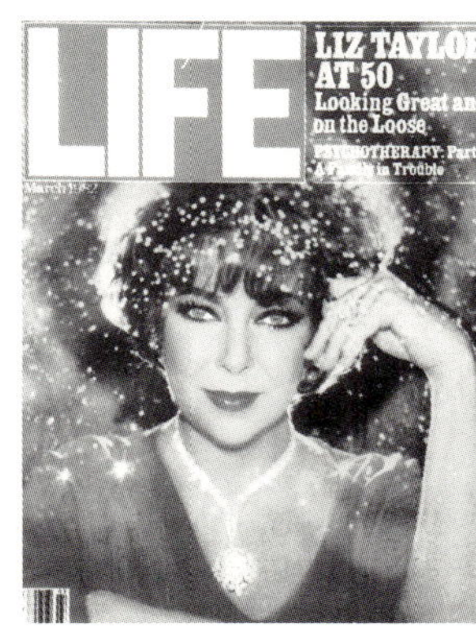

Life magazine cover, Liz Taylor at 50, 1982

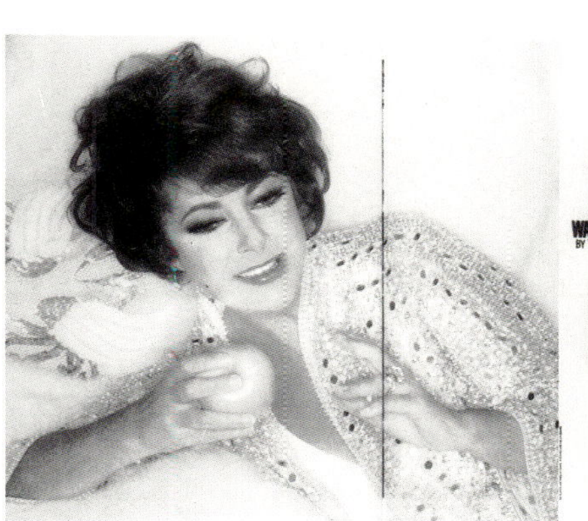

'Liz Taylor hardly needs an apple for Eve-like allure', Life magazine, 1982

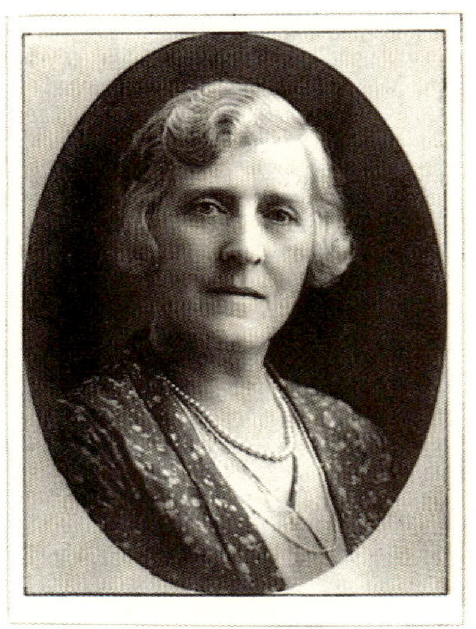
Speaight Ltd
157 New Bond Street W.

ROOTS

If there is a particular variety to be found in my photographs, it is possibly because my roots lie buried partly in the depths of the English countryside and partly in the great opera houses of Europe. The unlikely mixture of rustic and urbane genes that I have inherited makes me feel equally at home waiting patiently among the brambles over a badger's earth, or among the marble pillars and gilded ceilings of an Italian palazzo.

My father, named after the medieval names of Parkinson's *Paradisus*, was the elder son of a gardening butter-and-egg merchant from the West Country town of Malmesbury (which has a beautiful hilltop Norman Abbey, with a tomb in its churchyard that records the death of an unfortunate thirty-three-year-old Hannah Twynnoy within the 'jaws of Tyger fierce', in 1703). This grandfather, a passionate self-educator, married a Sarah Sealy from the neighbouring town of Tetbury (built of creamy Cotswold stone, it is now much favoured by the equestrian-orientated members of the Royal family). Possibly the most solid and beautiful of all the buildings to be found there is the collonaded covered market; at one end of this fine fourteenth-century edifice is the area that housed the smithy. The smithy was worked by the Sealy family for as long as records exist and I am very proud of the trickle of hoof-smoked blood that courses my veins.

Trained as a barrister, my father was for many-a-year without a brief. Undeterred he spent every unemployed moment walking the highways and by-ways and footpaths of his then home county of Surrey. I can well imagine the kind of scene that might have been witnessed at the turn of the century: an upper-crust family are gazing unsuspectingly out of their drawing-room windows, when suddenly my map-carrying father comes into view leading a motley crew of hikers across the lawns and through the rose beds in order to re-establish some long-forgotten public footpath that he has discovered was recorded by some dotted line in the Domesday Book. He was, on the surface, a quiet countryside batchelor until well after he was forty; then he met an impossible half-Italian widow, my mother. Louie herself was pushing forty when they were married, and little did William, my father, realize what a disciplinarian he had taken on. She was descended from Luigi Lablache, perhaps the greatest basso-profundo of all time. Louie's mother was the daughter of the union between Luigi's fourth son Henri and a budding soprano, a Madame de Meriec, singer to the Royal Court of St Petersburg, whom he met while Luigi was singing there.

I am recording the vagaries of my forebears not in any attempt to impress, but rather to explain that when girls are photographed by me in the cow parsley, or against dew-hung November cobwebs, you can be certain there are few errors.

Yet the broad sweep of the landscape with its carefully observed rural intimacies are only half of this photographer's palette. Fifty years of that sort of work would soon have become a real bore. Stars as glamorous and sophisticated as Elizabeth Taylor could never look good in muddy gum boots. They require the scent-laden alchemy of a soirée in Versailles or the languorous invitation of a cloth-of-gold tent hanging in the great hall of a Roman palazzo. And yet somehow this effect has to be created in Room 212 of a Ramada Inn . . . 'C'mon now, Parks, you've done it before – you can do it again . . . you know how we need that cover picture, honey!'

Those are the times that I bury the butter-and-egg man in me and call, looking back into my skull, to wake up the slumbering Italian Grandees. Sometimes it works. My non-overlapping, bi-lateral, diametrically opposed forebears, withdrawn quite exclusively into their tidy compartments, can send me some very satisfactory and practical signals to work upon. They may be part of the secret of why I think and see and work as I do.

The photographer's mother. First professional portrait taken while a pupil at Speaight & Son, 1931

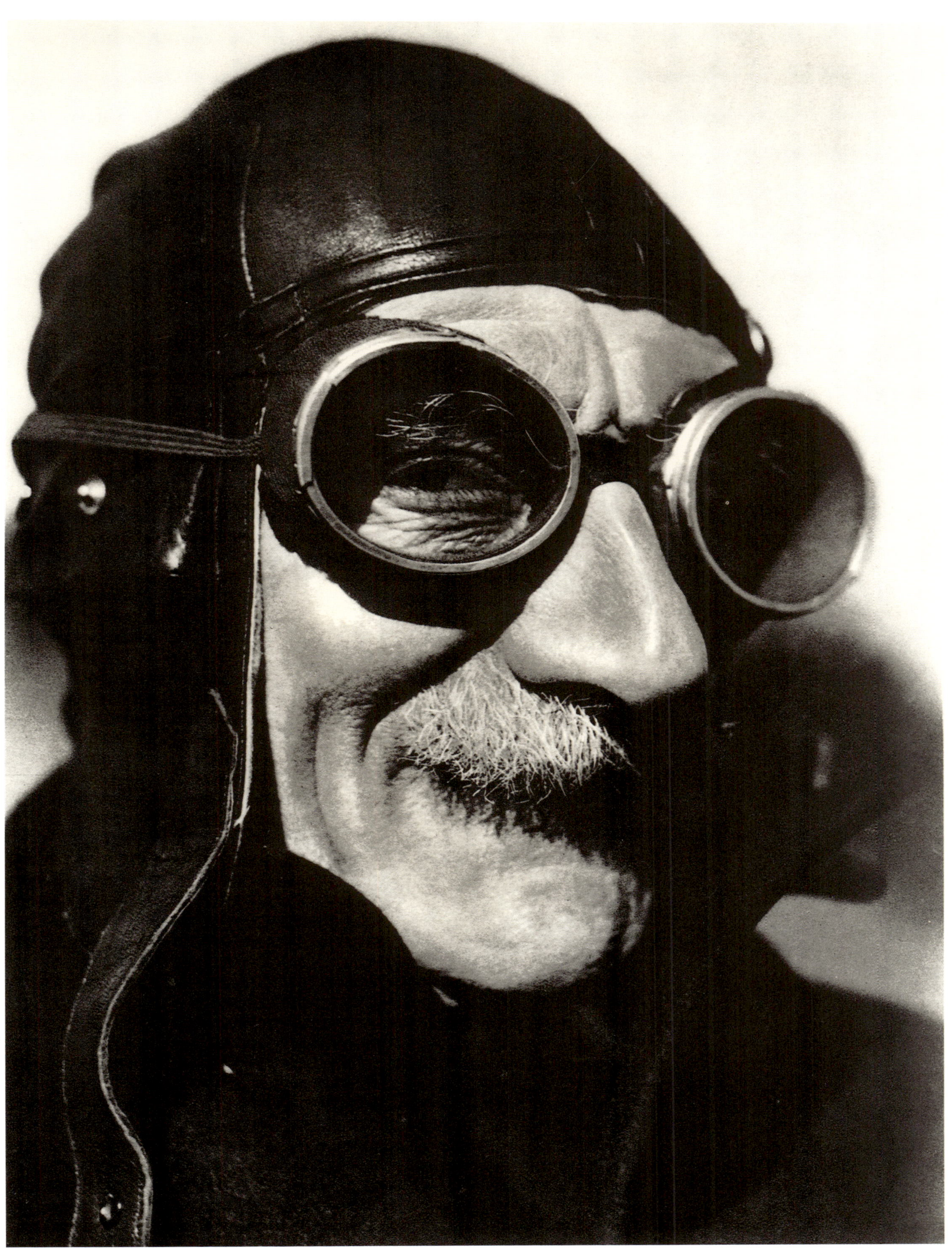

'The Age of Speed' A portrait of the photographer's father, 1936

1920s

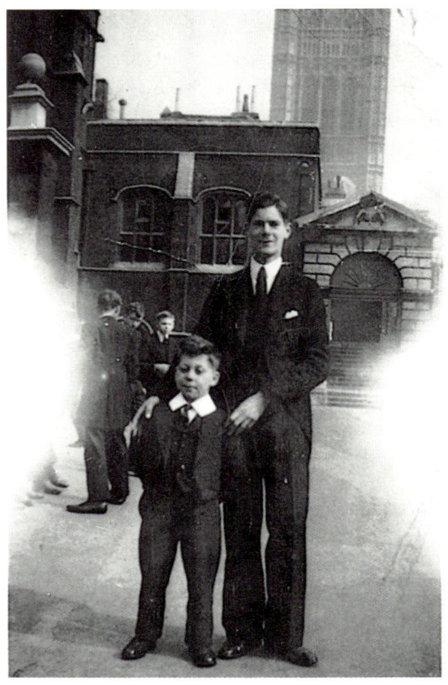

SCHOOLDAYS

In the late twenties, from 32 Landford Road, a cosy semi-detached in the purlieus of Putney half drowning in my mother's June roses, would emerge two youths indistinguishable from latter-day undertakers. My brother, Kenneth, and I were on our way to Westminster School in its top hat and tail coat days.

To reach the Underground at Putney Bridge we had to pick our way through the (then) slum areas of the Lower Richmond Road, which our mother had warned us was inhabited by 'guttersnipes'. Running the early morning gauntlet of abuse and over-ripe vegetables was certainly character forming, necessitating frequent defensive thrusts with well rolled umbrellas (obligatory regulation) and quick evasive rearguard actions.

When you started at the school, for the first month you were called a 'Shadow', tacked on to an experienced boy called a 'Substance'. For his own safety the Substance never left his Shadow's side, for the Substance was beaten for the Shadow's misdemeanours. The mystique and rigmarole of Westminster School life would fill a book, and without this kind of guidance new boys would never have survived. The day began at ten minutes to nine, when 250 boys of Church of England persuasion (there were others) would coincide their entrance into the Abbey from the Cloisters, through a small Gothic doorway. Half-washed boys, most unsuitably dressed (under 5ft 2ins in Eton collars and bum freezers, taller than that in tails), struggling frantically to get through an opening that only took one at a time. Once inside the high vaulted calm and coolness of that most important place, the vital history of Great Britain recorded on its tombstones, was deeply impressive. I remember the booming organ played by a Mr Lofthouse, and subsequently have often heard the spine-chilling fanfares that herald royal visits coming from that same organ loft.

Every spare moment from class work would find me sneaking back into the Abbey. Every day there was a new dusty corner, another new tomb, to discover. I knew a few of the vergers, and I had the run of the place. I often did my 'prep' sitting in the Coronation Chair but I did not, as others did, carve my name on it. My only distinction (for I was scholastically abysmal) was winning the Henry Luce Art Prize for a drawing of the Henry VII Chapel looking east while sitting on the Stone of Scone.

My affection for the secret corners of the Abbey was second only to my admiration for a thin, pale, tall dark-

Iredell and Parkinson, the shortest and tallest boys at Westminster School, 1929

haired master called Henry Williamson. With his spatulate fingers and his turpentine smell, he spoke hardly at all and I worshipped him with filial piety. He took about four Art classes each week for the form I was in. He had decided that of the thirteen or fourteen of us, only four or five would ever benefit from his tuition. 'Now the others,' he would announce, 'you all sit there and amuse yourselves. Do your prep, make your stink bombs or paper darts – but do not disturb us.' Never has there been more elitist tuition. I cannot recall any particular thing this talented man said or did, but I did hang on his every word. I did recognize that he seemed to be the pilot for the journey he had made me enthusiastic to take. He taught us, I suppose, to see and to see quickly, to make composition decisions and stick by them. He never attempted to bend or instruct one's vision, and we remained, all of us, exclusively individual. He cherished this, guiding only our personal tastes.

Other masters were not so patient. Monsieur Bonhote, who made us repeat at the outset of every lesson: 'Le vase brisé, par un coup d'eventail . . .' told me that I had the finest accent in the school but no words. And the Reverend Dams, white haired, diminutive, greatest living authority on Shakespeare, would send me to wait outside almost every period because of 'disruptive practices'.

I have found that moving house can be a rewarding time for finding memorabilia. On a recent removal, some of my term reports from Westminster School came to light and now that they have been fully digested by my family my position as paternal head has been seriously damaged. In précis, they read like this:

Latin	V. weak
English	Does not concentrate
Science	Could do much better
French	Should not look out of the window
Maths	Innumerate
Position in Form	14th out of 15

But in the column set aside for 'Headmaster's comments', the much-revered, stentorian prelate-figure, the Reverend Costley-White, later Bishop of Gloucester, had written: 'This is one of the worst reports I have ever seen, but I can't help liking the fellow'.

The end of the working day at Westminster on three afternoons each week was celebrated, if that is the right word, by a forgathering of the boys for short prayers in Up School. One particular November evening prayers I recall in vivid detail. The boys were seated; a few masters in their black gowns and mortar boards came strolling in from adjacent classrooms; gathered round an antique rough wooden table on a dais sat a handful of school monitors. A large half-open drawer faced the congregation which sprouted, from its opposite corners, two hefty birches. It was a very different type of altar from the one we faced each morning in Westminster Abbey, but there it was – the Hellfire de Sade version. The headmaster entered from the rear of the congregation with his beloved heavy and measured stride, noticing, or so it seemed, every horrible boy without turning his head. He touched me on my shoulder; it was an electric shock. 'See me afterwards in my study'. But worse was to come. As he made his way up the central aisle he likewise bent over three of my closest friends. 'My God,' we all thought in unison, 'WHAT has he discovered?' Our mutual anxiety was not to be speedily allayed. He turned and made this announcement to the school: 'It has come to my knowledge, from sources that I am not willing to reveal, that certain boys are telling each other filthy stories. Now this, as you all realize, is a very serious matter. The filthy story, with all its inherent exaggerations, not only soils the listener but also permanently stains the teller. I have given serious thought to hit upon a suitable analogy to bring home to you how objectionable this business is, and I pass on to you the following . . . Would you give your friend a glass of filthy water to drink?'

By the time we had assembled outside his study, our apprehension was almost out of control. 'But the Headmaster never sends for anyone, however serious the crime!' we were murmuring as the door opened and we filed in to a place that smelt of must and dubbin and old pipe smoke and brown-edged manuscripts. (Each master had his own smell. For those teaching the continental languages it was garlic or onion, while the sporting masters smelt of Harris tweed. All of them smelt of tobacco or snuff.) 'Mr Williamson, the Art Master,' he began, 'has given me your names as being, in his judgement, boys that he might recommend as having outstanding artistic talent and temperament.' We were fainting with relief as he continued, 'I have here a letter from a reliable Bond Street court photographer who wishes to ascertain if any boy from this school might take up the profession and wish to serve an apprenticeship to this trade. Have all of you decided what you are going to do next term?' Everybody else seemed to have their lives well planned out. So I got the letter to take to my parents from a Mr Richard Speaight, FRPS, of 157 New Bond Street, West One.

My mother, through some remote relation, 'knew' somebody in Kodaks and it had been thought a reasonable idea, with someone as untalented as the young Parkinson, to send him there to have 'some of the rough corners smoothed up a bit'. So, to my parents, Fate rhymed with Speaight and my father went off to have a chat with them meanwhile.

1930s

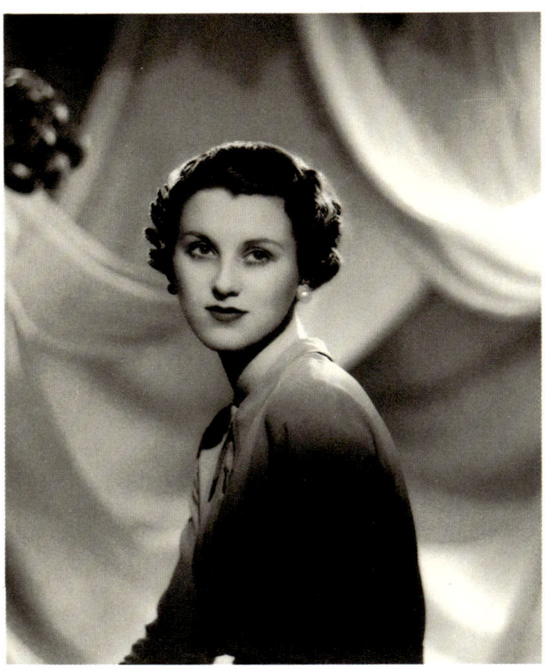

DOG DAYS AND COURT NIGHTS

William James Parkinson Smith, my father, could never be described as a man of the world, but he was a canny old bird. He soon discovered that the business manager of Speaight's studio, a Mr Fred Speaight, was inclined to tipple and was an undischarged bankrupt. Speaight's wanted a £500 fee to have me apprenticed to them for three years, and I was to be paid one pound per week. My father drove a hard bargain and I was ushered in for £300.

I spent the first few months as general dogsbody, sweeping up, dusting and throwing away the garbage. I was too inexperienced to be let near anything technical or seriously photographic. But I managed by enthusiasm to insinuate myself into the affections of a Mr Smart who was the Speaight printer (and what an amazing printer he was). I suppose that little man, with a large nose that almost overbalanced his five foot height, had spent nine-tenths of his life in the dark. I thought of him as a benign pit pony – except pit ponies do not chew on endless hand rolled cigarettes, or cultivate a multitude of blackheads. I worked for months by his side, hovering over him as we stood in front of the lead-lined teak sink. As his brown-stained hands flipped the next piece of totally clear photographic paper into the developer, I would wait and feel the excitement that I still feel today at the magic of the slow arrival of the perfect black and white image. Hardly before the picture appeared, he would announce 'Overexposed.' or 'We will have to hold this area back.' or 'It's not a very good neg., we'll have to underexpose and drag it.'

Slowly old man Speaight permitted further responsibility for his gormless apprentice. He taught me how to trim the carbon arc umbrellas, and focus and manipulate the great ten by eight bellows camera which rested on a slightly mobile iron contraption which looked like a coffee-grinder. In my second year I was allowed into the studio to assist. It was an excellent studio by any standards, with handsome late Victorian woodwork.

All our war time losses are taken for granted now. The bombers burnt up my pre-war negatives, they removed Up School, Westminster, on one dark night, and on another they got Speaight's handsome studio ... it has been replaced by the Time Life building.

On pianos in ancestral homes you might find a rather faded photograph of a rather stiff lady with three small ostrich feathers pinned up the back of her head ('Ich Dien'); elegantly arranged in a grand sweep on the steps

Lady Bridget Poulett, well-known society beauty famous for her almond-green eyes and jet black hair, 1935

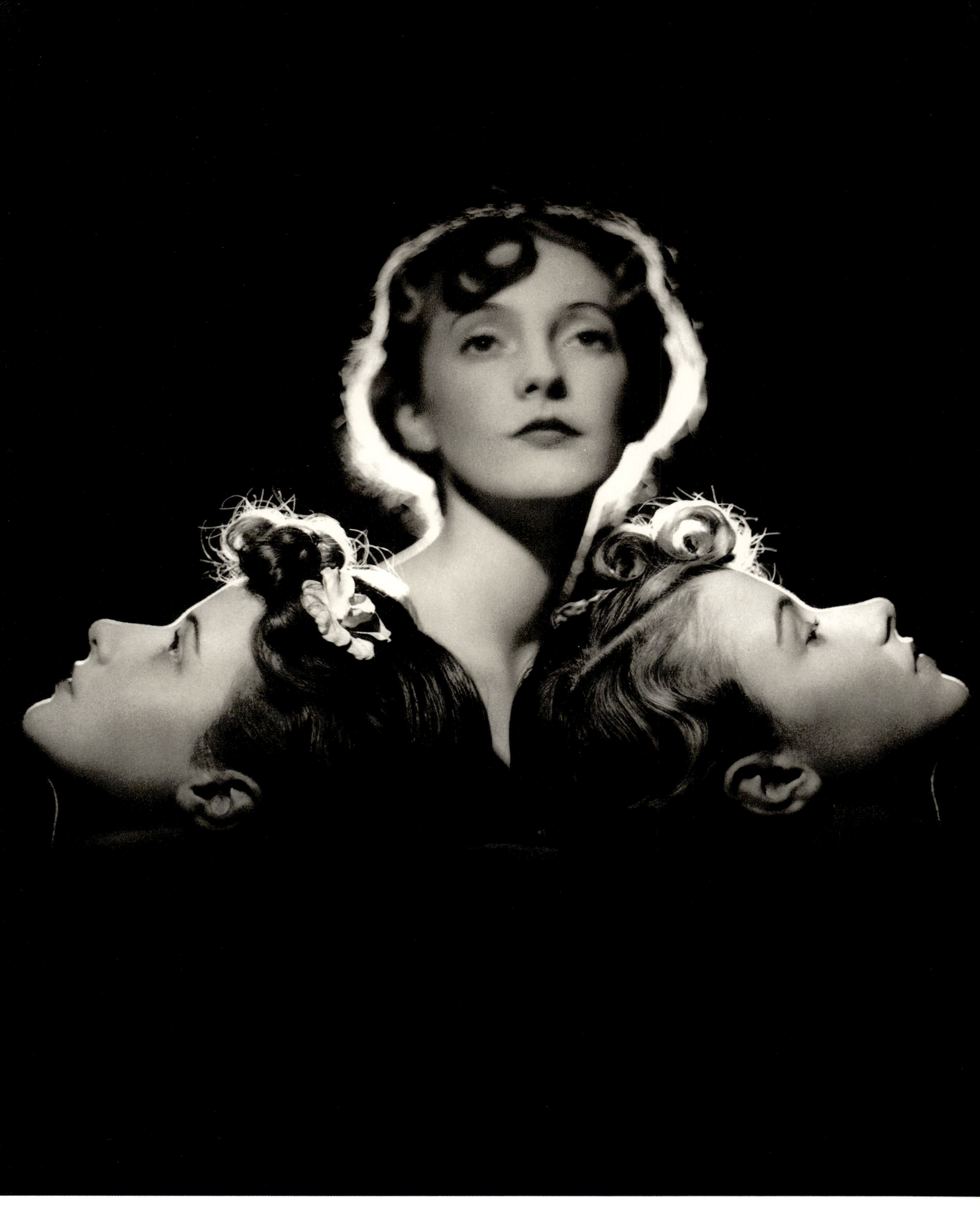

Debutantes Helen Trefusis (later Mrs Arthur Koestler) and the Paget twins (Celia and Mamaine), 1935

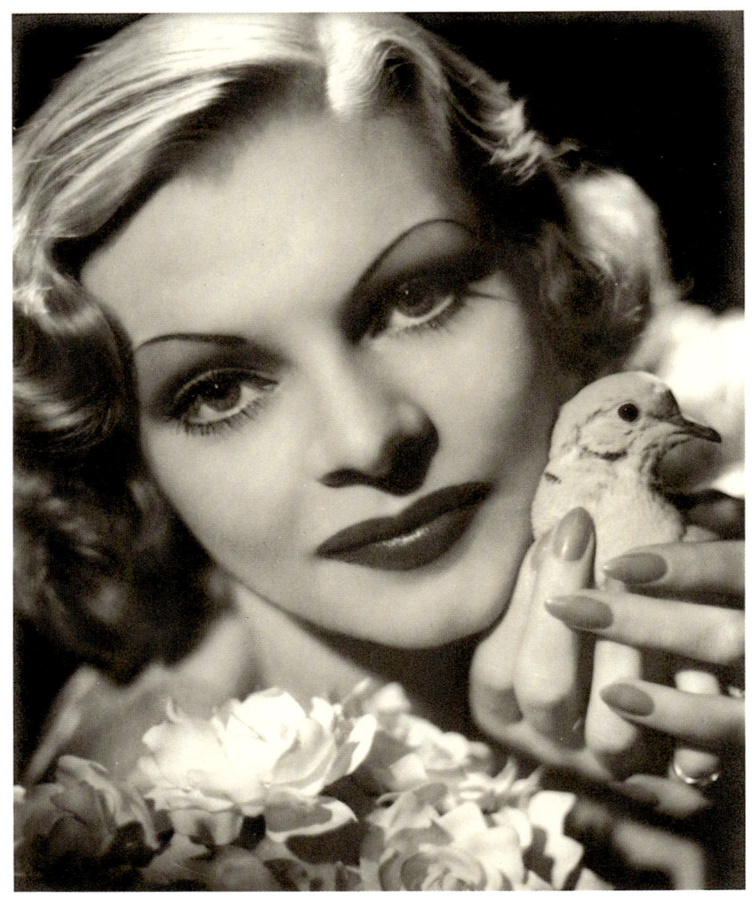

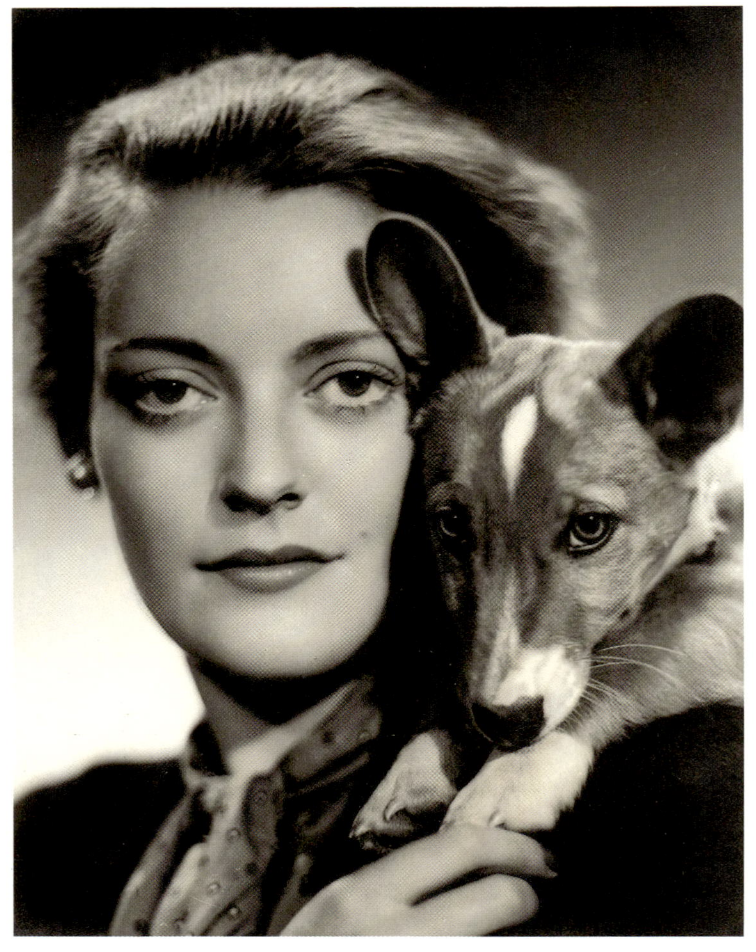

TOP *Claire Luce, actress, photographed after her trip to the Moscow Theatre Festival before leaving for New York and rehearsals for C. N. Cochran's 1936 revue, 1935.*
LEFT *Princess Dimitri of Russia with her Welsh Corgi, 1936*
OPPOSITE *Lady Pamela Smith, daughter of Lord Birkenhead, later Lady Hartwell, 1935*

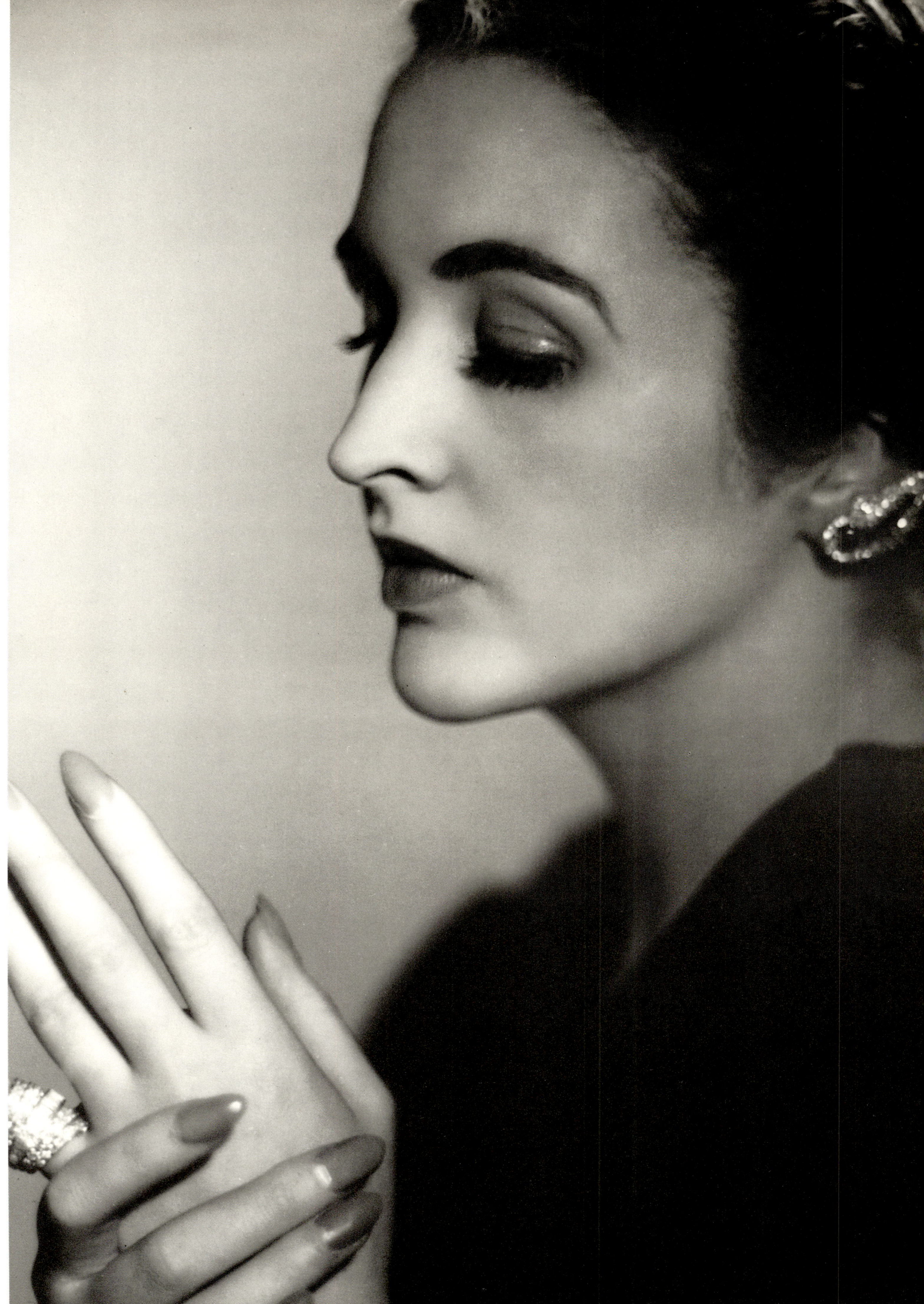

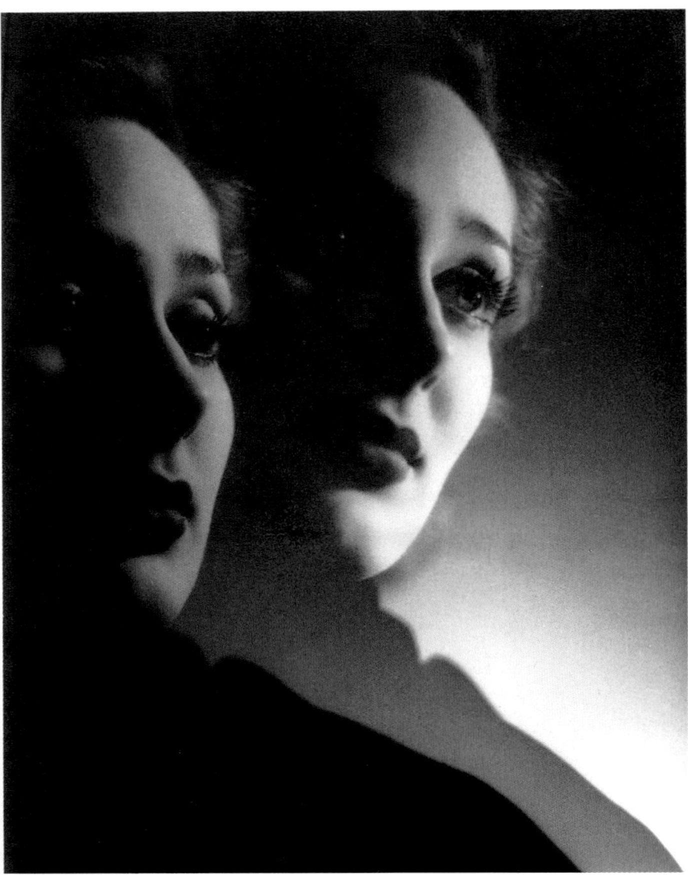

Margaret Vyner, actress (later Mrs Hugh Williams), 1937

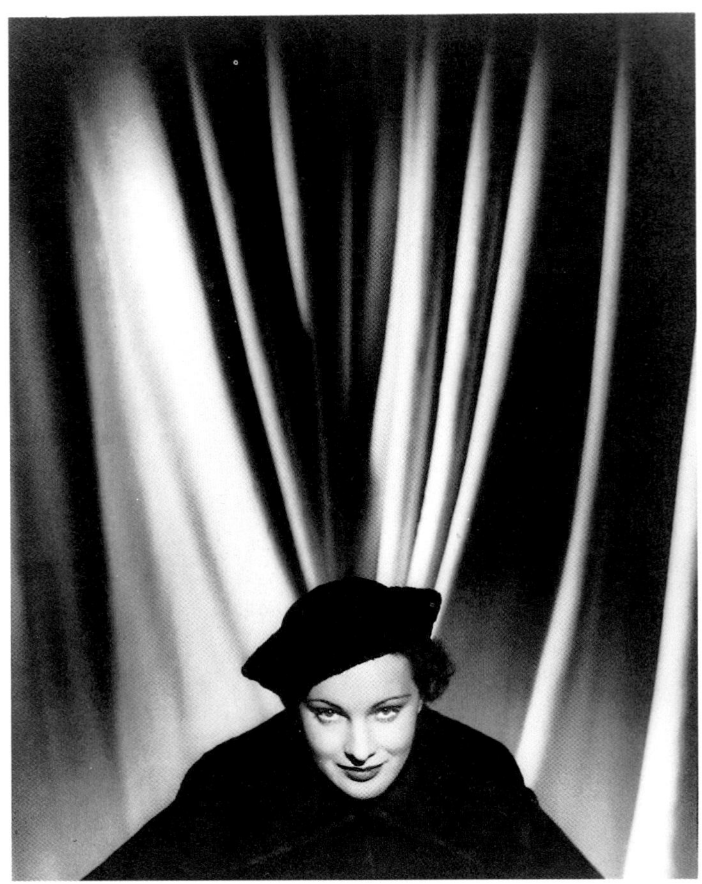

Diana Napier (Mrs Richard Tauber), actress, 1935

below her is the embroidered train of her dress. She wears tight white kid gloves to the upper biceps (which took her and a maid and a half tin of talcum powder about forty minutes to get on). She carries, at an angle, a fine ostrich feather fan from Duvelleroy. This photograph might have been taken by Speaight, with myself as the artful focusser, or Bertram Park, or Paul Tanqueray, or Dorothy Wilding or Yevonde or Bassano, or somebody who had such a mean geographic advantage called The Rembrandt Studios in the Buckingham Palace Road ... we hated them! These debutantes and their mothers, and sometimes their fathers in *levée* dress, would be summoned to the Palace of a summer night to be 'presented'. This was Court night, the night for the great photographic harvest. Each Court snapper would shamelessly advertise his talents to the disadvantage of his rivals. Free sittings were bandied about, free prints and even 'exceptional reductions'. It was a hard day's night indeed for the participants. Having got themselves dressed, they sat in their cars waiting in line astern in the Mall; eventually they entered the Palace and were, we assume, presented to Their Majesties and made their curtseys. At about eleven, the dispersal took place. The Daimlers *et al* whisked the clients, some distinctly the worse for wear, in the direction of their chosen photographer, and in the waiting rooms often one might view ten or fifteen couples waiting their turn to be 'taken'.

I remember my last Court night, or more correctly my last night at Speaight's, very clearly: it was towards the end of my second year of the apprenticeship and Mr Richard was finding me a little hard to handle. With his reluctant approval, I had taken certain measures to brighten up the seemingly interminable wait that was forced on the flagging debutantes. I had borrowed some records and an imposing and powerful radiogram. Frank Sinatra had just made an outstanding record, still a smash today, called 'On the Street of Dreams'. I was mad about this disc and played it continuously, to the debs' delight.

No doubt spurred on to finer things by Sinatra's song, I found Mr Richard Speaight's performance that night less than satisfactory. (I am sure I could not have done better.) Posing for her photograph was a real peach of a girl; for some reason Speaight did not always get the pretty debutantes so I think he was determined to make a meal of this one.

The train on the girl's dress was superb, the very best of pre-war Hartnell, and Speaight was keen to get it well shown. He threw it this way and draped it that; all the time he was telling the girl to look to her front which was unintentionally a good idea, for the sweat was pouring off the old fellow and falling, of course, all over the train.

It was his custom, when the picture or the dress were to his liking, to back slowly away from the sitter – his eyesight was not the best – holding up his right hand at shoulder height to receive the rubber bulb which was attached through an air line, to the shutter of the lens. He then took the photograph, and dropping the rubber bulb

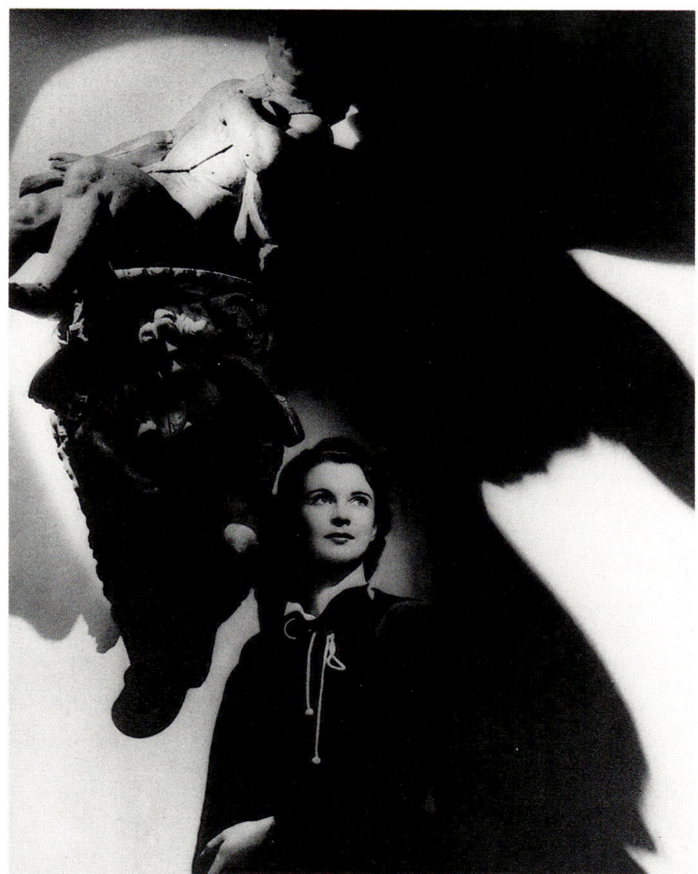

Vivien Leigh shortly after her success in the 'Mask of Virtue', 1935

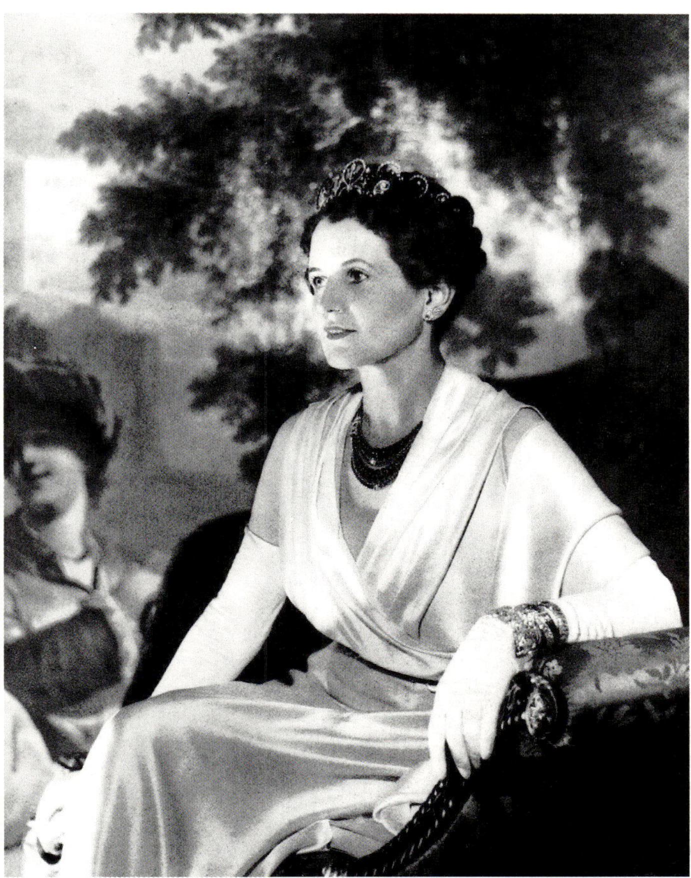

Rose Kennedy, wife of Joseph Kennedy, the American Ambassador to London, 1938

would say 'Another'. I would then replace the great film sheath, pull out the holder, reverse it to present the piece of film on the other side. As a fully fledged assistant my role in assisting was clearly mapped out: I focussed the camera and composed the picture on the ground glass at the back under the black velvet cloth which smelt of some rather unpleasant pomade that Speaight got from Trumpers. Patiently rewaiting with the rubber bulb at the ready, I caught the deb's eye several times while Speaight grovelled and perspired at her feet. A personal war had developed between him and the train. I got bored, the girl got bored, and the crowd downstairs were getting rather sick of Frank Sinatra. To relieve the tension, I unscrewed the camera from its monstrous base, climbed up a small staircase to a mock orchestral gallery above, clamped the camera on the balustrade and focused the picture up again just in time for Speaight, now satisfied with his new arrangement, to come walking slowly back, eyes fixed on the young lady. I lowered the rubber bulb and air line still attached to the lens, just in time to hit him perfectly on his waiting hand. 'Hold it, hold it, perfect . . . smile a little . . . that's right, now.' Click, clock. Speaight did not move for a couple of seconds, transfixed for he could not understand why the shutter sound, usually so close to his ear, seemed so far away. Already so seriously dehydrated, I felt he might faint when he slowly turned his head and saw no camera. The only evidence that he had that a photograph had apparently been taken was the bulb in his hand to which he now referred. Finding it still familiarly there, he followed upwards, with unbelieving eyes, the fine rubber hose. There, ten feet above him, the line terminated at the lens; alongside it a proud Parkinson was smiling.

He dispensed with my services next morning, but sent me on my way with a prophetic reference which read: 'It is possible that one day he may take a good photograph, he is a very original young man'.

During the twenties Richard Speaight was one of the most highly respected photographers in the trade, and recently the considerable contribution he made to the quality of post-First World War portraiture has come to be recognized. He was such a perfectionist with his lighting and technique, however, that the way he composed or tried to arrange his pictures often seemed laboured and unadventurous.

Portraiture died with the First World War, the death knell of vanity, and as the potential clients dwindled, so the number of photographers at work within two hundred yards of Mayfair who were eager to scoop up the remaining few, increased. Next to Douglas, the smart coiffeur in Bond Street opposite Speaight's studio, was the new rage, Dorothy Wilding. She employed a famous retoucher to paint the same sideways eyelashes on everyone, including, on occasion, the men. Round the corner in Grafton Street there was competition from Hugh Cecil – a smart photographer of the greenery-yallery. At the bottom of Dover Street on the left Marcus Adams took his famous soft-focus children's pictures against a background of cumulus clouds. Bertram Park and his wife, Yvonne Gregory, were also there, taking theatrical pictures.

In this scene Speaight was a little old fashioned, almost Edwardian; perhaps this endeared him to the Duke and Duchess of York (now the Queen Mother) who were most faithful to his camera. During my apprenticeship I remember working behind the camera for several sittings with them and their two daughters. In fact Speaight took the first official pictures of Princess Margaret.

Undoubtedly his most famous photograph is a portrait of King Albert of the Belgians in the trenches in 1917. The effective dark quality of the picture is most moving, reminiscent of Rembrandt. Speaight had told me that it was taken during a bombardment on the Western Front and the reflected light was provided by a bed sheet. I did not endear myself to the proud photographer by enquiring, 'What was the exposure, Sir, a fortnight at five point six?'

Looking back I realize I was most fortunate that fate and financial circumstances let me learn my trade with this great technician. If I have had success with my camera, and was asked the over-simplified question, 'How come?', my reply would be: 'Two hard years with Speaight.' Like riding a bicycle, you never forget.

BELOW *Lady Marguerite Strickland photographed for an early advertisement for Matita fashions, 1936*
OPPOSITE *Italian-born Duchess of Leeds (née Irma Amelia de Malkhozouny), first wife of the eleventh Duke, 1938*

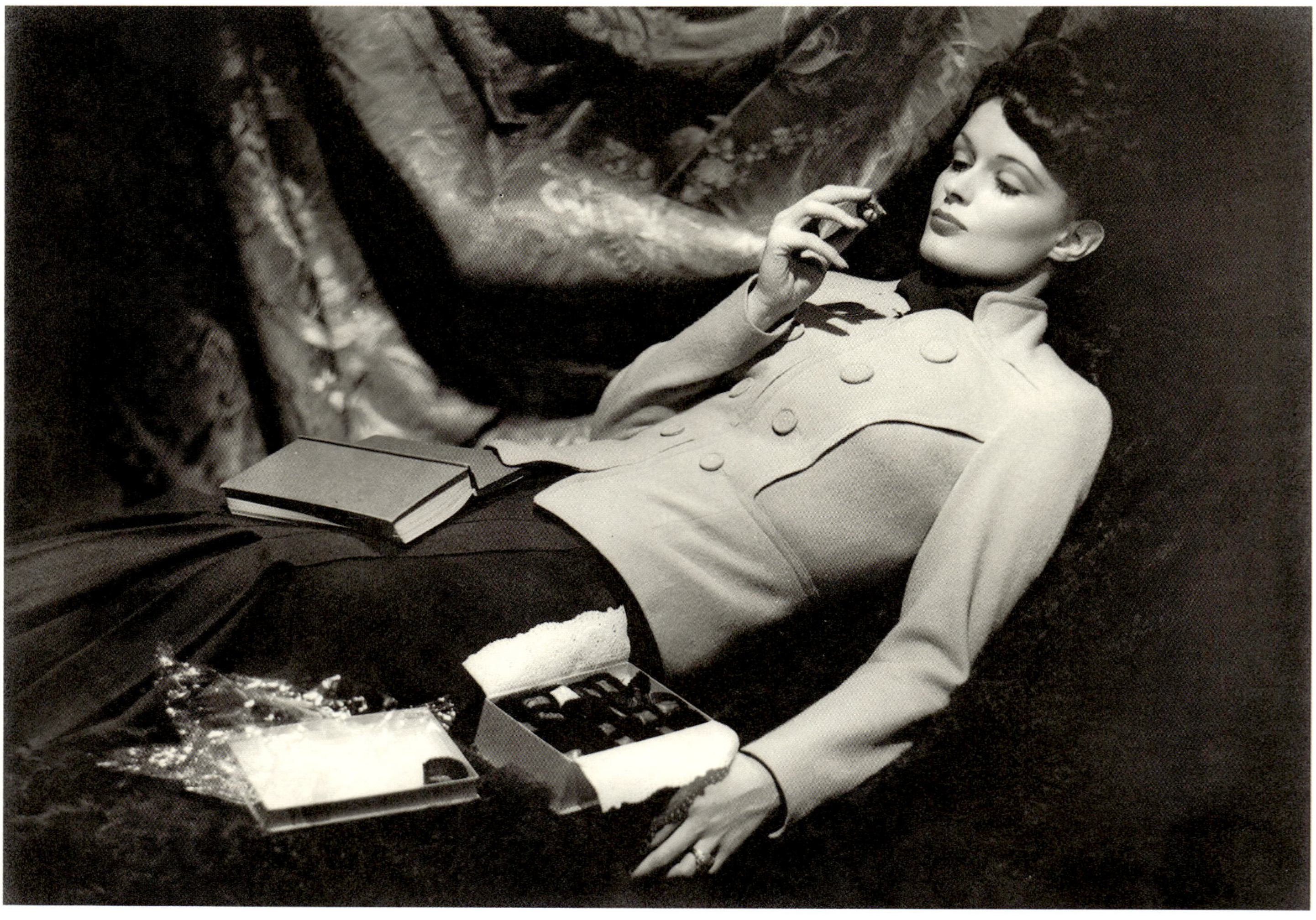

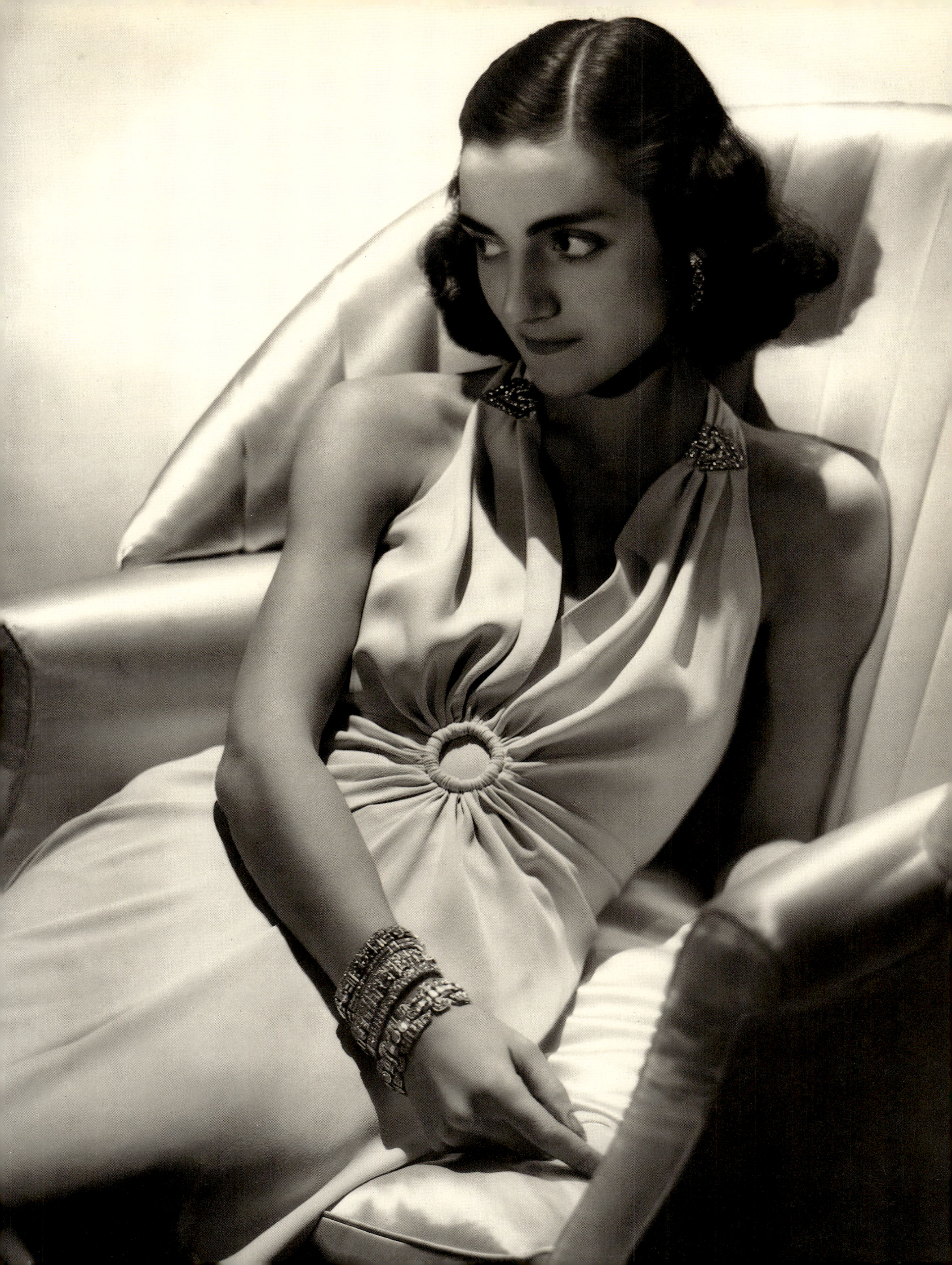

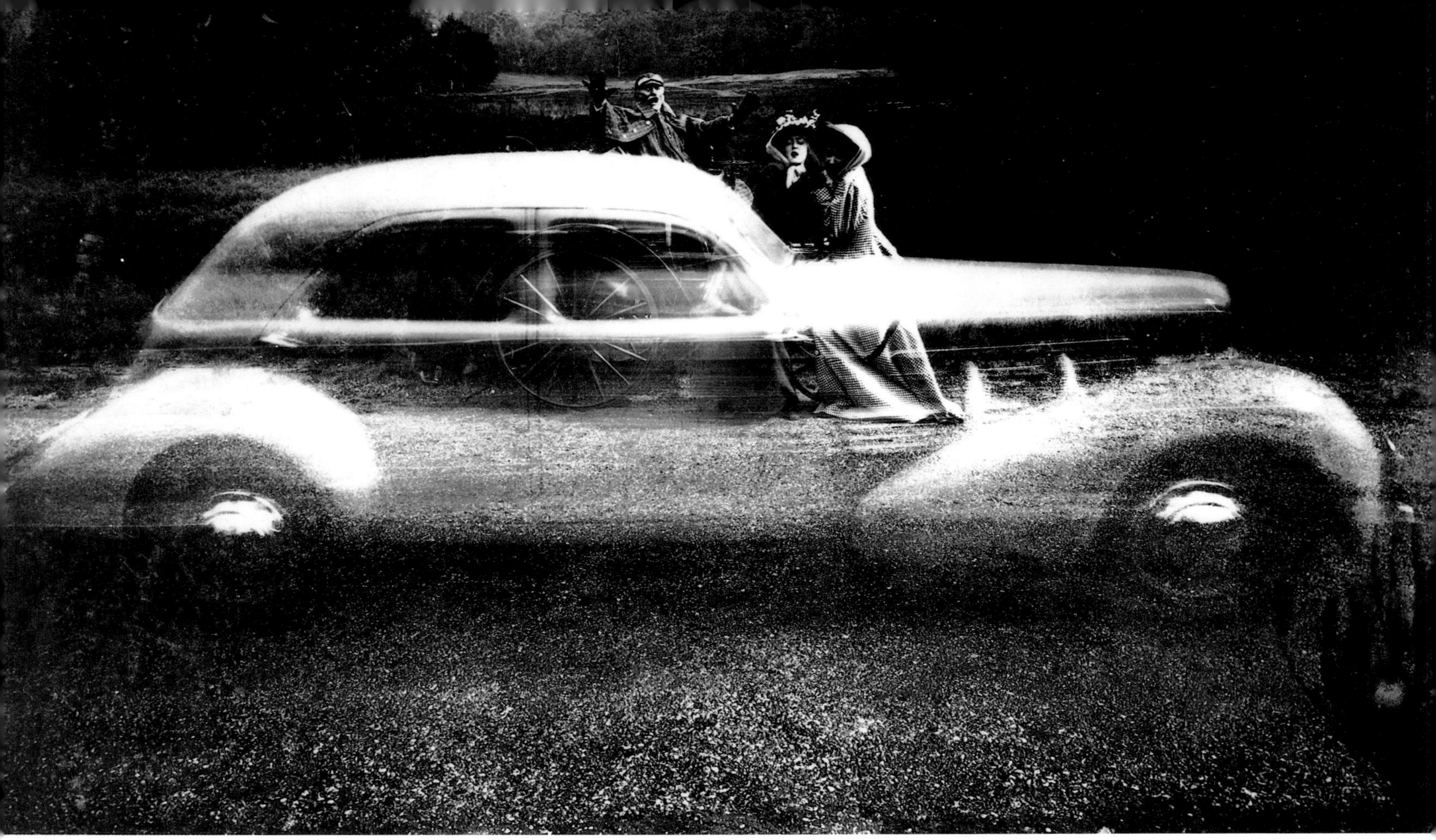

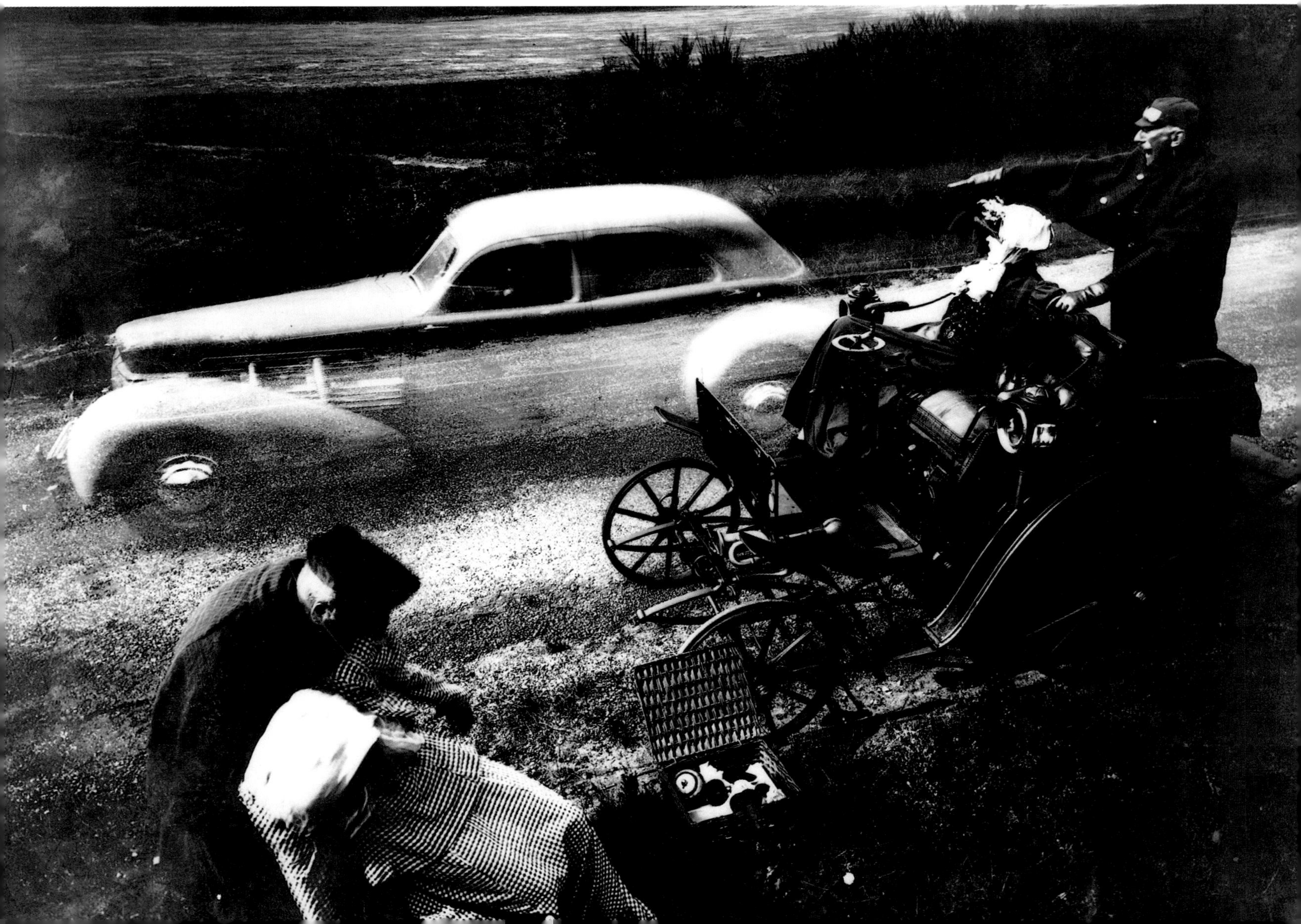

NUMBER ONE, DOVER STREET

The next view of the photographer's apprentice is of a disconsolate figure sitting on a solitary chair in Green Park. I had signed the lease on the first floor of Number One, Dover Street, for £400 a year. I sat there tapping my twenty-one year old scull as I repeated 'You have to earn, with your camera, over £10 a day to pay the rent alone.' Ringing in my ears was my father's very sensible admonition, 'Why do you always have to run before you can walk? It is madness to try and break into the smart areas of Piccadilly, you are a Putney boy. Open your studio in Putney High Street, and move up West if it succeeds.'

The first year or so was not too bad. I was something of a 'deb's delight'; I had the first of some very fetching motor cars and I have always prided myself on being rather a 'whizzo' driver. It was the lovely days of Brooklands and Maseratis and dashing guys like Whitney Straight. (He became a good friend later, though I was never in his class.) I drove an OM four-seater tourer, a most stylish vehicle, if I may say so. Only about half a dozen ever arrived in the UK, and it seemed as though the debs were queuing up for a spin or two. Eventually I would spin them into the studio and, if they agreed, would sell one of the resulting pictures to the *Bystander* for a full page for five pounds. My portraits, all beautifully mounted with a folder round each, cost ten guineas a dozen. (Pedigree items, I like to think; only thoroughbred horses are still sold in guineas.) After a while the deb business palled; they rarely paid their bills, and even a Smart Young Thing each day could not keep me solvent.

Once again, Fate took a hand. About this time P. Joyce Reynolds, Editor of English *Harper's Bazaar*, had to visit Number One Dover Street – perhaps to admonish a photographer, Cannons of Hollywood, who had a studio on the fifth floor. Fate ordained that the usually reliable elevator should break down that day and P. Joyce had to climb the stairs. In so doing she had to pass some enlarged black and white prints that I had taken with a friend's camera on an earlier trip into Italy. They were very much of the period, rather Germanic – lowering skies, silhouetted trees, but they must have impressed her, for later that afternoon I got a call from Alan McPeake, who was her Art Director. 'I hear you take some very good photographs out of doors. Would you like to work for us?' 'But', I replied, 'I only work in my studio.' 'But you did take those pictures that you have on your walls?' 'Well then, go out and buy yourself a camera to use outdoors, and be over here in Grosvenor Place at three o'clock tomorrow afternoon.' I heard in the friendly Scottish voice of Alan McPeake the saviour of my business. I dashed a block and a half along Piccadilly to the Westminster Photographic Company. 'Do you have a camera, second-hand, for about £12 that I can hand-hold outside?' They did. It was a quarter plate camera which they sold with three film packs.

The following afternoon I was to be found in Green Park near Buckingham Palace with two 'smart' ladies in tow, the Hon. Mrs This and That, and I had to photograph their hats. This is exactly what I did, leaning against some statue or other. I enjoyed myself, and the prospect of my new career. Taking my leave, I headed off for the developing tanks at my studio. I could not believe my eyes as every film, one after the other, that I lifted dripping from the hypo, was totally and absolutely blank. At that instant, I learnt a lesson I have never forgotten: never, ever use a camera that you have not tested.

Next morning I was wiping the floor with myself before Alan McPeake. But the little man was not fazed at all. 'It's quite simple, get yourself a camera that works, turn up here tomorrow, again at three, and your ladies will be ready. Don't worry, I hear the ladies enjoyed themselves and won't mind doing it again I'm sure.' I bought a Graflex for £15.10s and this time we were in business.

The star photographer of English *Harper's Bazaar* at that time was Peter Rose Pulham. He was brilliantly creative and I was quick to perceive that I could never approach his artistry. So how then was I to become as valuable to that magazine as he was? With a little espionage I discovered, regrettably with some glee, that despite his undoubted talents, Rose Pulham was unreliable. On some of his sittings if he turned up with his camera he had forgotten his film; if he turned up with the film he had mislaid his camera. If he did get his entire act together, it would take three weeks to get hold of the results, and then someone would have to be paid extra to clean them up and spot them. As Alan McPeake says, 'I think he developed his pictures in sand.'

So I bought a camp bed that fitted neatly in my darkroom. I would work during the day for *Harper's*, and at night I would process and contact the results. The last

OPPOSITE *The 1938 Cord appears to the motorists of 1903*

I was struck by an American motor car that came out in 1938 called a Cord. In many ways it was revolutionary. I had this idea of finding a veteran car and filling it up with antique ladies who would be in a state of total consternation when the Cord passed by. It was a ghost picture that I wanted to create. I realized I could do this photograph if I could give it a ten second exposure in full daylight. If you want to take a picture of a car streaking by, you have to start the vehicle in the picture and move it backwards. Then it will look in the photograph as if it's moving forwards. You don't do it the other way round. The characters here include my father and my brother's wife, Nancy Sandys-Walker.

underground train on the Piccadilly Line in those days was the 12.45 am, and almost every night I heard it rumble westwards. In the morning I would be off down to *Harper's* and have the previous day's shoot ready on McPeake's desk before he arrived. It was a simple process, but it paid off; *Harper's* used me more and more, and so I was able to gain the experience to discover and exercise what talent I had.

I was using, on location, my by-now faithful Graflex quarter plate camera, and was trying to make moving pictures with a still camera. Many photographers who attempt this technique have come to realize that if you *see* on the ground glass the image you are striving for, and it is a moving or air-borne image, you are too late. The secret is to direct the shot and to have the luck to anticipate it. It was discovering that I had the exceptional good fortune to be able to do so that convinced me and I was hooked for all time on photography – I am recalling the moment when I pulled from the developer that picture of Pamela Minchin mid-air between the breakwaters of the Isle of Wight in 1939 (see page 37).

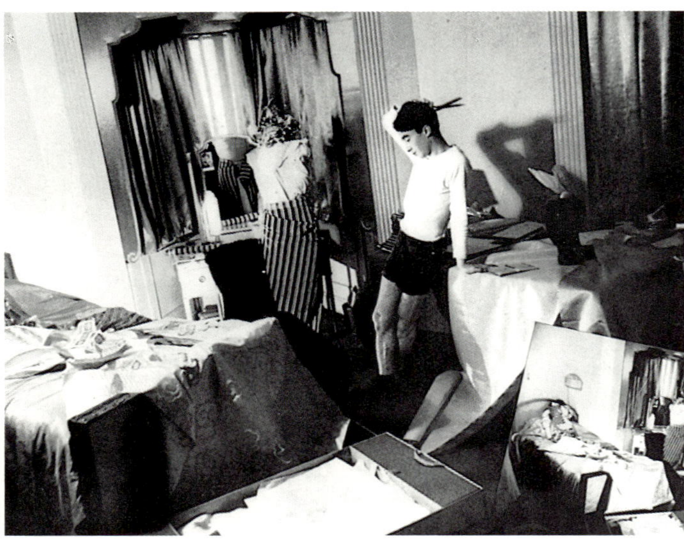

Charles James, American couturier, Dorchester Hotel, 1937

'There is a designer staying in a suite at the Dorchester that we want you to go and photograph tomorrow afternoon', commanded *Harper's Bazaar* Editor, P. Joyce Reynolds, in the midsummer of 1937. So, sure enough, I was there the next day with my second-hand quarter-plate Linhof (the Graflex was an outside hand-held camera). The bellhop showed me into a crazy, totally messed up bedroom. Taffetas and silks, bolts of them, were just everywhere, hanging from the curtain rails, draped over the bathroom door, and pillows pinned with them. I can admit now, although I could never have done so then, because in your early twenties you pretend that nothing fazes you, I was not totally at ease with this dark, thin young man. I understood nothing about him; he was mad, of course, I recognized it immediately; but then there was a directness, an impetus about him, so perhaps I convinced myself that he was not really mad, just talented. He had the figure and movement of a bullfighter and when he seized a large pair of scissors, long before I was ready with my camera, spun into an unfurling roll of fine puce shantung (was it shantung?) which fitted him perfectly and shouted 'Olé!', I understood I was in for an interesting sitting. I suppose I managed it all right, for the magazine liked the pictures and used them. It was not until I went to work in America after the War that I fully comprehended what a great and important designer he had become.

Charles James might have been the first, he was certainly the last of the American high-elegance evening dress designers. He would have had a fit if ever confronted by a jean, let alone a pair of designer jeans. He could do as much with folding, turning and flying fabric as Balençiaga in his heyday, and perhaps he could do it with just a shade more flair. There will be some who will agree with me about this. He was certainly the first designer to conceal a woman within a dress so that the accepted 'in here and out there' was flatteringly hidden. He became the darling of all the great ladies who could pay; 'My dear you just cannot be seen out in the evening without your new Charles James!' It always seems to happen to one's most talented friends – they take on too much, their clients are desperately fickle, and as they become social butterflies, confusion and disorganization take over.

There is a story, that might well be true, which involved his more important clients and his most successful frocks. It was an era of evening dressing *par excellence*. Perhaps subconsciously trying to avoid embarrassment for his ladies meeting one another in the same model, he would, quite simply, make one special dress and sell it to a small handful of people. They would have to be about the same size, though fit was not the essential thing about his look. So for a ball on Tuesday a grand hostess would wear her faille dress with the great pleated collar. On Wednesday morning, about the time that her breakfast tray was being removed, she would be handed the telephone by her maidservant saying, 'Madame (or Your Ladyship), it is Mr James for you'. 'Hullo Charlie, what is it?' 'Well, darling, I saw you last night at the Metropolitan Ball. You were a sensation in my dress, everything about it becomes you – you were the star of the evening, I promise you.' Thus would Charlie eulogize and after the lady's fulsome, 'Oh how kind of you Charlie, thank you, thank you ...' he would say, 'Listen darling, there's just one thing that I couldn't fail to notice ... now you know what a perfectionist I am? Well, give the dress to your maid in the same box, because I am sending round for it now. I want to have it back into the workroom because I am certain I can improve the look of the back – I will only need the dress for two or three days and it will look much better on you.' That same evening another lady who had chosen the dress would be wearing it to the Opera, and on Thursday it would be on the next lady's back at another place of high society – and so it went on *ad infinitum*. Charles James is reputed to have made, most beautifully, one or two dresses for five or six important women. That, I think, is real talent.

OPPOSITE ABOVE *Pamela Minchin in clothes by Sequoia on a 35-foot Seaflash built by the British Power Boat Company on the Adriatic, near Dubrovnik, 1937*
OPPOSITE BELOW *Tweed fashions by Jaeger, near Little Compton, 1937*

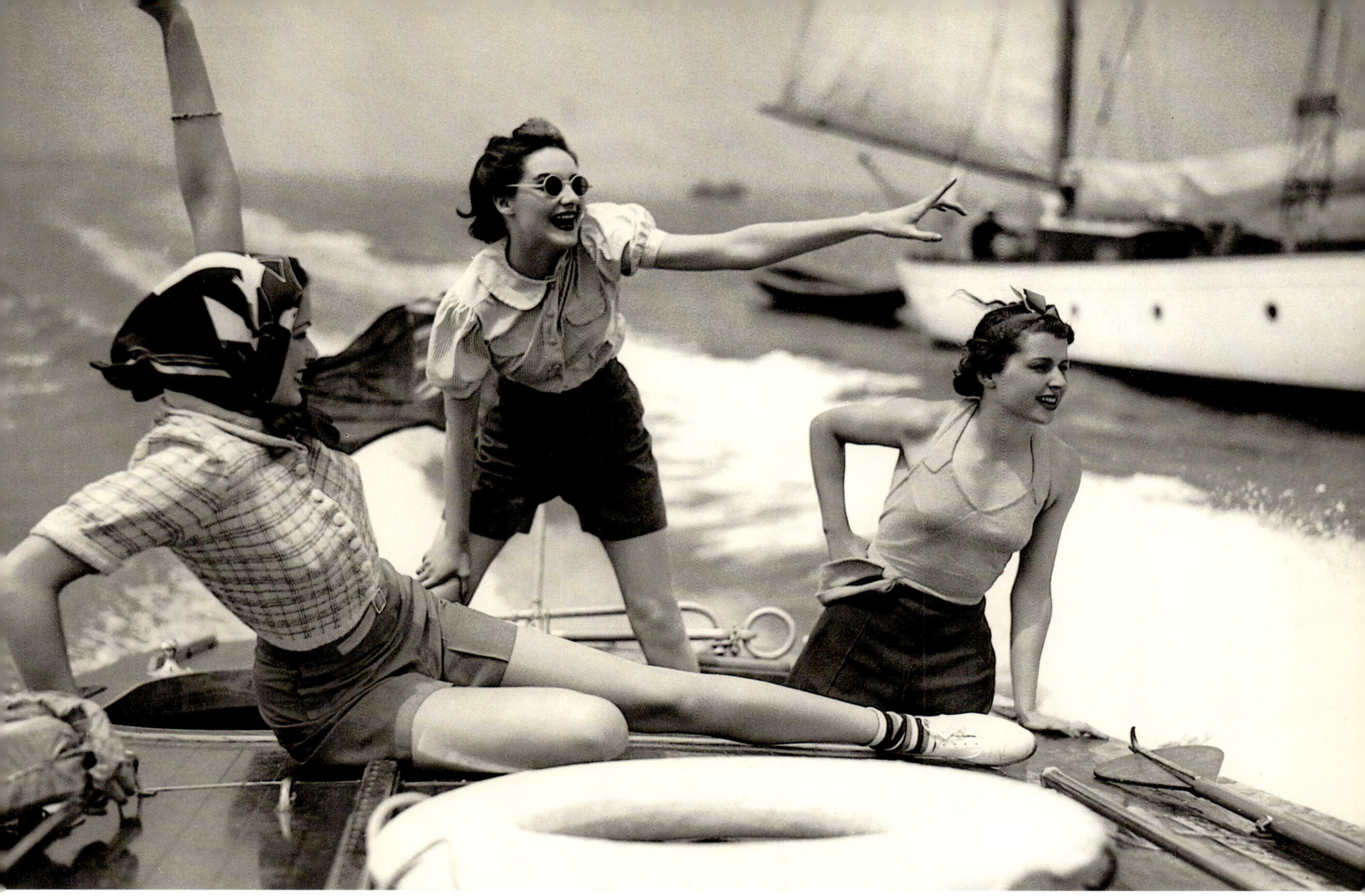

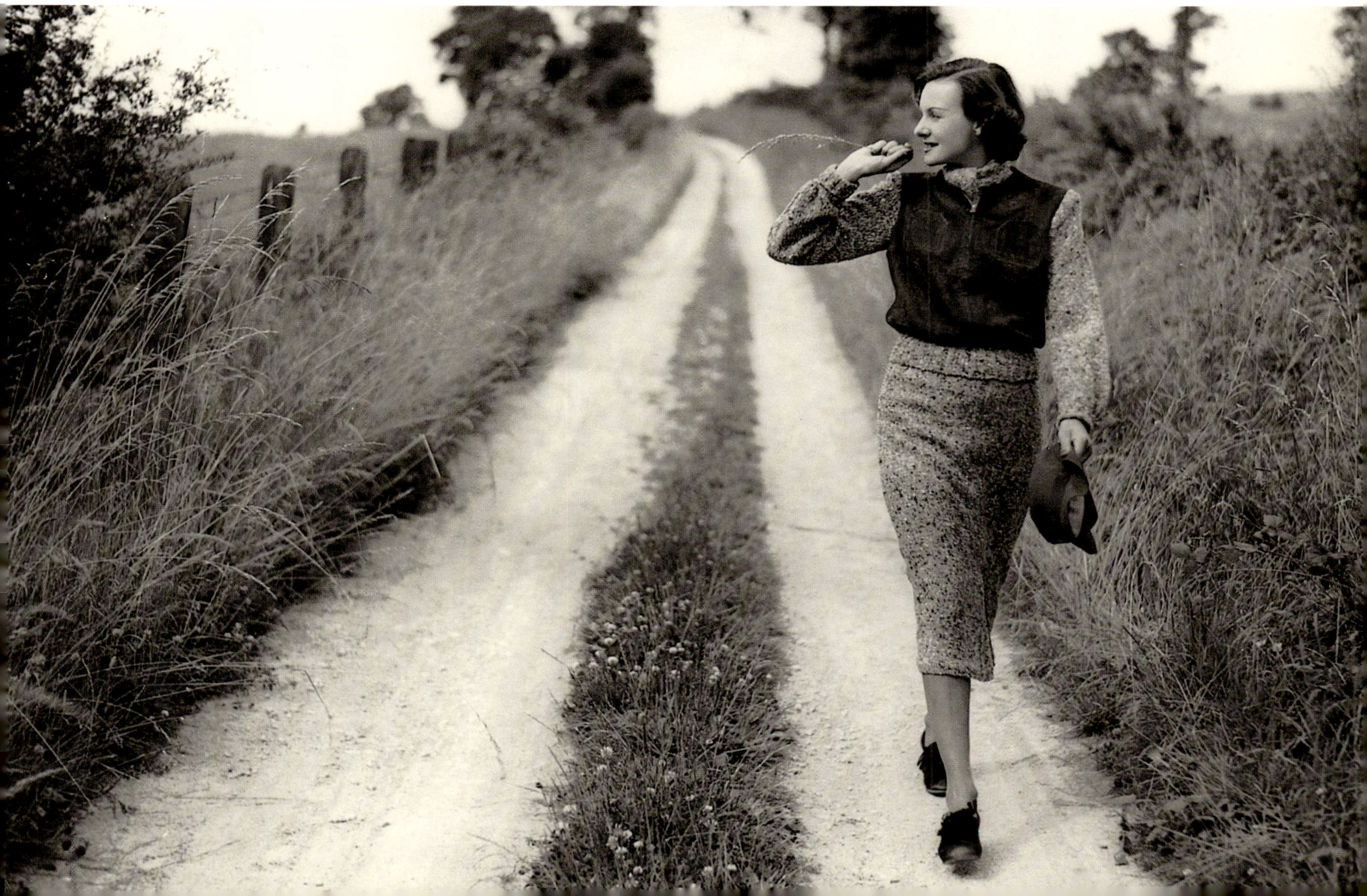

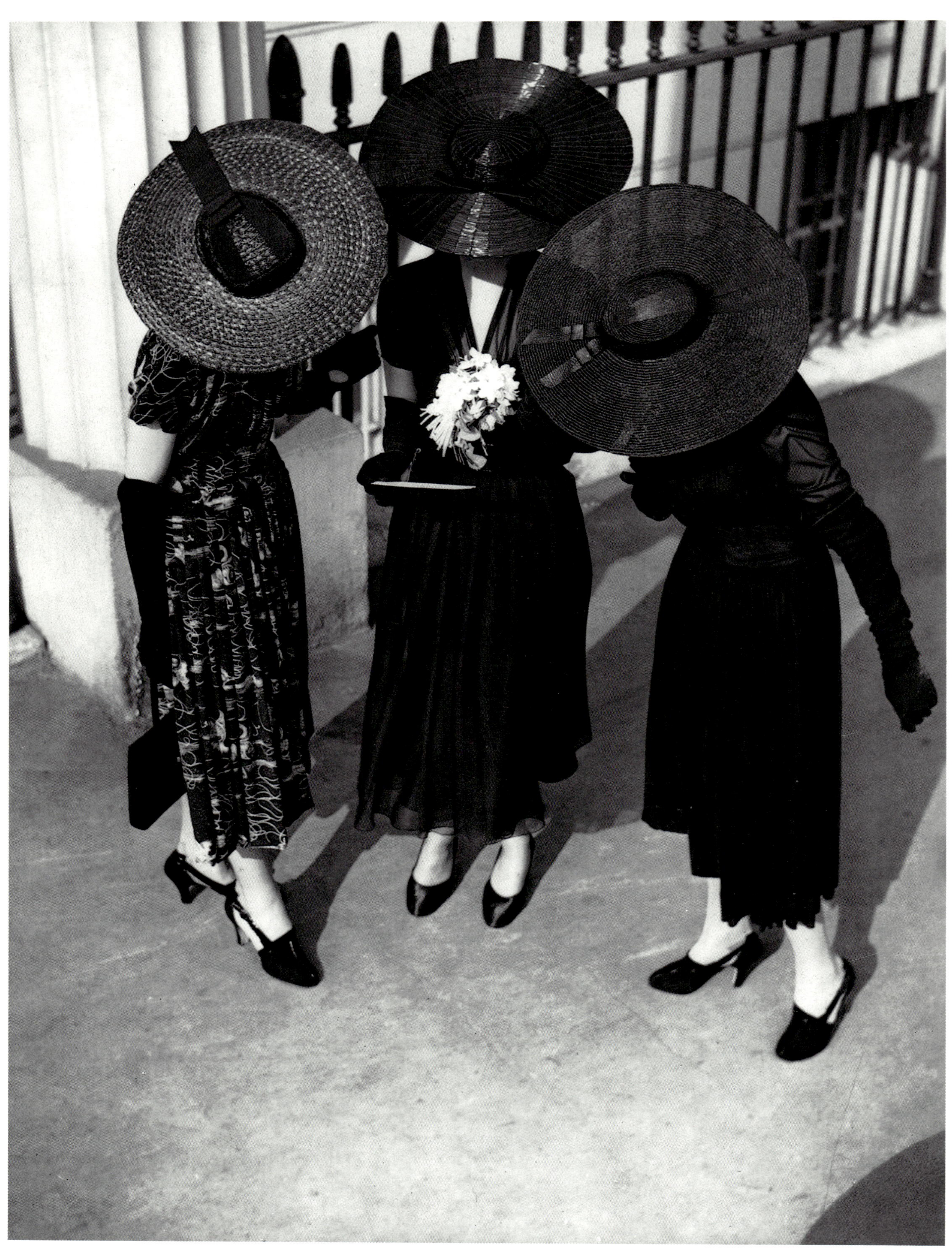

Wedding outfits, dresses by Victor Stiebel, taken from on top of a taxi in Eaton Terrace, 1938

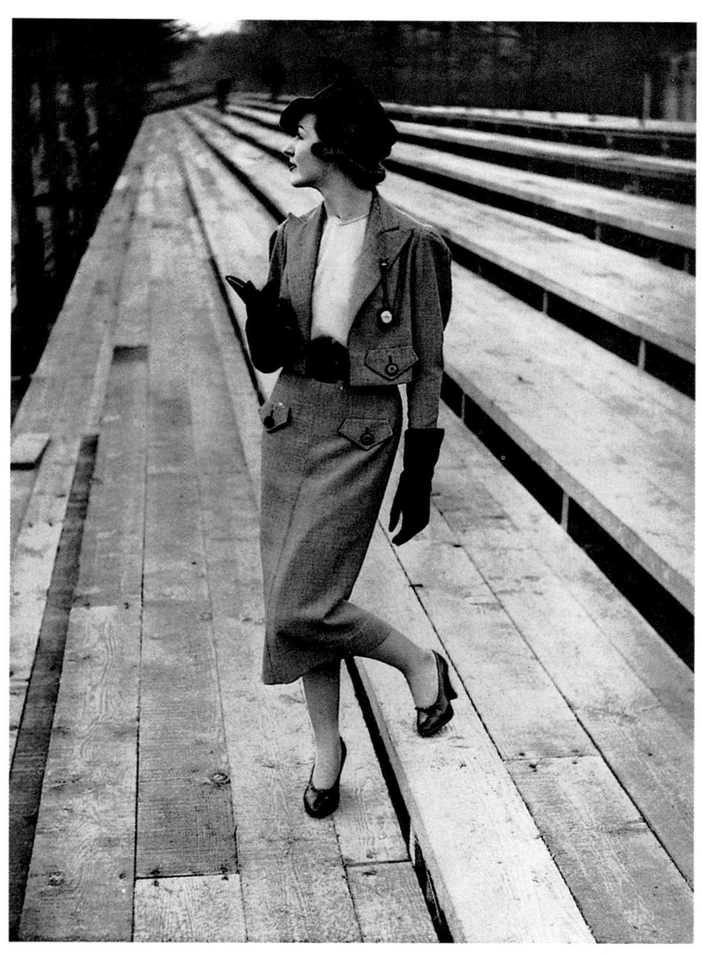

Short jacket by Isobel, posed on stands for the forthcoming coronation, 1937

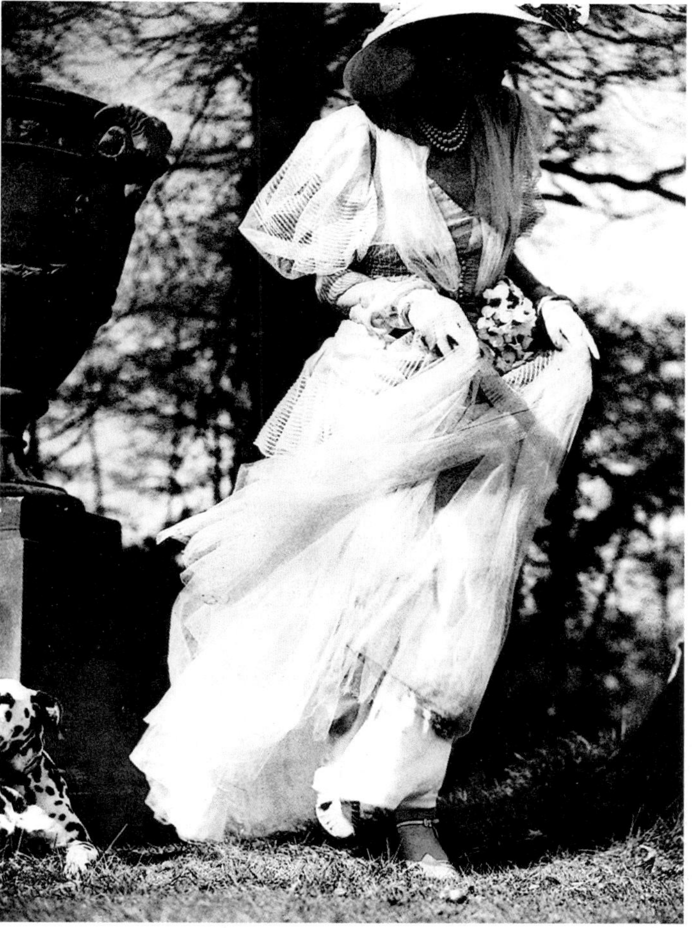

A dress from Harrods to wear to Ascot, 1937

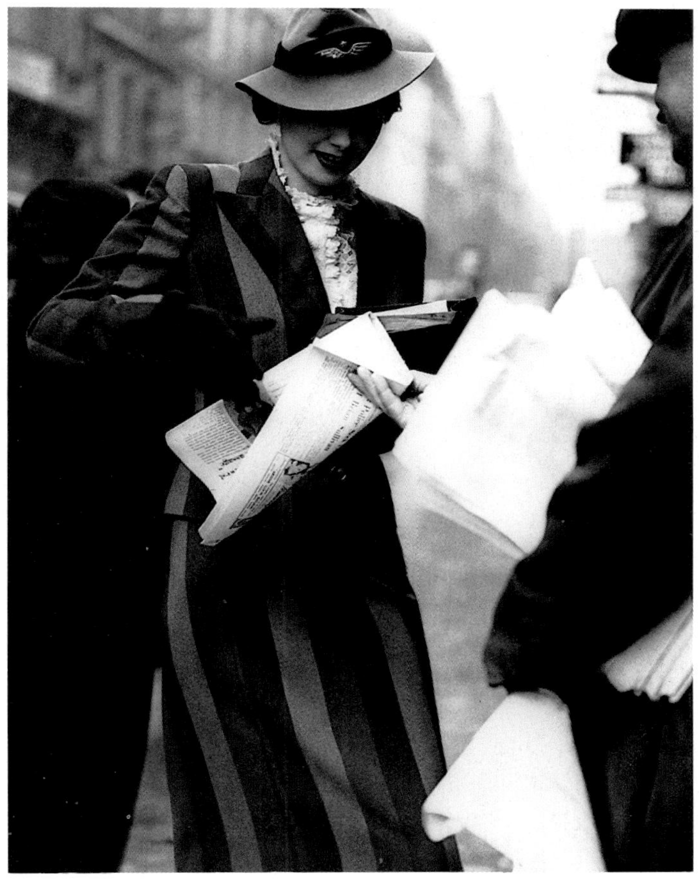

Slate blue tailored suit by Busvine, hat by Le Monier, 1938

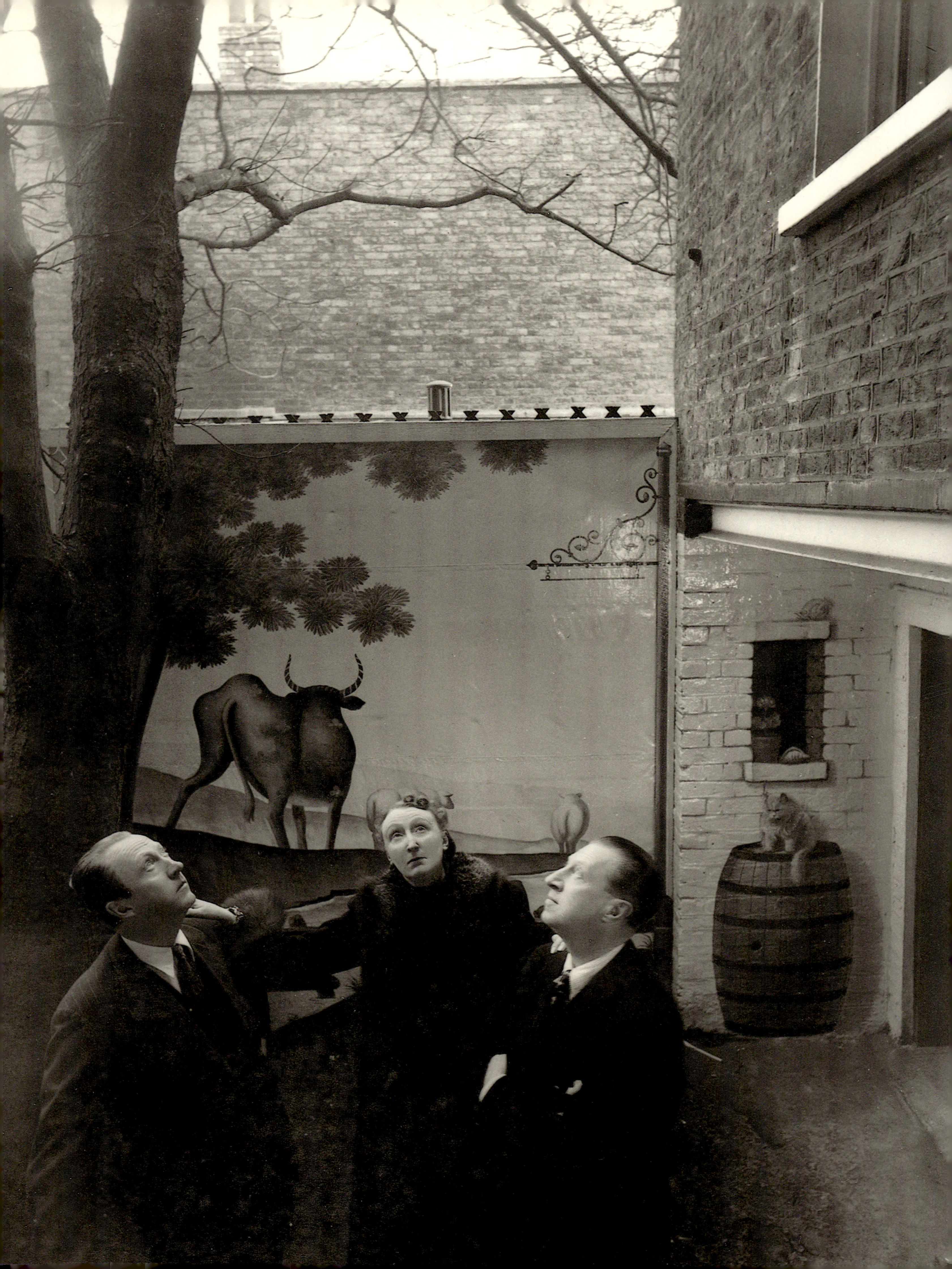

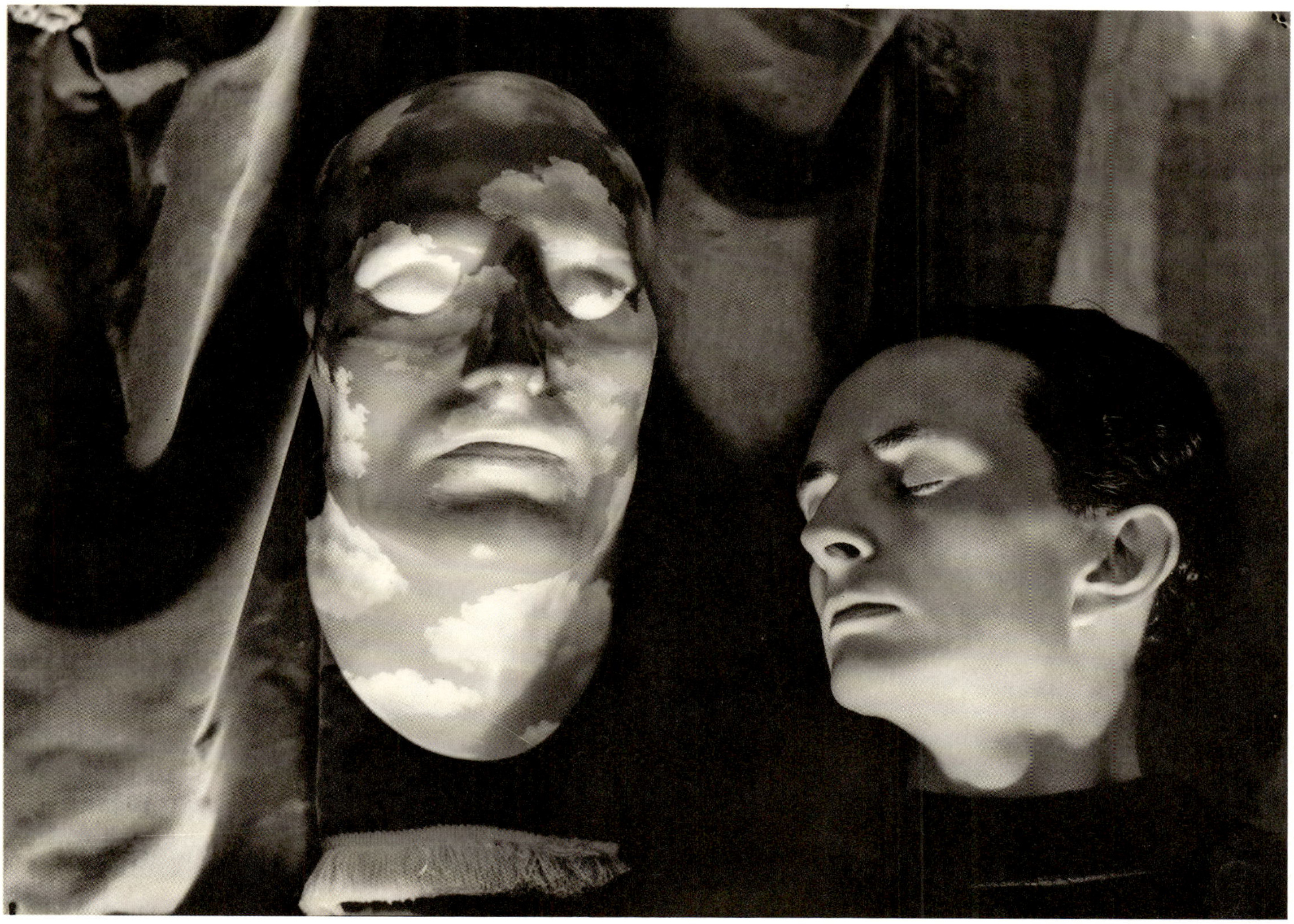

Edward James, patron of the Surrealists, photographed with the death mask of Napoleon painted by Magritte, 1939

Apart from the Sitwells, and Edward James with his rarefied ménage in Wimpole Street, I think the most memorable person that I met quite often before the War was Noël Coward. He came to the studio for a sitting in 1938 with Gladys Calthrop in attendance. I had the mistaken idea around that time that I was a bit of an artist – an idea that I have attempted to dispel over the past forty years – and dressed even more outrageously then than I do now. I affected sandals, rather a lot of leather and suede, and a mid-calf length cape affair, made from blood-red Harris tweed. That garment was the real McCoy; it smelt, as it should, of a sheep byre, and I belted it with a well saddle-soaped stirrup leather. On my head I wore a peaked cap that Locks had made for me. Aware of my interest in fashion, when my father died he left me the hounds-tooth trousers that my grandfather was married in. A peculiar bequest you will rightly say, particularly if I mention that, for reasons known only to my grandfather, the moth had entirely devoured the crotch. When Noël Coward viewed this Bruderhofian apparition (after he had received, with considerable pleasure, the results of my photography), he looked up and down my curious garb saying, 'Parkinson, your photography is very good, but you will learn that people who have talent dress like stockbrokers.'

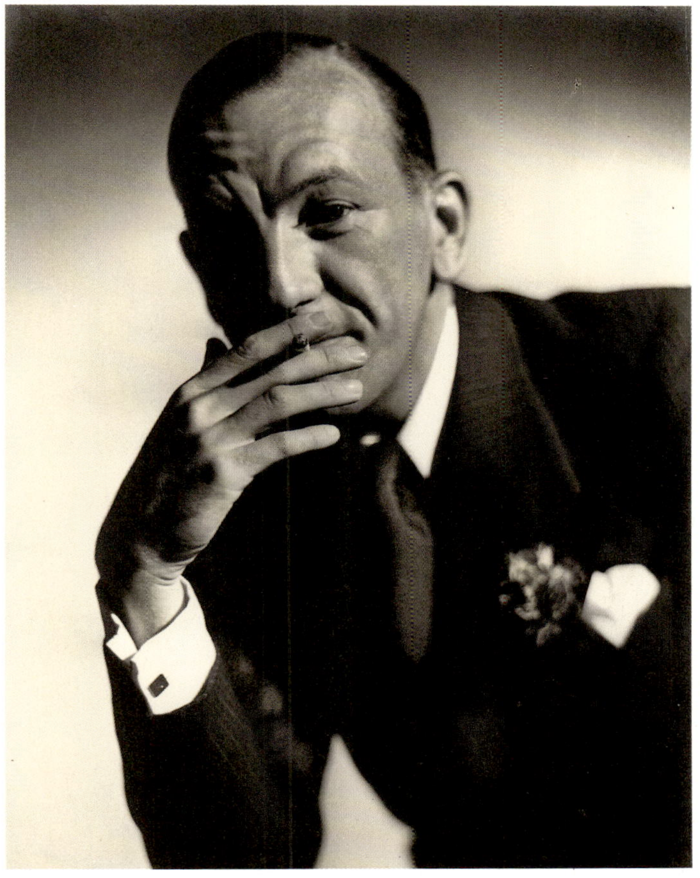

Noël Coward, playwright, composer and wit, 1936

OPPOSITE *Sacheverell, Osbert and Edith Sitwell in the courtyard of their Chelsea house (trompe l'oeil wall painting by Gino Severini), 1938*

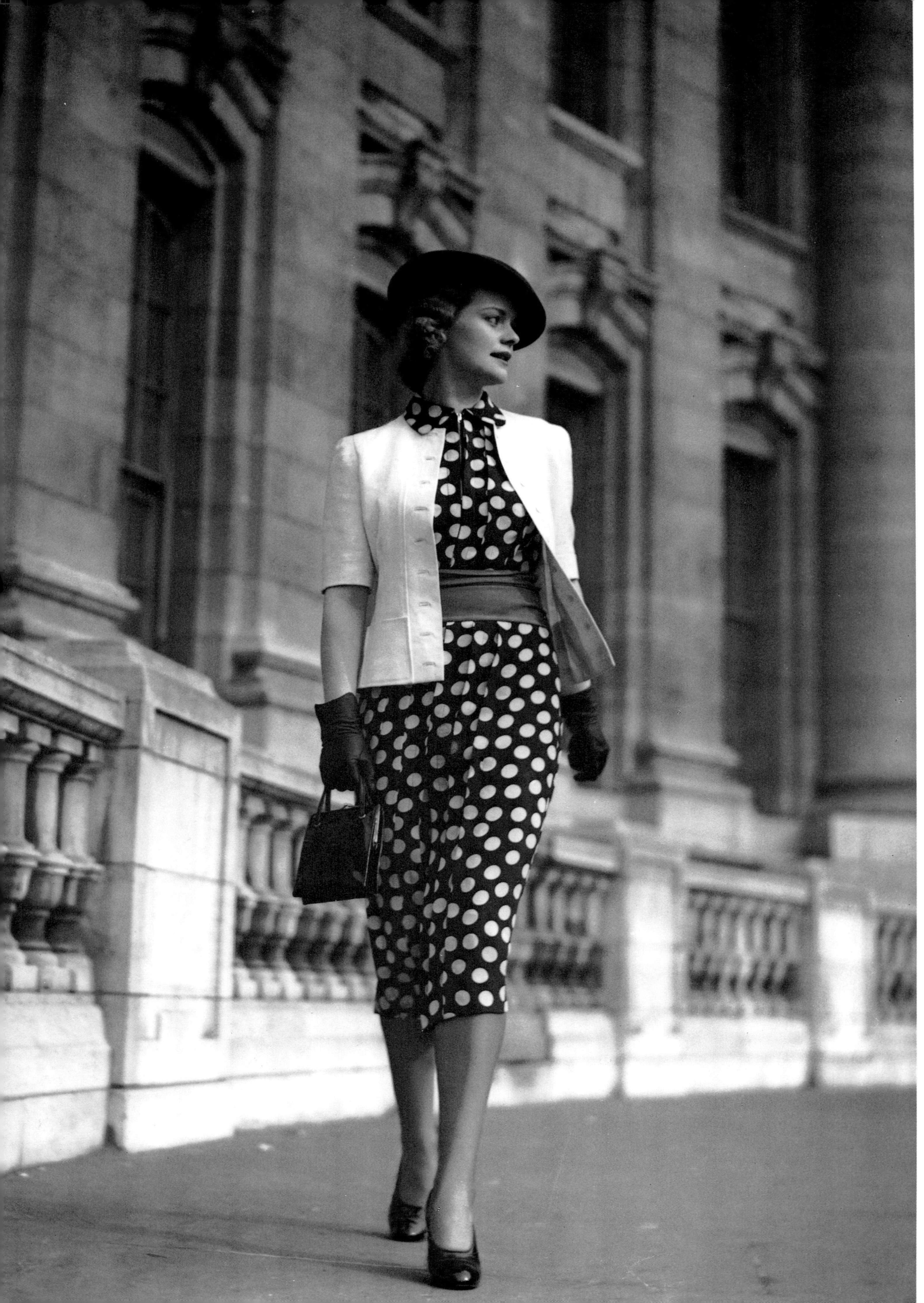

I was hardly aware of other photographers' work until I went to *Harper's* when I learnt about Steichen, Hoyningen-Huene, Durst and Beaton. But the women in their photographs were a rarefied few, an elitist handful. My women behaved quite differently – they drove cars, went shopping, had children and kicked the dog. I wanted to capture that side of women. I wanted them out in the fields jumping over the haycocks – I did not think they needed their knees bolted together. There was always room in a magazine for the scent-laden marble-floored studios with lilies falling out of great bowls of flowers. But there was also room for my sort of photography.

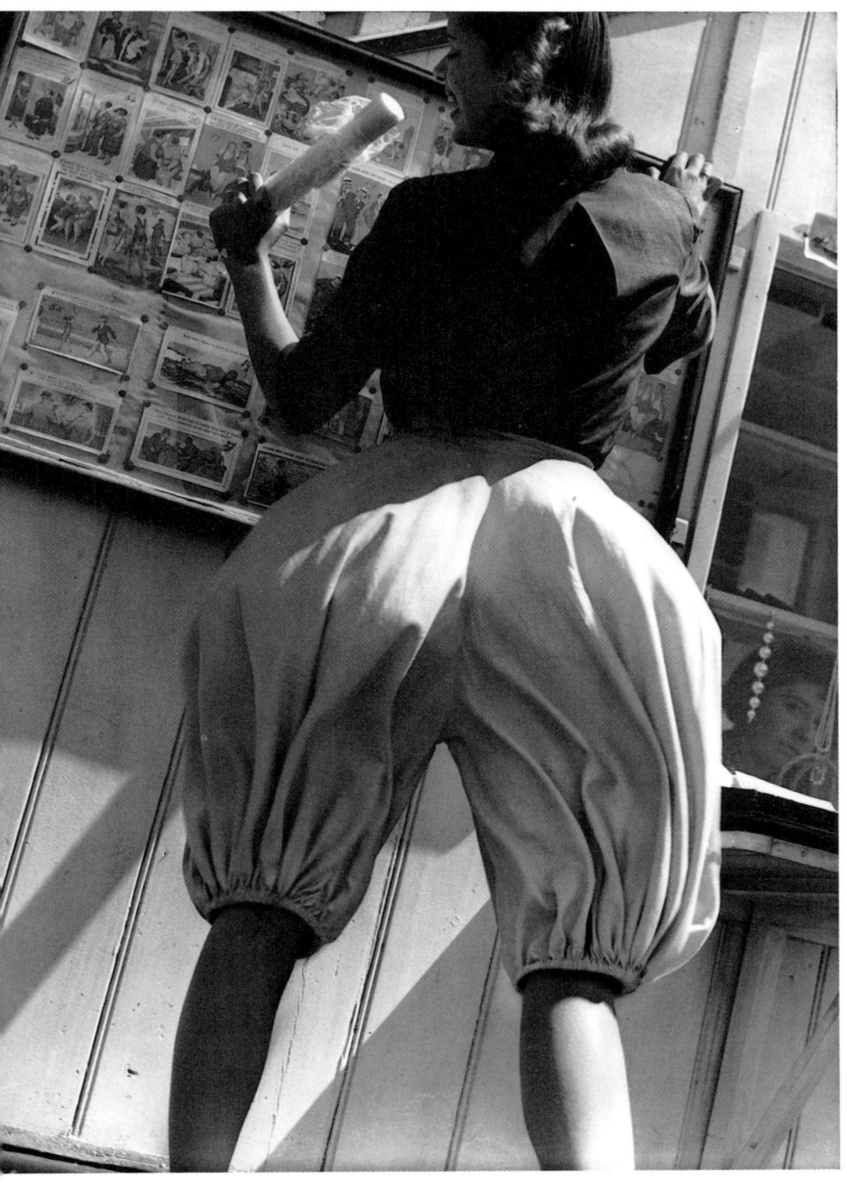

Pamela Minchin in pantaloons, Brighton, 1938

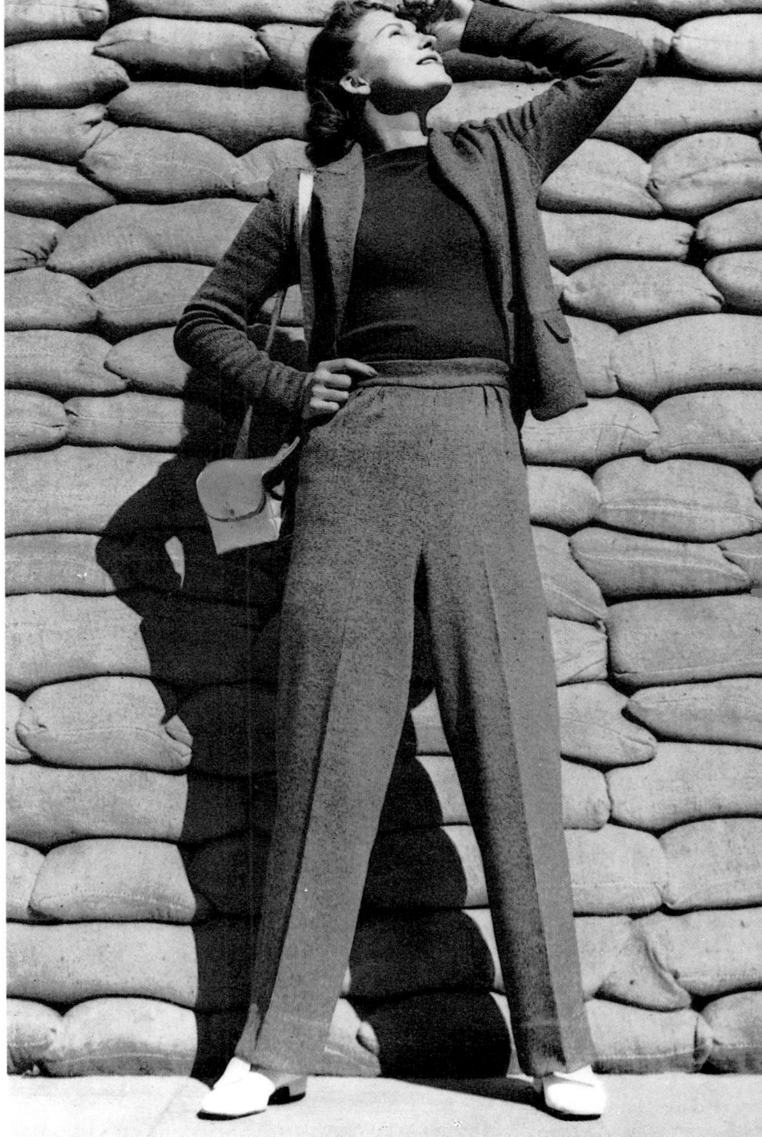

'The War girl of 1939, practical and ready for anything' in a Debenham & Freebody two-piece suit

OPPOSITE *Polka dot fashion near Admiralty Arch, London, 1930s*

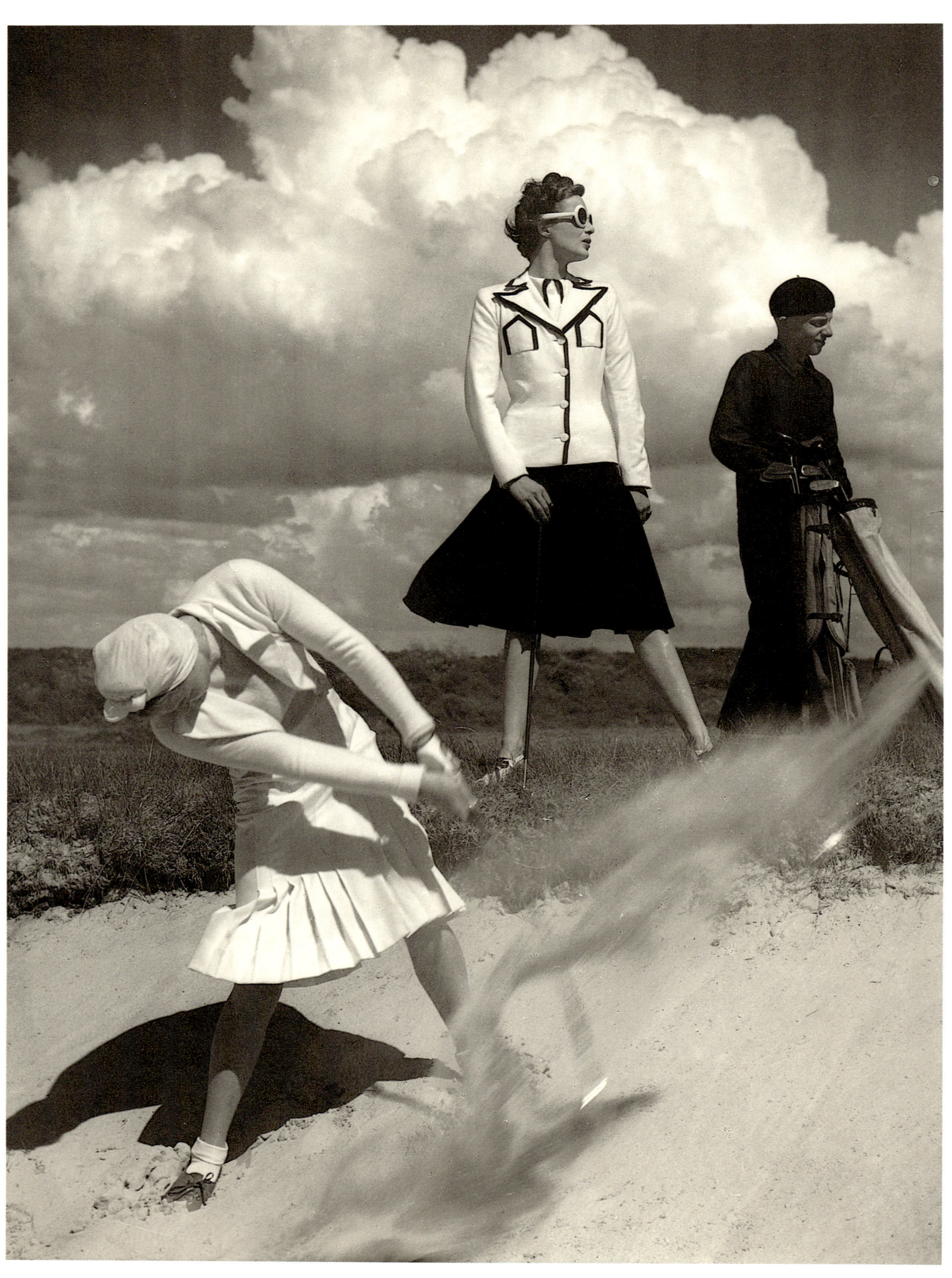

ABOVE *Simpsons' suits photographed at the links, Le Touquet, 1939*
OPPOSITE *Pamela Minchin in a Fortnum & Mason swimsuit, Isle of Wight, 1939*

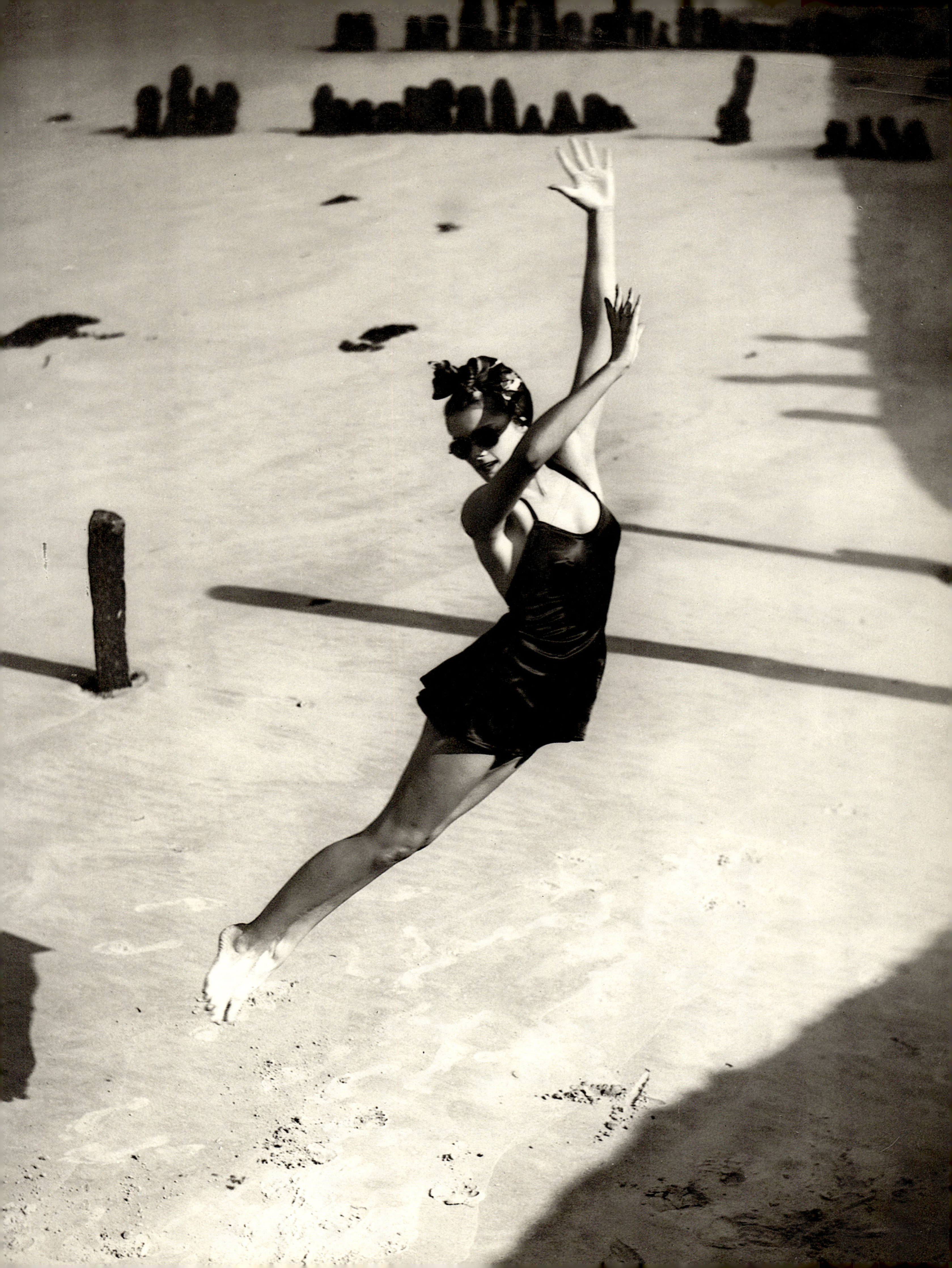

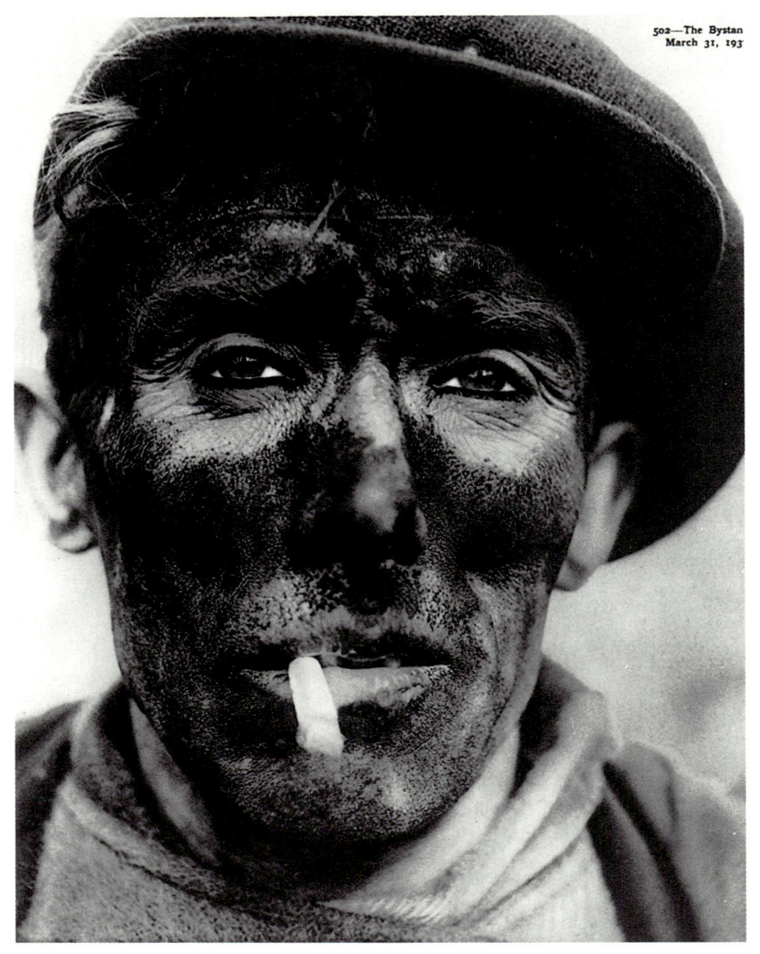

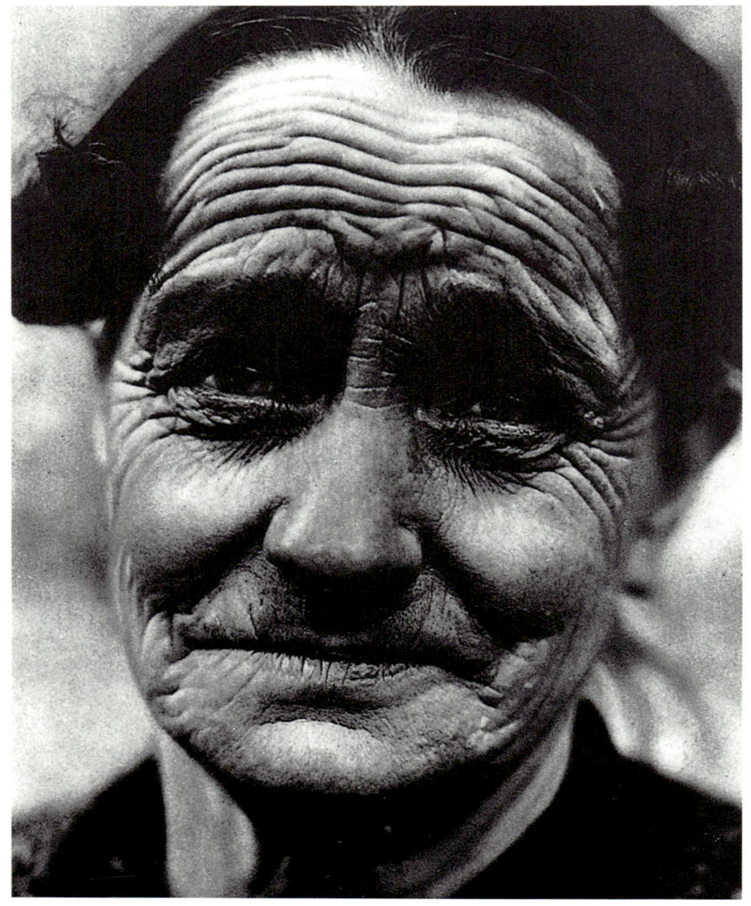

LEFT *A coal miner and his wife, South Wales, 1937*
OPPOSITE *'The Old Lady of Bath', 1939*

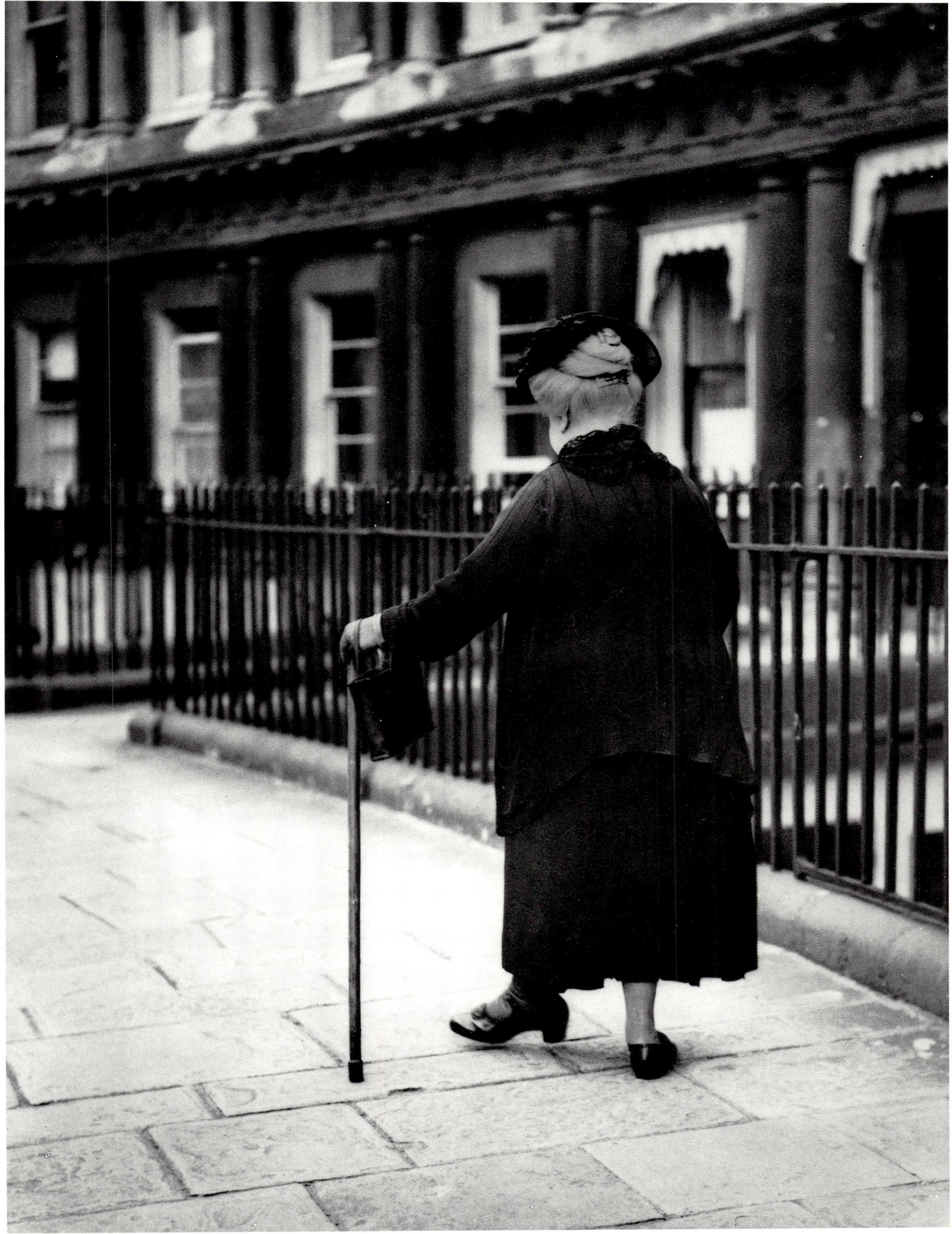

1940s

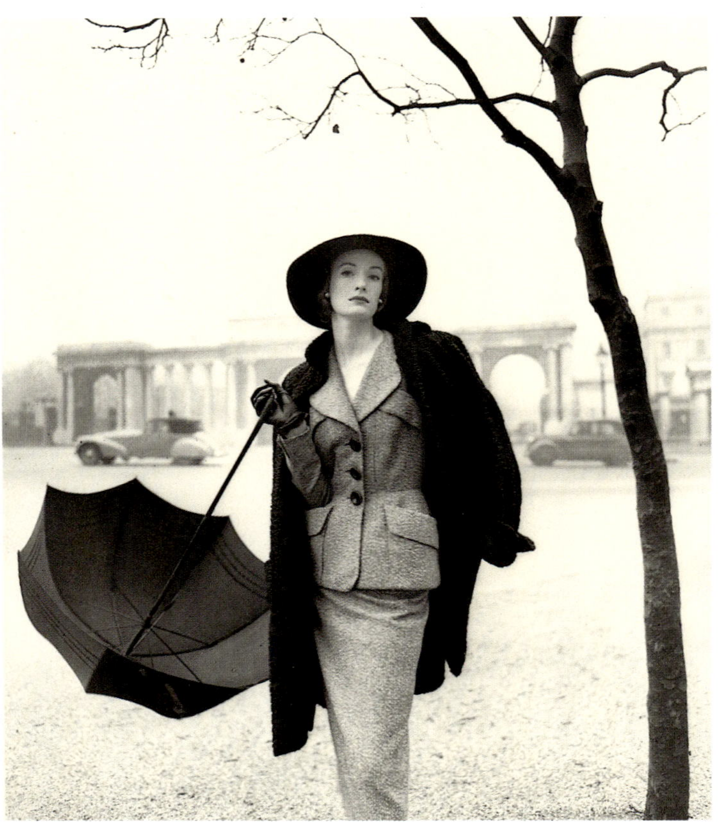

WENDA

Rembrandt had his Saskia; Romney had Emma Hamilton; Goya had the Duchess of Alba; Dante Gabriel Rossetti had Lizzie Siddal (whom he shared with other Pre-Raphaelite painters); and Picasso had Fernande, Françoise and Jacqueline.

I do not promote the idea that photography is an art form or that, compared to the great artists who have done it all before us, photographers are anything but small fry. Any association, therefore, between the foregoing great names and those that follow is only to make the point that history has shown that an aesthetic communicator often seeks, for periods of his work, a mate, an inspiration. Through this person, by their presence and by their manipulation, some of the artist's most important work comes about.

Irving Penn has his Lisa Fonssagrives, Richard Avedon his Suzy Parker; Helmut Newton had Bronwen Pugh and Denise Sarrault and Mercedes and Lisa Taylor among others*; David Bailey had Shrimpton; and Norman Parkinson had Wenda.

A couple of years after the end of the War *Vogue* Studios were in Rathbone Place, a barn of a place but convenient for the Rag Trade. (It was at the back of a manufacturer of false teeth; china clay dust was everywhere.) I was doing a feature on travel clothes, and the editors, I remember, were all excited over a new model that Cecil Beaton had discovered in a play at the Arts Theatre. 'She's such a good actress, you know Parks, you'll love her.' Well, the person in question was produced from the dressing-room;

*When I asked Helmut Newton which model he would like me to include here, he produced, after some days of deliberation, the following list: Bronwen Pugh, Margaret Hibble and Maggie Tabberer in the fifties, Denise Sarrault, Mercedes, and Willie van Rooy in the sixties, Aria-Emanuelle in the early seventies, followed by Lisa Taylor and Rosemary McGrotha and, in the eighties, Sylvia Alexandra and Arielle.

ABOVE *Wenda in a Hardy Amies suit, near Rotten Row, Hyde Park Corner, 1951*
OPPOSITE *Wenda in a Molyneux satin evening dress with a 1907 Silver Ghost Rolls-Royce, 1951*

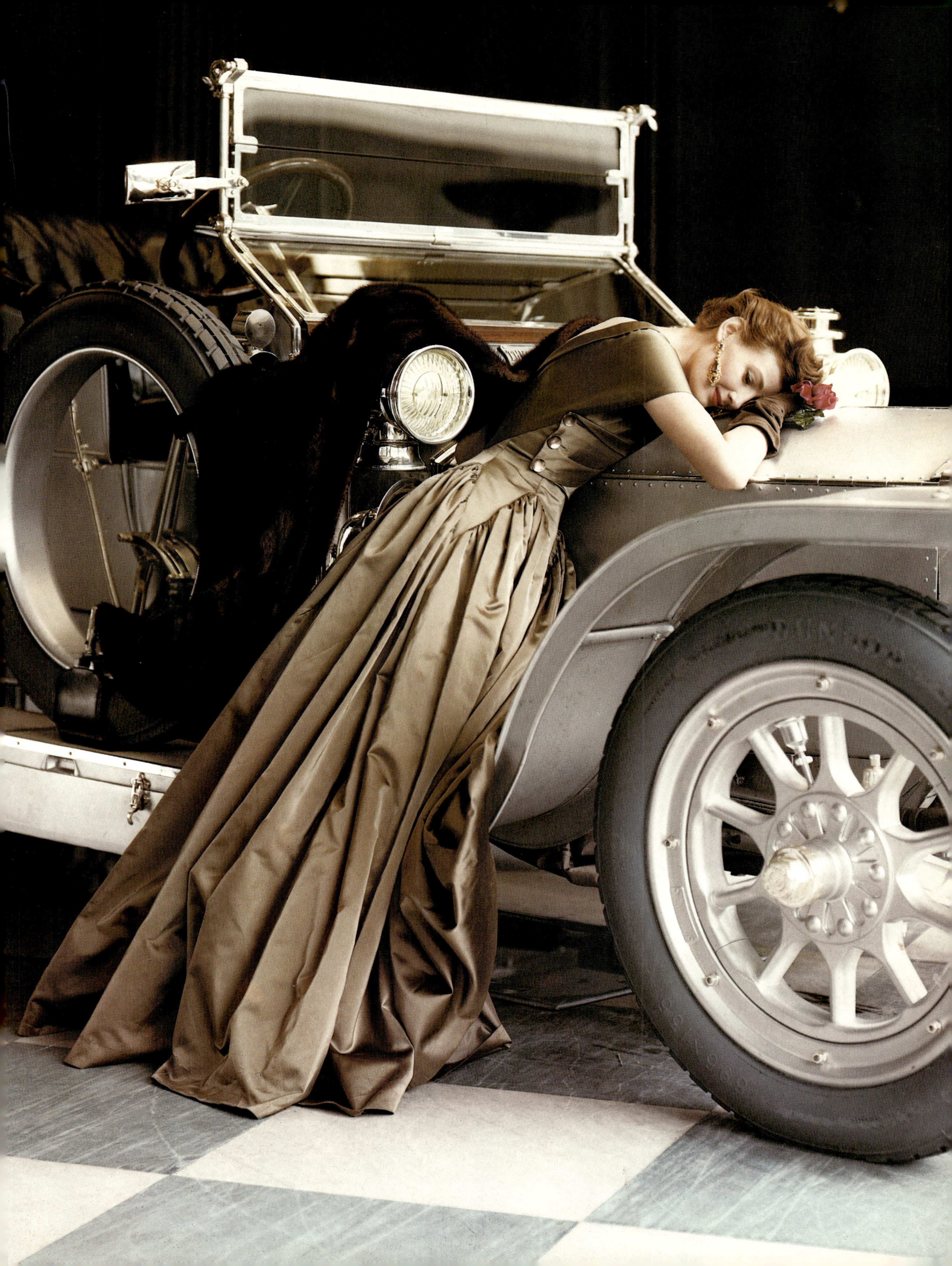

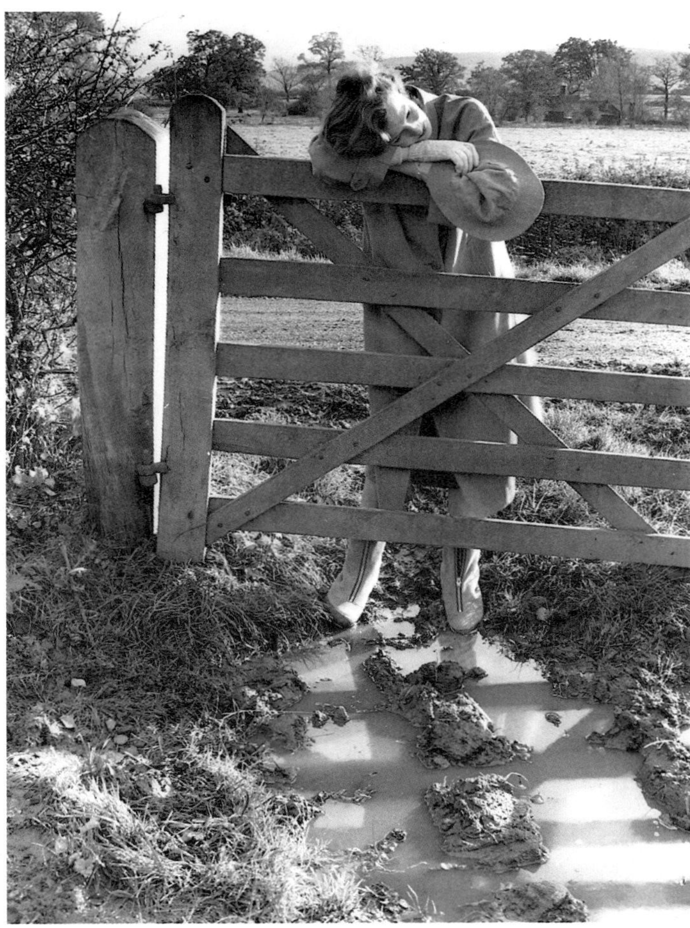

Wenda in a Burberry raincoat, 1951

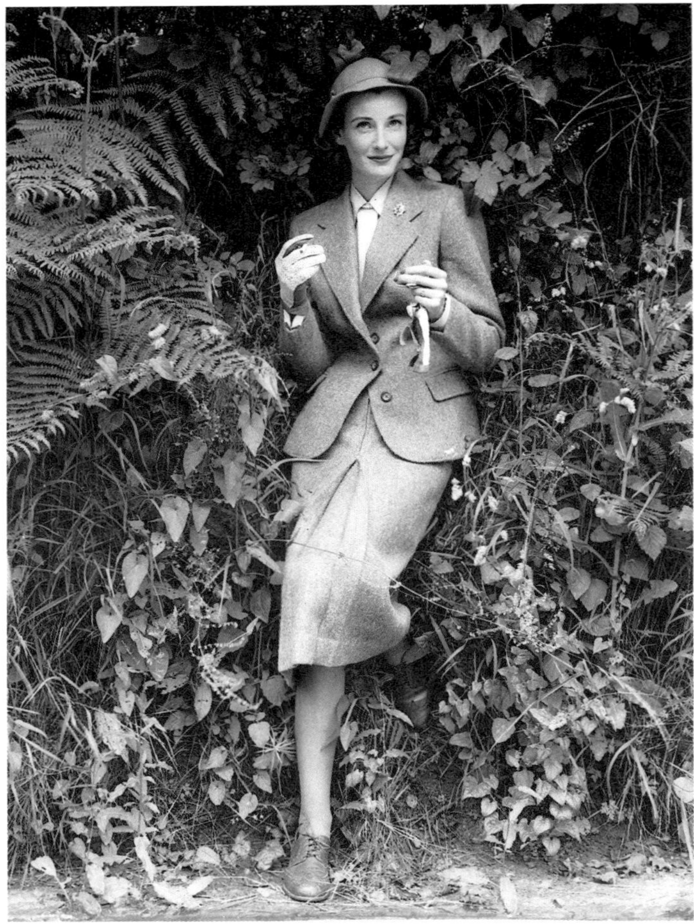

Wenda in a Scottish tweed suit by Sumrie, 1951

apparently ready to go motoring, she was half-hidden in a heavy tweed coat, while on her head was plonked an all-enveloping hat. 'So, what's under the hat?' I asked – a question which Wenda recalls to this day as absolutely devastating. I found it entirely straightforward.

She was working with Peter Ashmore who was directing the shows at the Oxford Playhouse, and at the age of twenty had got just about the best review that I have ever read for a theatrical performance. Stanley Parker, the *Oxford Mail* critic, devoted his whole piece to her first appearance in *Gaslight* and was almost beside himself in his admiration: 'In the interval [she] was compared with ... Miss Gwen Ffrangcon-Davies, who created the role, and Miss Diana Wynyard, who played it in the film, but this, I think, does her insufficient justice for she has more depth and width than either of them ... Without the slightest hesitation, or the veriest qualm, I foretell fame for Miss Wenda Rogerson. At the final curtain she was the cause of a quite extraordinary demonstration. Flowers, cheers, and insistent demands for "Speech" showed that all Oxford recognized a great actress in the bud. And she received her homage like a baby Bernhardt. Miss Rogerson is 20 years old today. Many happy and laurel-crowned returns.'

She moved to the Arts Theatre Club when we started to 'walk out'. I do not recommend the courting of an actress when she is working. Your evenings are bleak and lonely, you cannot make up your mind whether you should drink too much or eat too much – or both, as you wait endlessly for the last ten minutes of the last act. You feel such a Charlie hanging round the Stage Door exits. The stage doorman hates your face – he soon learns to recognize it well. Since he despises you anyhow, you have all the time to have a personal altercation on the merits of handing him a hefty tip or just snarling and playing blasé; you feel in your gut that he would see through the tip as just 'sucking up'. So, if the weather is not too ghastly you just stroll up and down in a highly unconcerned manner until he pokes his head out of those swing doors and announces: 'She'll be down in five minutes'. That really stops you in your tracks – how on earth does he know who you are waiting for anyway?

Without a doubt Wenda was a great actress with a great future. There is a handful of theatrical directors and stage personalities who feel that I wooed her away from the boards while she stood on the threshold of a shining career. She will tell you, I am sure, that it was entirely her decision. One or two incidents took place, not unrelated to the casting couch, which disenchanted her and we left London never again to hang around theatreland. We were married in a tiny Cornish village – it is so long ago I even forget the place. But the occasion is vividly remembered. It was a very hot spring day and a very small registry office. The open windows were almost larger than the room itself. We managed to find a couple of girls as witnesses in a nearby W.H.Smith shop. The ring, a fine worn golden strap second hand, cost 3s 6d from a pawn broker's.

OPPOSITE *Wenda in a hand-knit cashmere twinset, the public bar, Hobnails Inn, Little Washbourne, 1951*

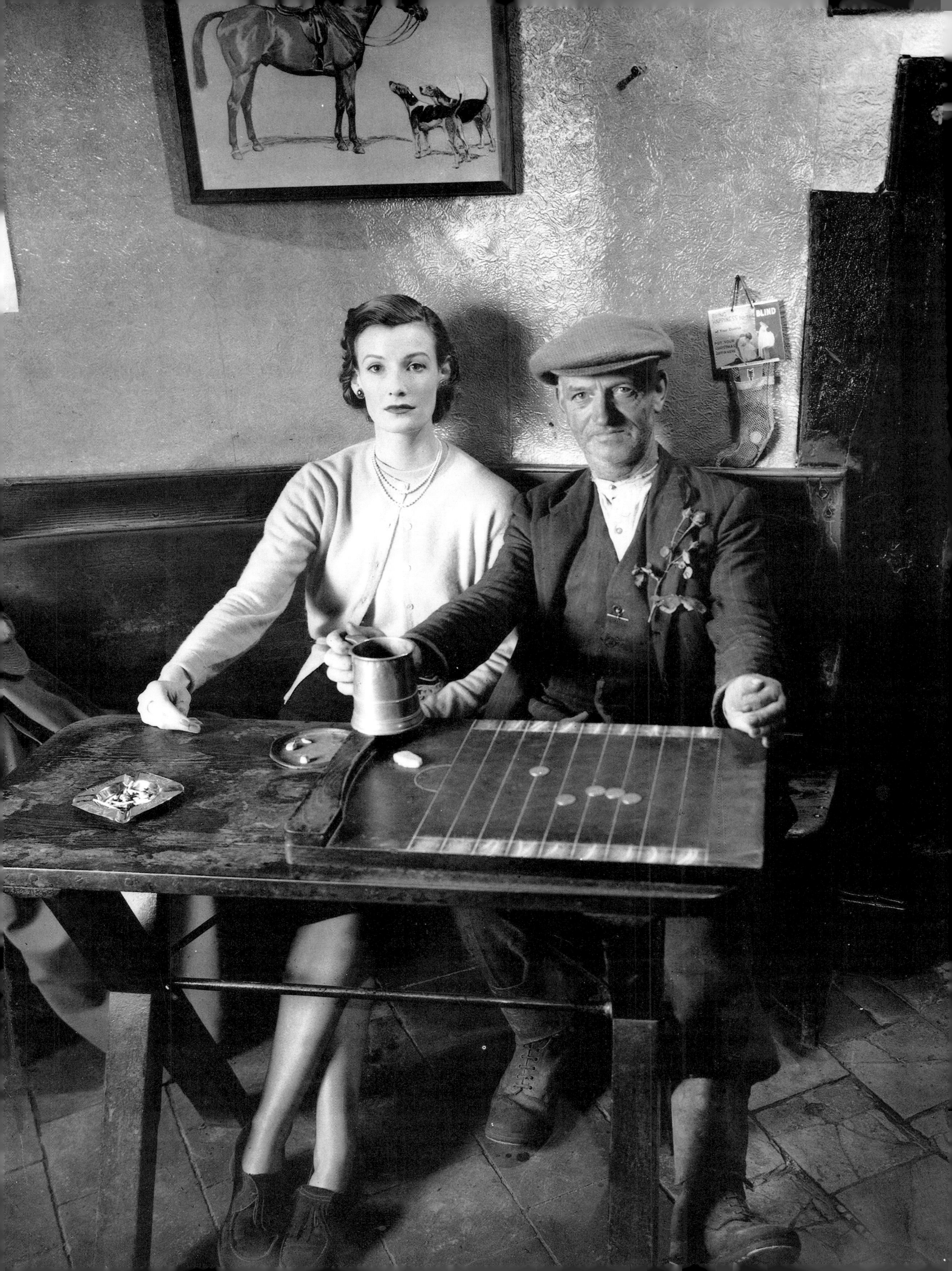
BLIND

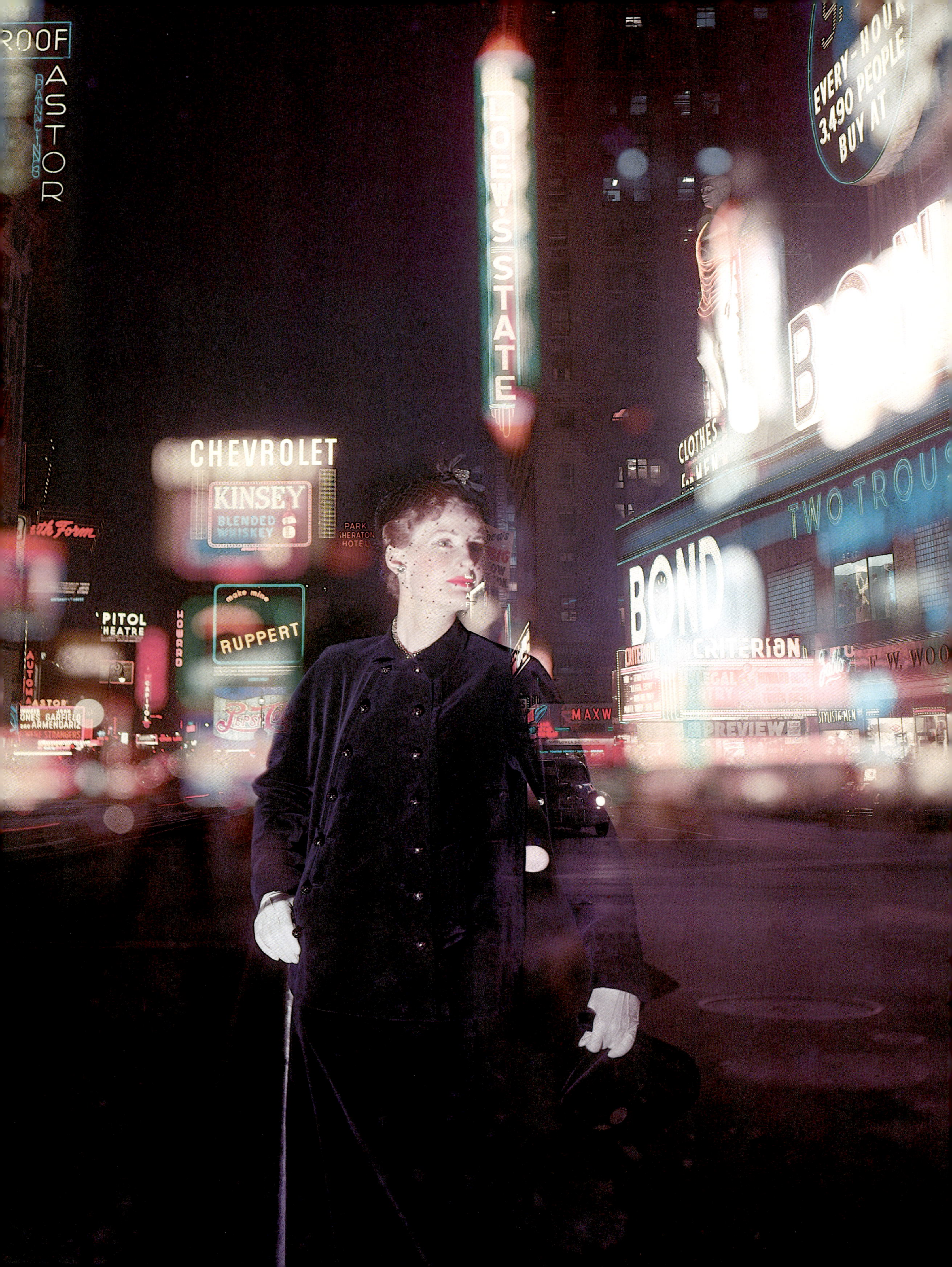
ROOF
ASTOR
LOEW'S STATE
3,490 PEOPLE
BUY AT
CHEVROLET
KINSEY
BLENDED WHISKEY
PARK SHERATON HOTEL
make mine
RUPPERT
CLOTHES
BOND
CRITERION
PREVIEW

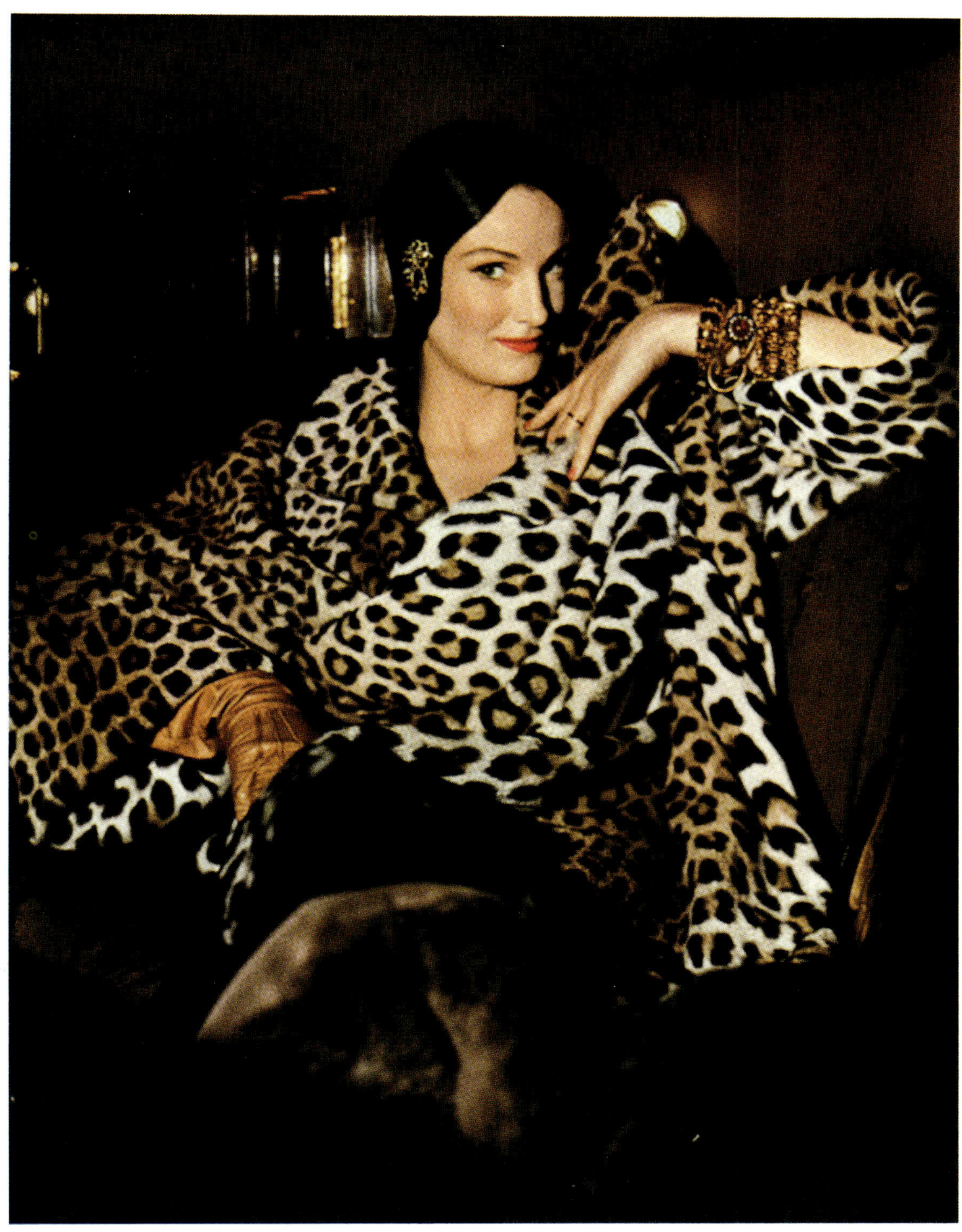

Wenda felt undressed in her springtime frock without a bouquet, so together we picked a bunch of primroses from the roadside moss. The timid and seedy registrar was barely audible above the double *forte* cacophony from a large rookery outside, and slightly frowned upon me because I kept saying 'I will' every time he faltered. I never heard at what point in the brief ceremony we became man and wife.

Wenda and I walked out into the sunshine feeling no change had taken place in our lives. Do all just-married couples have this numbness, this curious feeling that a troth that has been arranged by the private consent of two adults has recently been besmirched by the law?

Wenda's mother was a fanatical gardener, and was proud of being able to bask in the questionable glory of having been arrested in Kew Gardens for filling her handbag with rare magnolia seeds. Wenda inherited a green thumb which left me with little alternative but to buy a George I terrace house in Twickenham, with a large magnolia in the front garden and, climbing up its 1720 redbrick wall, a contemporary meandering and twisted wistaria. Together we rooted up the rather hideous borders and planted a flourish of French roses: Centifolias, Fantin Latour (I imagine he would sleep with a rose), Caroline Testout and on and on, filipes and Bourbons, and the

OPPOSITE *Wenda, Times Square, New York, 1949*
ABOVE *Wenda in leopardskin coat, New York, 1949*

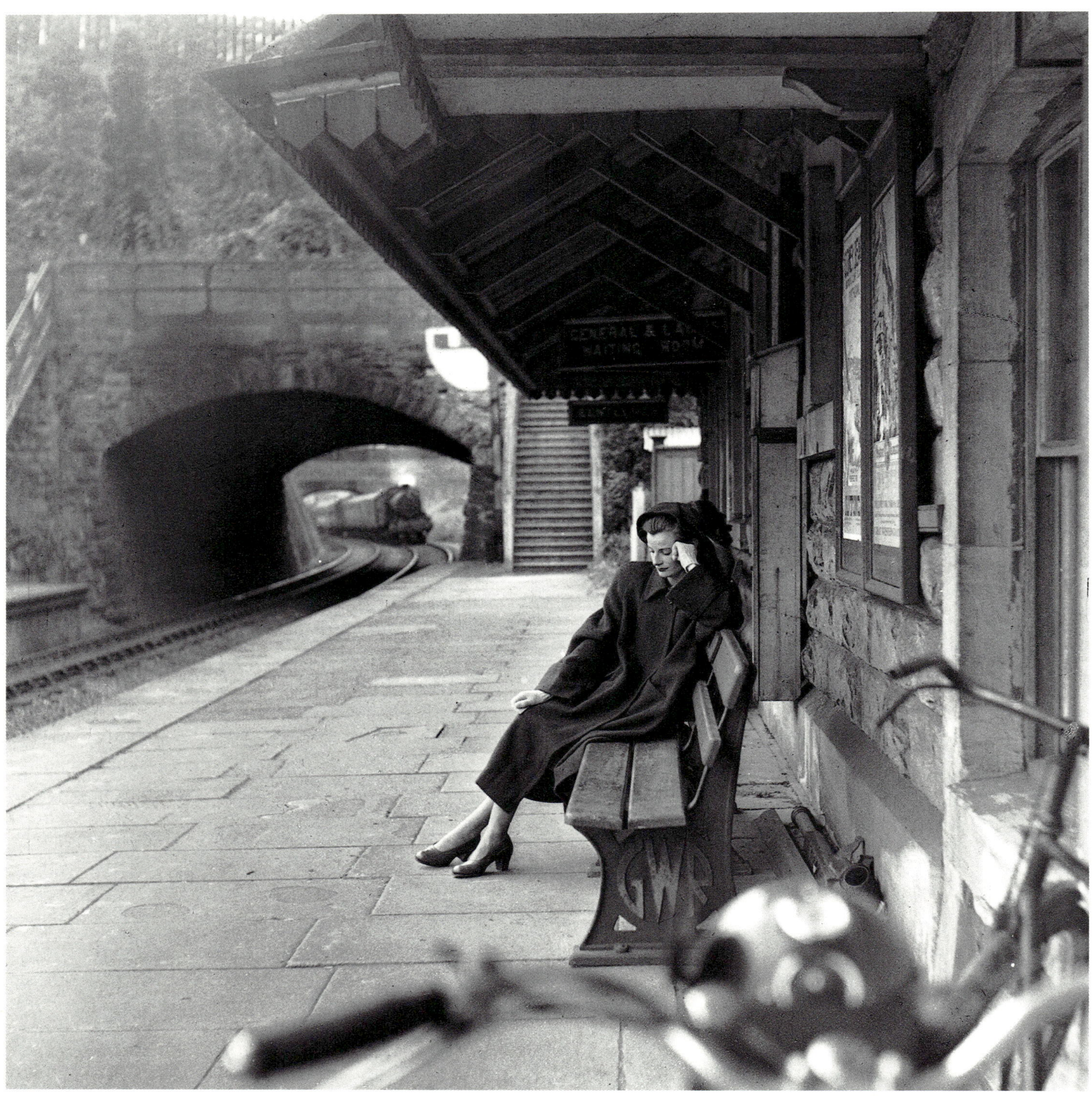

Wenda in a coat by Aquascutum, 1947

Penzance Briars – a family which is a joy to be with for the month of July; after that it is a battle with black spot and rust and greenfly. But we were always home in July.

Twickenham has always been a magic riverside place to live – Alexander Pope and Walpole and all that Strawberry Hill business was no accident – for centuries it has been the most privileged part of London. And I was extra privileged for Wenda filled our house with roses in the summer, and at Christmas time she would emerge from the cellar with bowls of heady hyacinths; she staggered under the expert plenitude and we all reeled for weeks from the wonderful scent, which is rivalled in these days only by that white marble Hall of Perfume at Harrods.

This set of pictures, all of Wenda when we first married, offered to my camera a quiet beauty that does not look so out of date today. Girls change, clothes change, but beauty itself, in whatever form it is viewed, is sealed there forever – it is frozen, it is permanent and it does not age. Perhaps there is a vintage quality to beauty, and to mood too, which makes those early attempts to capture that beauty in many ways more successful.

OPPOSITE *Wenda, Simon Parkinson and 'Baba' Hope Hatch, Connecticut, 1949*

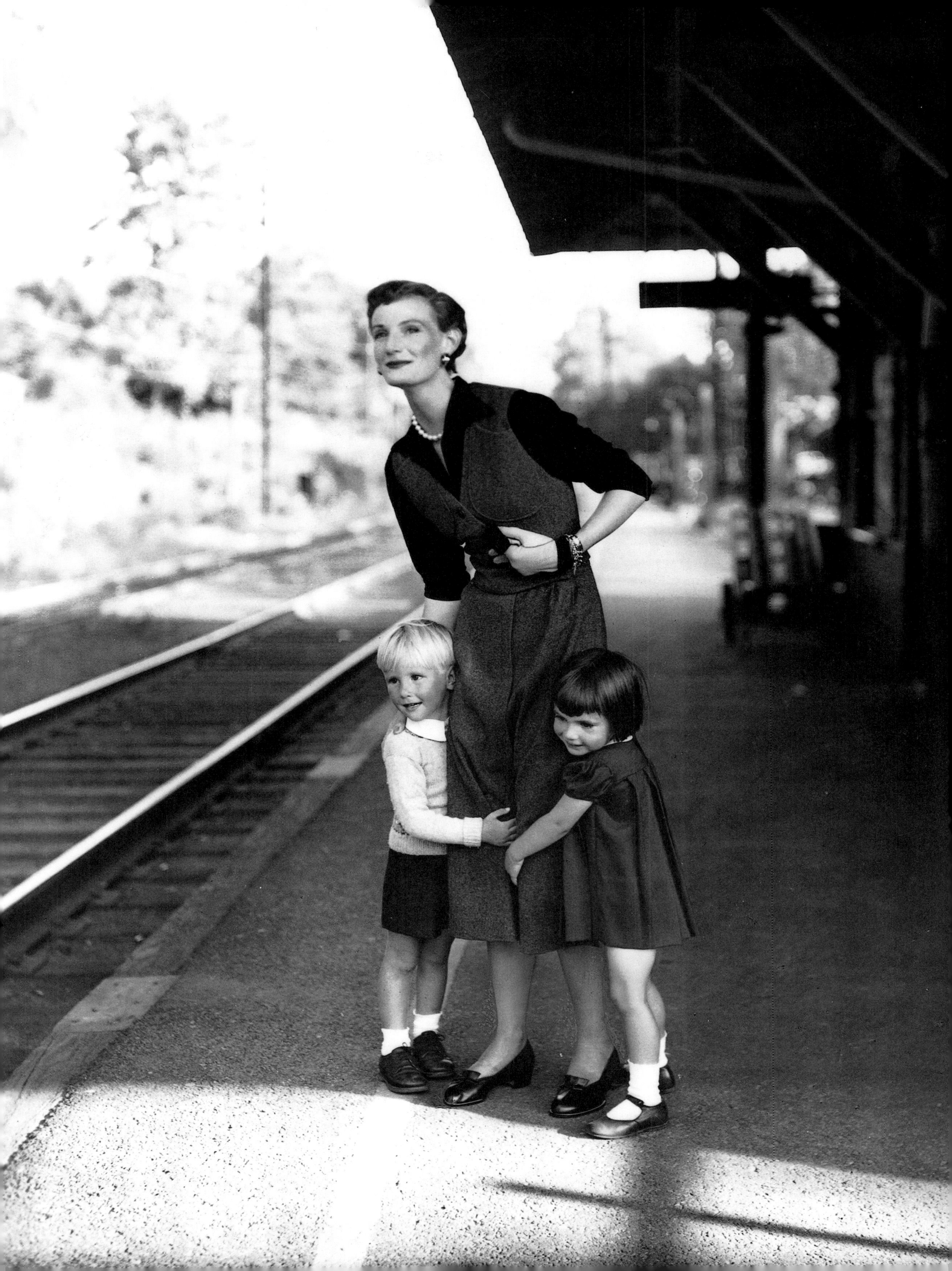

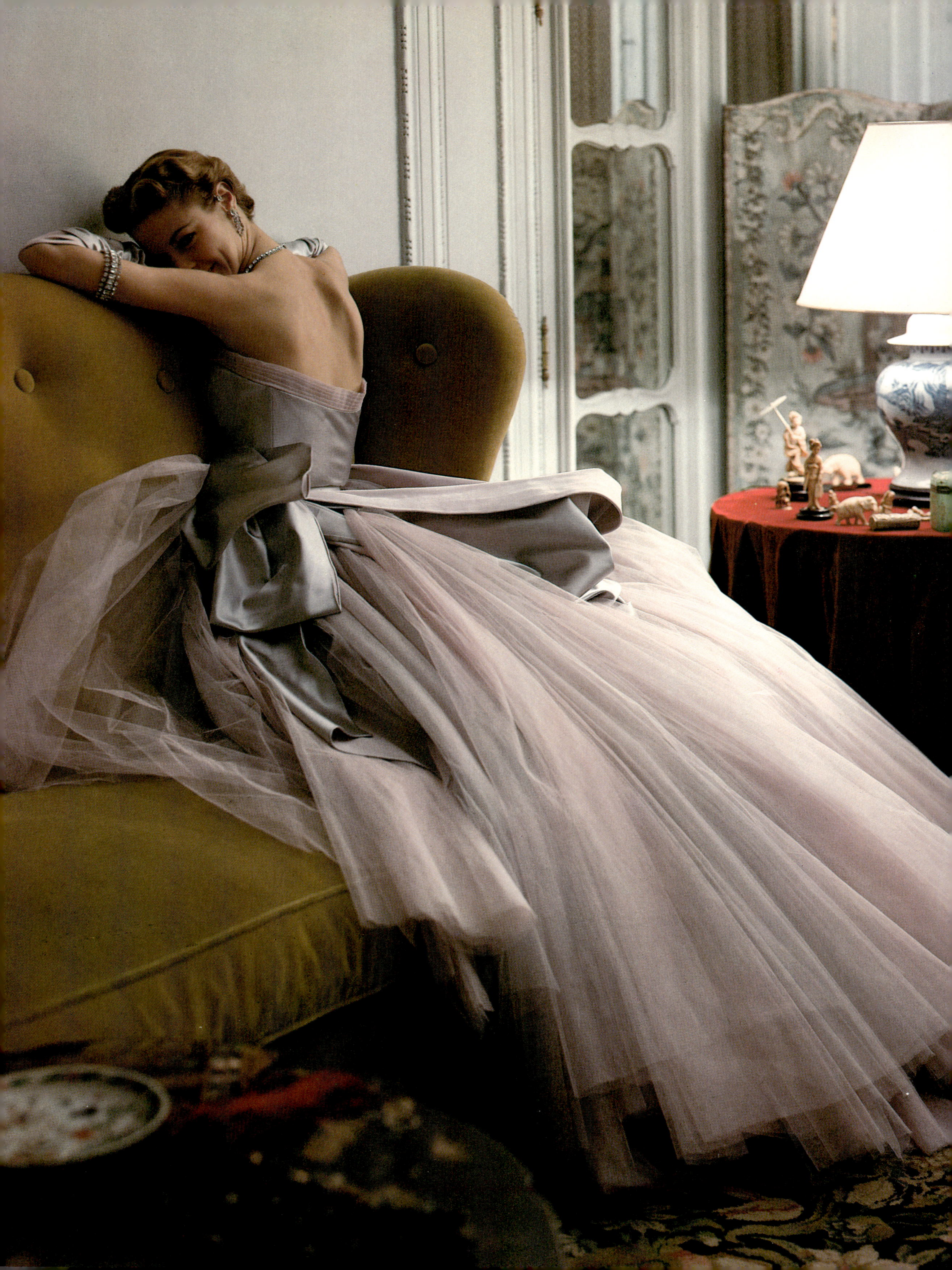

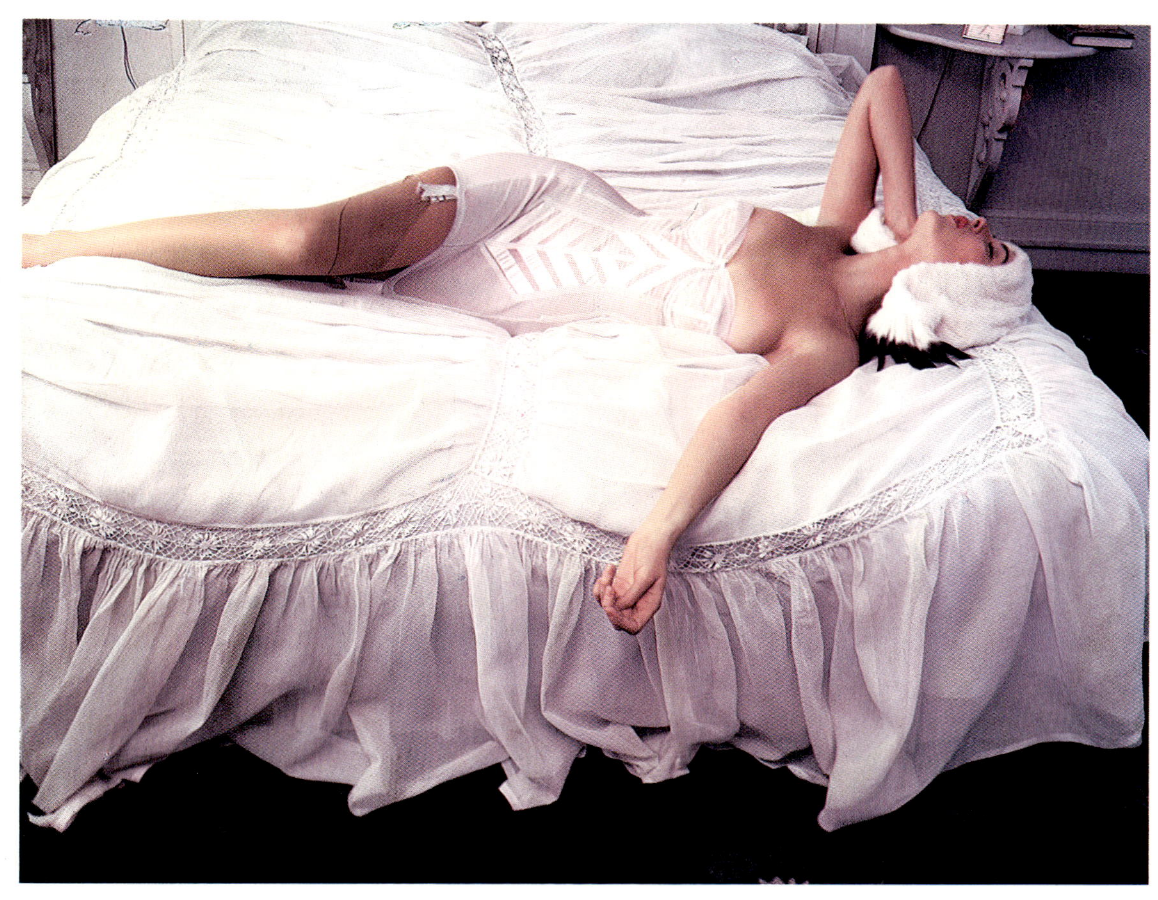

ABOVE *Carmen in a strapless corselet, photographed for the 1953 'Vogue Beauty Book'*
OPPOSITE *Jean Patchett in a Jean Dessès evening dress, Paris Spring Collections, 1950*
BELOW *First nude in colour, photographed for the 1951 'Vogue Beauty Book'*

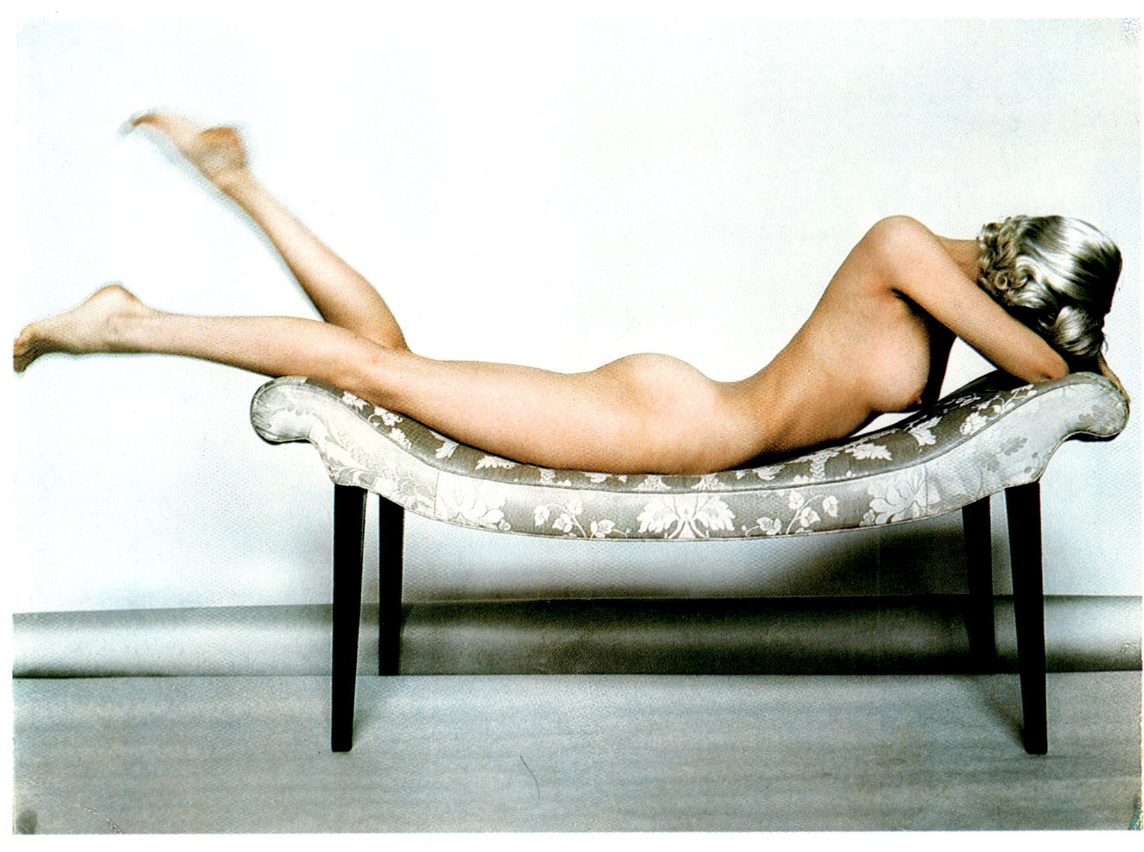

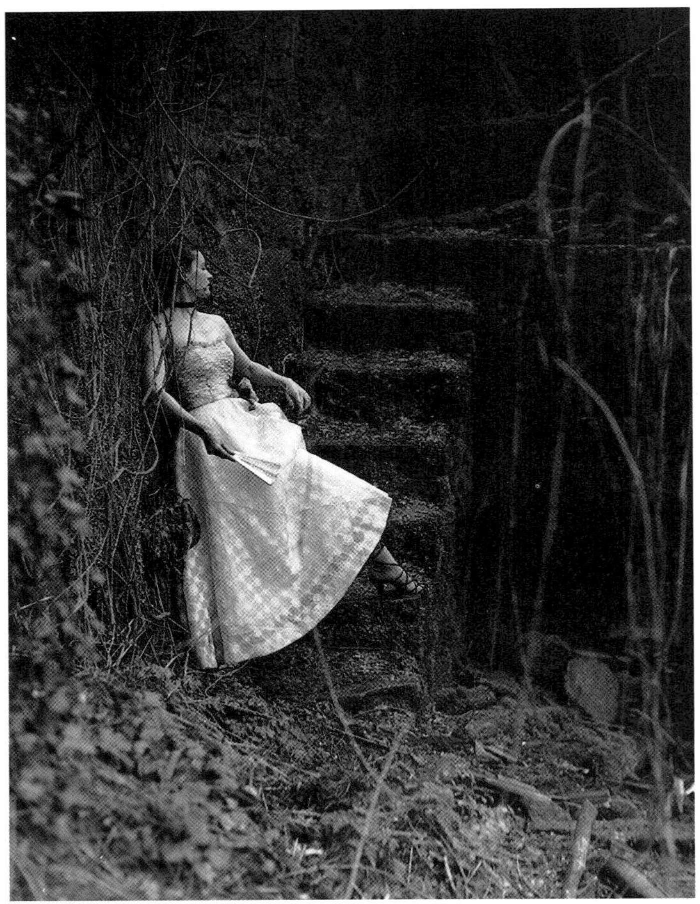

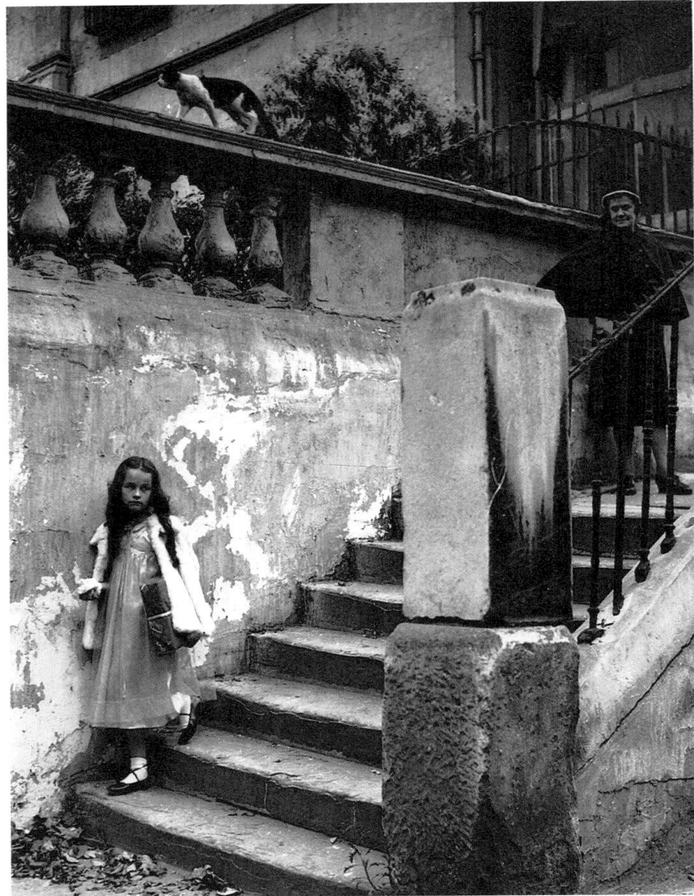

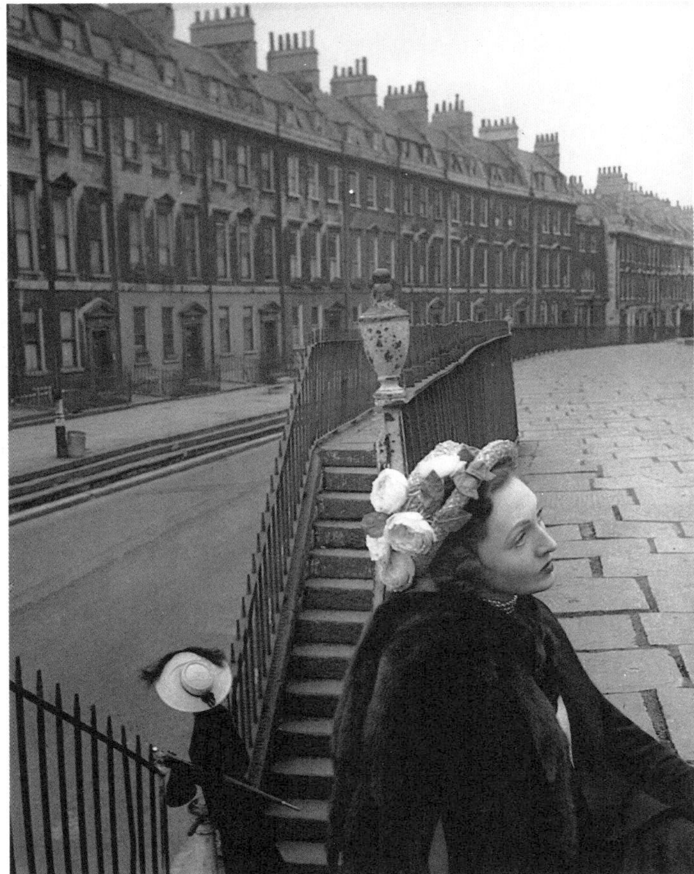

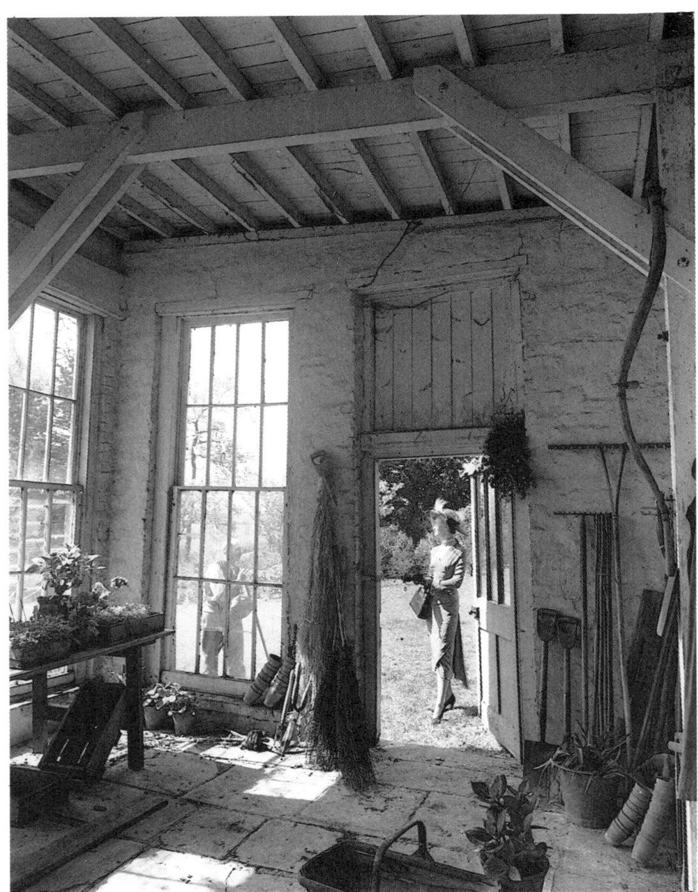

TOP LEFT *A dress by Kitty Foster, Tintern Abbey, 1947*
TOP RIGHT *Susan Gibbs in a white fur party wrap by the National Fur Company, Regent's Park Terrace, 1947*
BOTTOM LEFT *Anne Chambers in a Vernier hat, The Paragon, Bath, 1948*
BOTTOM RIGHT *Anne Chambers in a Hartnell dress, 1948*
OPPOSITE *'The New Look' Wenda Rogerson and Barbara Goalen in Hardy Amies and Molyneux coats outside the National Gallery, London, 1949*

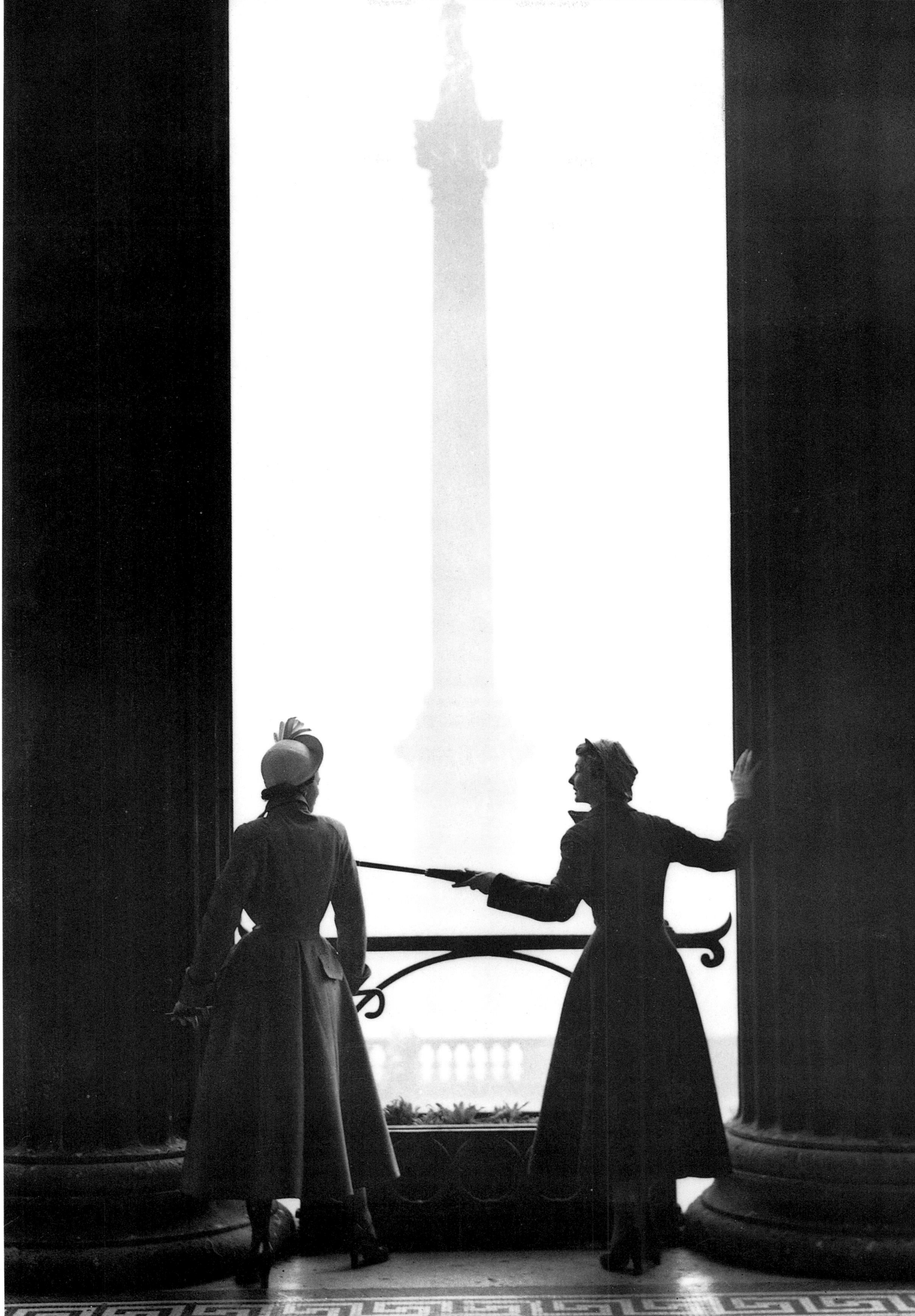

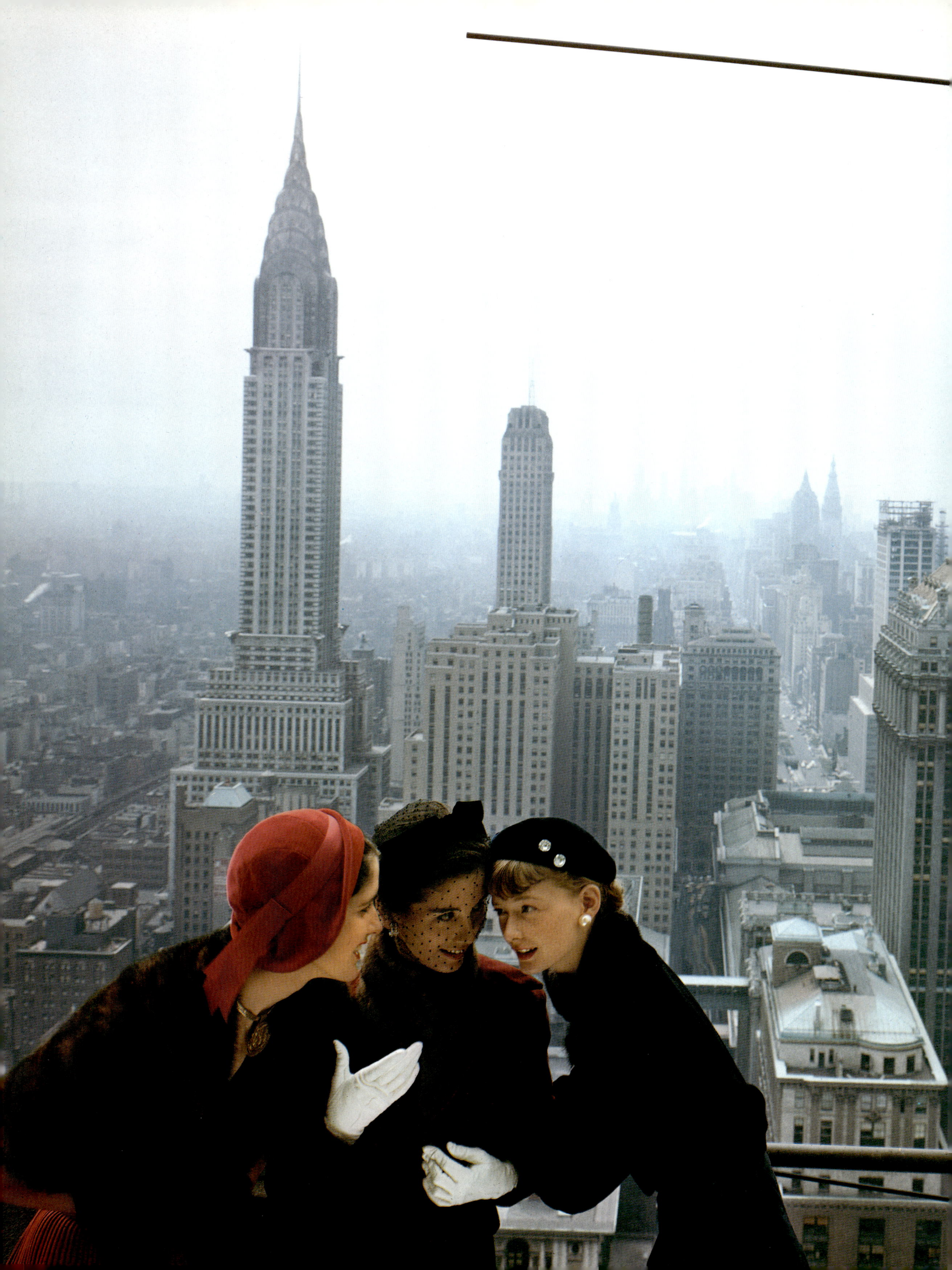

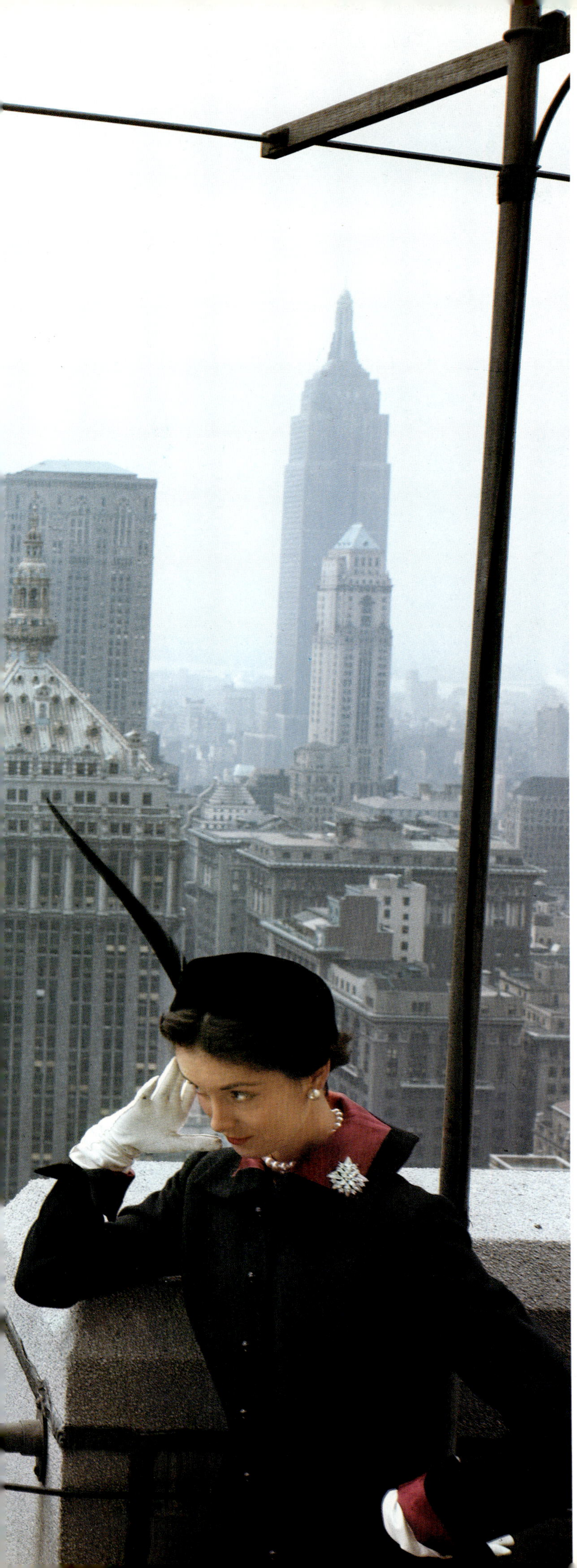

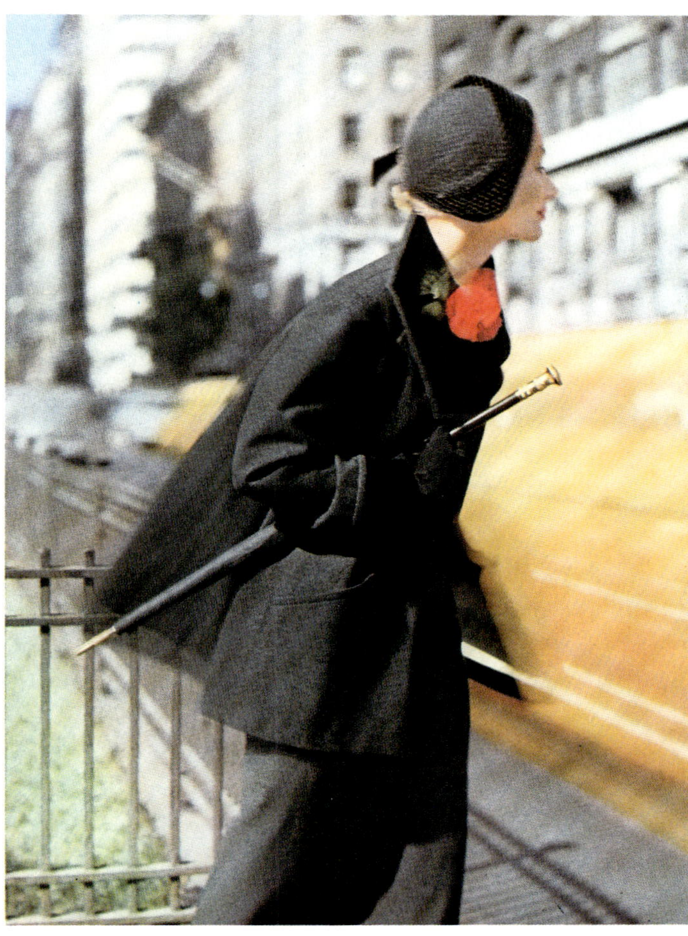

LEFT *Hat fashions, the New York skyline from the roof of the Condé Nast building on Lexington Avenue, 1949*
ABOVE *Lisa Fonssagrives (later Mrs Irving Penn) in an Oxford flannel finger-tip coat by Hattie Carnegie, Park Avenue, New York, 1949*

MAD MANHATTAN

One golden day in 1947 I was sent forth with a model, a fashion editor, three evening 'gowns' – as Norman Hartnell called them – a cumbersome wooden 10″ × 8″ camera, an underfed assistant bowed under the weight, and four sheets of Kodachrome with a speed of 6 ASA, commanded by the Editor of British *Vogue* to get three colour pages with admonitions to use the fourth sheet of film only 'if the girl moves'.

There is no harder way to learn the trade of fashion colour photography. When I had heard that Irving Penn could often use twenty or thirty sheets of 10″ × 8″ on a still-life sitting, my gaze turned longingly westward across the Atlantic. I scanned the plush pages of American *Vogue* and *Harper's*; beautifully lit and reproduced full pages were appearing every issue in 'glorious color' – such a lift to be enjoyed by contrast to drab London in the full grip of rationing. My longing for New York was always there and eventually I summoned my courage to write Alexander Liberman, the new Art Director of American *Vogue*, the following letter: 'Dear Mr Liberman, I am thinking of travelling to New York to take a job as a soda-fountain attendant. Is there any chance that I might take a few photographs for you on my days off?' Fools certainly rush in . . . but I was determined to try my hand alongside the great photographers working there in the late forties – Penn, Avedon, Rawlings, Coffin, Joffé, Frances McLaughlin, Cassidy, Blumenfeld, and Rutledge.

Much to my surprise. Alex wrote back with a most enthusiastic invitation: 'Forget the soda-fountain, come and work for us and I will personally vouch for you and your family with the US authorities.'

It was in May 1949, I think, that I flew to America. Wenda and small son Simon arrived later in June on the little Cunarder, the *Parthia*. When I think back upon the arrival of the rather bleary-eyed Smith Family Parkinson in New York I am always reminded of Ford Madox Brown's painting, *The Last of England*, and the words inscribed both on the base of the Statue of Liberty and the walls of the (then) Idelwild Airport: 'Give me your tired, your poor . . . Send these, the homeless, tempest-tost to me . . .'

I had found an apartment with *Vogue*'s help, and after our first few days spent at the Barbizon Plaza (it is still there by Central Park), we settled in rather nervously. Fresh from rationing, we were stunned by the quantities of wonderful food, a stroll round a supermarket was more entertaining than a visit to the cinema. We drooled at the contemplation of so many different types of bread – even bread was plentiful!

All the emigrant and stranger-in-paradise apprehensions that we felt upon our arrival were speedily dispelled. The New Yorker is so much more friendly than the Londoner and very soon we needed baby sitters for Simon three or four times a week. Dinners, lunches, cocktail parties, theatres, and weekends in Connecticut followed, and we spent high summer on Fire Island.

I was swept away into the capacious commissions (and arms) of Mrs Bettina Ballard. At first she totally took my breath away. She was large, forthright, indestructible and totally tireless. She had an infallible fashion instinct, a tough exterior of impeccable style, a caustic wit and a great heart. Beneath the forbidding countenance there must have lurked a tiny seed of Anglophilia. She gave me, obviously with Alex Liberman's approval, lots of sittings. I was working for her two or three times a week, and she was the unassailable, the High Panjandrum Fashion Editor of American *Vogue*, and I was totally out of my depth with this lady. But we worked and we were fêted and people were so pleasant and delighted.

It still takes eight or ten weeks from the time of a photographic sitting for the issue that you have worked on to appear on the news-stand. But the time did arrive and the pages that I had produced with Bettina began to be seen. A cover here, a lead there and the pages started to add up. My pride in the Ballard patronage was dampened by my awareness – I know I am not wrong about this – that I was being received in this and that office with a marked coolness. It started to worry me when friends who had earlier hosted parties to make us welcome would cut me in the corridor – or was it my imagination? Was I being too sensitive? Finally I could stand it no more and off I went with my query to my over-lifesize new-found friend. 'Bettina, is it my imagination or are the people who made us so welcome to New York a few weeks back starting to cut me and be thoroughly unfriendly . . . should I worry?' 'Parks, darling,' was the reply, 'you worry when they say hello'. (Success, alas, in the competitive world of journalism can breed enemies, not friends.)

Wonderful fashion editors put *Vogue* together then – Connie Thayer, Kathy McManus, Muriel Maxwell, Scully Montgomery and Bridget Tichenor. What a team . . . led, of course, by Bettina Ballard.

Edna Woolman Chase was the Editor-in-Chief, though when I arrived in New York her tenure was coming to an end. She was about to hand over to Jessica Davies. Mrs Chase was a diminutive, serious and Edwardian sort of American; a very conservative lady. She permitted no smoking to appear in the photographs, and, if you wanted to run headlong into a retake (having to shoot the picture again), you dared to show shoes with open toes. She really hated open toes, and smoking. I got into continual trouble, but she modified her wrath for she felt I was British, conservative like herself, and, underneath it all, well mannered.

She would often take us to lunch or dinner at the River Club, until I made the cardinal error of complaining about the dining room murals which depicted the most ferocious sea battle of the War of Independence in which every White Ensign hangs forlornly in tatters or is about to sink beneath the briney. She said, 'How true, you know I eat here all the time and have never noticed'. She was a lovely lady, rather tyrannical – though you would never have guessed it from her appearance; she was short and blue-grey haired and not unlike a suet roly-poly, from the front or the back.

I was called in one day, perhaps two days too late as it transpired, to the *Vogue* office and given the following directive: Muriel Maxwell is out getting a wonderful ballgown; they are tearing down the Ritz, the marvellous staircase is just still visible; dress Wenda quickly in a taxi and get the picture. The bull-dozers were working even faster than they normally do in New York and there was practically nothing remaining to remind one of the hotel's former elegance. Of course, the building foreman would not allow us on the site. 'Much too dangerous', he kept murmuring. 'You gotta wear hard hats and take out an Insurance Indemnity Clause', and all the time the background that we wanted was disappearing in clouds of

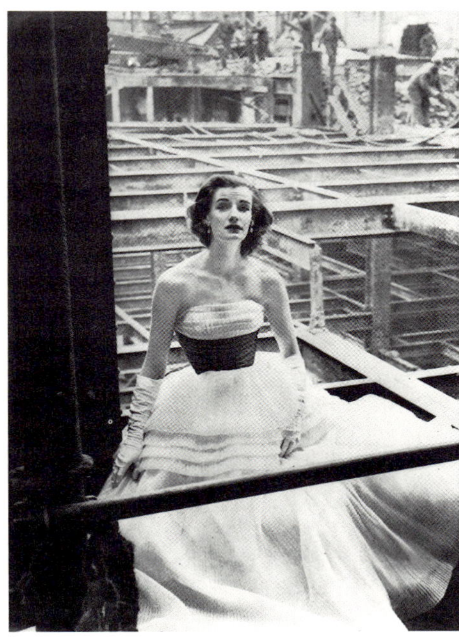

Wenda in a ballgown on the site of the demolition of the Ritz, New York, 1953

dust. I pushed Wenda, in an enormous Mainbocher evening dress, about twenty feet onto the rubble, and I climbed up a lamp post, steadying myself with my feet on the chest-height mailbox. I had taken a couple of shots which were beginning to please me when I found a postman emptying the box under my feet. I quickly assessed that he was a jolly soul and asked 'Is the box the property of the Postal Authorities?' 'Sure, I guess so', was the reply. 'Well, as their Agent, do you mind if I stand on the box for a short while to take this photograph?' 'Not at all. You can stand on my mailbox as long as you like'. Encouraged by that invitation I went to work in earnest, shouting at Wenda above the noise of the razing, and did not notice that quite a crowd was gathering. In the centre, legs astride like a Colossus, one hand thrust deep into his trouser pocket, his night stick waving slowly as a pendulum, stood a New York cop. 'Come down off there', he ordered. I pretended not to notice and took a couple more quick snaps. 'I said, Mister, come down off there', he persisted. 'Oh hello there Officer,' I began in a sycophantic manner, 'it might be of interest to you to know that the postman who owns this box just passed by and gave me permission to stand on it at any time and for as long as I wish.' Surprising as that simple phrase might have sounded, the cop suddenly became very angry. 'Mister, you and your lady are under arrest'. There was an audible murmur of disapproval from the attendant crowd. I stole one last shot as this determined lawman was pulling very seriously at my ankle. In a trice I was eye to eye with him on the pavement and soon a motley crew were observed making their way Up Town (I fancy he was bruising my arm more than Wenda's otherwise she would have been screaming). He pushed us around the corner and got out his notebook, which heralded the arrival of Muriel Maxwell who, wisely, had been watching everything from a distance. She got her name taken too. The crowd, who appeared to have nothing better to do, became inflamed by the spoilsport attitude of the cop, and they started to barrack him seriously. 'Leave them alone . . . they're nice people . . . they've done nothing wrong . . . Go and catch a mugger instead'. Through all this harassment we were being marched slowly towards the Police Station (but there they are called something else like Precinct 45). We walked about a block with this police protection when suddenly we were told to 'Move on. Get lost. Go home. Forget it.' And the cop abandoned us – but we did get the picture.

It is a curious habit adopted by the Americans that if a place is popular, or even pretends that it is popular, the management erect a barrier. If you wish to enter an acceptable New York night club you must initially, if you are not recognized, be insulted and made to stand, in all weathers, behind a crush barrier. If you are recognized you enter immediately for free. There was a finality about the red plush barrier at El Morocco that was more impassable than the Ligne Maginot. The contemplation of suicide was the only alternative to rejection from that silver-haired pearly gate. Once inside the desirable customers were shepherded onto the banquettes covered in mock zebra upholstery or the nearby dining tables. Earnest young couples, however, in from the suburbs for a night out at the 'famed' El Morocco, would promptly be shown to the 'bleachers' – the horror of horrors, an unmentionable Siberia. One night we felt so sorry for these *ingénus* couples, so roughly treated by the management, that in a body we moved all our tables and glasses into the bleachers and directed the underprivileged into our seats.

I am quite prepared to confess now that our behaviour at 'Elmers' was unforgivable, though never quite outrageous enough to make us totally unwelcome. The one night Pud Thayer did rather overdo it, he was banned. Within a week we were all back *en masse* with eager smiling faces. We had had the foresight to buy a collar and lead and attached Pud's mannish neck to Wenda's handbag. He played the part well on all fours, but was soon discovered by the gauleiters who ran the place. 'Mr Thayer', they began 'is banned from this club'. 'We know that', replied Wenda, 'but this is my dog'. They capitulated and we were in.

Our first summer in America we shared a house on Fire Island with two of our earliest New York friends, Bruce Knight and Robert Viret (some thirty-five years later they are still our very good friends). Together they were the Art Directors on *Glamour*. Robert had only adopted the USA as a temporary measure. None of the Frenchmen that I have met have ever had the slightest doubt that they were the world's most superior beings – and not just superior, but the out-and-out winners of an unequal contest. Robert believed, with some justification because of his uncanny likeness to the man, that he was Napoleon Bonaparte reincarnate. Tongue in cheek and with a certain humour, he played the role to perfection with his right hand thrust inside his jacket; his Saturday evening after-dinner speeches in the finest early military French were harangues that we never forgot. He was extremely brave during the War, being a senior member of the 'Maquis'. He had forgotten how many enemy soldiers' heads he had removed by the stealthy use of a cheese wire. For his services to La France he had been awarded a Legion d'Honneur Militaire of the highest order; he wore the *bouton* very rarely – it seemed as large as a cherry tomato. There is a story, it could well be true, about Robert and Mr Patchevitch, the overall boss at *Vogue*. Mr Patchevitch was awarded an ordinary Legion d'Honneur in the early fifties by the French Haute Couture for American *Vogue's*

Anne Gunning, in a Jaeger pink mohair coat outside the City Palace, Jaipur, India, 1956 (When Diana Vreeland saw this picture she said 'How clever of you, Mr Parkinson, also to know that pink is the navy blue of India.')

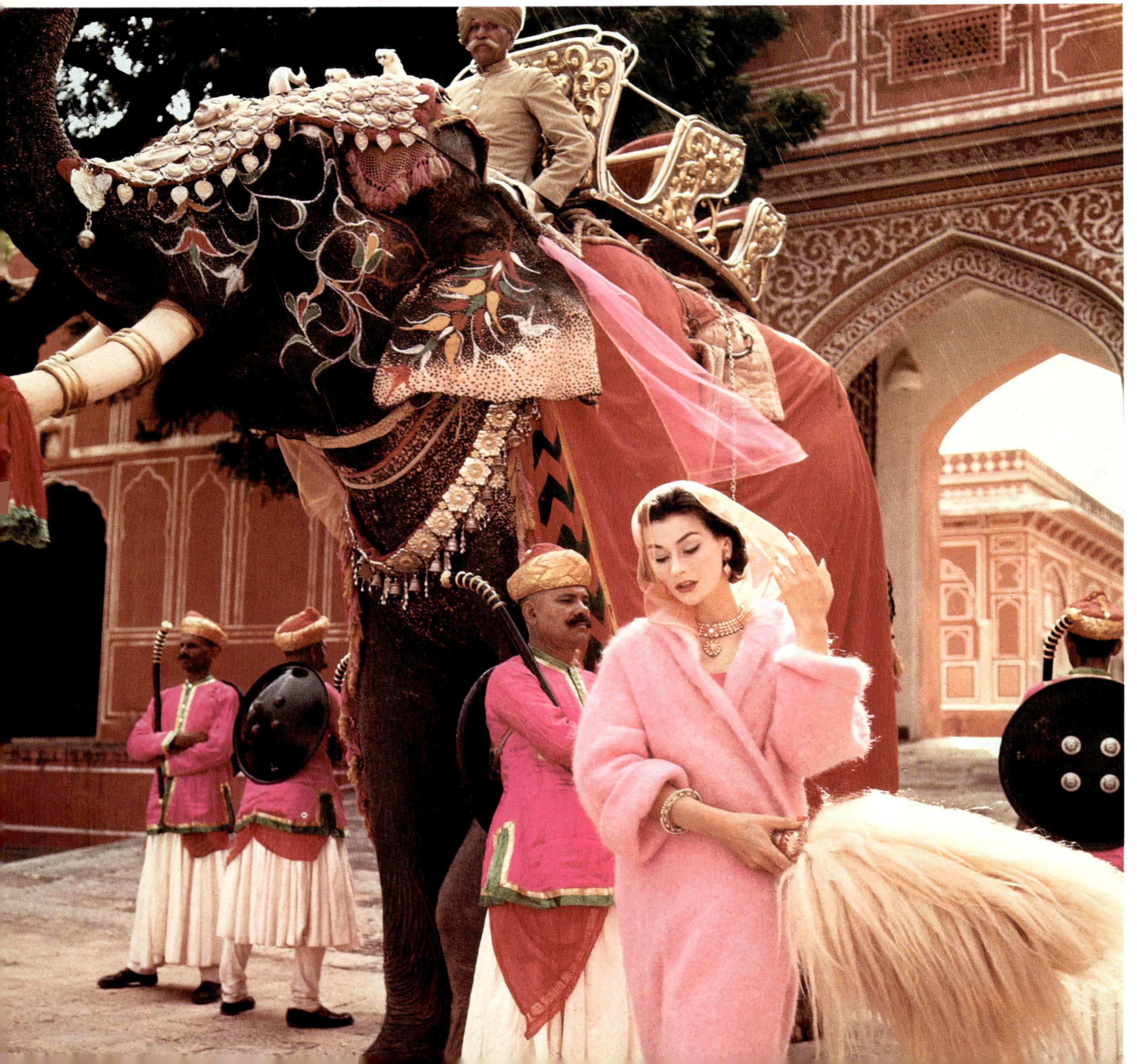

coverage of the various Paris designers. One day, Viret, wearing his enormous *bouton*, got in the same elevator at Lexington Avenue as Patchevitch who was wearing the more humble variety for the first time. They stood side by side in frigid silence for nineteen floors, and I believe they were never introduced, then or subsequently.

New York was a wonderful town in the late forties and early fifties; I wish I could remember all the silly and very sane happenings that contributed to the great pleasure of being there at that time. Simon can never remember how fortunate he was, and why should he? The brilliant photographer Maria Martell gave a wonderful fourth birthday party for him. Irving Penn, living alone in his mouse-brown apartment eating delicious black bean soup, would often kindly babysit Simon. There are some valuable pictures that Penn took of Simon, and I believe that somewhere there is a roll or two that Simon took of Penn. For his eighth or ninth birthday present, Dick Avedon telephoned us, asking if Simon and I could be down on a certain East River pontoon at 10 o'clock the following morning. There we saw a small sea-plane drop out of the sky. Through the skyscrapers they went, Dick and Simon, for a birthday present. That's New York; and gift-bearing New Yorkers are people who have so much to do and who are so busy, yet invariably make the time to give others carefully planned pleasure.

Anne Gunning in a cotton mousseline dress by Atrima, Dal Lake, Kashmir, 1956

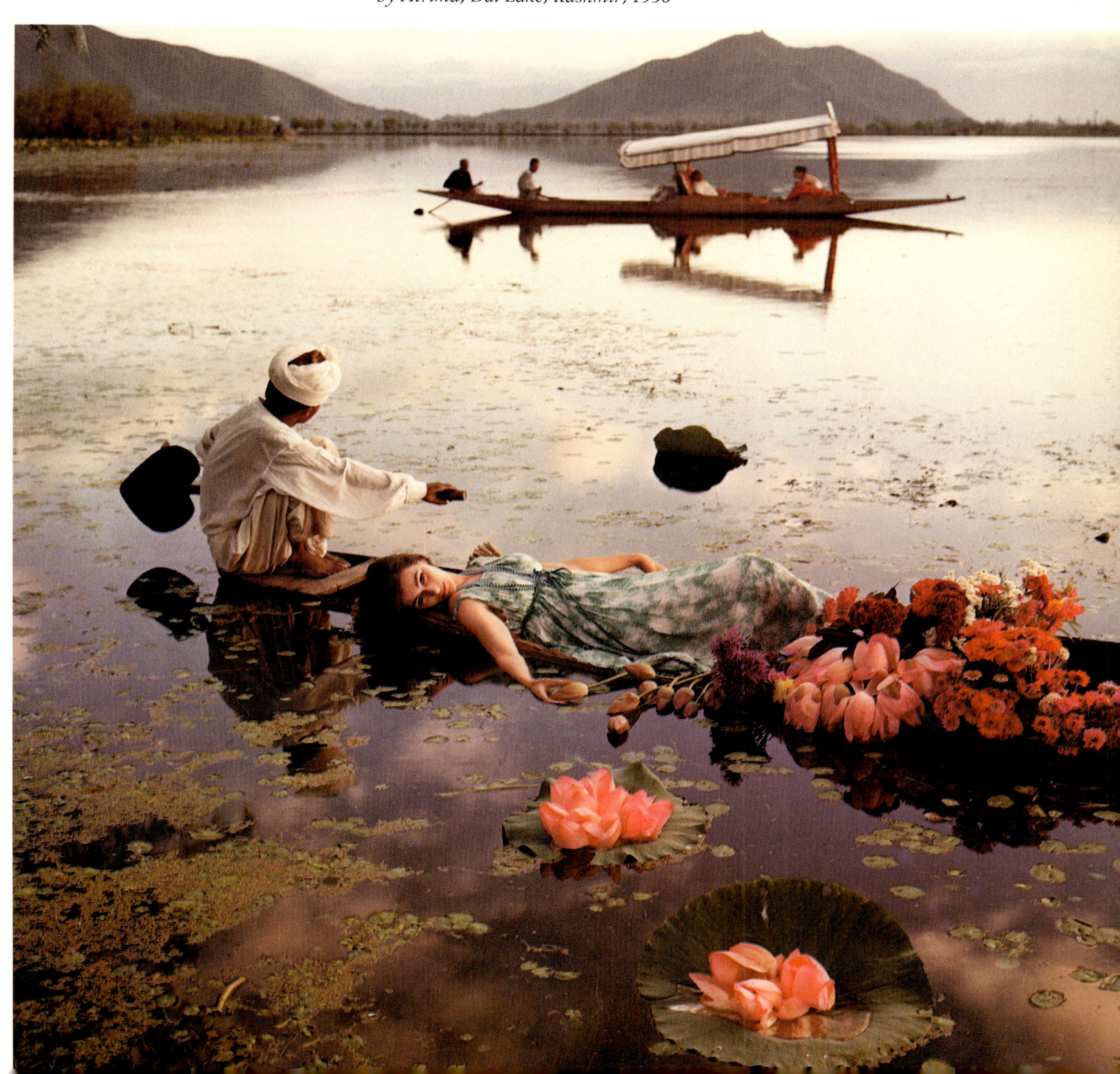

1950s

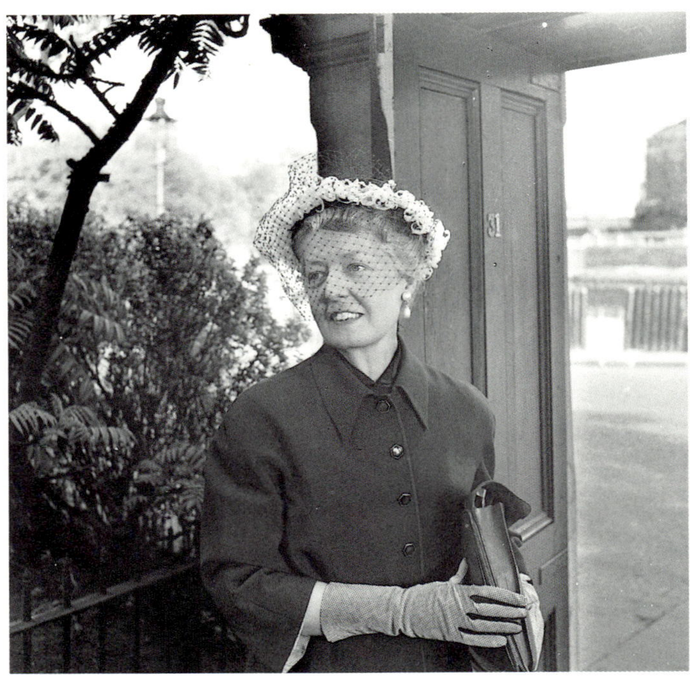

THE EARLY GLOSSY WORLD

From about 1940 onwards British *Vogue* was edited by a brilliant and paradoxical woman, Audrey Withers. Her presence was imposing, but you could never label Audrey as dull; her humour and creative talents were always part of the paradox. She once angled more and more photographic opportunities in the direction of a considerably untalented photographer who was a confirmed alcoholic because her generous and loving nature was convinced that with more creative opportunities he would mend his ways – in fact he would mislay a camera each week. She demanded and received unswerving loyalty from her staff and absences from the office were written off without question as bouts of 'flu or other genuine indisposition. She was a confirmed Fabian who presided over a publication with a strict Tory and capitalist image. An intellectual who knew very little about it, she found fashion slight and ephemeral and in consequence she delegated much to her Fashion Editors to organize.

The first Fashion Editor I met there was a very neat, white-haired sparrow lady, the much-respected Gertrude Pidoux. She was followed, for she was far from young in 1947, by a loveable and memorable lady entitled La Vicomtesse D'Orthez. I suspected she knew as little about fashion as the Editor herself – certainly much less about photography. But Audrey put together a very fine British *Vogue* in particularly difficult post-war years. It would be true to say that together with Harry Yoxall as publisher, the future success of *Vogue* in Britain was assured; from their early partnership it has never looked back.

The Art Director under Audrey and Harry was John Parsons. Nervous and desperately sensitive, and a brilliant draughtsman, he shone for me a penetrating beam on the rustic elegancies of England, which I was almost too close to notice. He was quiet but when he whispered . . . Zoffany . . . Devis . . . Gainsborough . . . Wyatt . . . William Kent . . . Capability Brown, I looked again.

At the end of the forties the British *Vogue* studios moved to a location in Shaftesbury Avenue above Jack Jacobus shoe shop between the two theatres. The offices remained in a corner of Golden Square.

Among some photographs of one of the London Collections I had taken a particularly pretty picture of a Stiebel dress which I hoped *Vogue* would use as a full page. I had only taken four transparencies and I had marked my choice by snipping off the corner. When I enquired of John Parsons which one he was going to choose, he

ABOVE *Audrey Withers, Editor of British Vogue from 1940–60*
OPPOSITE *Wenda by the 365-foot sheer drop of the Howick Falls, Natal, 1951*

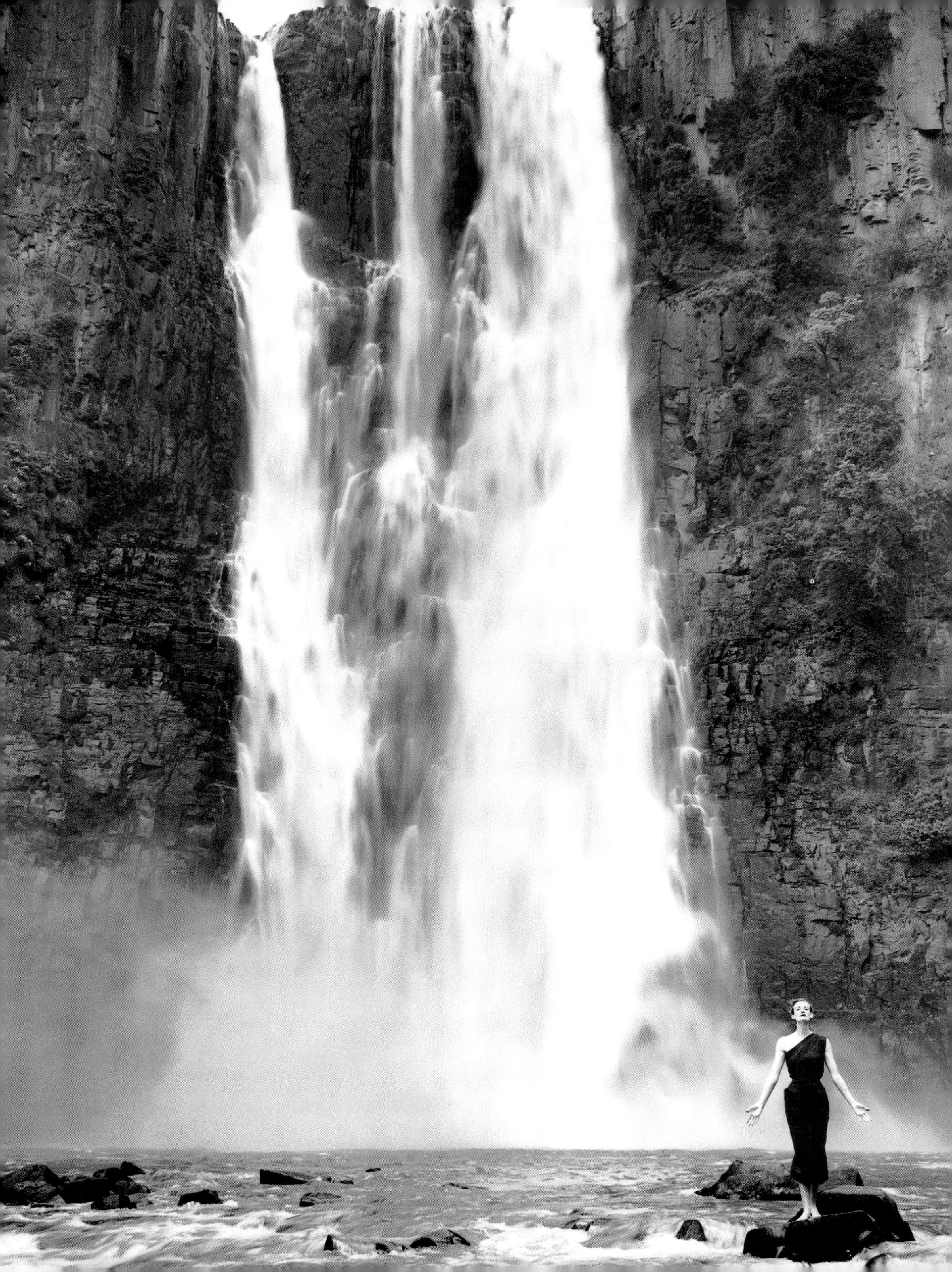

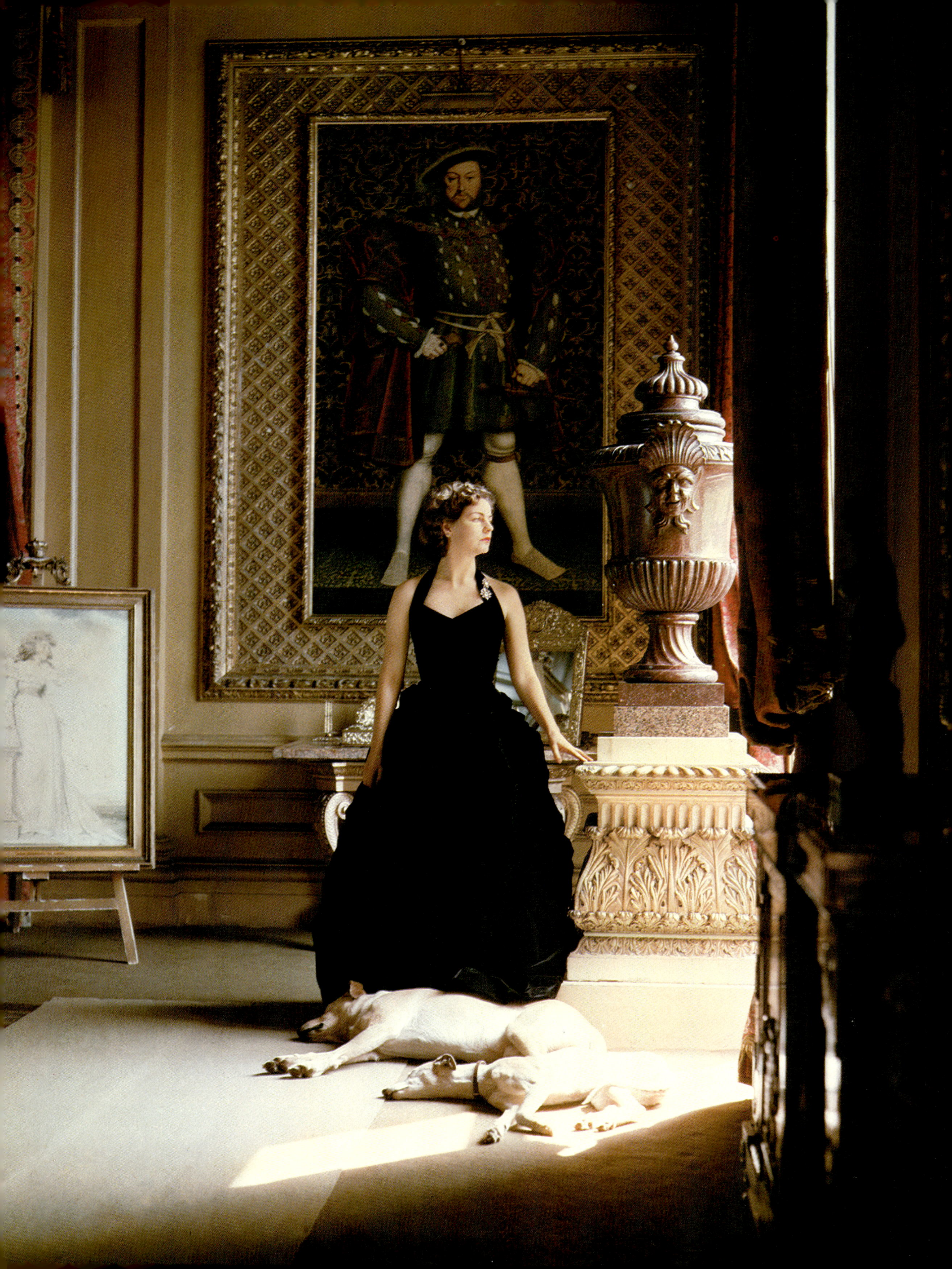

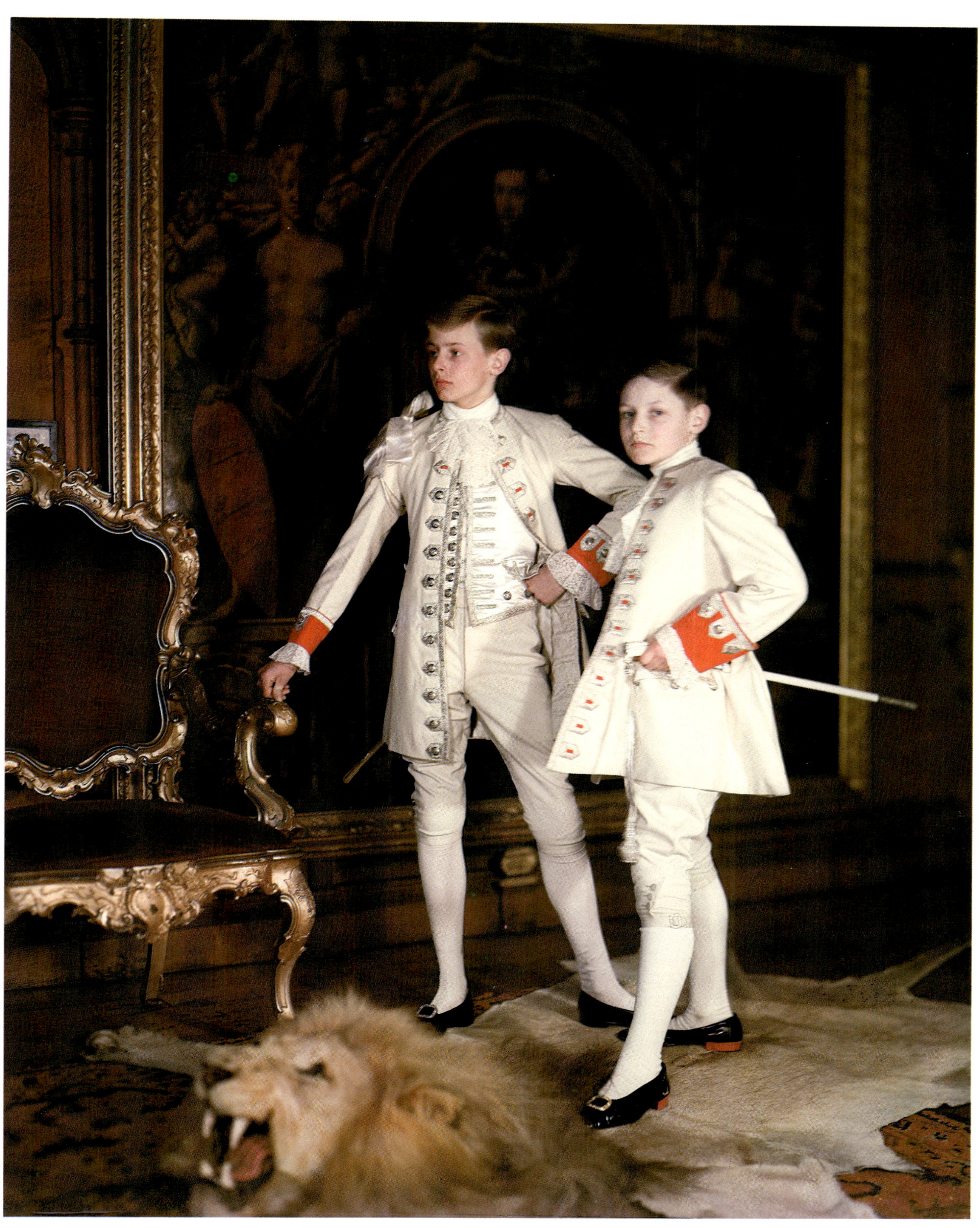

OPPOSITE *The Duchess of Devonshire (née the Hon. Deborah Freeman-Mitford). The Gold Drawing Room, Chatsworth, 1952*
ABOVE *The Hon. James Drummond and Master Duncan Davidson, Pages to the Duke of Norfolk, Arundel Castle, 1953*
Both photographs taken for the occasion of the coronation of Queen Elizabeth II

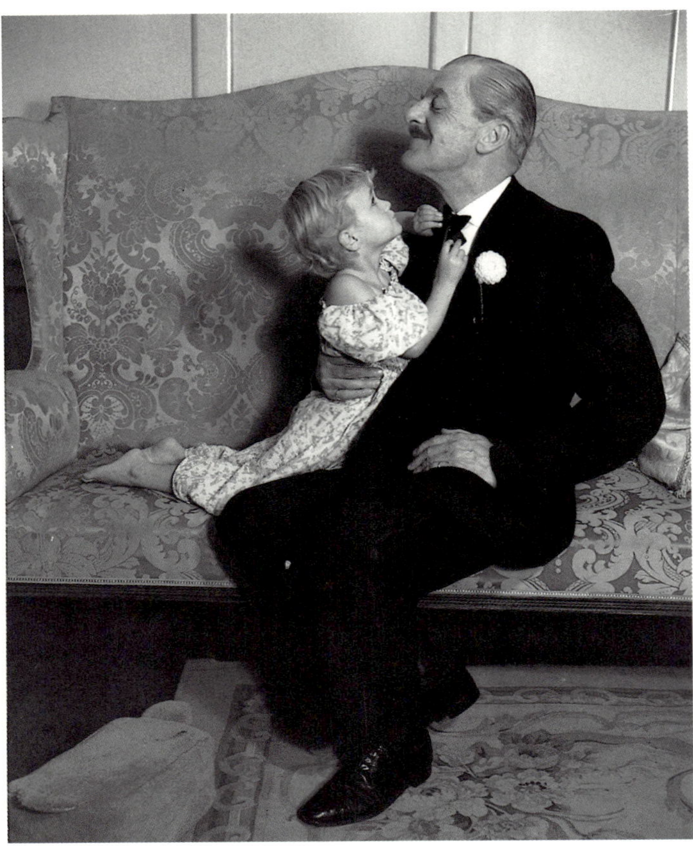

Aquascutum dinner jacket advertisement. Josephine Robertson and Archie Campbell, 1954

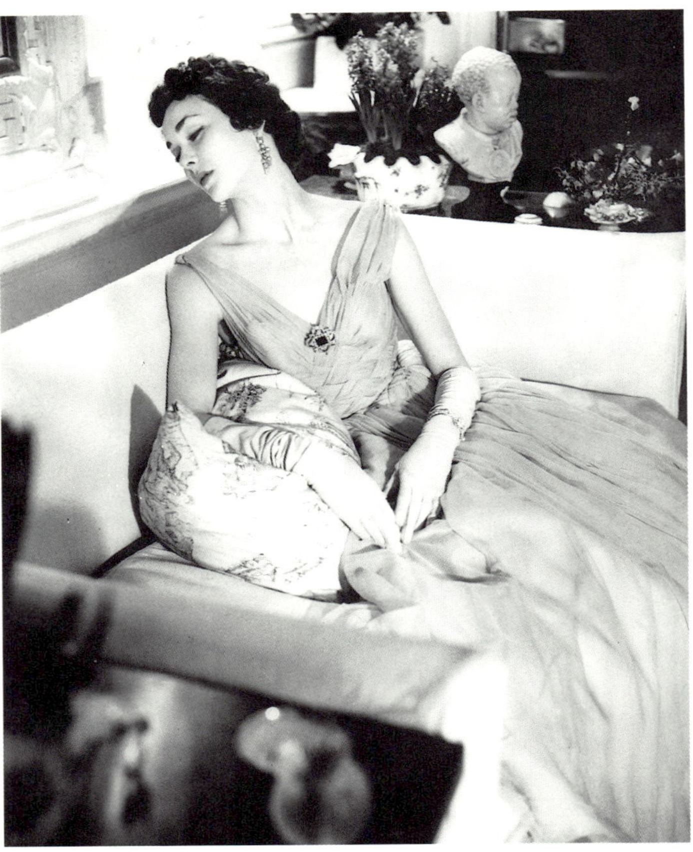

Mrs John Wyndham (later Lady Egremont) at New Grove, Petworth, 1954

softened the blow in his usually sensitive way by telling me that he loved the sitting but my choice had been relegated to second place. 'Both Audrey and I agree that another is better'. This rebuttal blew a fuse in my brain for I was convinced my choice was the only picture.

I then meticulously embarked upon a course of behaviour of which I am not very proud. I told the model I was working with to go to the dressing room, and asked the Fashion Editor to send someone out for lunch. 'We are taking one hour's break', I announced. I sought out Ted Knowles who did the colour processing in those days, borrowing from him three or four reject colour transparencies which I proceeded to practise tearing into small pieces. Not an easy thing to do, I soon discovered, but I was determined, desperate, and very angry. Eventually I found that the thick 10″ × 8″ colour transparency would rip well enough if you started it with your teeth.

Convinced now about the righteousness of the mission ahead, I set off from Shaftesbury Avenue towards the magazine offices. Five minutes later I walked into Audrey Withers' office and asked her secretary to summon John Parsons with the colour transparencies from my last sitting. He soon appeared carrying them. 'Which is the one that you intend to use?' I enquired. John handed it to me. For an instant I held it up to the light to be certain that they might not have changed their minds. (Once in a lifetime things can go better than we plan them.) By using my teeth as rehearsed, the large transparency was in four pieces in as many seconds. I heard an upper-class breath-catching hush of shocked astonishment as I threw the pieces on the Editor's desk, and, not being brave enough to face their peeved wrath, I left the room and made my way quite quietly back to Shaftesbury Avenue.

It was not very long before the telephone rang in a nearby studio and a young secretary handed me a note which read: 'When you have finished your photography, would you please go and see Mr Yoxall'. (Harry Yoxall was the moustached major-domo of *Vogue* at that time.) My emotional response went straight back to schooldays and I felt a twinge of remorse, preparing myself for trousers down and four of the best.

I knocked nervously on Harry's door and stood before him for the expected admonishment. 'Parkinson, you have done a very bad thing; you have shocked both Audrey and John because they are your good friends and you have no right to offend them so. However the damage is done; please never do it again. You have made a serious mistake, your behaviour is unforgivable, but please understand I cannot afford to employ people who don't make mistakes.'

There are few men in the magazine publishing business that I admire more than this very sane man. He is still with us mercifully and enjoying to the end his great love of good wine. 'Floreat Yoxall' I cry.

Back in the late forties the supreme accolade for the magazine photographer, and I suppose the same thing could be said today, was to be given the chance to 'do the French Collections'.

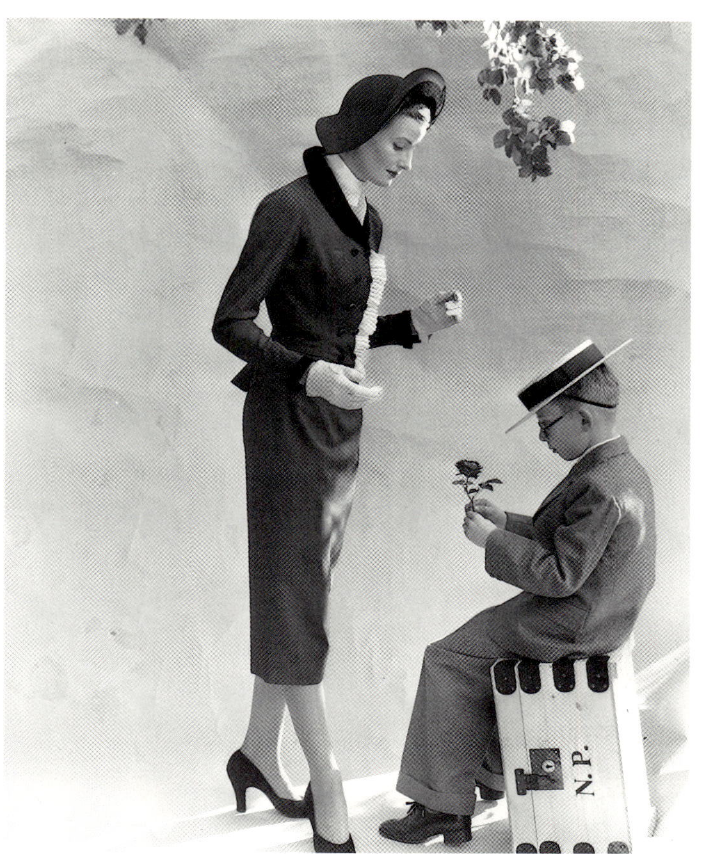

Wenda Rogerson in a Charles Creed coat-dress, and Noel Patrick, London Collections, 1950

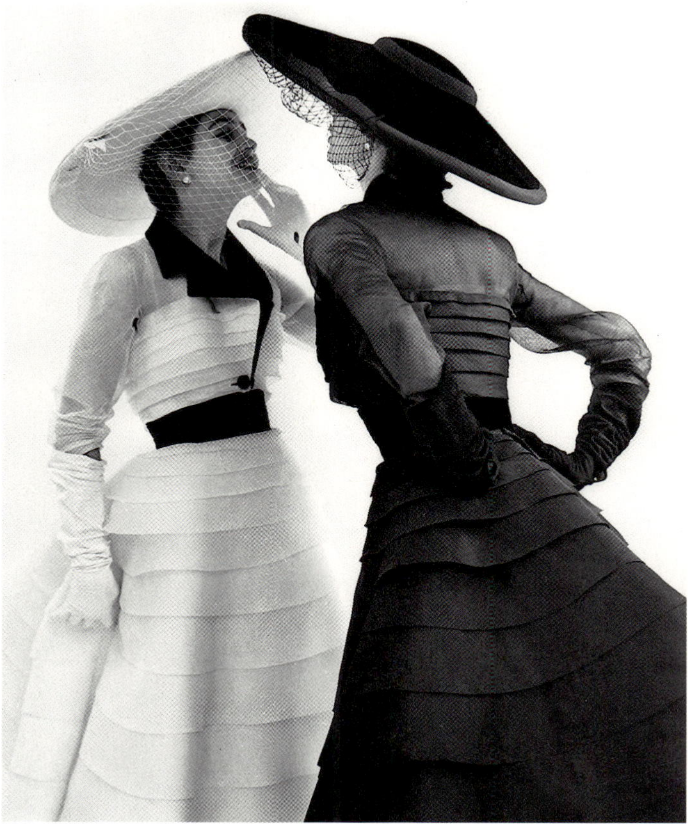

Organdie dresses by Jacques Fath, 1952

Paris has always been the unassailable fashion capital of the world. Twice a year the great couturiers 'pass' their 'Collections' which dictate the fashion look for the season ahead. These jamborees happen at the end of freezing January, when the summer clothes appear, and the end of stifling July, when the winter heavies arrive. (Incidentally this is brilliantly planned by the Parisians – for all the restaurants and half the offices shut and their patrons go on holiday as the invasion arrives in mid-July, which makes after-work survival doubly difficult.) These bi-annual explosions circumscribe the careers of the professional writers on fashion who converge on Paris from all the magazines and newspapers to sit through about twenty shows in considerable discomfort balanced on undersized gold cane chairs in suffocating salons – a five-day marathon of endurance. The photographers who accompany them also need unlimited quantities of stamina, strength and speed, and patience.

It was in the summer of 1950 that American *Vogue* offered me this great and prideful opportunity. The few hectic days that make up the photography of the Collections would be my nadir, I thought to myself, and the way forward photographically could only be down.

At the back of your mind you appreciate that the world's best fashion photographers are all gathered in Paris to photograph the same clothes that you face. Furthermore, while you may get the garment for ten minutes, they may be obstinate and insist on retaining it for two hours. The designers 'pass' their summer and winter Collections first to the Press, then on following days to their clients. They show twice daily at a pre-appointed time so that the buyers from the large American stores, who scramble for one of each of the more popular designs, and buyers from Japan and elsewhere, who choose designs from the racks to copy *en masse* (this is how the designer makes his largest profit, *not* from private clients), monopolize the clothes before and after the shows. This ensures that the 'house' will delay sending out any model to the studios to be photographed for the magazines until there is no further chance of a sale 'in house'.

You might have been told you would get dress number 84 at 10.30 pm. So you wait and wait. The model girls probably fall asleep in their make-up and curlers on a divan in the corner; you sip Algerian plonk in an attempt to wash down a rather stale roll. The bell rings just before midnight. 'Parks, they've sent 92 from Balmain.' (You have spent the day setting the scene for 84.) 'Oh . . . Well, wake Janice up and put her in it.' Janice staggers back to the dressing room stretching and cursing. Soon you discover they forgot to send the earrings and the shoes are far too small for Janice's large foot. The bell rings again: 'Parks, it's the messenger from *Bazaar*. He wants the Balmains that you have.' 'Tell him to wait.'

By 3 am you may have two shots under your belt which you are not too convinced about; there are two messengers from other magazines glaring at your back waiting for garments that have been sent from Dior and St Laurent (one without a skirt, the other with no hat; and yet your Editor

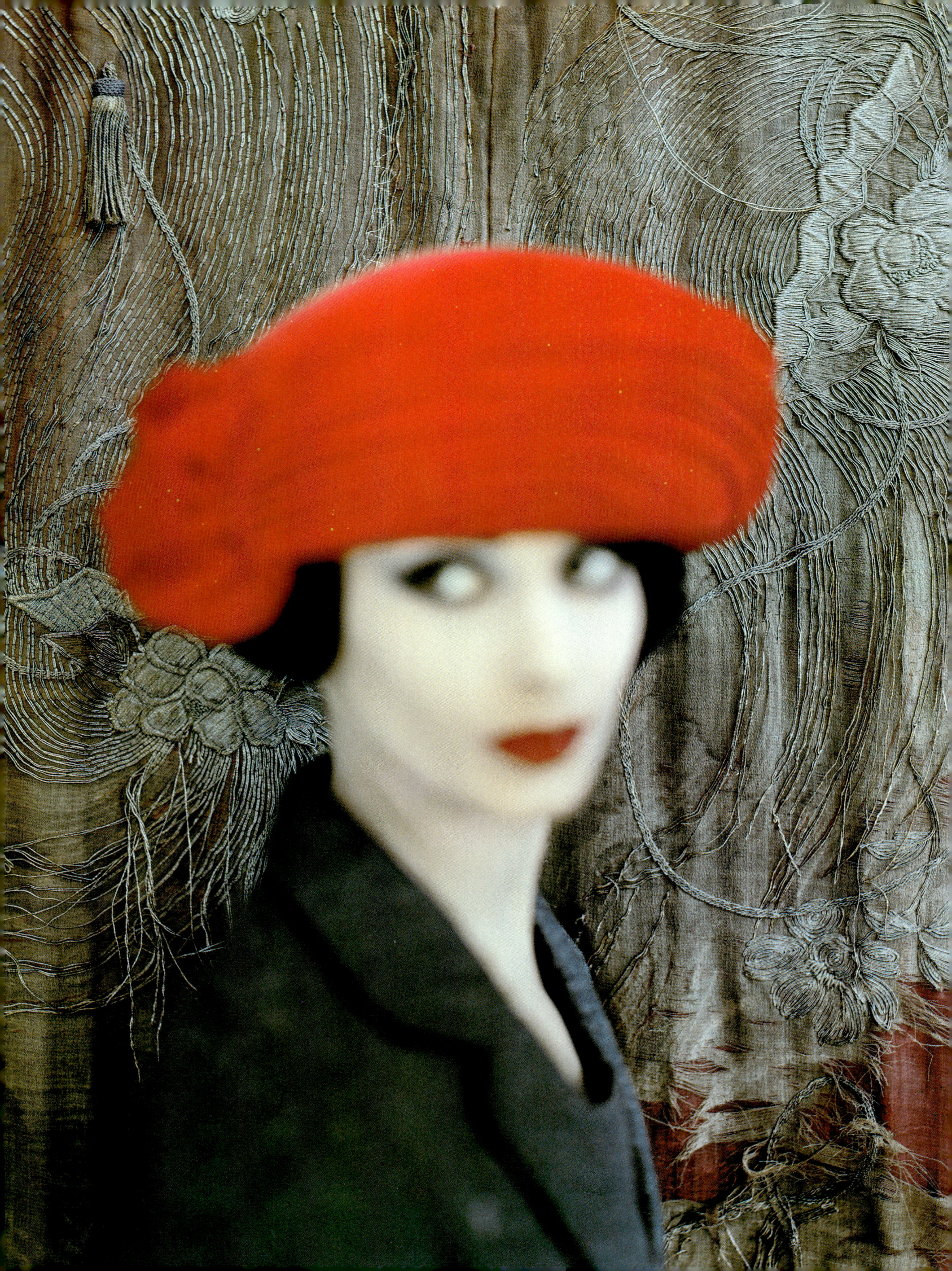

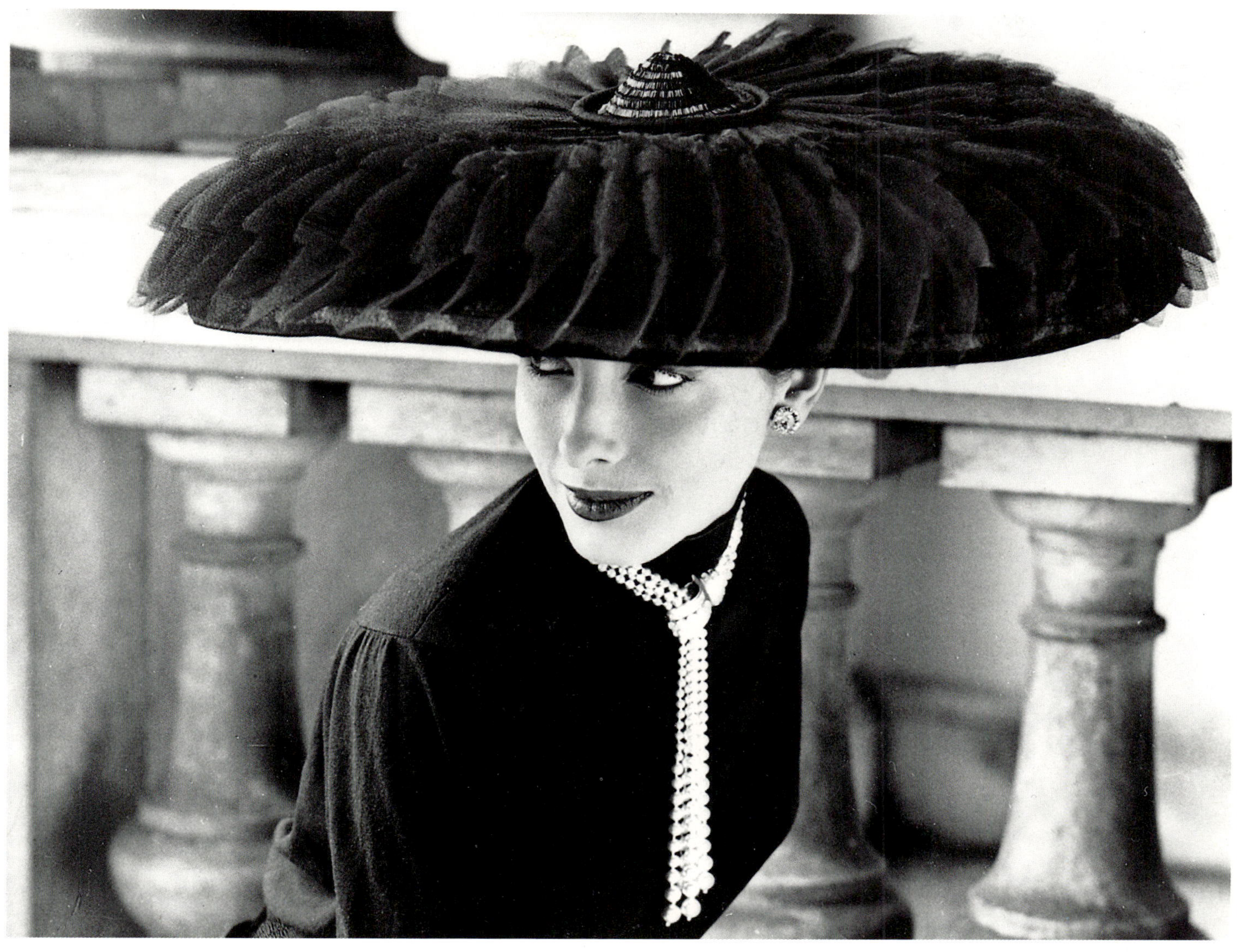

wants a cover try on the latter). By breakfast time you are either demented or exhausted or both. You all break up, promising to start again at 6 pm, and struggle to bed. Your Editor calls at noon: 'I managed to snatch the hat from St Laurent. Are you strong enough to try the cover? Mabel is awake and says she'll do it.' 'Sure,' you mumble and go off to the studio again. This goes on for four or five days. The magazine is anxious to get to press with the material so the pressure is constant and retakes are impossible. 'No time, no time' is the constant cry.

So it was with some trepidation that I went back to Paris, grateful that Bettina Ballard, *Vogue's* Fashion Editor, would be there to guide and orchestrate us.

The early days of August were beautiful while we worked all over Paris. The entire fashion world was just about recovering from the hammer-blow impact of the 'New Look' projected a couple of years earlier by Christian Dior. A highly feminine image – nipped-in waist below a neat fitted jacket and above a full swinging skirt – it blew right out of the window all the War year austerity of clothing coupons, 'sensible' brogue shoes, mannish tweed suits and studded leather shoulder bags with brass mock military insignia which could conceal a gas mask. Dior swept all this dowdiness away in one Collection and femininity never looked back.

One afternoon we were working in the Versailles gardens and I complained to Bettina Ballard that a particular Dior ball gown would look much better if the bodice was pulled down tighter into its enormous skirt. 'You're right,' she said, taking hold of the model's arm. 'Come with me.'

Nearby there was a small copse with bushes which Bettina immediately thought might offer the necessary 'cover'. She half-dragged the somewhat unwilling model into the shade and, facing the girl, bent down, throwing the many petticoats upwards as she dived forward to grab hold of the bodice. The two of them locked in this extraordinary position presented a bizarre shape. Bettina, bent like a croquet hoop, was under the model's many petticoats, and as she fumbled for the base of the bodice, only her posterior was visible. A passing pedestrian, having stopped for a few seconds to take in the scene, became as fascinated by this extraordinary sight as we were. His curiosity got the better of him, and walking forward, he tapped Bettina on the back: 'Pardon, puis-je intervenir Madame? Je suis medecin.'

ABOVE *Legroux Soeurs hat, 1952*
OPPOSITE *'After Van Dongen', Adèle Collins in an Otto Lucas toque, 1959*

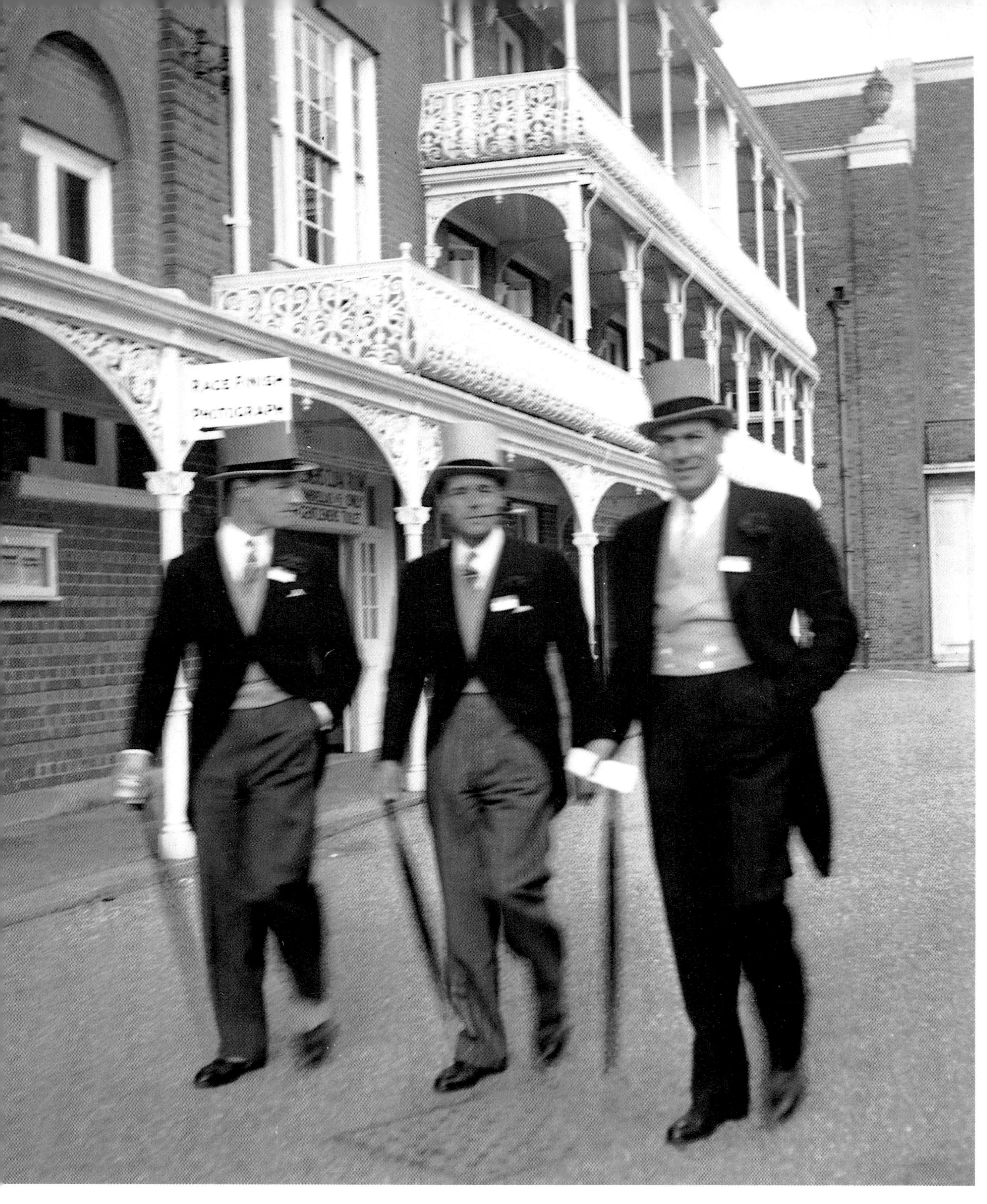

ABOVE *The Royal Enclosure, Ascot, 1958*
OPPOSITE *The new Mayfair Edwardians: Peter Coats, William Aykroyd, and Mark Gilbey, Savile Row, 1950*

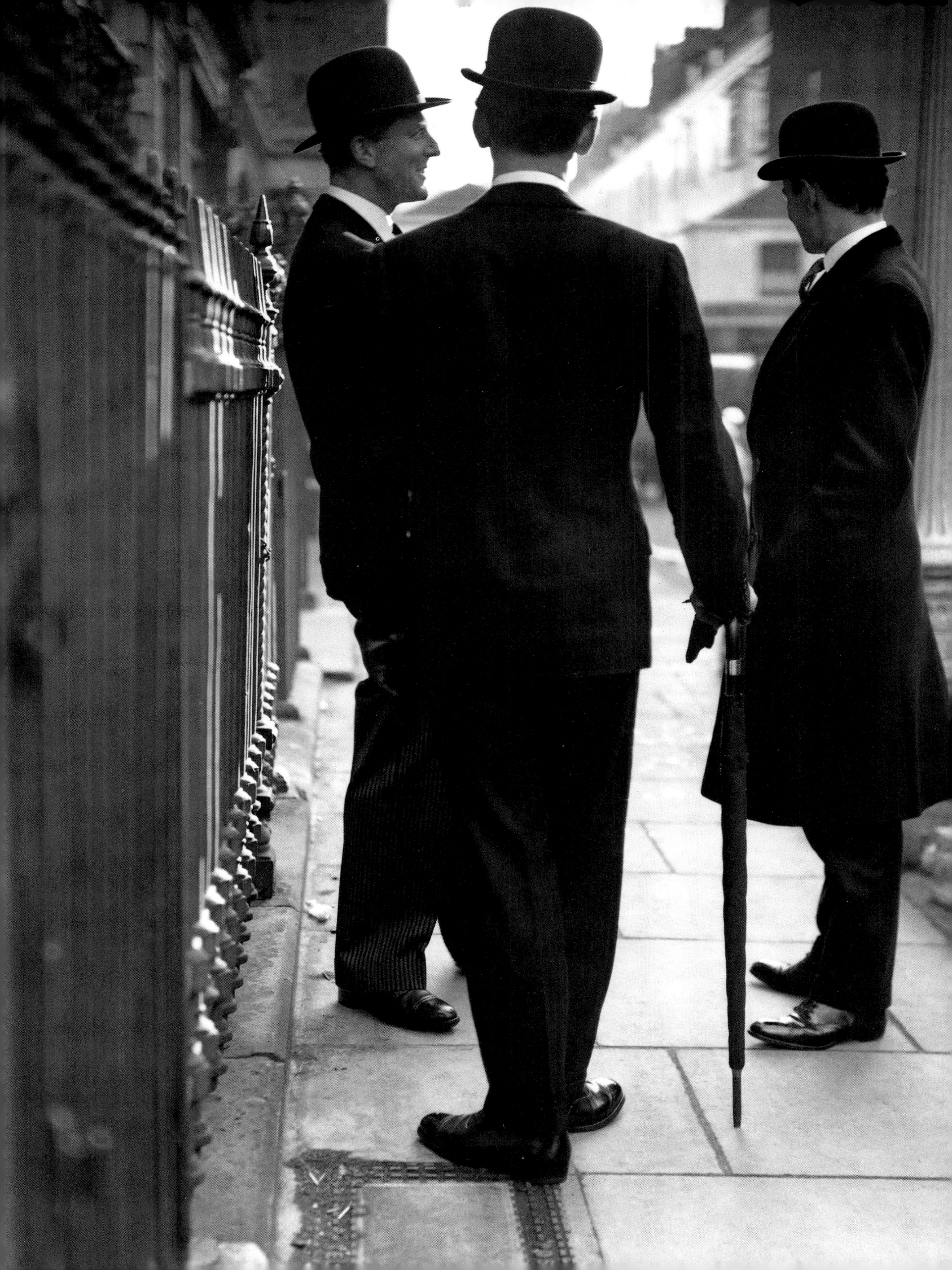

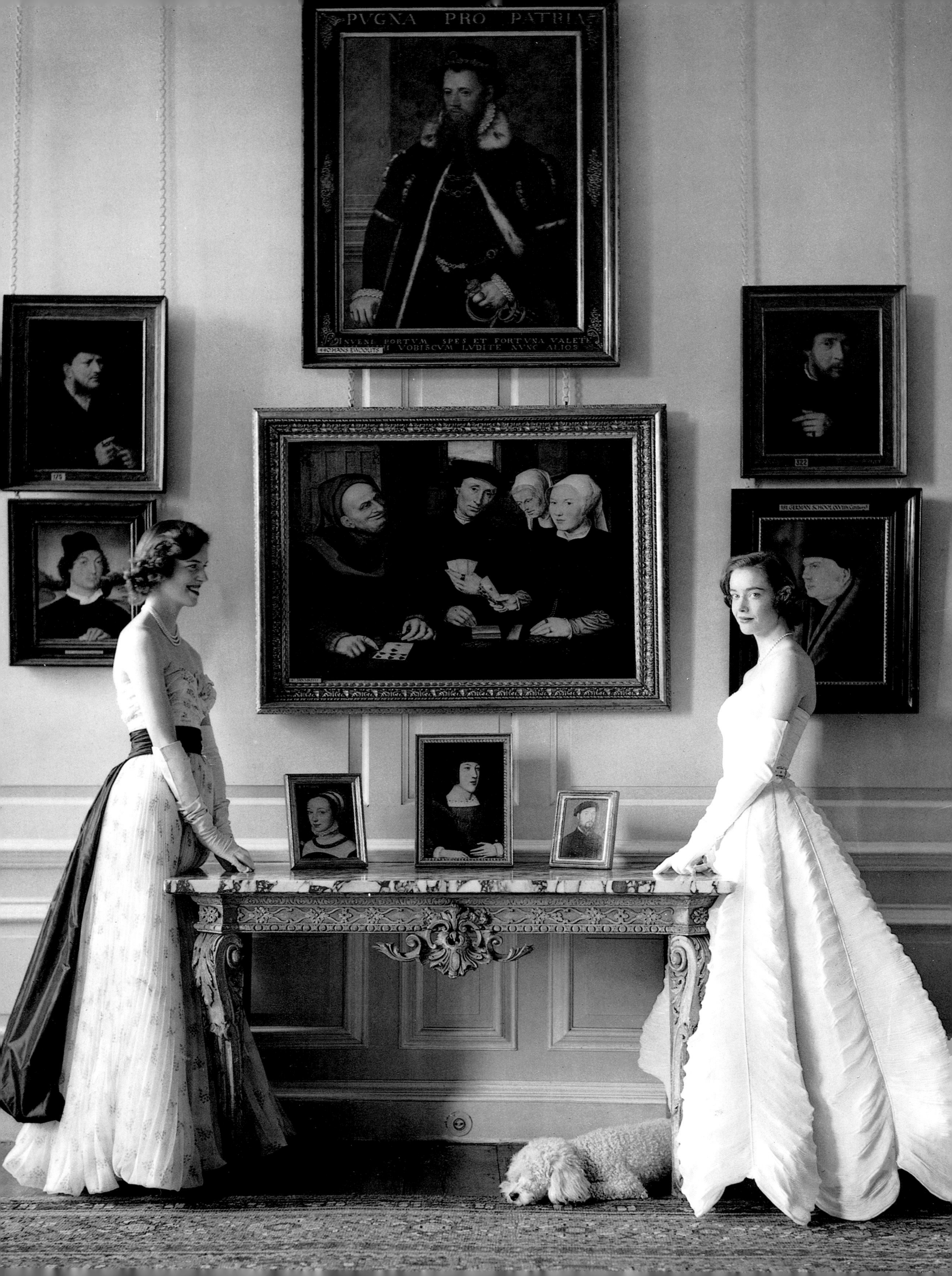
PVGNA PRO PATRIA
322

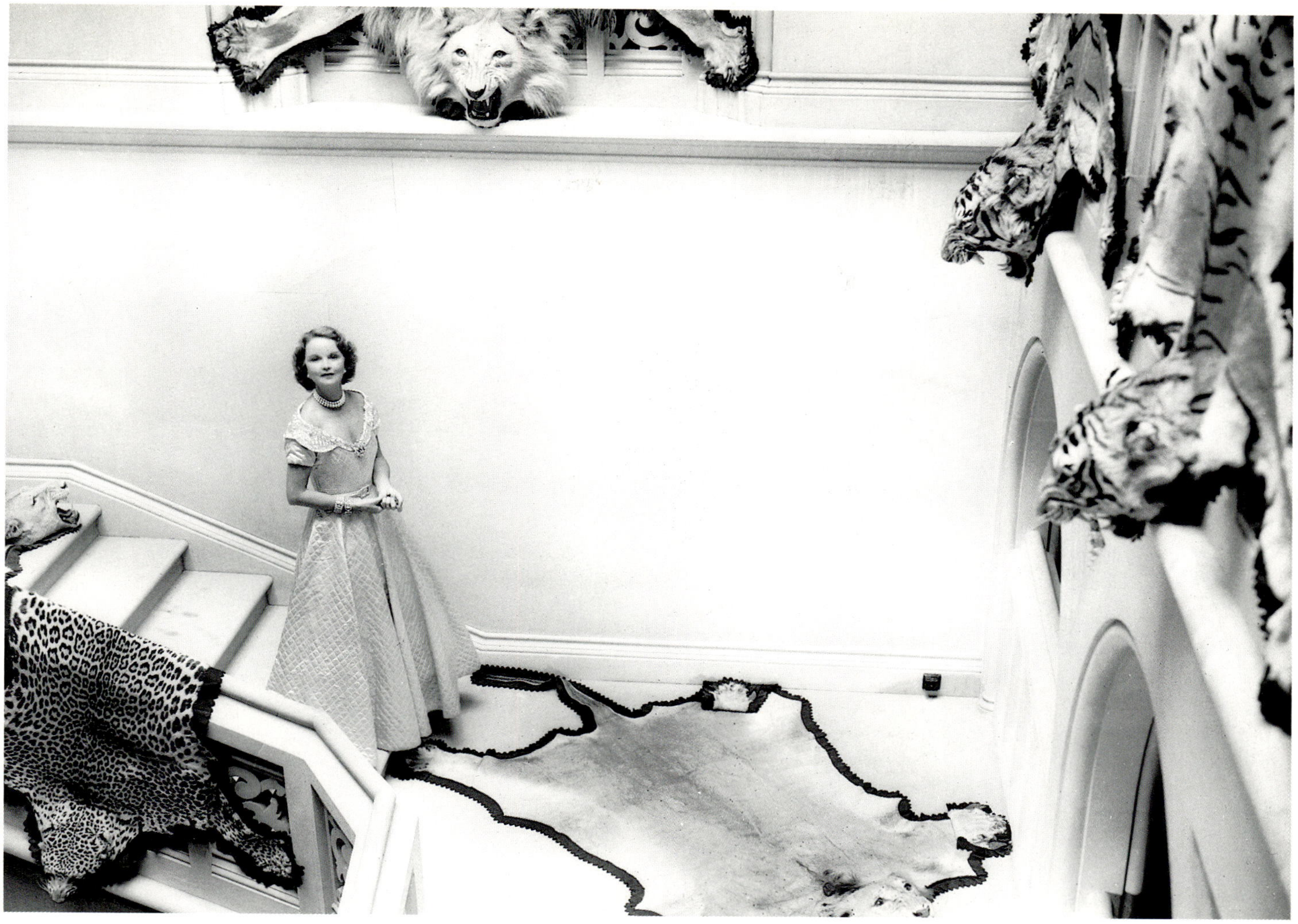

The Duchess of Sutherland, Dunrobin Castle

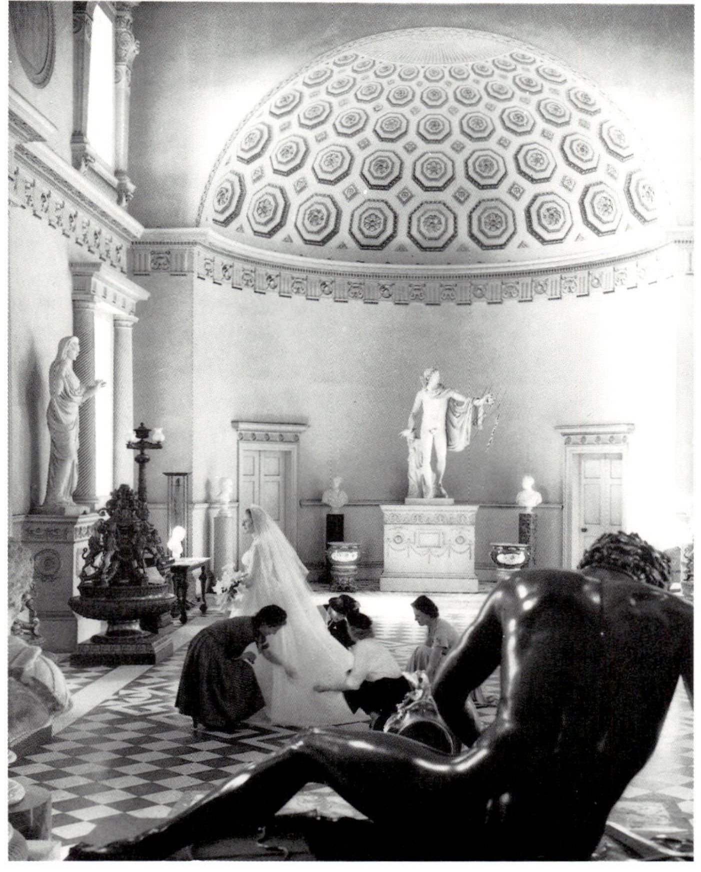

Lady Caroline Montagu-Douglas-Scott on the day of her wedding to Sir Ian Gilmour, Syon House, 1951

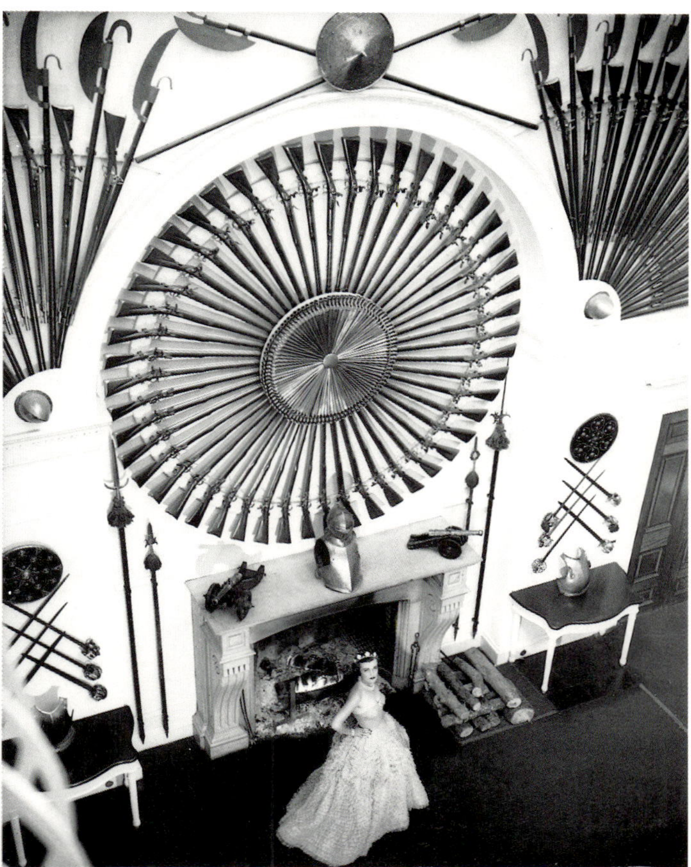

Margaret, Duchess of Argyll, Inverary Castle

OPPOSITE *Lady Melissa and Lady Caroline Wyndham-Quin posing in Sybil Connolly dresses, the Little Dining Room, Petworth House, 1954*

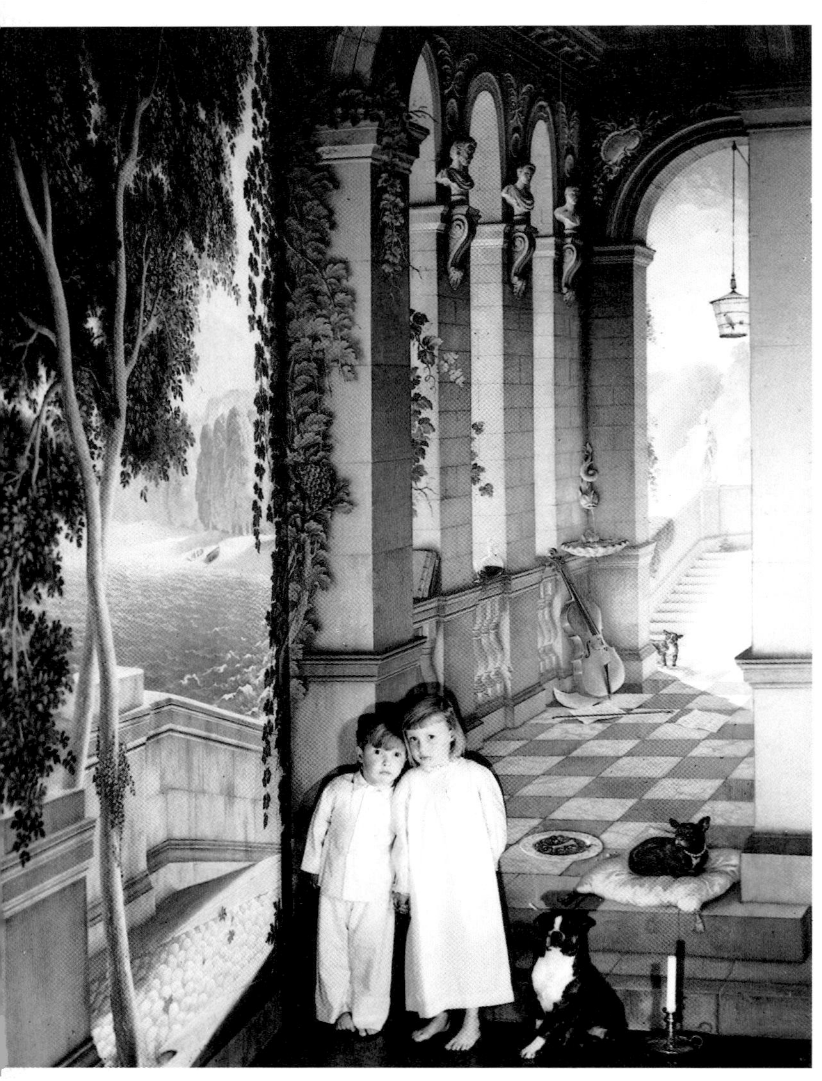

The Earl of Uxbridge and Lady Henrietta Paget, children of the Marquess and Marchioness of Anglesey, in front of Rex Whistler's trompe l'oeil murals at Plas Newydd, 1953

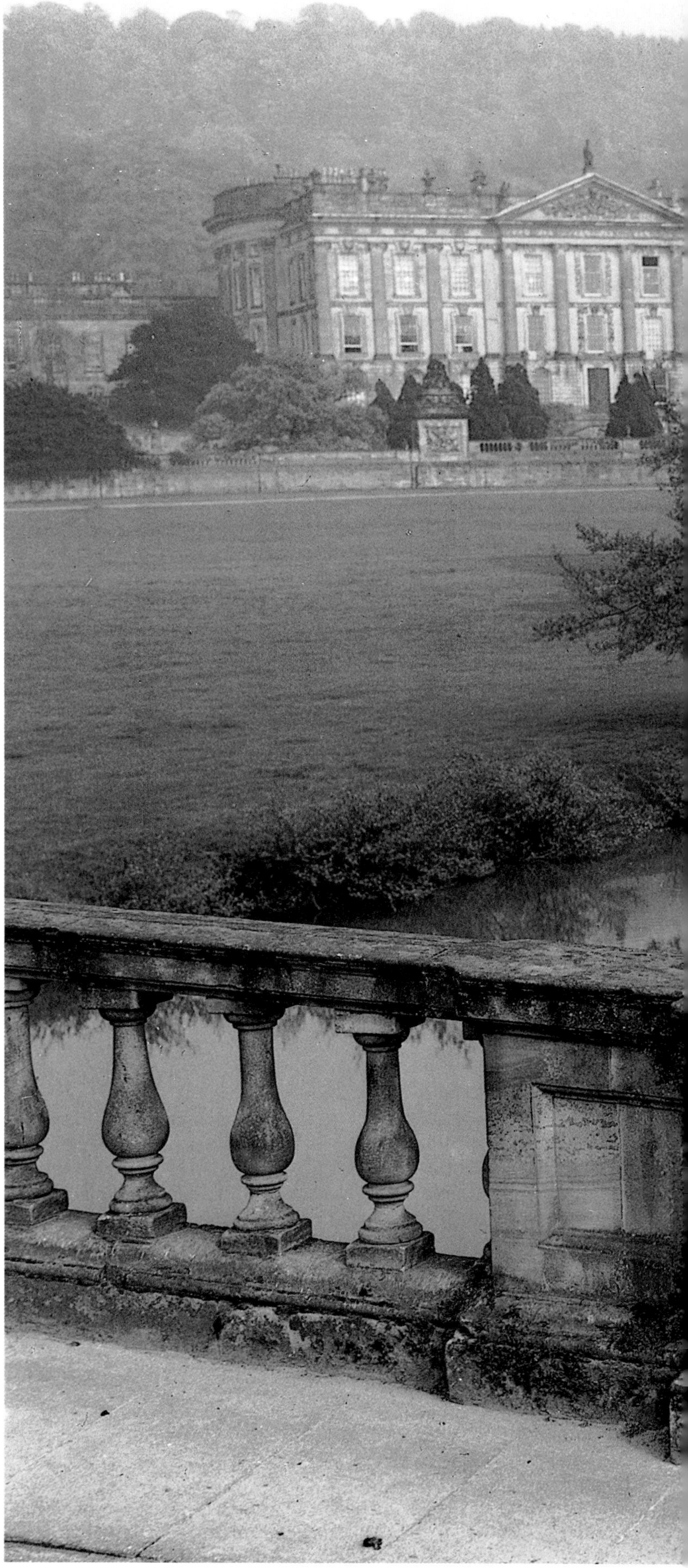

Lord Hartington and Lady Emma Cavendish, children of the Duke and Duchess of Devonshire, Chatsworth, 1952

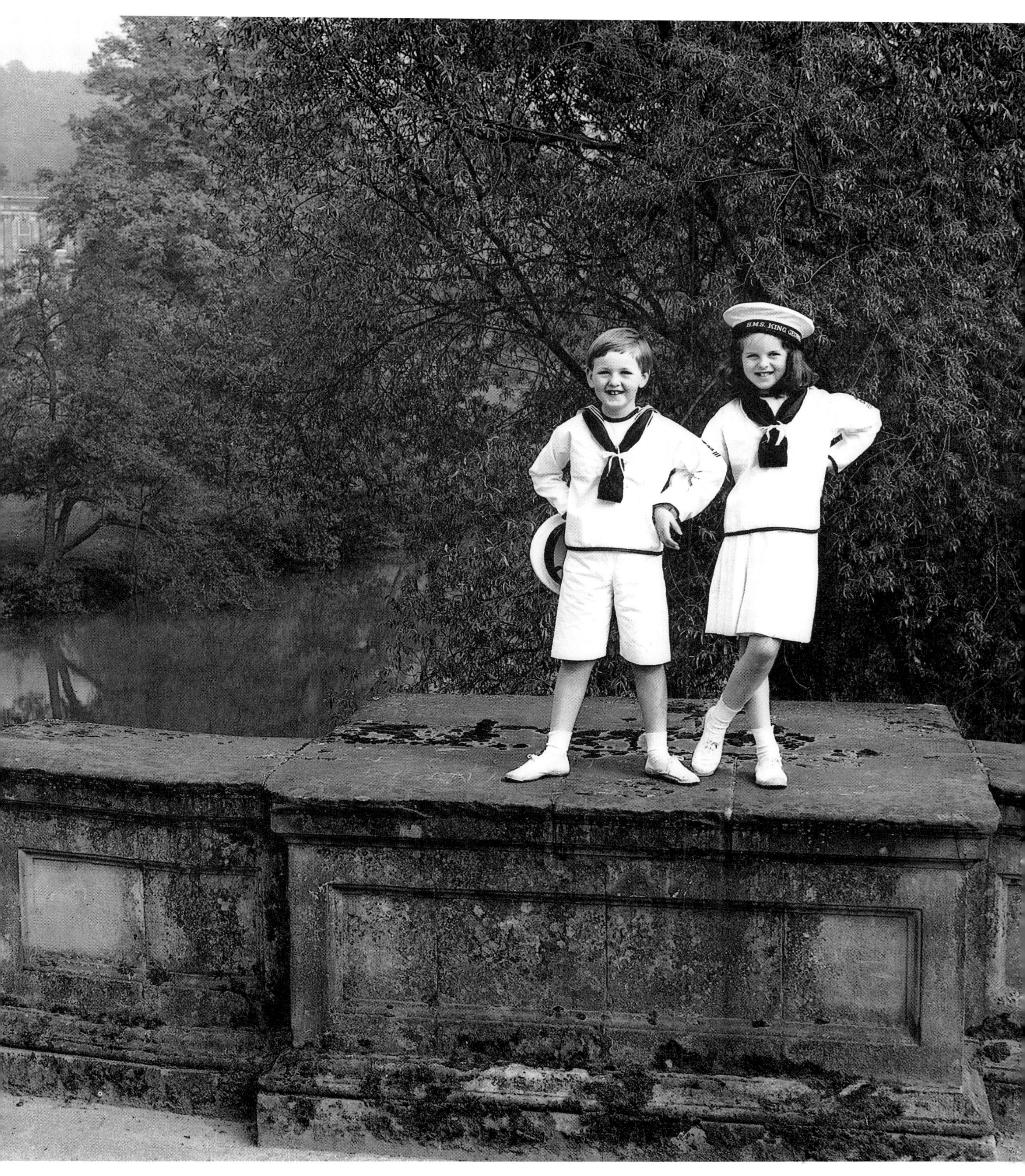
H.M.S. KING

ERIC AND BOUCHÉ

When it comes to dapper, Eric Ericson was extra dapper. He was a pale and elegant William-pear of a man with a relaxed round face. His eyes were typically those of an artist, darting and seeking everywhere. As his name implies, he was Swedish and specialized in just-better-than-good watercolours. He could put down in an accomplished manner the cold northern lights of his homeland. From these early clean, quiet, polished seascapes it was a giant's stride to illustrate, with such facility, the world's vogueish posh spots. I believe Harry Yoxall, the post-war boss of British *Vogue*, discovered him.

(I have left the first paragraph above as I originally put it down, because after many years of acquaintance this is the way I thought of him. I imagined that he had arrived from the outskirts of Stockholm with his large folder of watercolours aged about thirty-nine just before the Second World War. But all that is apparently a myth. While looking for long lost negatives in the *Vogue* library in New York recently I came upon an early fifties laudation for Eric. The disillusioning truth from his biographer is as follows: Carl Oscar August Ericson was born to American parents in 1891 in Joliet, Illinois; his father was in the whisky business; he arrived in New York with his watercolours in 1914; he did his first freelance illustrations for *Vogue* in 1916. Whatever the truth, I still cannot think of this brilliant and active individual as twenty-two years older than myself – he was like a contemporary and that is how we behaved together.)

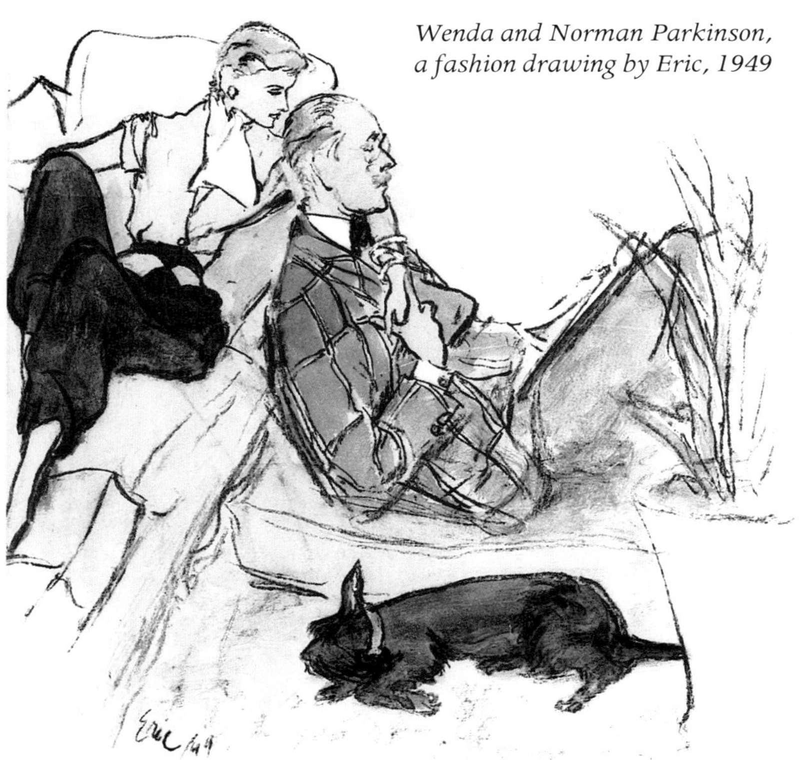

Wenda and Norman Parkinson, a fashion drawing by Eric, 1949

When the history of twentieth-century glossy magazines is fully written, we shall learn more about the roles played by Frank Croninshield, Condé Nast, Alexei Brodovitch, and Carmel Snow; and Eric's work will emerge as the most talented contribution to the formative years. Contemporary with him were Bouché and Williaumetz and, to a slicker degree, Gruau. But Eric had the edge, for he was a consummate draughtsman. He would stand before an easel on which was fixed a large block, two feet by three, of crisp thin white paper. He drew in charcoal – little thin sticks from Lechertier, Barbe of Jermyn Street. It was a magic revelation to watch the images spring from his hand, later they were finished off in pale washes of watercolour. He would create quick elegant scenes for the background of his fashion illustrations. The *salles privées* at Monte Carlo, the aft deck of a yacht at anchor off Newport, RI, the Royal Enclosure at Ascot, *dîner intime* at Maxims, would emerge as if from a camera obscura, for in his mind's eye he had recorded all the references. His eye was so expert that the veracity of his crowd scenes could not be bettered by any photographer.

During his most productive period in the early fifties he was well patronized by American *Vogue*, which enabled him to give rein to his appearance as the St James's Street boulevardier – perfect dark navy English tailoring, handmade shoes and shirts finished off with the sincere Sulka tie and, of course, to crown it all, a fine bowler hat from Locks. I seem to remember that once he carried pale lavender gloves – but perhaps I exaggerate. There was a single eccentricity in his immaculate appearance which provided the hint that this elegant Englishman might have been born elsewhere – he wore his bowler slanted over one ear.

As a *bon viveur*, he looked forward to his trips to London and Paris to work with Bettina Ballard. He did his best work, inspired by the important fashion openings and social highspots, from the late forties to the mid-fifties, and then, to everybody's chagrin, it was all over even more quickly than it had begun. He discussed his alcoholism quite openly, and we would talk about it without embarrassment. His drinking was not a real problem, the problem was that he could not draw as he wished to draw when he was sober. He preferred to work at odd times. We became good friends and would often dine with him so that he could draw us in the evening. Sometimes he stood with difficulty and would fall asleep during our meal together, but in this condition his ability was critical and his draughtsmanship of the highest order. Paradoxically, I would say that during this wavering blindness he saw most clearly. I remember an occasion in Paris when he was drawing Wenda. He supported himself against the panelled wall of his suite at the Crillon; head lowered, he studied her carefully for some seconds and then, lunging a little at his easel, he drew a meticulous eye towards the top of his large sheet – just one eye. He then hesitated at the

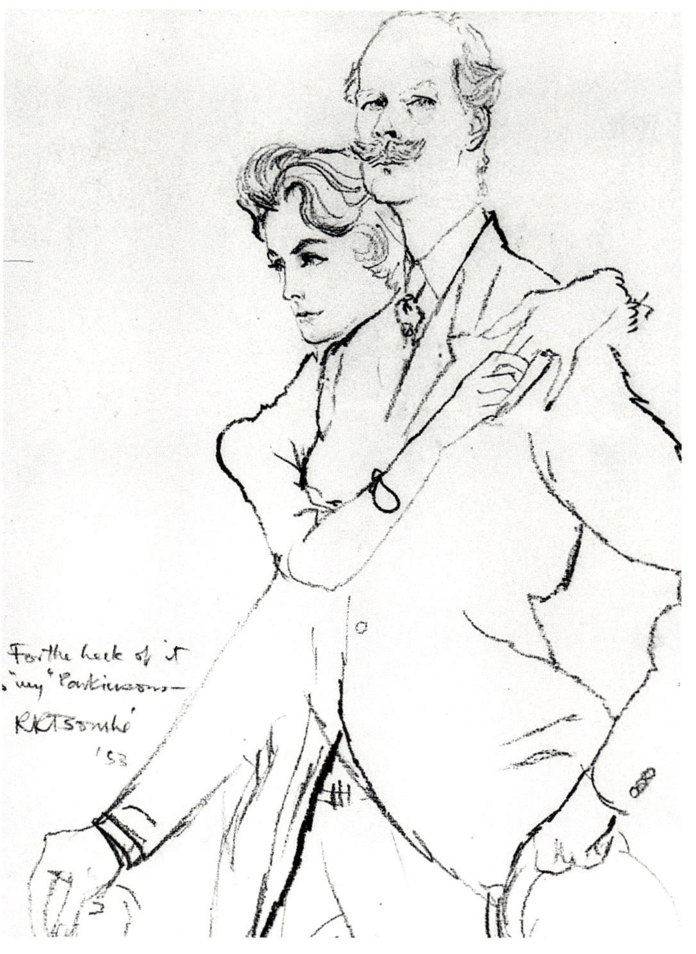

Wenda and Norman Parkinson
by René Bouché, 1953

base of the paper and started to draw a shoe; when this was finished to his satisfaction his charcoal turned the ankle and, as if following the numbers in a child's drawing book, he scratched up the calf, behind the knee, along the hips, the waist, and suddenly conjured from the air an arm, a hand and its bracelet, the shoulders, the neck, and now his bent stick of charcoal circumnavigated the skull, with miracle intention enclosing in its correct position the original eye. He stood back and smiled a small smile of pleasure as he recognized that his outrageous gamble had paid off. He turned to me and winked, pleased that I had been a partner to the joke. In his considerate and gentlemanly way he then asked Wenda to rest, while he added some more detailed touches to the drawing from his memory. Later Wenda stood before him again in the same pose and the drawing was completed, preparatory to the waterwash. He loved to draw Wenda; she was one of his favourite models and he drew her constantly when their visits to Paris or New York coincided. There were also quite a few illustrations of us together. The illustration that is included here was done in New York before we sat down to a delicious meal with him in his apartment. He did not eat very much and fell asleep after the steak. We waited a while and then tip-toed from the room shutting the door behind us. The dog and spiky plant must have been put in the next day for they were not in the drawing when we left.

Vogue magazine and his family became very concerned, for different reasons, about his long and unpredictable disappearances into the noontide backwaters of Third Avenue. *Vogue* needed his regular and most valuable contributions so that they could make their Press dates, and his family were obviously worried about his health and safety. When the sum total of his absences became greater than his available productive time, his protectors, to his displeasure, made a concerted move in an attempt to effect a cure. Some months later he told us about his terrible experiences in the alcoholic hospital where they attempted to balance things by injecting him with alcohol, producing, as he described it, the most frightening DTs – little mice and dwarfs everywhere, squeezing out from under the rugs and running up the walls. He often spoke of the panic and delirium which had affected him deeply, but he did stop drinking and his family had every right to believe that the somewhat violent cure had been successful. Certainly he did not drink, but more importantly neither could he draw. His inimitable flow of elegant style had been extinguished with the liquor; his subsequent illustrations were generally unusable and Eric was frantic. With the evidence of his sterility before them, his protectors suggested to the doctors that a small intake of wine, and wine only, might regenerate his prowess. We saw him quite often at the time that the shaky charcoal was beginning to rediscover its former brilliance. He made the suggestion that as we had been such good friends; 'I want you and Wenda to have all the drawings that I have done of you – I've put it in my will and the family knows my wishes'. Shortly after this he started drinking again and was found dead soon after. About a year later the family arranged an auction of his illustrations for the assemblage of his estate. It was held in New York, unbeknown to us, and everything was sold except some that Condé Nast Publications wished to retain. Somewhere, on somebody's walls, there must be dozens of his best illustrations – all of Wenda.

René Bouché was an acquaintance, whereas Eric was a friend, so we did not know him as well, which was our loss. He was smaller and darker and more active than Eric with his understated Scandinavian phlegm. Bouché was like a greying curly headed terrier, and very susceptible to the opposite sex. He filled in for *Vogue* during Eric's absences, but no derogation here, he was a very fine illustrator in his own right.

He was preparing an exhibition of his drawings and paintings for New York and London when he asked us to sit for him. He signed the drawing included here with the words 'For my Parkinsons just for the heck of it'. (Later he completed an oil painting of the same subject.)

We remember vividly our sittings in his Central Park South studio. He arranged that we should be locked there in an embrace and as he paced the room like a caged feline, the growls and moans as he wielded his charcoal would have rivalled the furore emitted from the big cat house at the Zoo at feeding time just across the Park. Furthermore, the moaning and teeth-sucking were secondary to his climbing around the room over the furniture. It will be a long time before we forget being drawn by the great René Bouché.

MADISON AVENUE

In the early fifties Condé Nast operated five or six large studios (now torn down) at 480 Lexington Avenue, just a block or two up-town from the magazine offices at 420, with all the facilities for producing colour and black-and-white photographs. We all worked from there except Rawlings, who had his own place, and the whole operation was managed by Clare Mallison.

About this time it was decided that I should chance my arm at some advertising photography which is more lucrative than the editorial work. So, in the prescribed manner, I got together a book of samples. Moreover it was also decided that Ms Mallison should be my agent (taking 20%, and another 25% went to the studios), and she would attempt to sell my talents in Madison Avenue. I would occasionally go round with my newly acquired agent to meet some of the big New York agency art buyers and I would sit there like an aspiring harlot, while my Madame extolled my virtues, not convinced in my gut that I was going to enjoy the man who was about to hire my services.

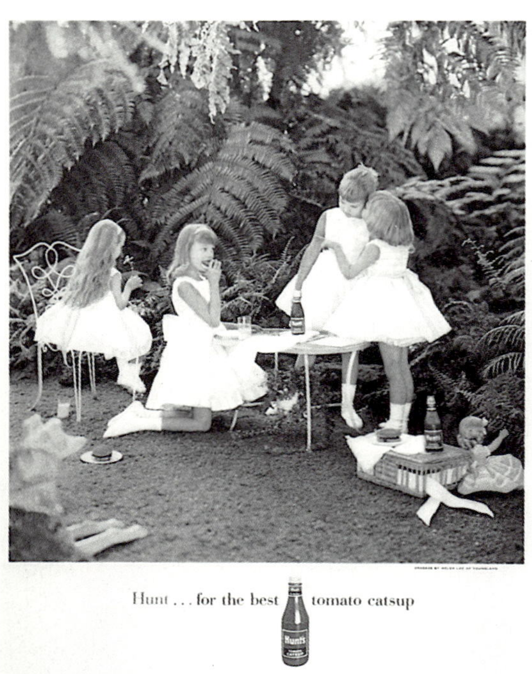

Hunt's catsup advertisement, 1956

On some such occasion, an art director flipped through my sample book which contained twenty or thirty prints and tear sheets, of most of which, in my ignorance, I was rather proud. There were photographs of almost everything – ravishing girls dressed for winter or summer; prize snaps taken on location in Jamaica and Peru; springtime in Washington, chic cars in fall colours in Connecticut; every visual cliché was intentionally included. The art director person closed up my book, and turning towards my agent, excluding me from the conversation, he said, 'Your photographer has a good book; I like his work, but unfortunately there are no photographs in it of television sets. I was going to offer you a big account for television set advertising but how do we know that he can handle this type of work?'

In the early fifties I worked on several assignments with Fran Healey at Young Rubicam. Fran was a kind and exceptionally pleasant person who seemed slightly out of place in the harsh hurly-burly of Madison Avenue. One January afternoon, I remember, she arranged for me to see an art director who opened the conversation with, 'Listen Parkinson, we handle the Hunt's Catsup account and we want, for our summer campaign, a colour picture of a summertime picnic with five little girls in flimsy white lace dresses eating hamburgers in buns with red catsup oozing out.' I was momentarily speechless and standing up I pointed a purposeful finger at the window behind him where a heavy snowstorm was driving horizontally down Madison Avenue so hard that the opposite side of the street was almost obscured. 'Do I understand you correctly?' I spluttered. 'You want me to arrange a high summer picnic in this weather? Can we go to Florida?' 'No, Mr Parkinson, it has to be taken around New York and we want the transparencies in a week.' 'Goodness, you have fixed me with an awful problem.' 'Look Mr Parkinson,' he replied almost without a hint of sympathy, 'I have my problems, now you have yours.'

Six days later, by the intervention of a meteorological miracle, I delivered my high summer picnic transparencies of unanticipated beauty, and some twenty years later they still remember that sitting at the agency.

As an epilogue, perhaps I should say how the pictures were achieved in the foulest of weather. The day after my meeting at Young & Rubicam I had a hunch and drove out to the Bronx Botanical Gardens through the gently falling snow. The gardening officer, for a fee, agreed to allow me to work inside the largest hothouse, now dark and murky with the snow cover and grey skies, but I noticed an area within the tropical vegetation where we might have been able to shoot our picnic if we were to lay down a carpet of artificial grass. I booked the sitting for a couple of days hence. It snowed hard for the next twenty-four hours and near-panic prompted me to hire quantities of tungsten light and a four-wheel drive caravan truck. The dawn of the chosen day revealed cloudless skies and I said a silent prayer of thanks. I telephoned the mothers, collected the children and we ploughed our solitary journey to the Bronx through a foot of snow.

The reflected light in the tropical hothouse was brilliant for the sun had thawed off the excesses of snow from the roof. We laid down our grass, and the primly dressed children had their picnic round the Catsup bottle. As I focussed the scene on the ground glass of the camera I could barely believe my eyes, for there before me, in sub-zero weather, was a high summer picnic which I readily admit would have been difficult to take in June.

SWIMMING FOR SIMON

Simon was a typical English boy with a shock of white hair – he soon captivated our new American friends. With this captivation there naturally followed requests that he should appear in some of my pictures for the magazine. In the first month or so he earned some nice pocket money for his model fees, but quite soon he became a bit bored with the business and we had to resort to bribery – not with money, for that meant nothing, but with toys. One afternoon I did a sitting that included an elegant mock grandmama taking tea with her grandson in the Palm Court of the Plaza Hotel. If young Simon, now becoming slightly blasé through over exposure would be a 'very good boy' and do exactly what his papa said, we would go across the road after the photography and buy him a lovely big boat. It worked like magic, even to kissing the mock grandmama several times.

Divested of his Merrimite clothing he downed an eclair, and the family moved across the road to F. A. O. Schwartz. It did not take him very long to choose the largest and most resplendent motorboat, the price for which was fortunately well covered by the anticipated model fee. Within a very short time, still under pressure from the successful child money maker, we were walking towards the lake in Central Park. The vessel was persuaded to make short loops, returning almost immediately to the bank some few yards further on. Becoming frustrated with these unadventurous forays, and since the boat seemed to have an impressive quantity of residual power still available, we directed the ship straight to the opposite bank some two hundred yards away. It took off with an impressive wake but after about a third of the journey its effort started to waver and, as might have been expected, lost power completely, right in the centre of the almost circular lake. Simon started to cry and his parents looked at each other disconsolately. What to do? A crowd of passersby and small boys with yachts gathered, full of helpful hints. The best advice came from a youth who claimed to have rescued his similarly stranded ship by throwing a line with a stone on the end of it over the vessel. It was beginning to get dark and was long after Simon's bedtime, so after taking him home, Wenda returned carrying a long reel of good thread. Meanwhile a crowd of marauding ducks had converged upon the stranded vessel, mounting it in a body, either attempting to sink the intruder or perhaps to mate it, so only the bow appeared clearly above the water. With superhuman effort and unerring aim, we managed to get a line or two beyond the speedboat but its sleek superstructure presented no protrusion upon which the thread or the stone might catch. Night fell and the prospect was bleak indeed. 'There is no alternative', I announced, 'I must swim for it.'

With considerable trepidation, I entered the water stark naked but with my shoes on, aware of broken glass crunching under my feet. As soon as the water was deep enough I started to swim to conceal my nakedness. I was out of my depth when I arrived at the by-now half submerged wreck which I seized with considerable disaffection, for the water was perishin' cold. I then turned on my back and placed the boat on my stomach. As I set sail for shore, I began to see the real humour of this absurd occasion, and to illuminate the absurdity even more brightly, an advertising blimp suddenly appeared about five hundred feet above me with flashing lights recommending Lucky Strike cigarettes.

Simon was very pleased to find his boat beside his bed when he woke up next morning; it is unlikely that he will ever believe what I went through to retrieve it, but then why should he, it was probably my own fault anyway.

Simon spent many months each year growing up in New York. He holds the happiest memories of it and was delighted when, after Westminster School, he was accepted for Harvard University, which gave him the ongoing weekend opportunities of jumping the shuttle from Boston to renew earlier acquaintances. Our earliest memories of Simon when he first arrived as a three year old attempting to get to sleep in the mid July humid heat, were his hysterics at the screeching, howling alarms of the New York Fire Brigade going about its business. He became inconsolable and it took us many weeks to comprehend why they terrified him to such an extent. Eventually we got the truth – because of the menacing noise put out by the fire engines to get through the traffic, he believed that they rushed here and there to light fires. What else would a fire engine do?

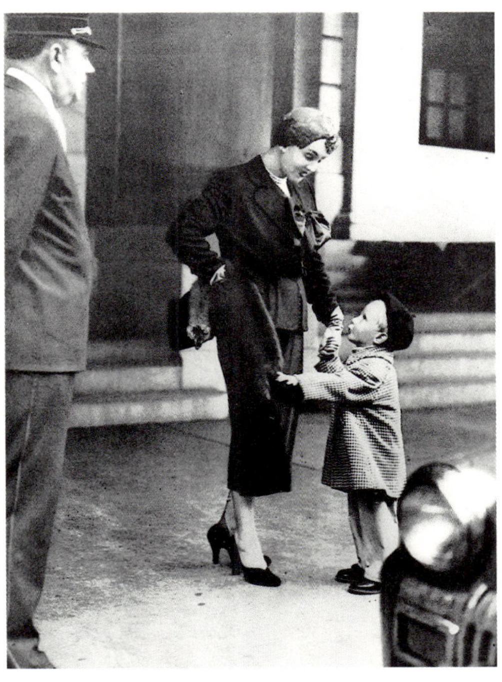

Simon Parkinson as a child model,
Plaza Hotel, New York, 1952

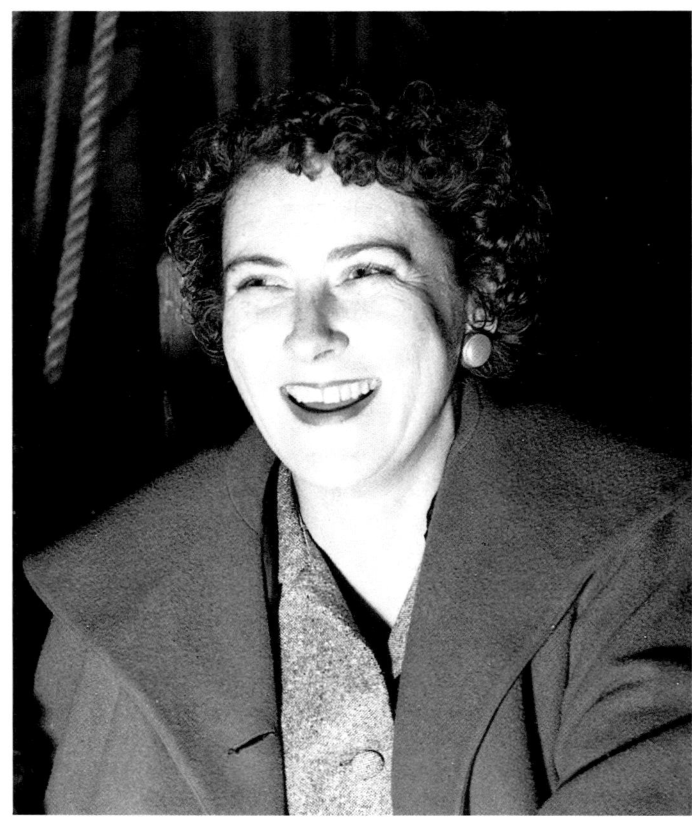

TRIBUTE TO SIRIOL

I wanted my photograph of Siriol, that does her no justice, together with these rather scratchy memories of her, to precede the following group of photographs. These erudite gentlemen, many no longer alive, are the props under the solid platform of mid-twentieth century scholarship. I am very proud to have recorded them (perhaps inadequately) but beyond and above this, these portraits are a memorial to Siriol who knew and admired these men; she took me to them and is the natural mother of this collection.

Siriol was promoted Features Editor when Lesley Blanche left British *Vogue*. She was recently down from Somerville College, Oxford, where she had enjoyed a meteoric scholastic career. She once took me back to her old school, Cheltenham Ladies' College, where her name, I noticed, was recorded on many a *cum laude* board.

I cannot remember where or when we met or when I last saw her, but ours was one of those lifelong associations when no introductions were necessary. Her erudition was so complete and impressive that I always felt inadequate in her presence. She was a brilliant girl, but never serious or the least bit overpowering about her superior knowledge. She was like a lovable dark brown Welsh vole. A jolly creature but very humble with a lot of 'do you think so?' She never pushed or made heavy suggestions, for although quite certain herself, she would never assert her personality directly enough to prevent you arriving at your own decision as to how best to solve the photographic problem. She led me on a silken thread into an endless photographic treasure trove. With her tinkling Welsh chuckle she drew aside the arras to reveal pictures, as yet untaken, that took your breath away. 'Look, Parks,' she would say, 'isn't that nice?'

She returned, for she was most welcome, to her old hunting grounds – if that could be the right analogy – and she invited me along with my camera. The Gilbert Murrays and the Lord David Cecils and the Bertrand Russells spoke another language to me, my ears could not digest such erudition. So Siriol, rewelcomed in the seats of her former scholastic triumphs, did the chatting and I was there modestly doing my snapping. We were a great team, and here are the spectators.

ABOVE *Siriol Hugh-Jones, Features Editor of British Vogue from 1947–55*
OPPOSITE *Lord David Cecil, essayist and biographer, Oxford, 1950*

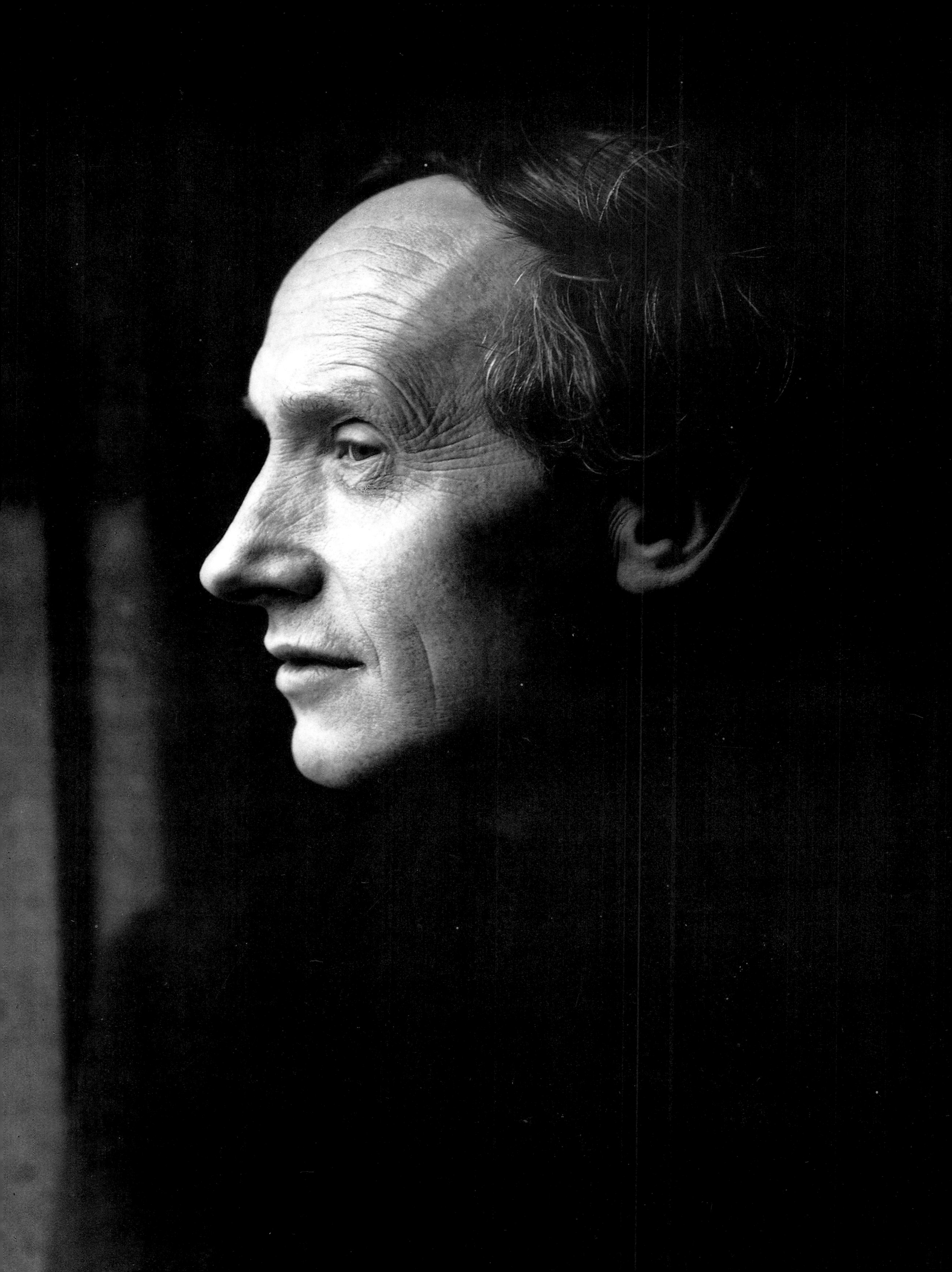

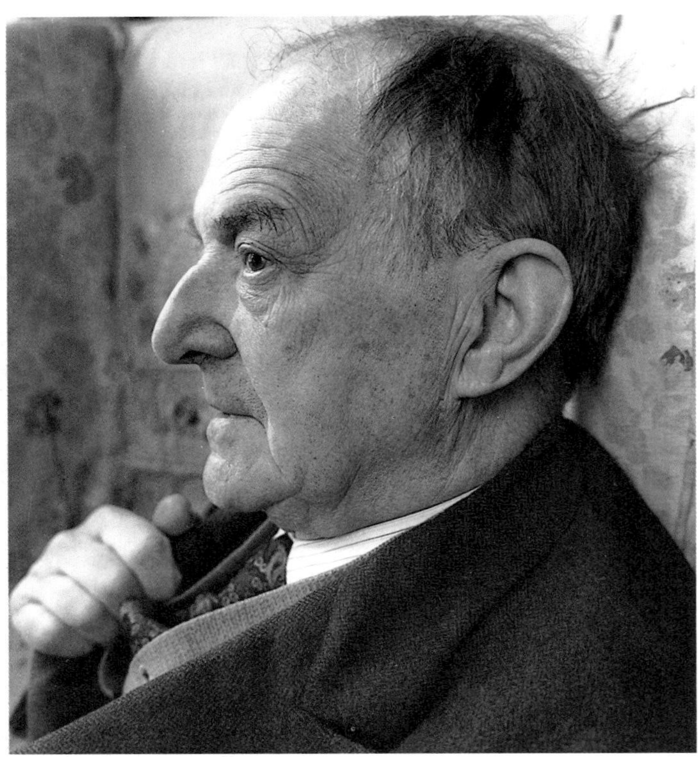

Ralph Vaughan Williams, composer, at home, 1951

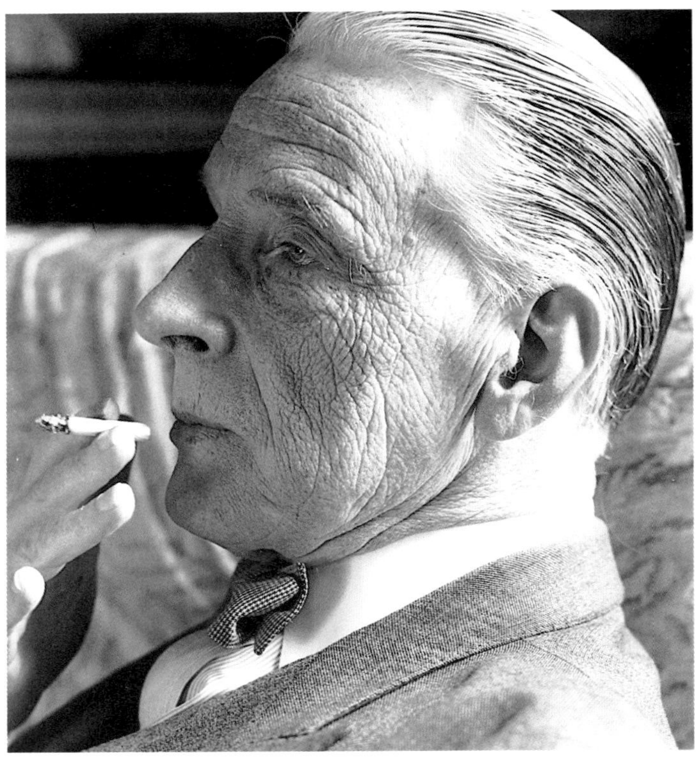

Charles Morgan, novelist, dramatist and critic, 1952

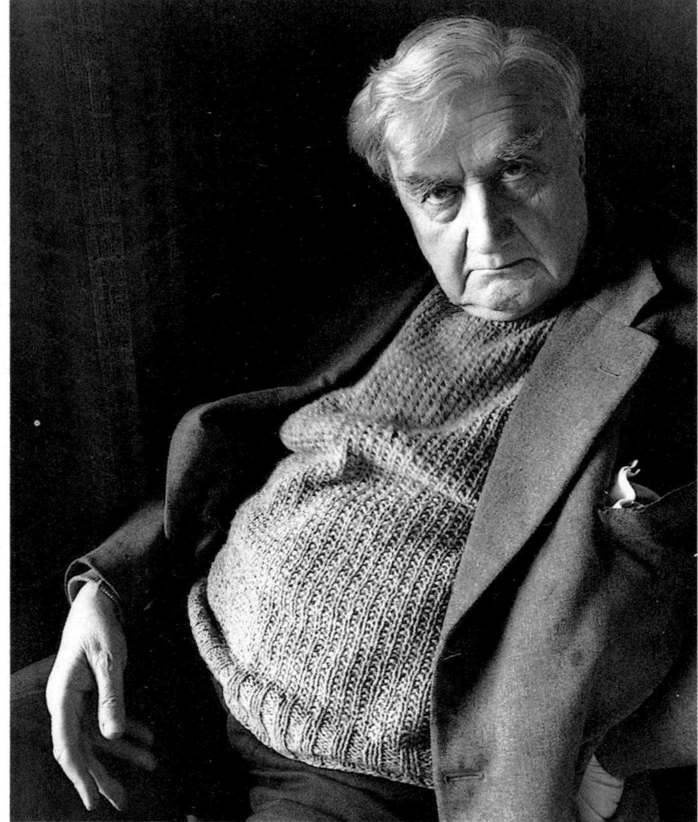

Walter de la Mare, poet and novelist, 1951

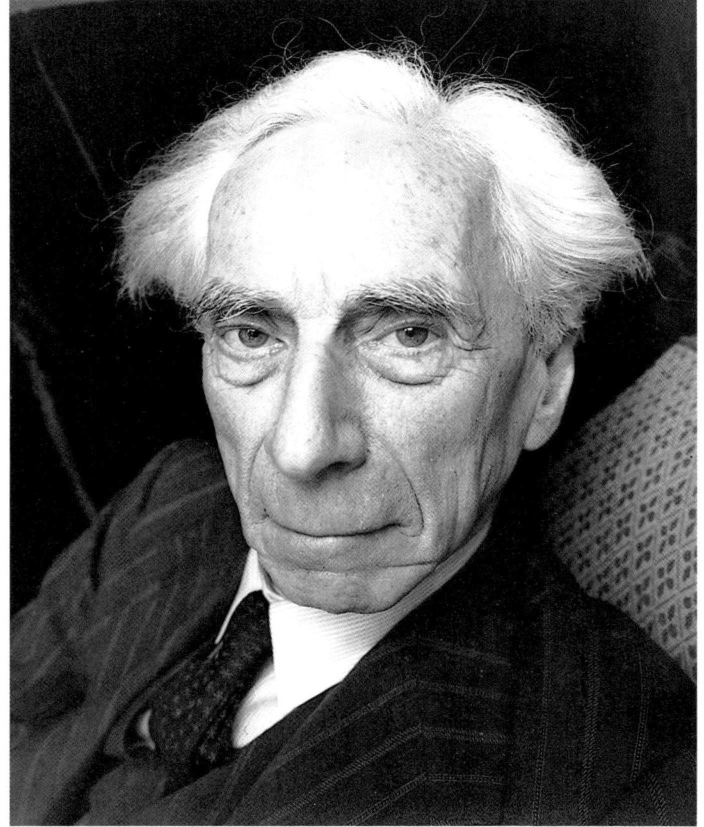

Bertrand Russell, philosopher, 1951

OPPOSITE *Georges Enesco, conductor, composer and violinist. A Romanian in exile, he was pupil of Fauré and teacher of Yehudi Menuhin. Salisbury station, 1953*

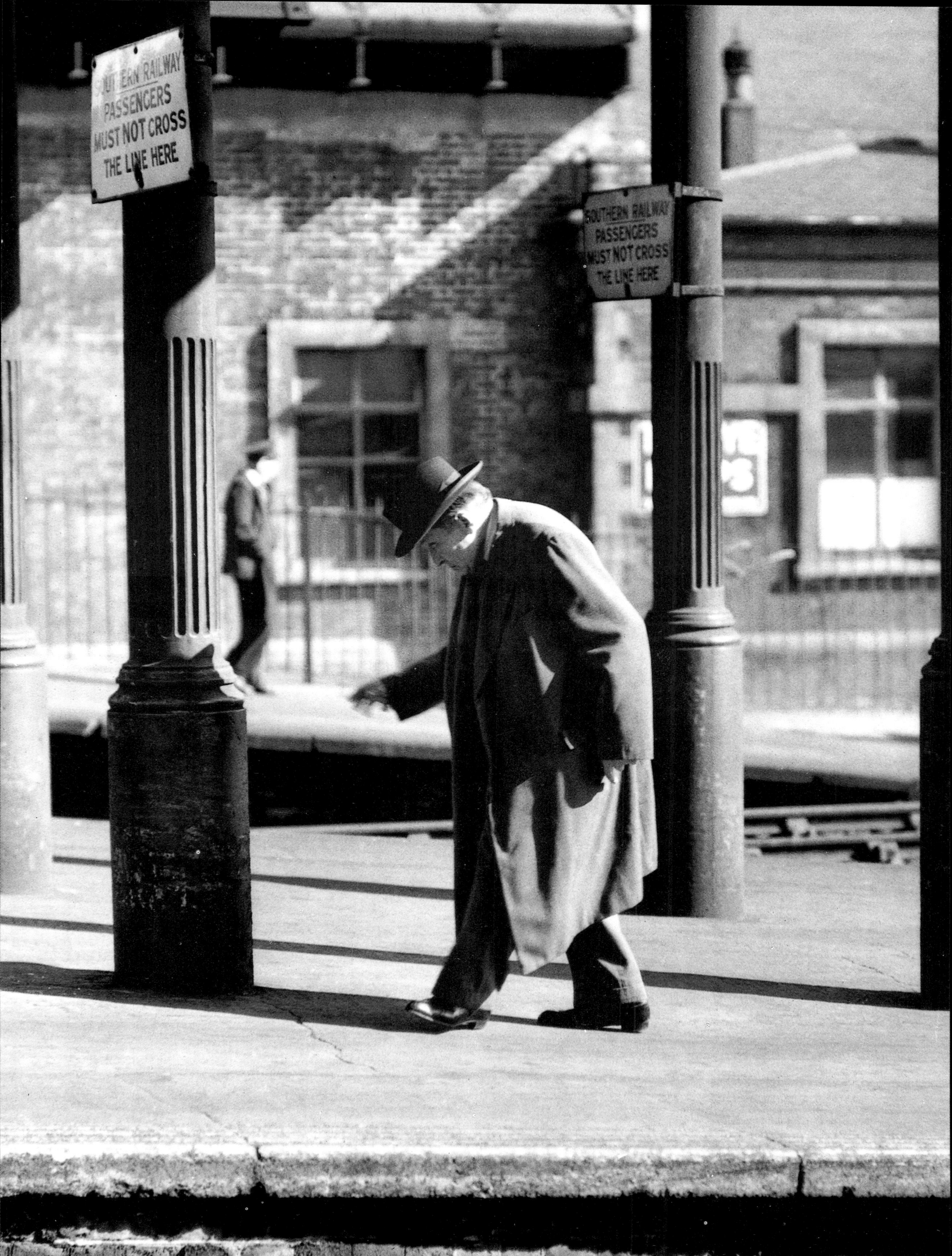
SOUTHERN RAILWAY
PASSENGERS
MUST NOT CROSS
THE LINE HERE
SOUTHERN RAILWAY
PASSENGERS
MUST NOT CROSS
THE LINE HERE

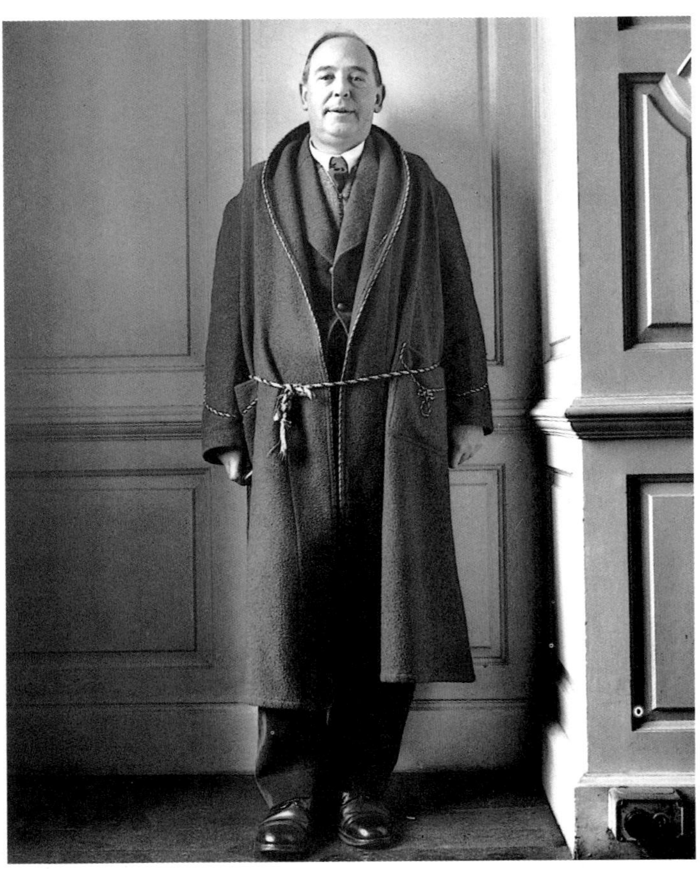

C. S. Lewis, Christian apologist, literary historian, writer of children's books and science fiction, Magdalen College, Oxford, 1950

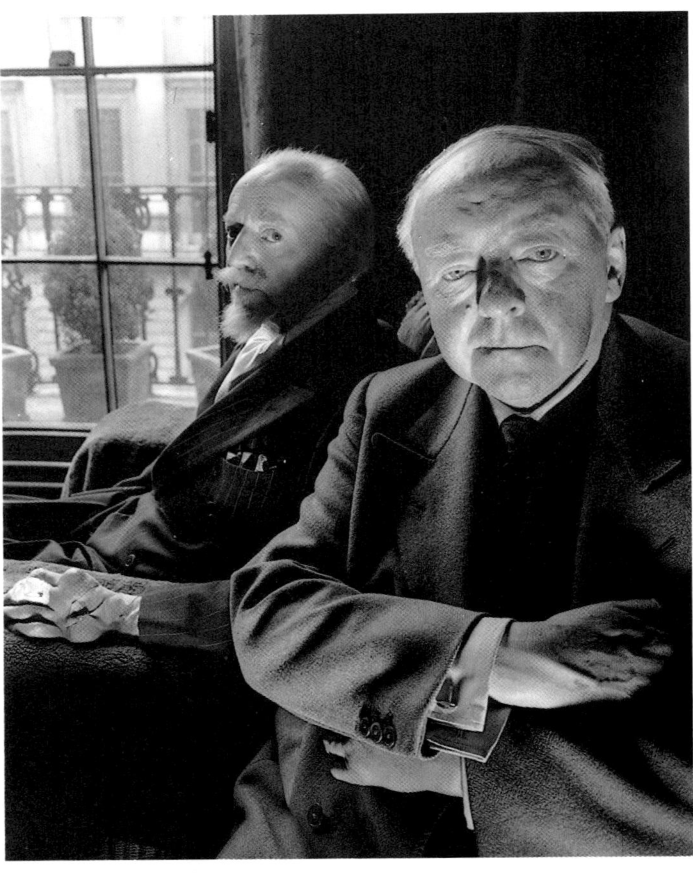

Clifford Bax, dramatist, with his brother, Arnold Bax, composer, Hampstead, 1953

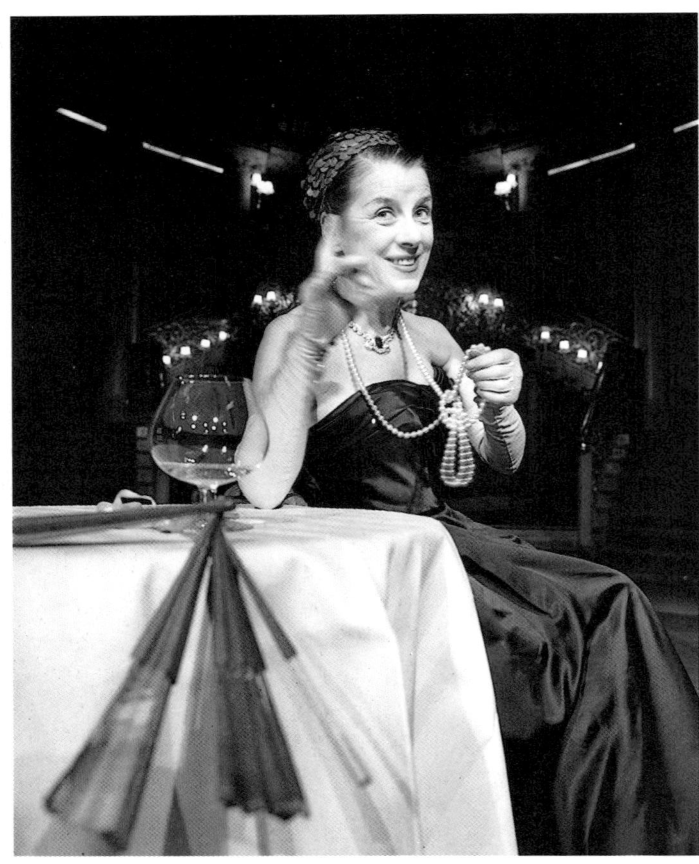

Beatrice Lillie (Lady Peel), actress and comedienne at the Café de Paris, 1951

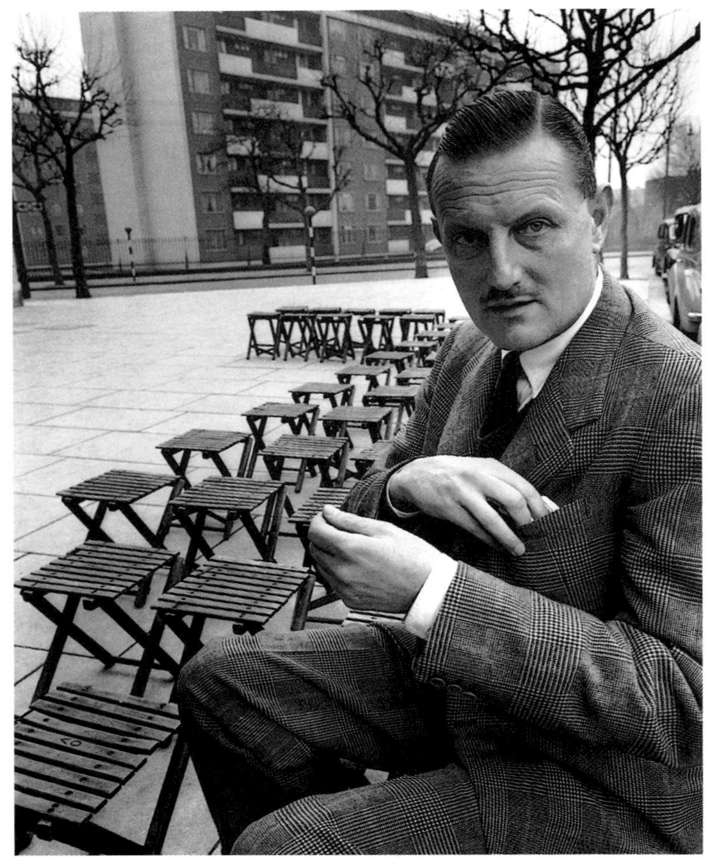

Tyrone Guthrie, theatrical producer, outside Sadler's Wells Theatre, 1951

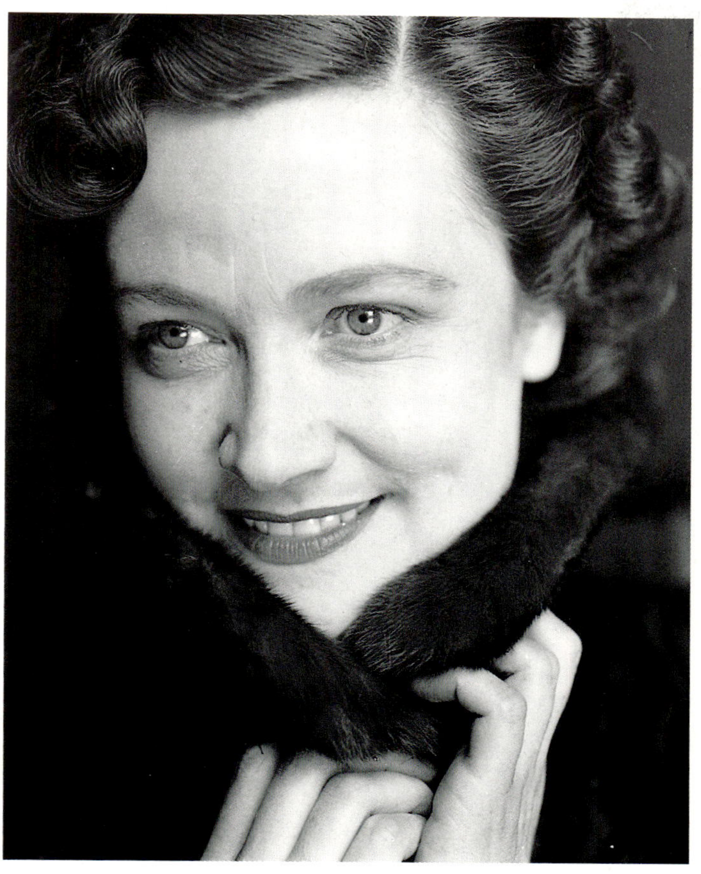

Kathleen Ferrier, contralto, before her performance at the Edinburgh Festival, 1952

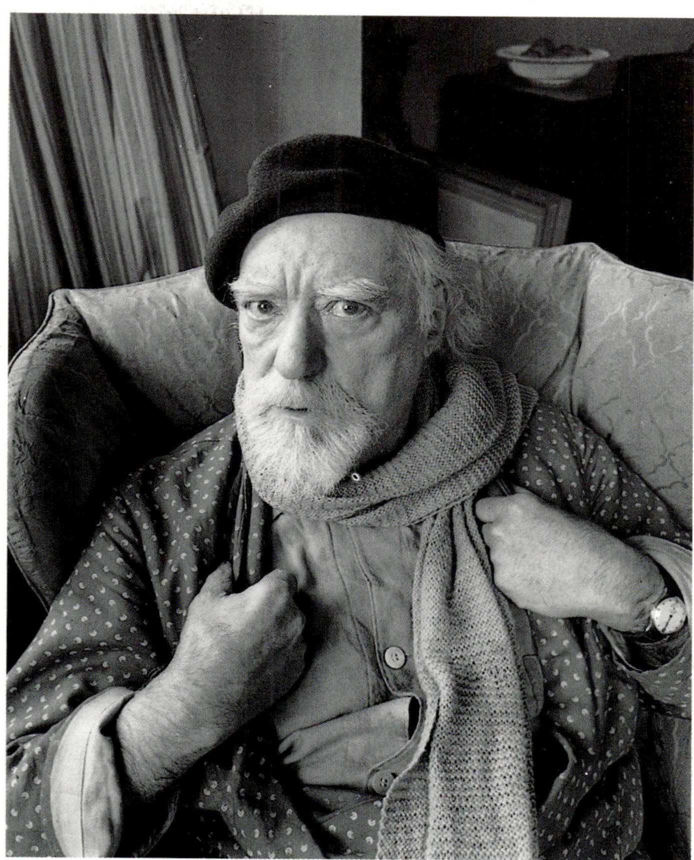

Augustus John, painter and bohemian, 1951

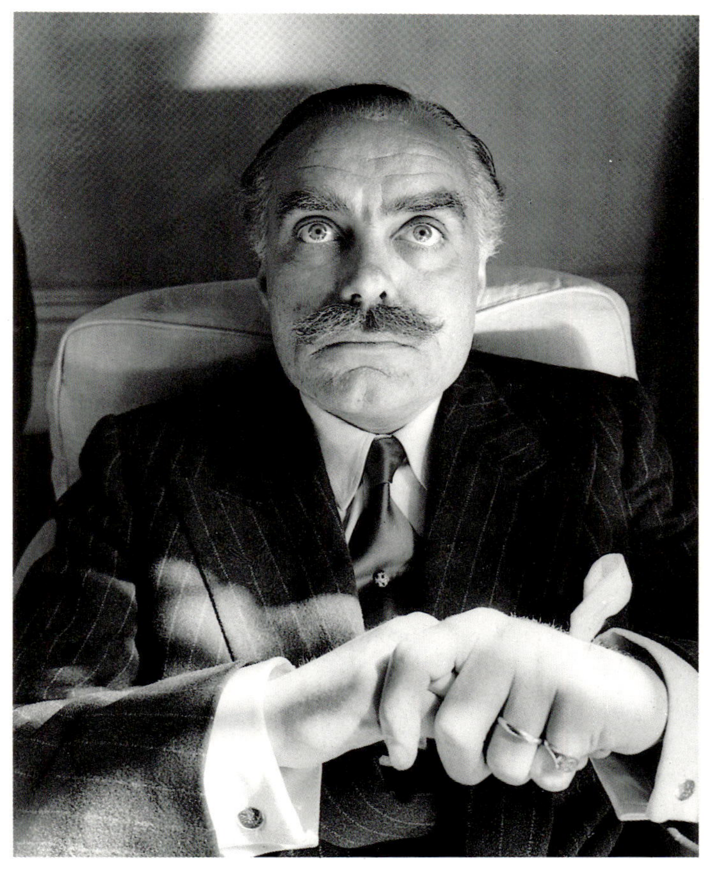

Algernon Blackwood, novelist and short story writer of the supernatural, above Park Lane, 1951

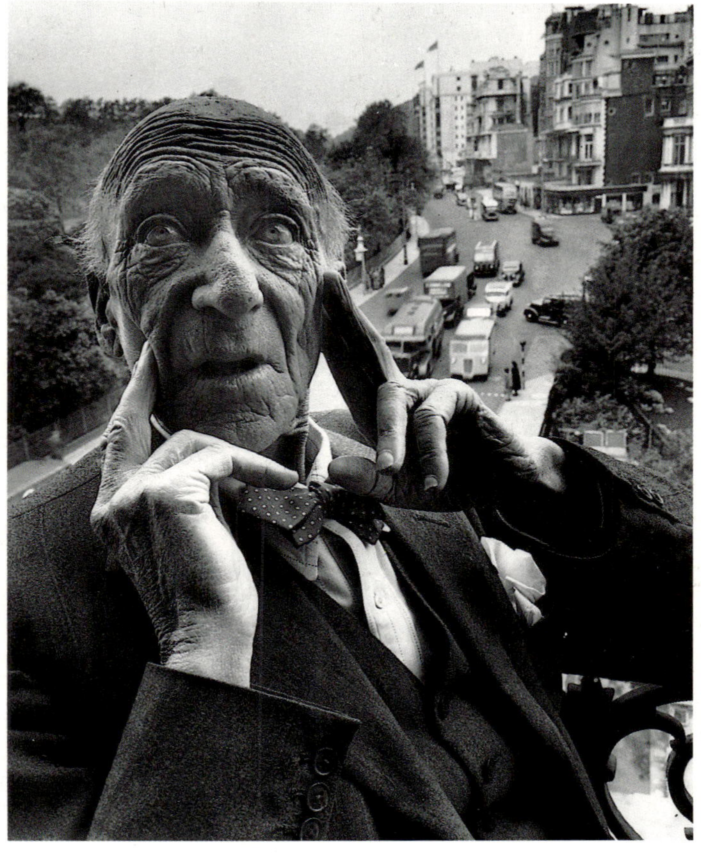

Osbert Lancaster, cartoonist and humorist, 1952

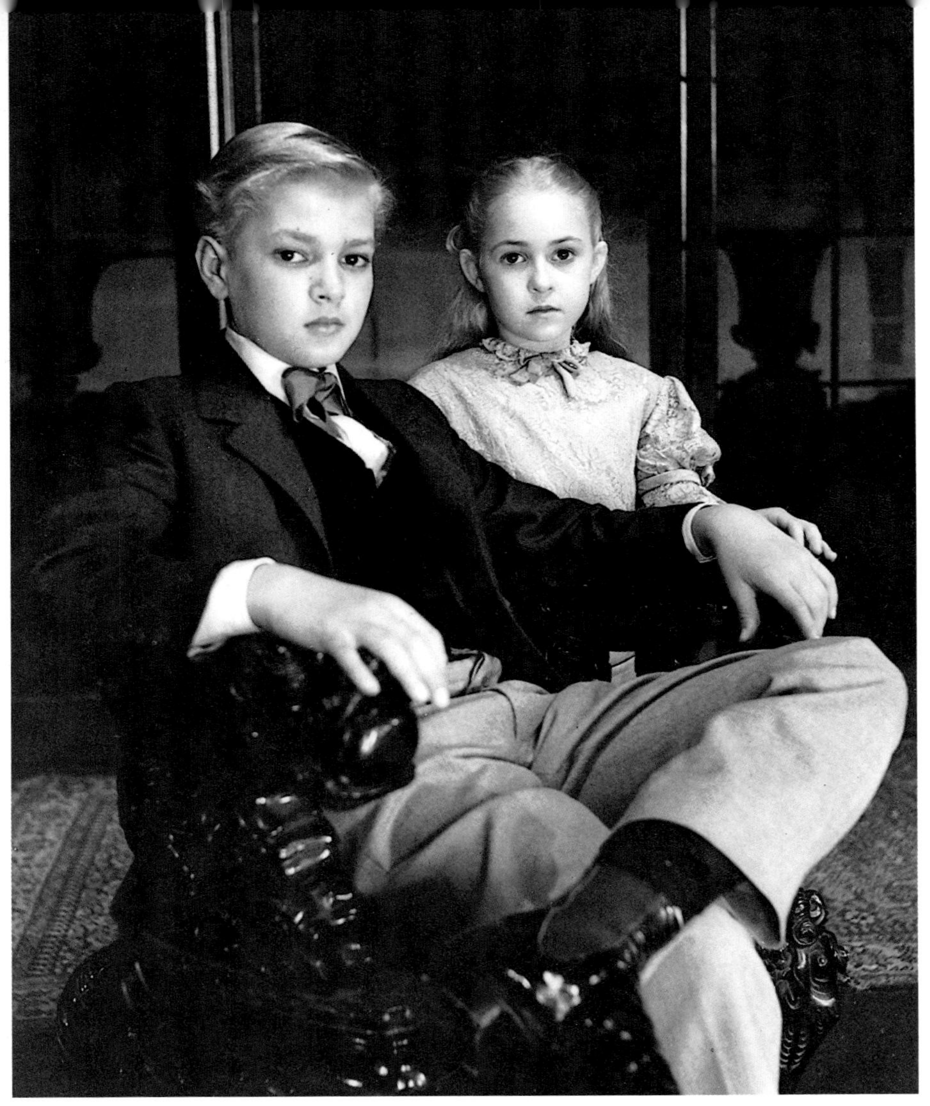

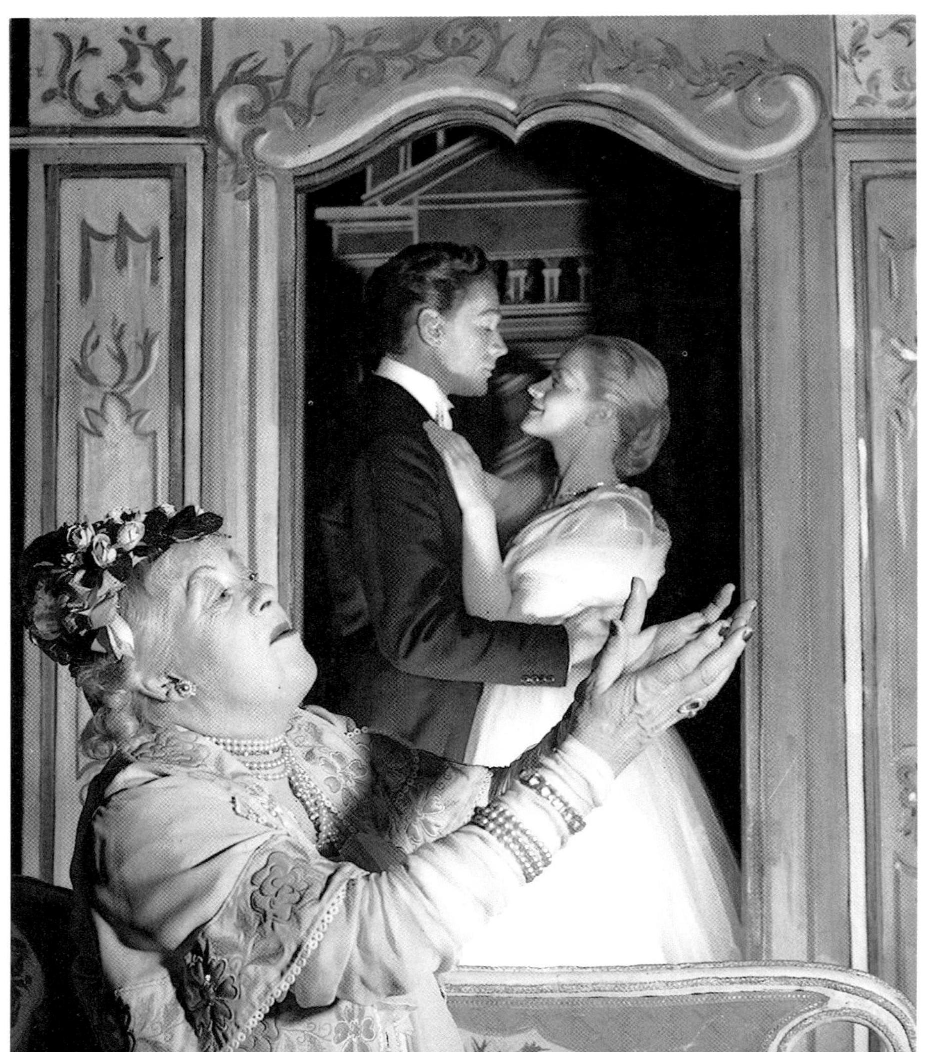

LEFT ABOVE *Jeremy Spencer and Carol Wolveridge as 'The Innocents' in a play of the same name, a stage adaptation of Henry James's 'Turn of the Screw', 1952*
LEFT *Margaret Rutherford as the Duchess with Paul Scofield as Prince Albert and Mary Ure as Amanda in the production of 'Time Remembered', a translation of Jean Anouilh's Play 'Leocadia', 1955*
OPPOSITE *Emlyn Williams as Charles Dickens, reading from 'Our Mutual Friend', 1951*

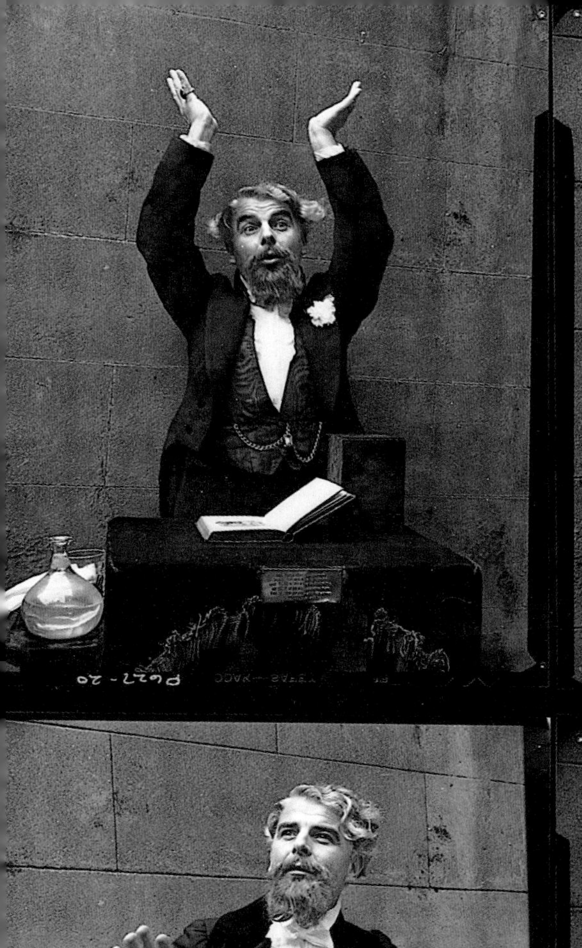
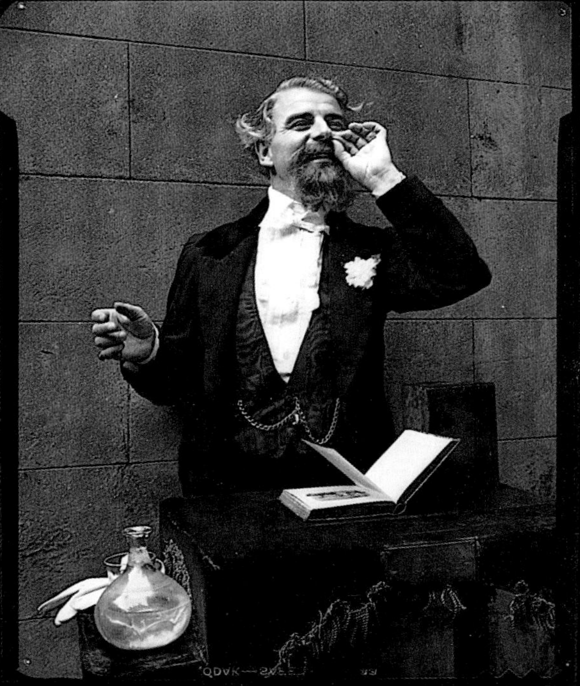
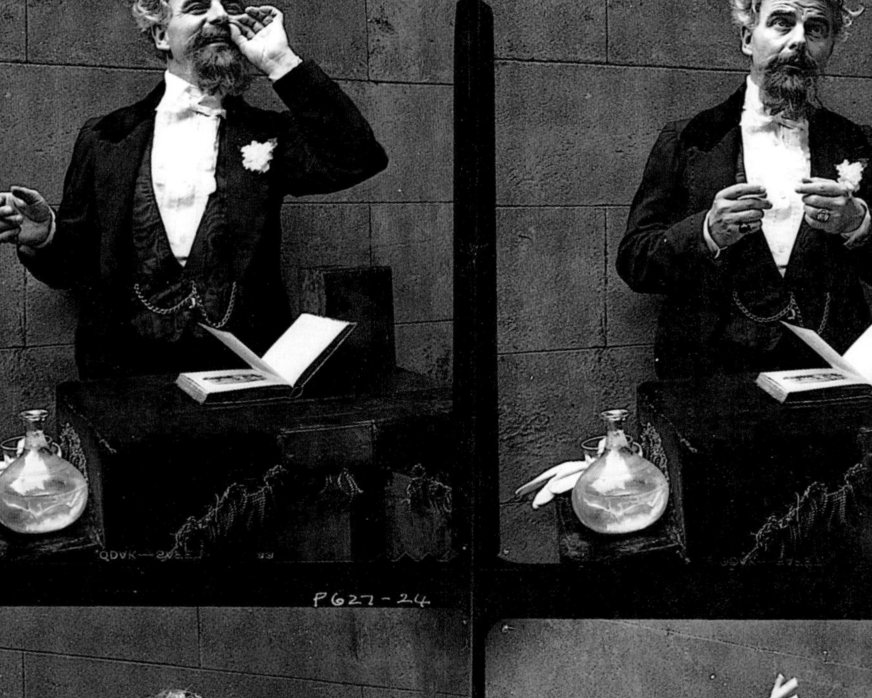
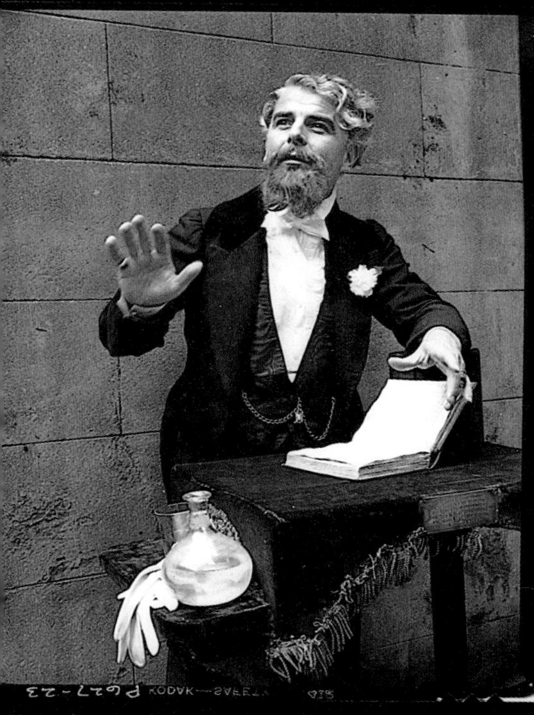
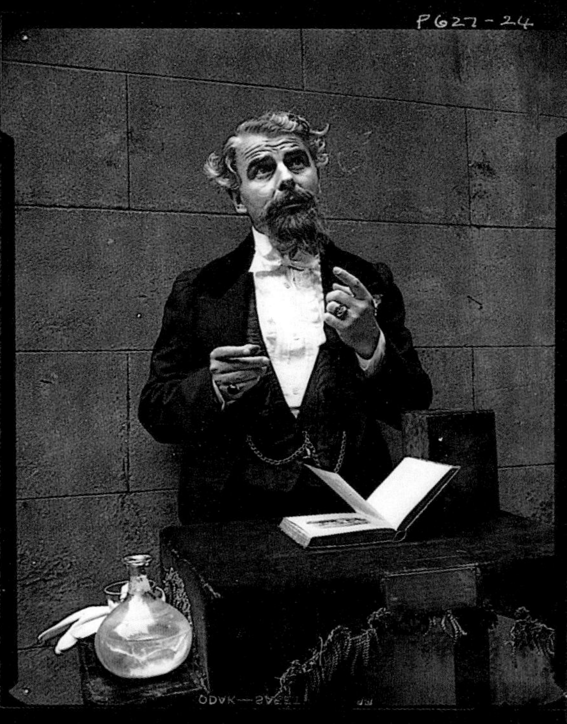
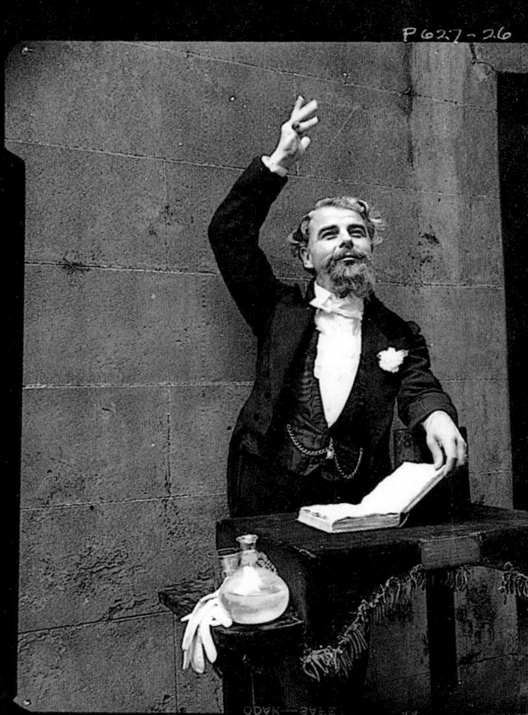
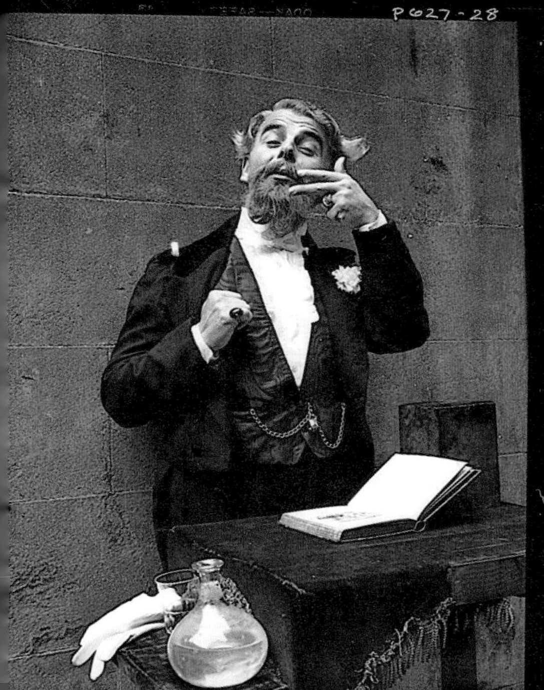
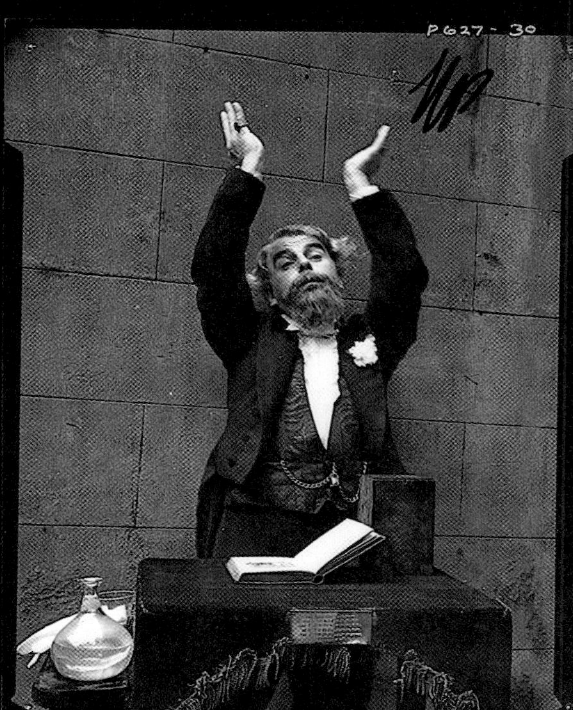
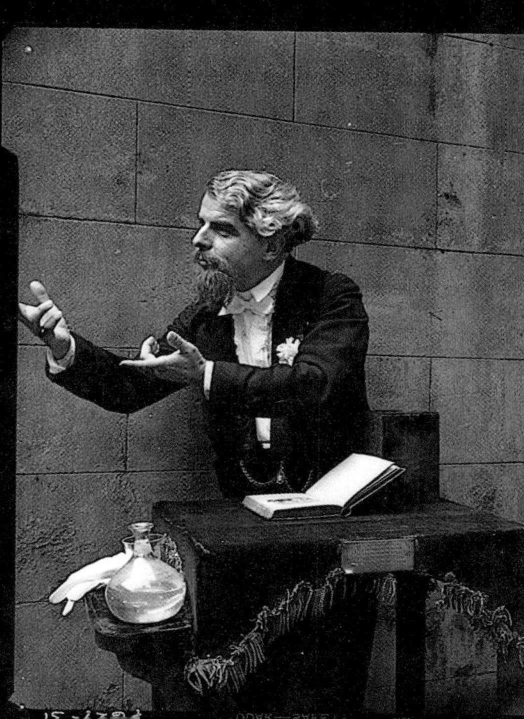

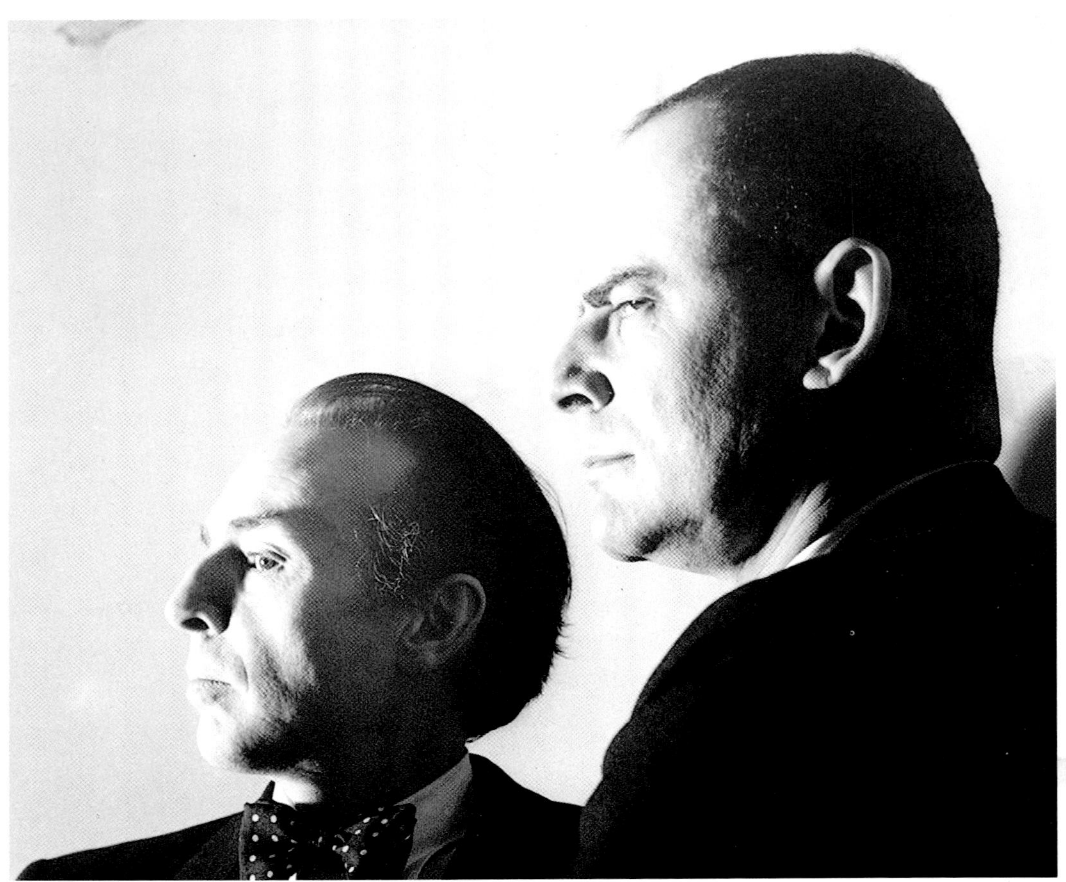

George Balanchine and Lincoln Kirstein, Artistic Director and Director General of New York City Ballet, 1952

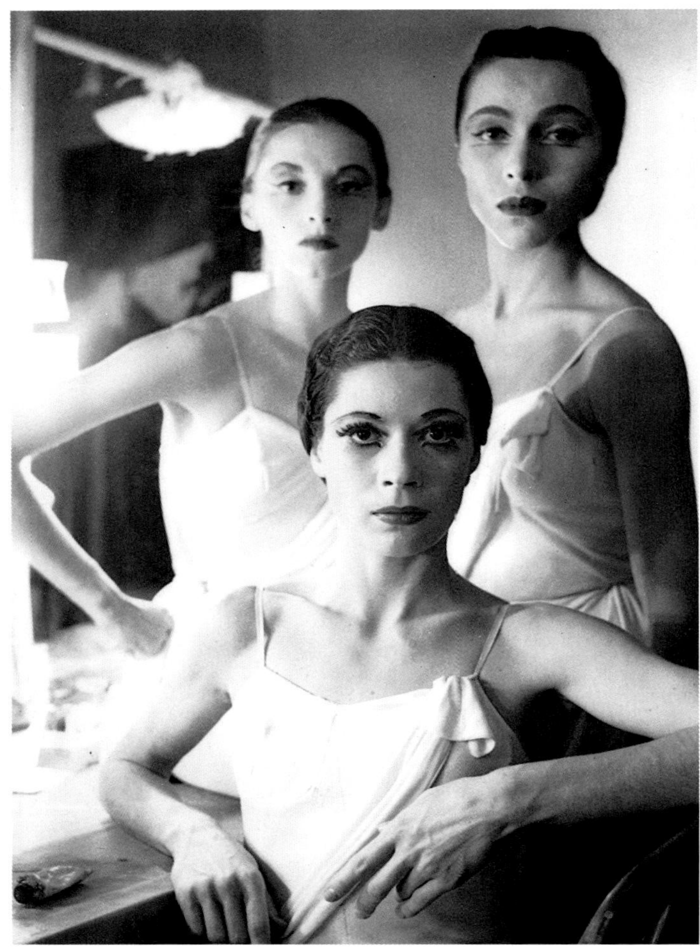

Diana Adams (front) Maria Tallchief (centre) and Tanaquil Leclerq (back), ballerinas of New York City Ballet, 1952

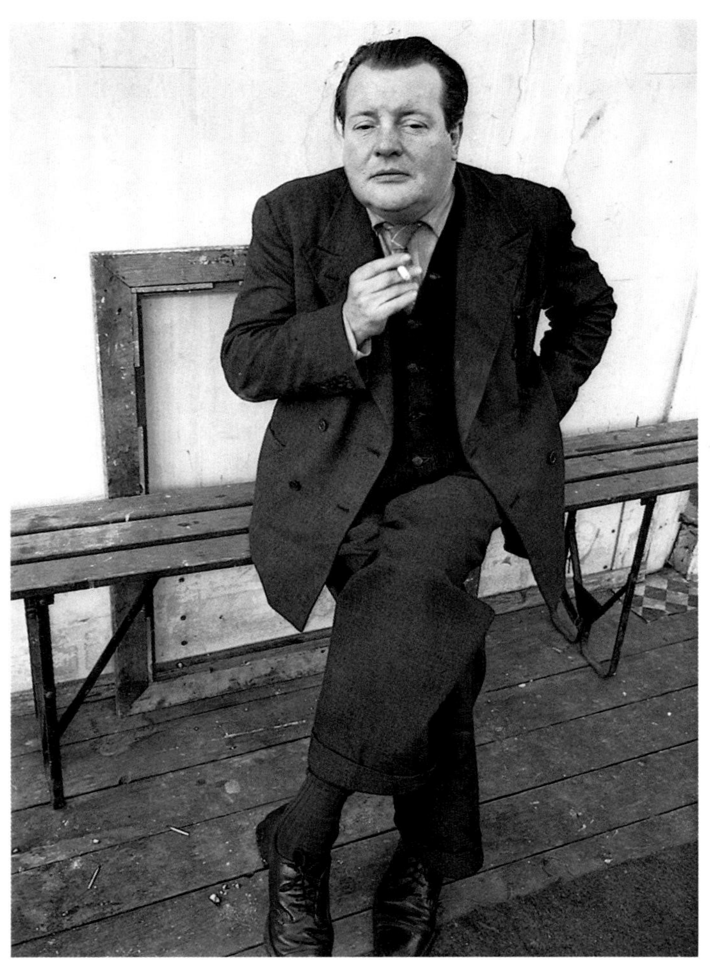

Constant Lambert, composer, 1951

OPPOSITE *Robert Helpmann and Margot Fonteyn, 1951*

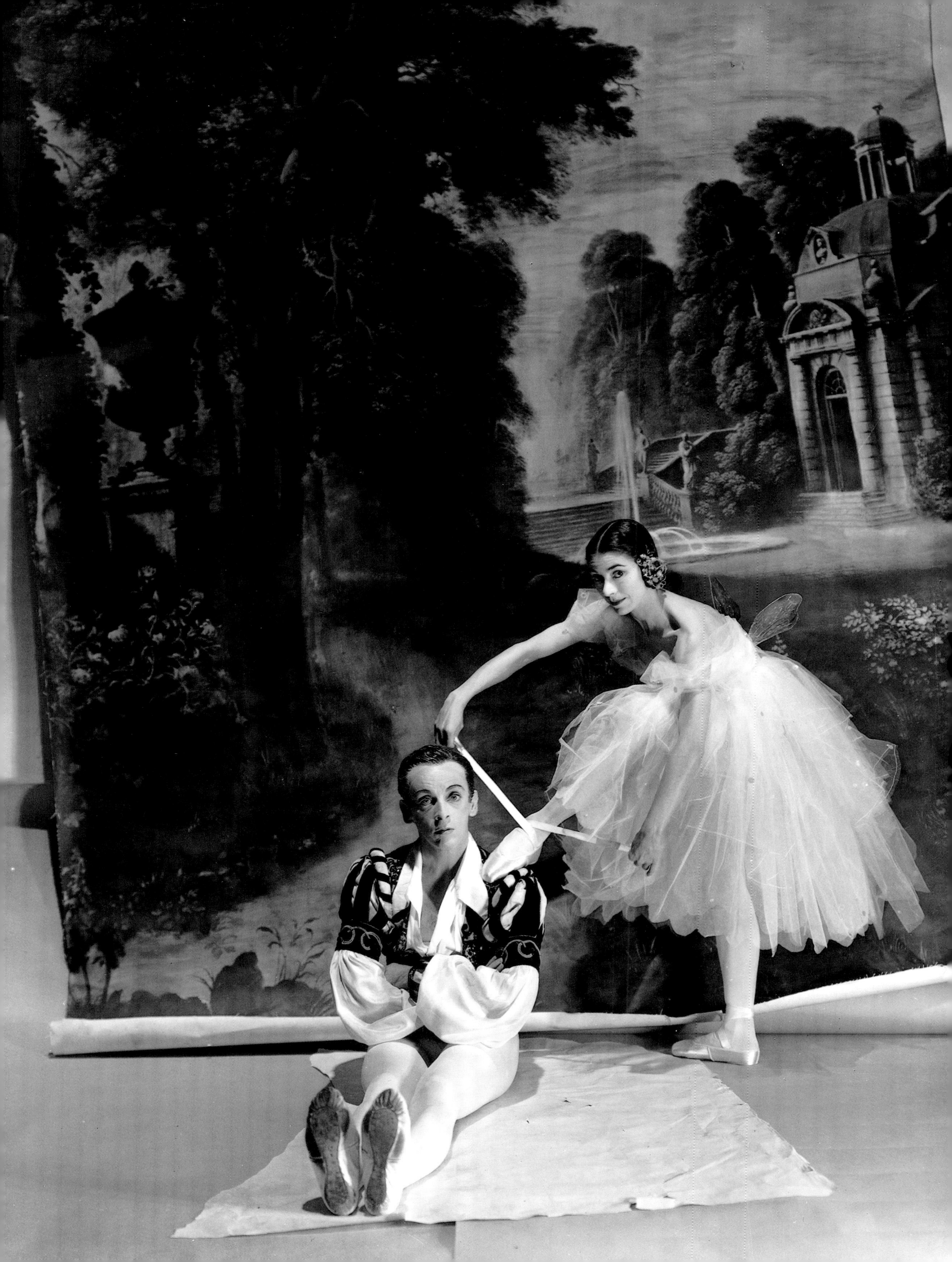

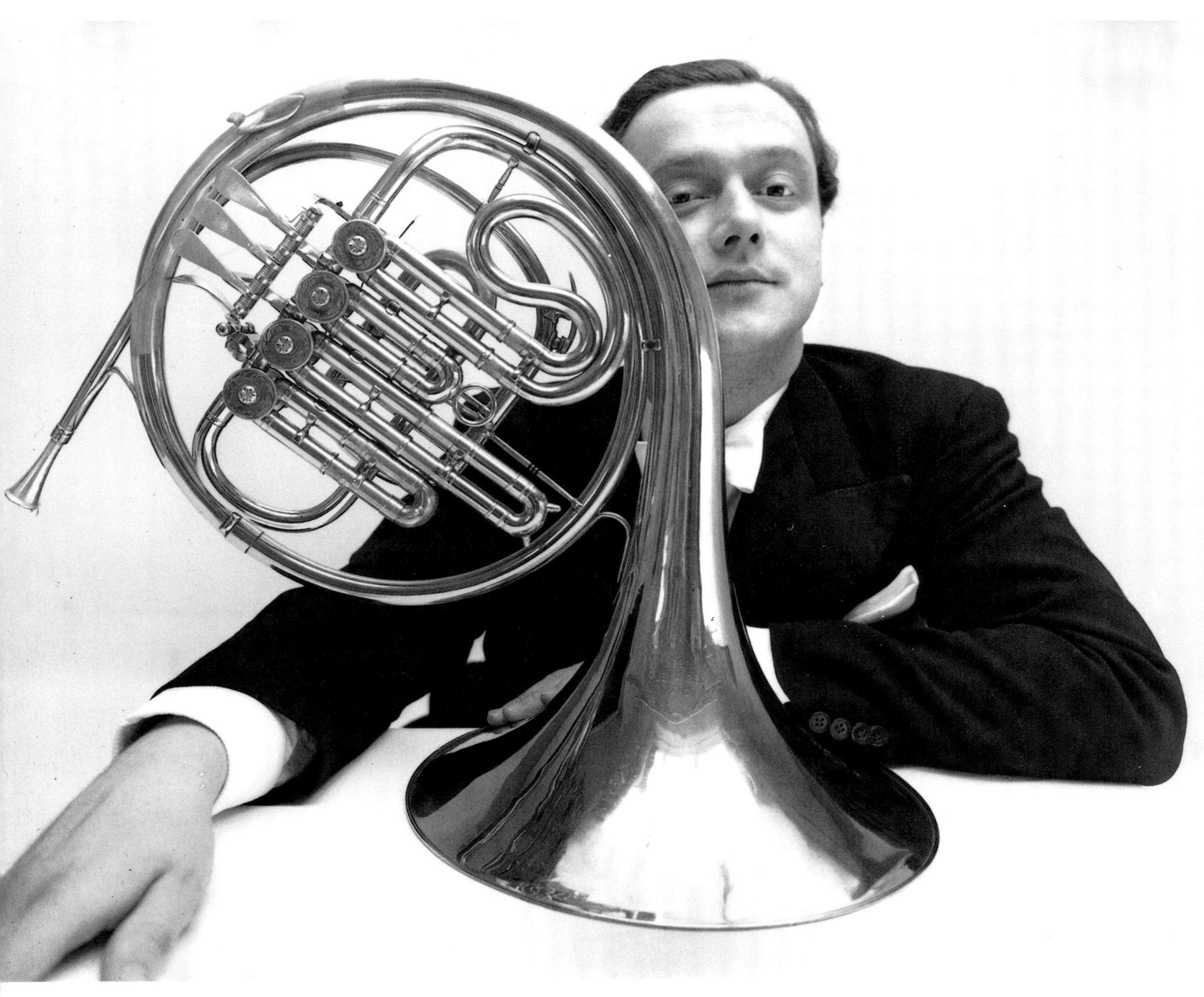

ABOVE *Dennis Brain, virtuoso horn player, 1953*
OPPOSITE *George Eskdale, first trumpet in the London Symphony Orchestra, 1953*

Anybody who sits down to be photographed feels it is contrary to their natural instinct. They feel narcissistic, immodest. So you have to remove the feeling that they are not being true to themselves, and make people enjoy it. You are like a snake watching a mongoose. You give your whole attention to them. You never turn your back. You persuade, you talk, you have non-technical asides to your assistant, but you never take your eyes off your subject.

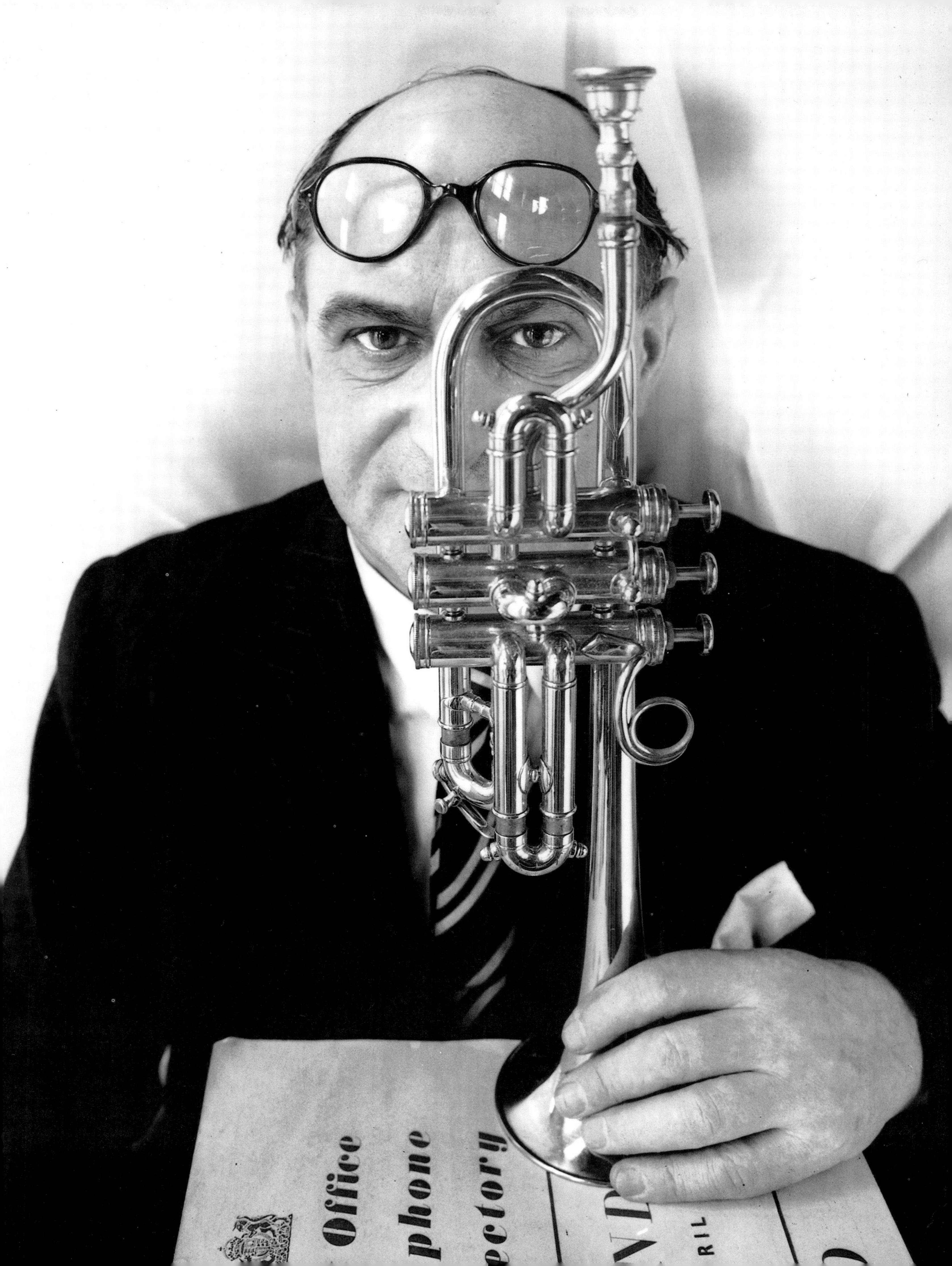
Office
phone
ectory

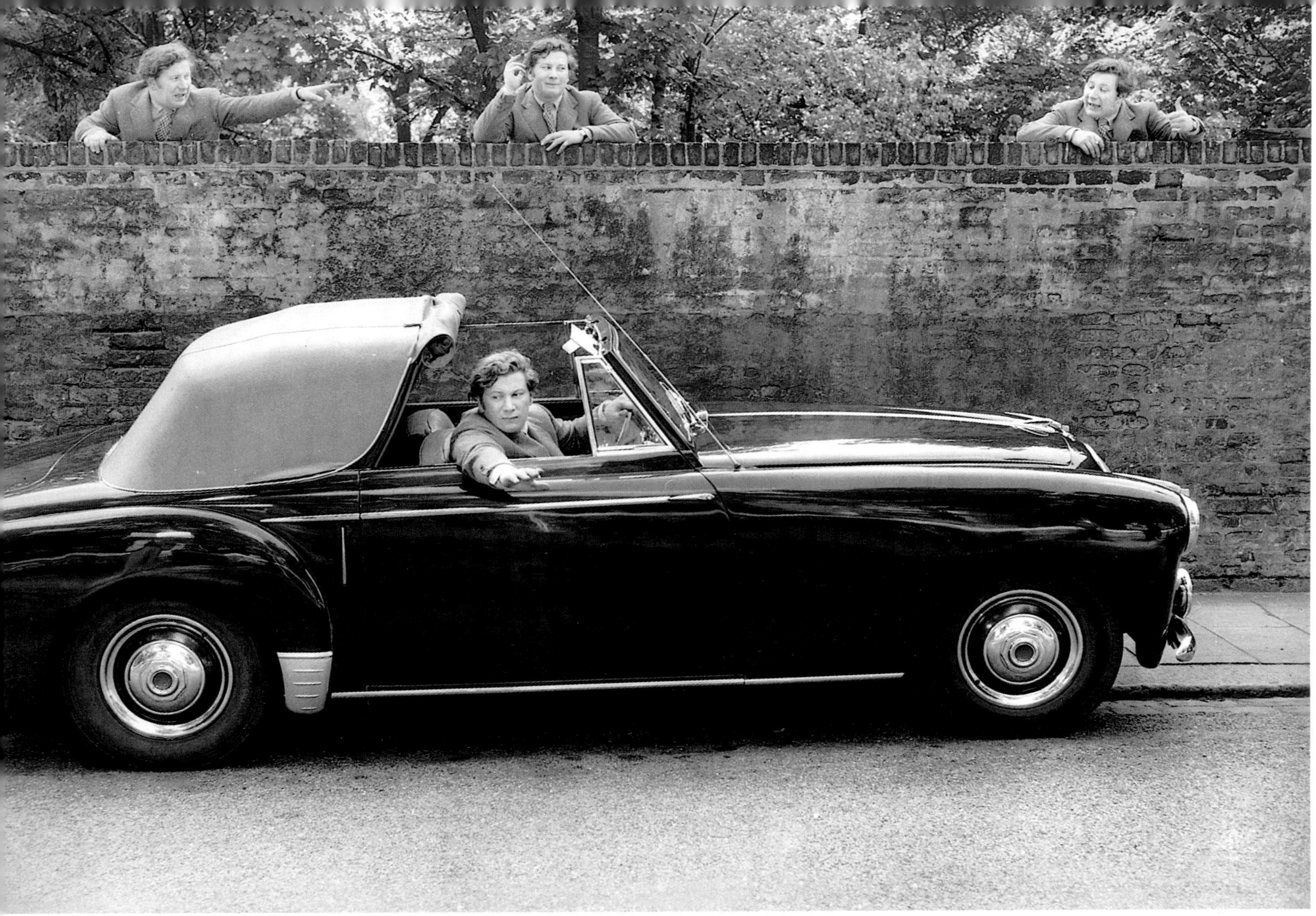

Peter Ustinov, playwright, producer, actor and motorist with his dark blue drop-head coupé, three litre Lagonda, 1953

Hugh Casson with his 1927 Rolls Royce, Knightsbridge, 1953

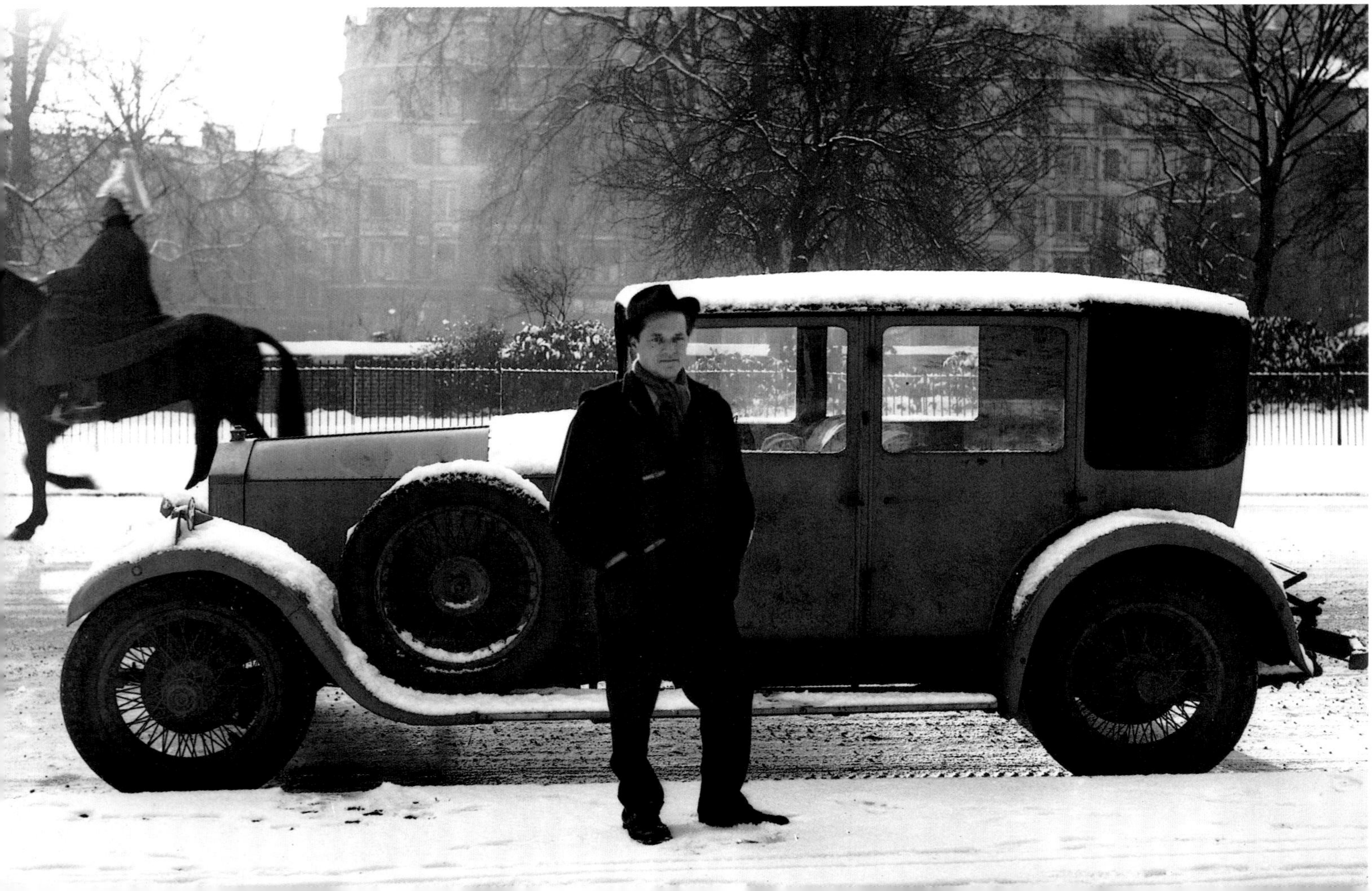

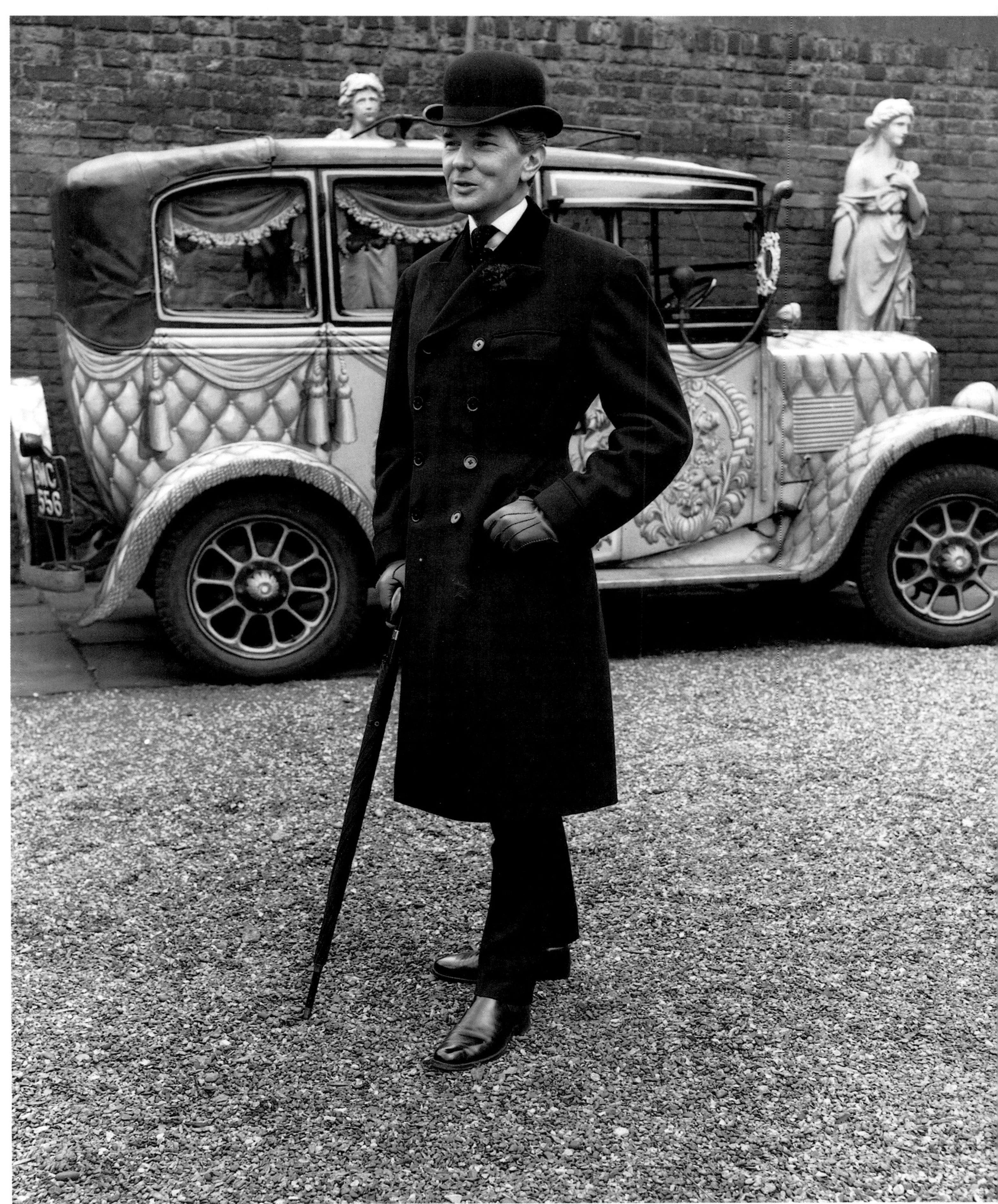

Neil 'Bunny' Roger, fashion designer, with a pink 'quilted' taxi painted by Roy Alderson, 1954

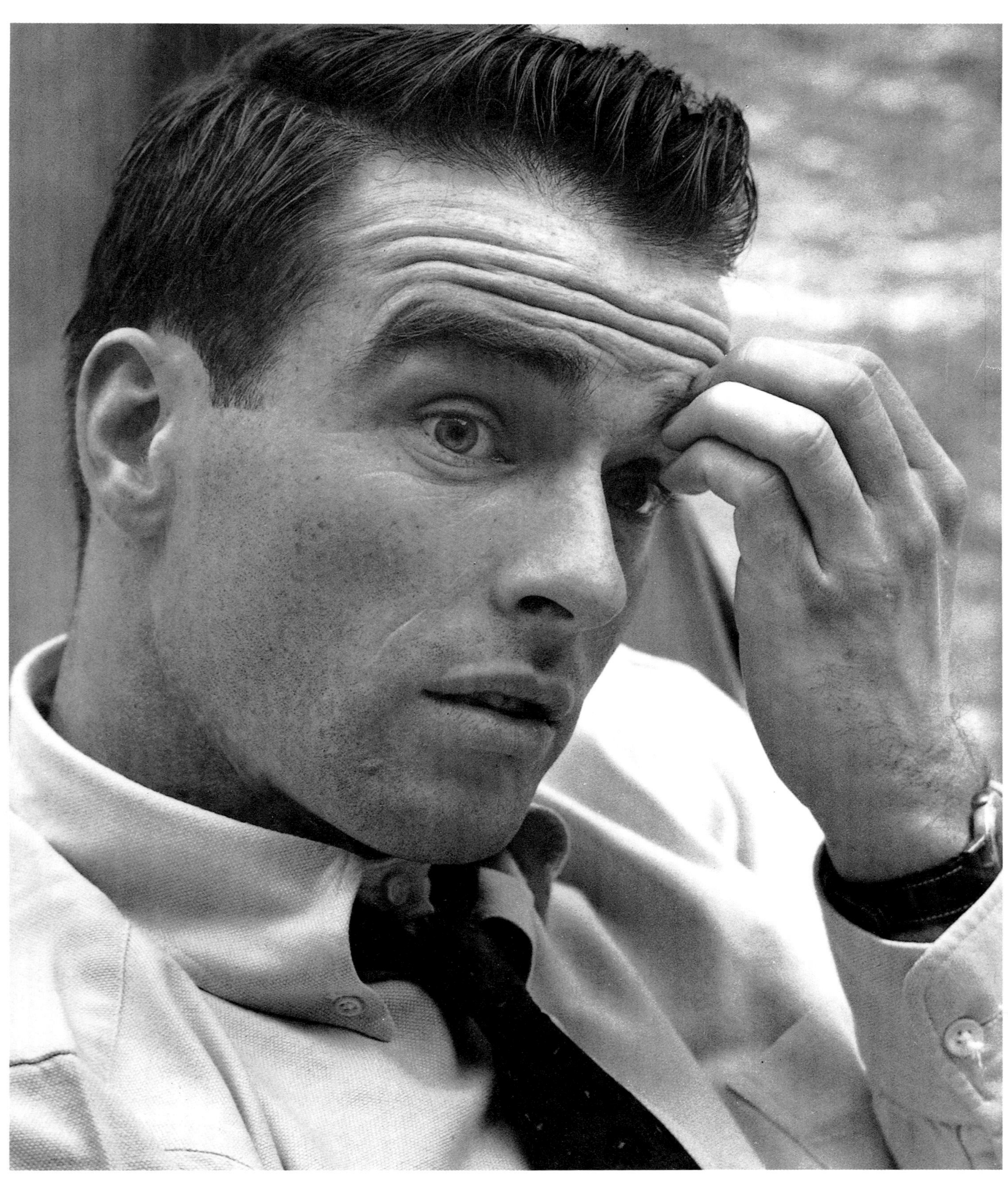

ABOVE *Montgomery Clift, actor and film star, New York, 1951*
OPPOSITE *Audrey Hepburn, during the filming of 'War and Peace' near Rome, 1955*
OVERLEAF LEFT *John Houston, between takes of the filming of 'Moby Dick' at Elstree, 1955*
OVERLEAF RIGHT *Marlene Dietrich, on stage at London's Café de Paris, 1955*

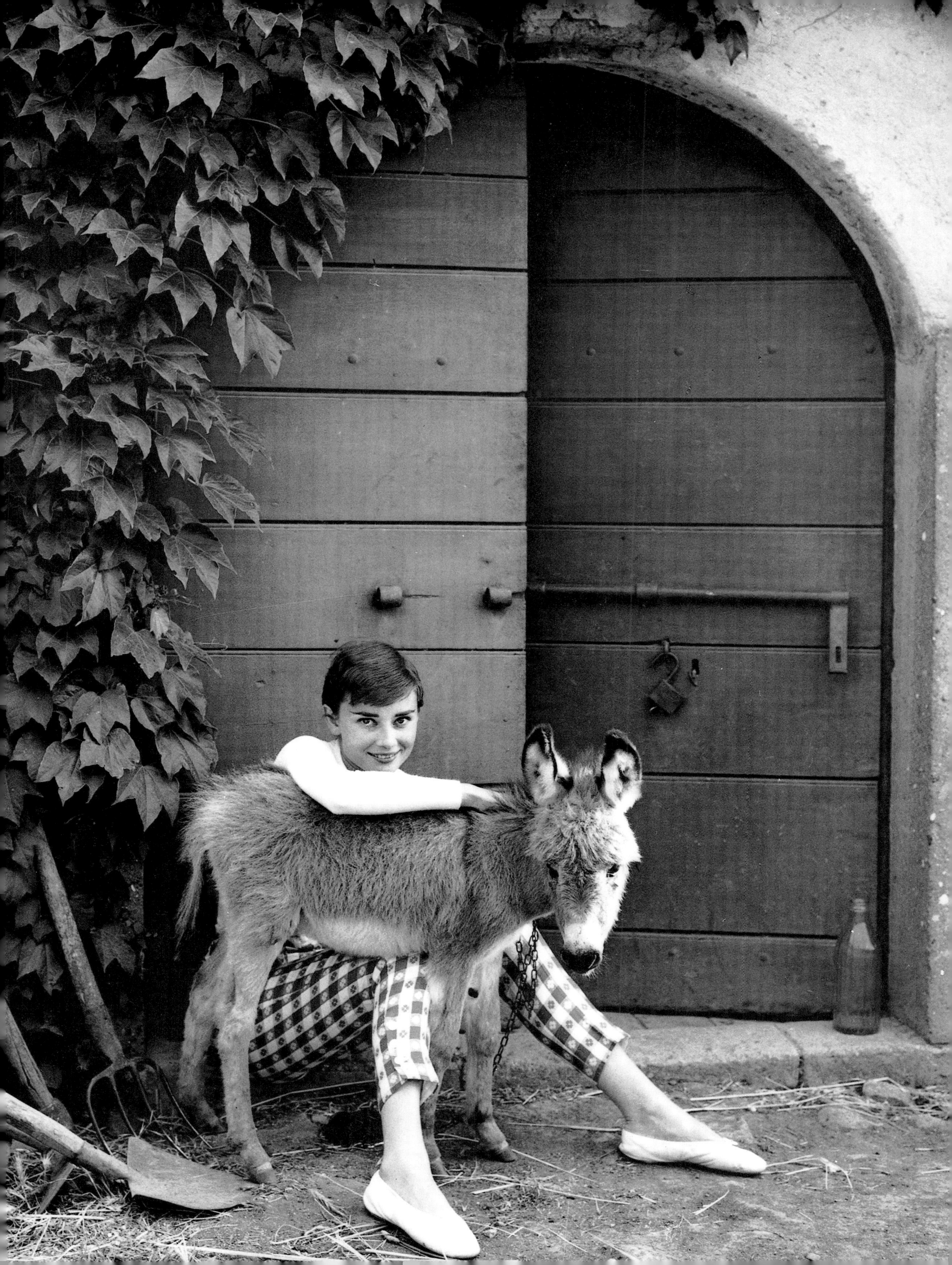

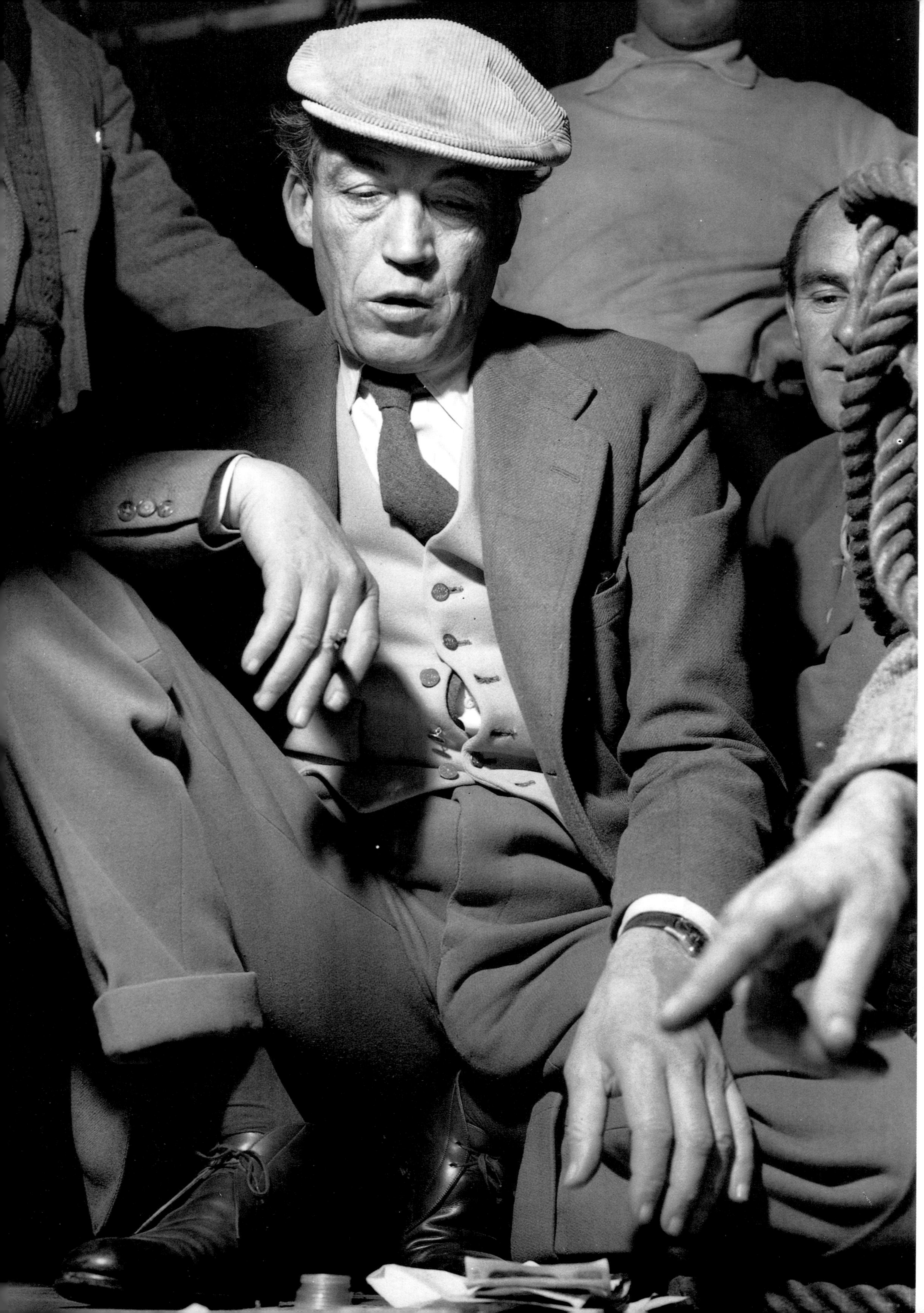

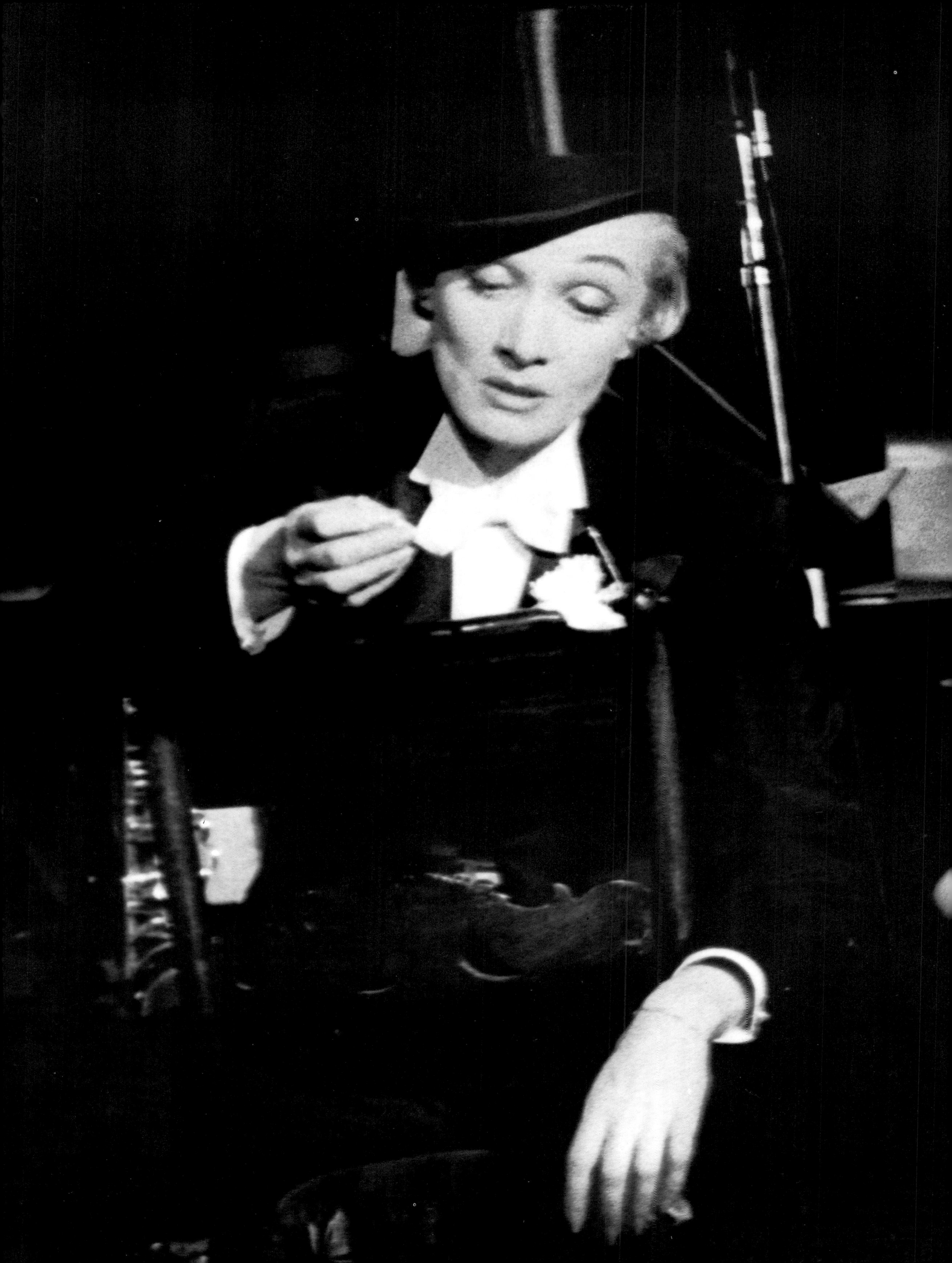

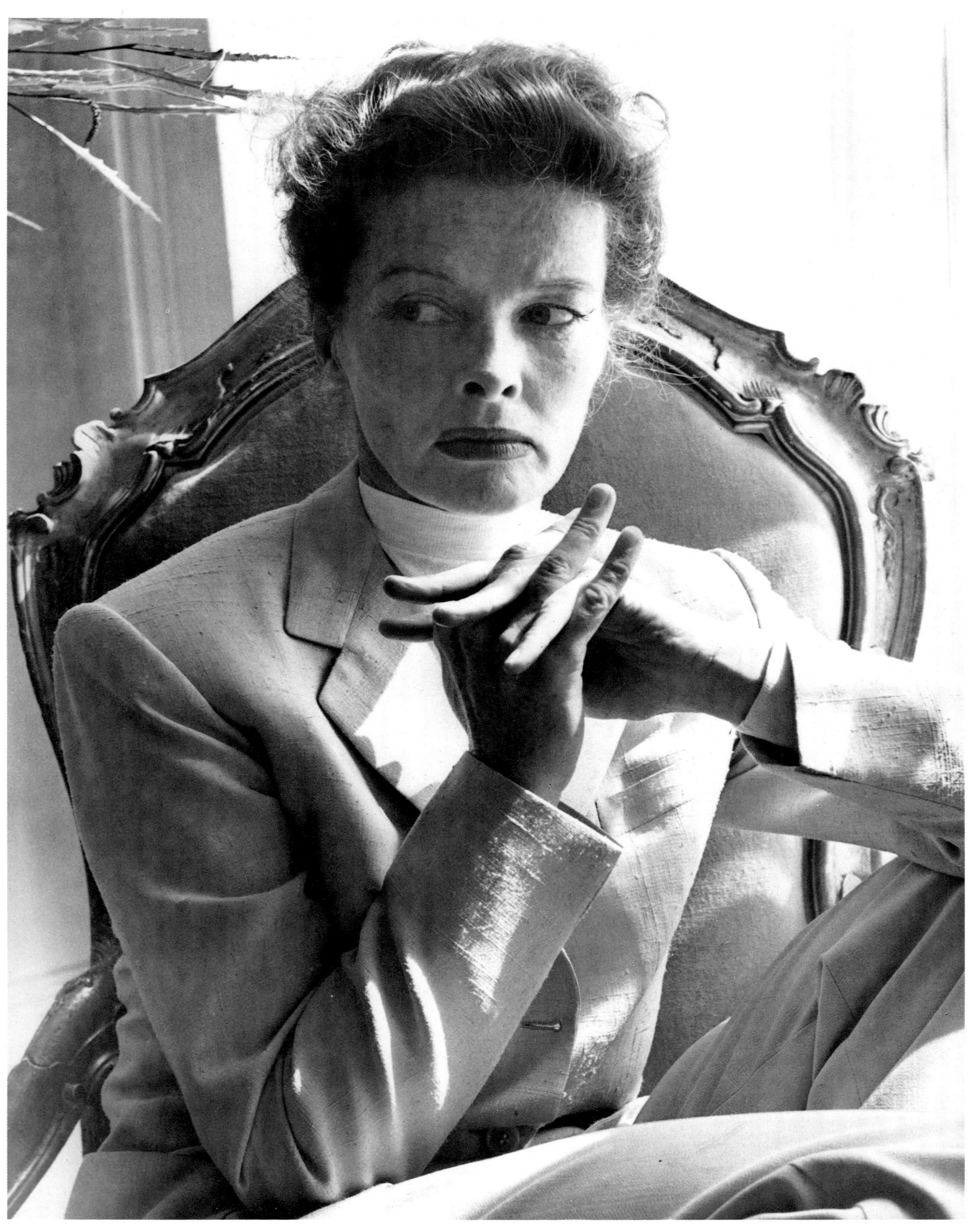

ABOVE *Katharine Hepburn, in London at the time of her appearance in George Bernard Shaw's 'The Millionairess', 1952*
OPPOSITE *Ava Gardner shortly after filming her role as Queen Guinevere in the 1954 film 'The Knights of the Round Table', 1953*
OVERLEAF LEFT *Jean Seberg, off the set of Otto Preminger's film of 'St Joan', 1957*
OVERLEAF RIGHT *Carroll Baker, as Tennessee Williams' Baby Doll, 1957*

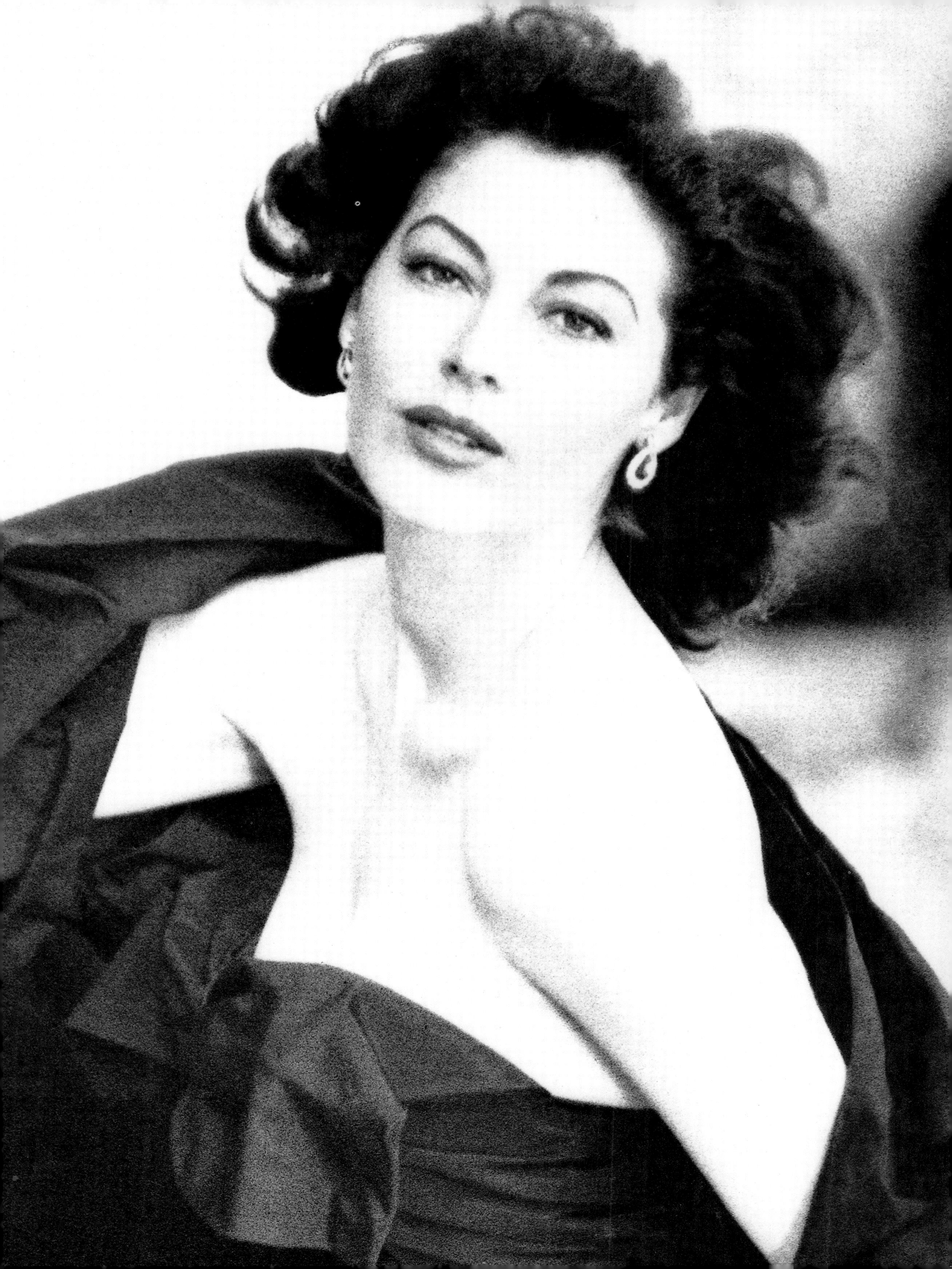

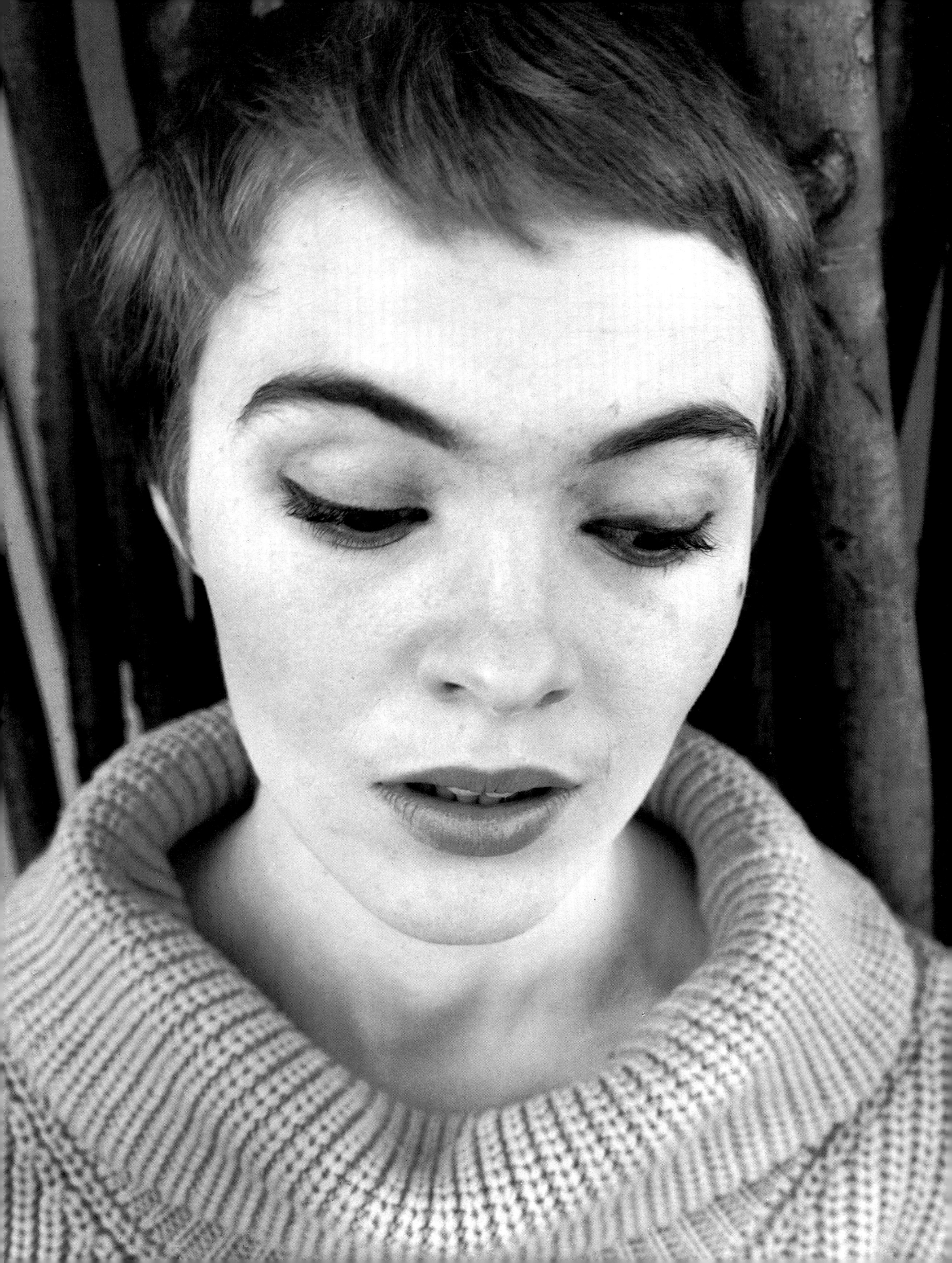

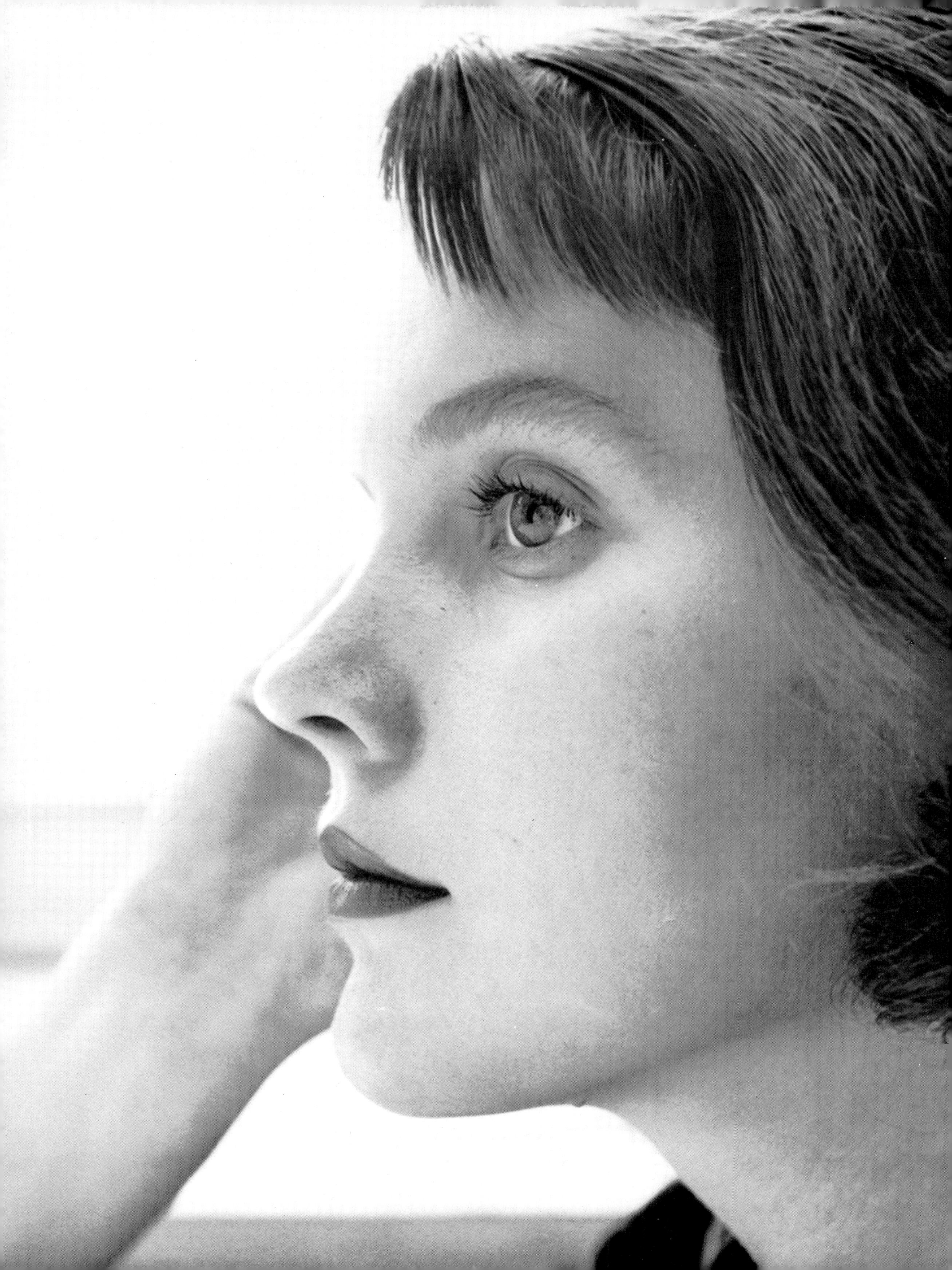

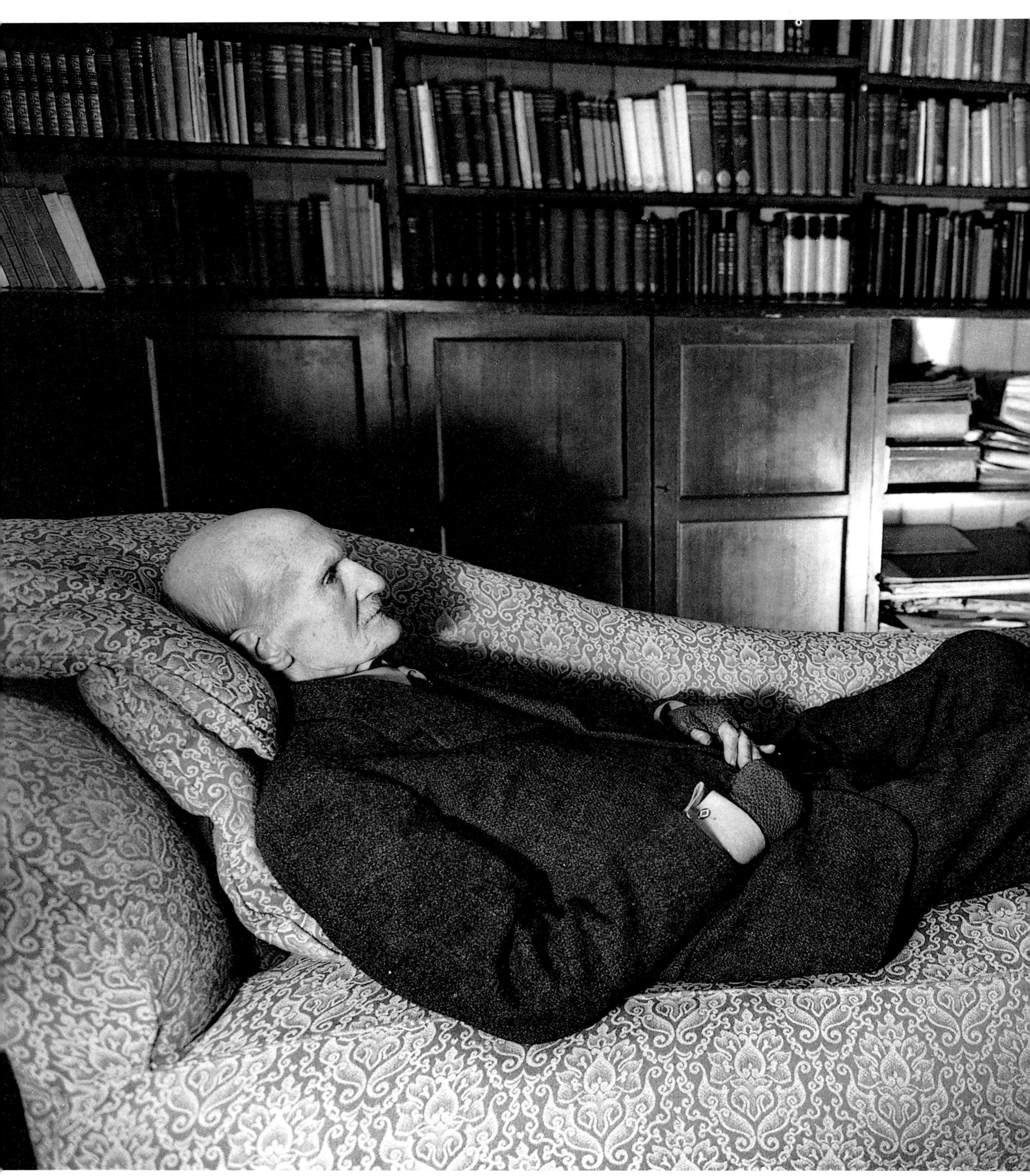

Professor Gilbert Murray, classical scholar, in his room at Oxford shortly after his 91st birthday, 1957

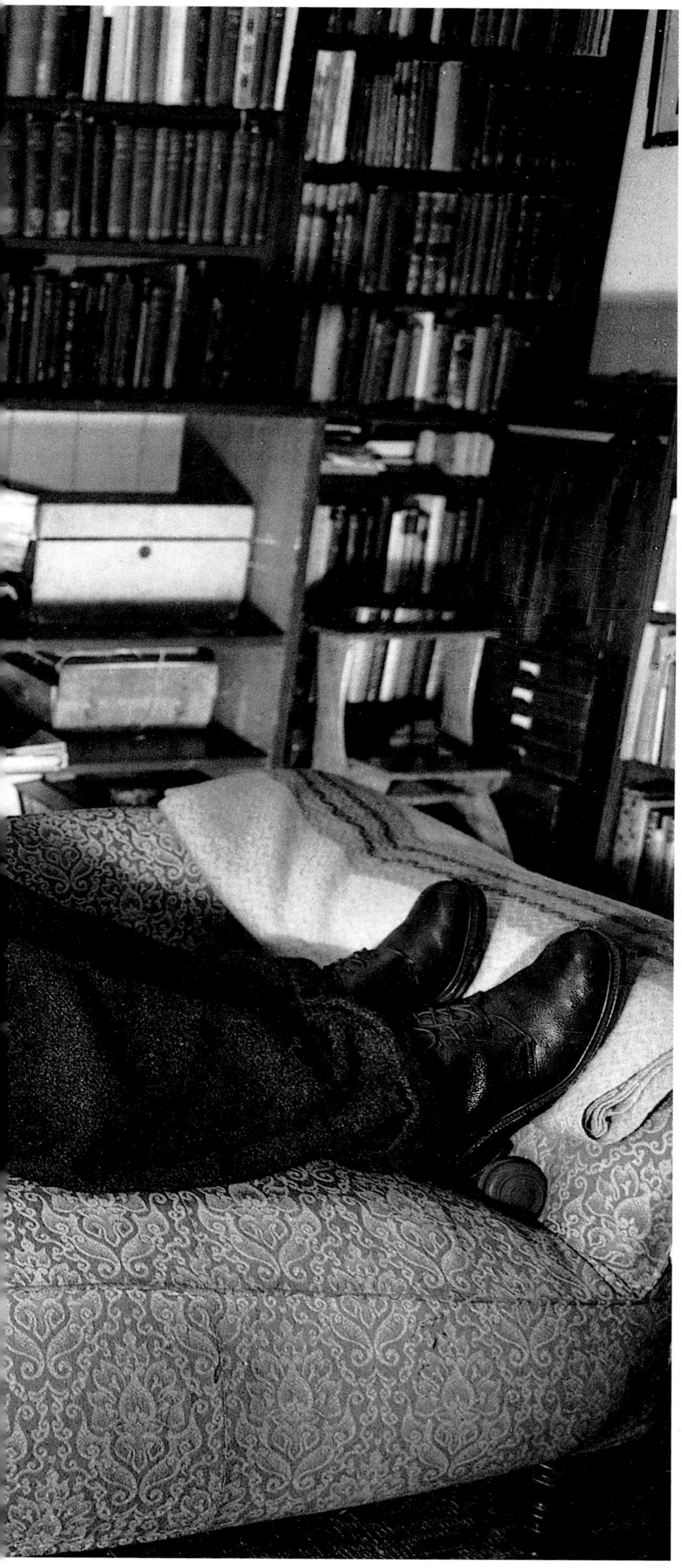

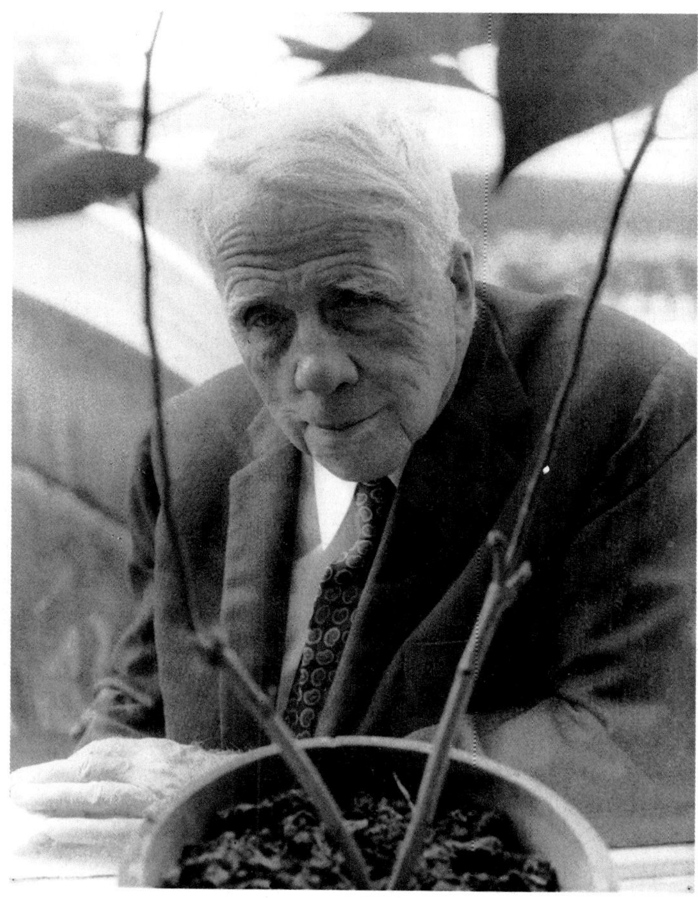

Robert Frost, America's national poet, on a visit to London, Grosvenor Square, 1958

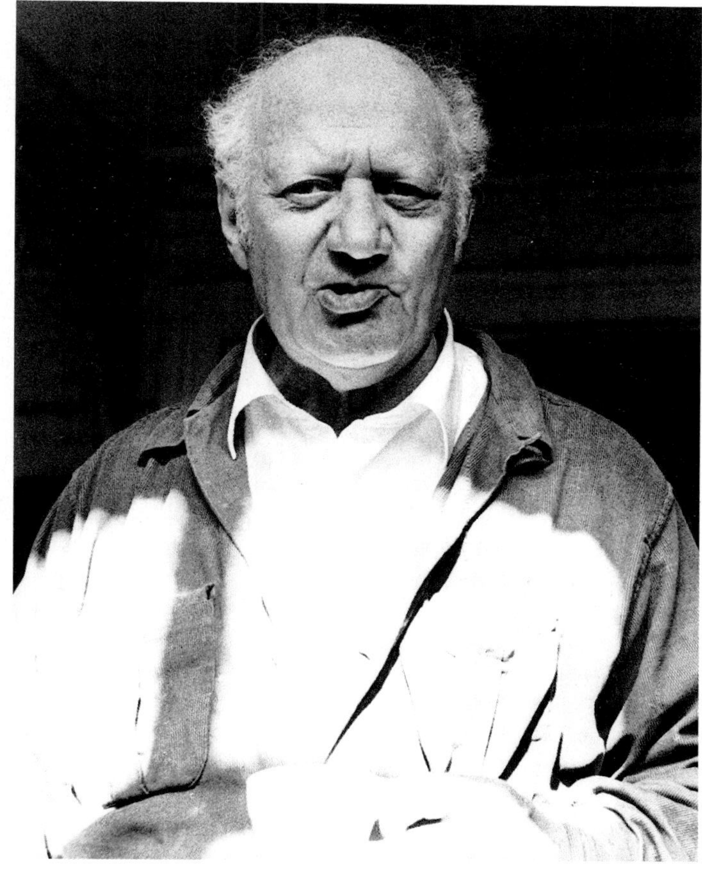

Jacob Epstein, American-born sculptor, 1956

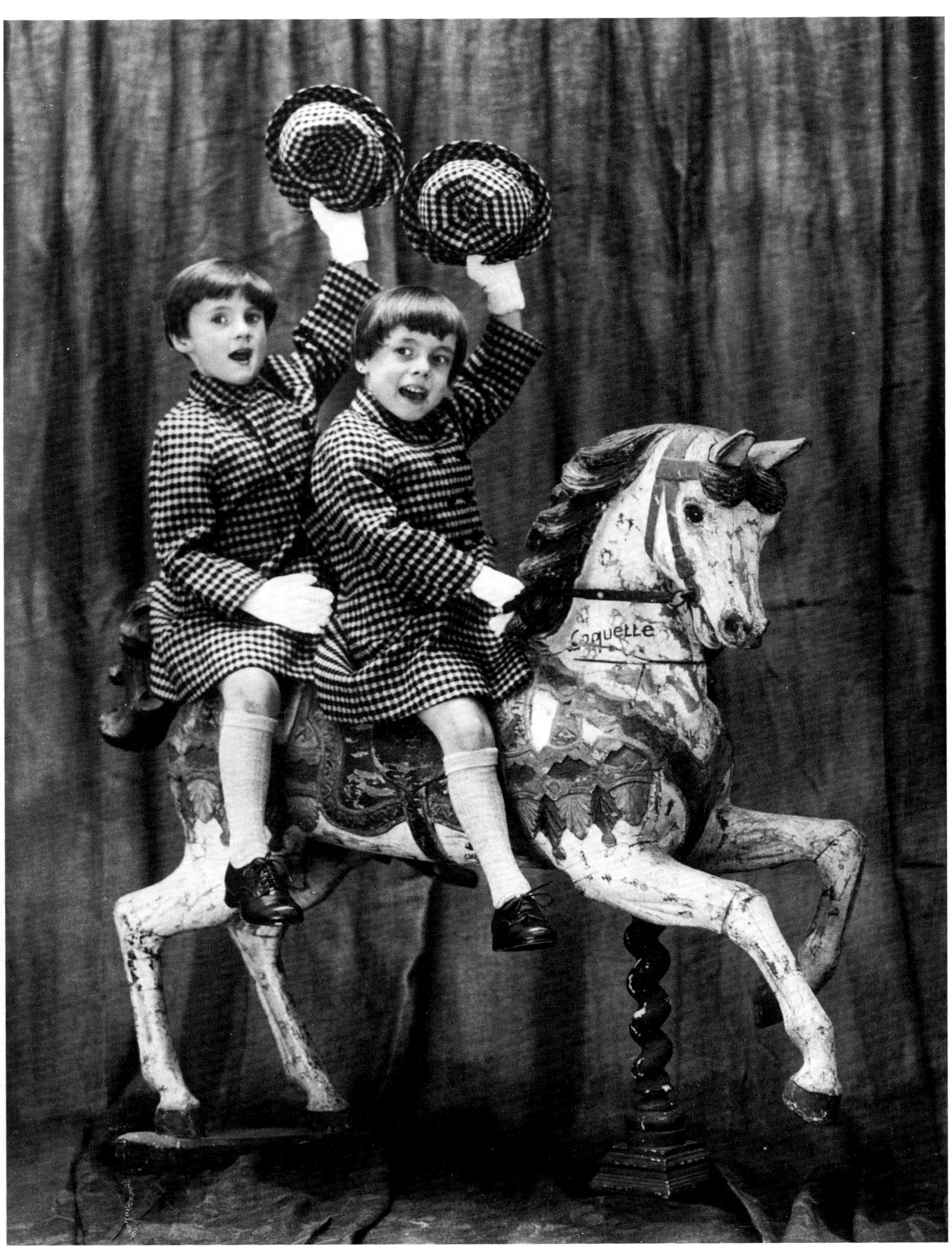

Rupert and Bruno, six-year-old twins of Professor and Mrs Richard Wollheim, 1959

 OPPOSITE *Sabrina and Miranda, the four-year-old twin daughters of Mr and Mrs James Guinness, 1959*

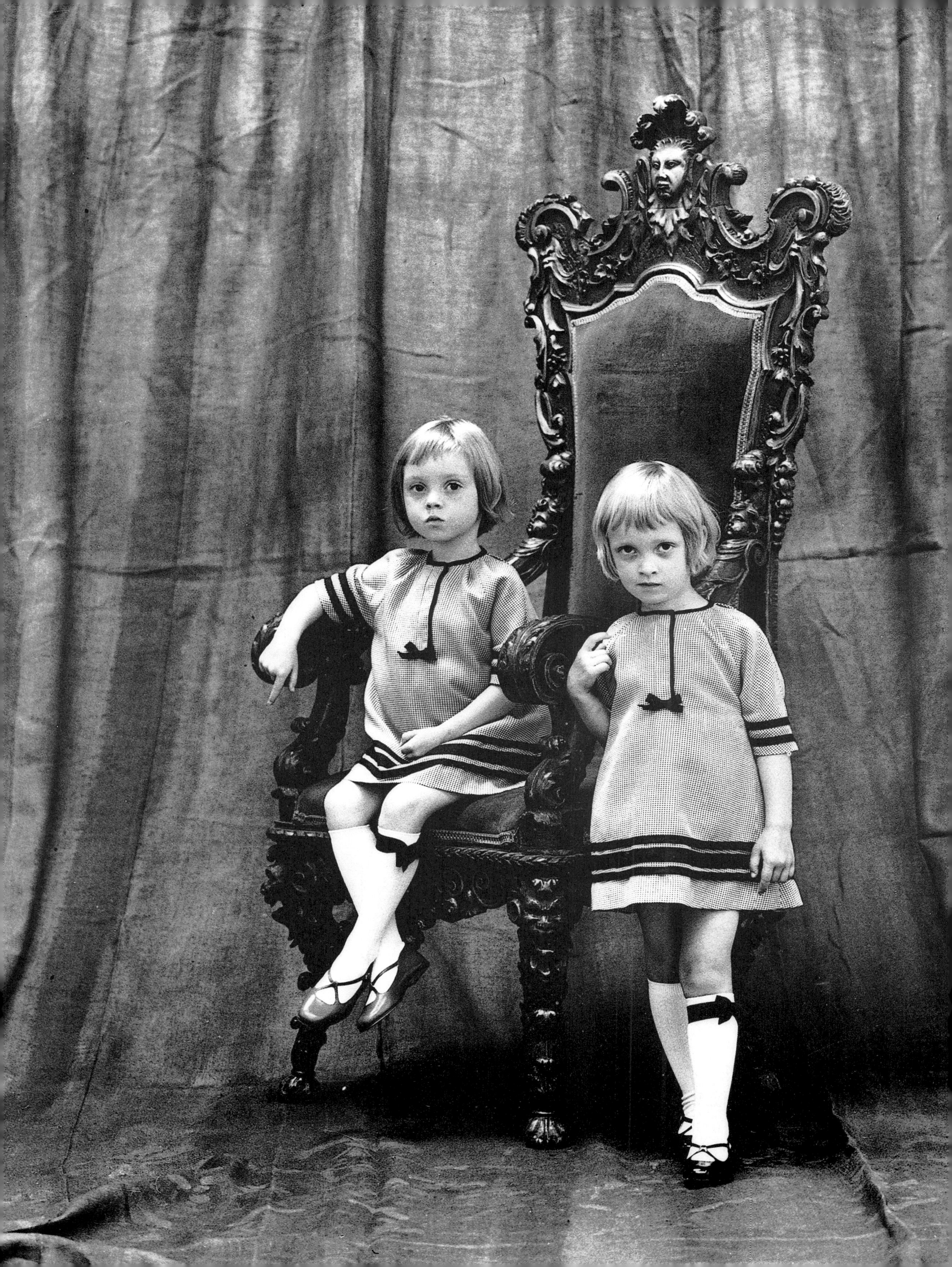

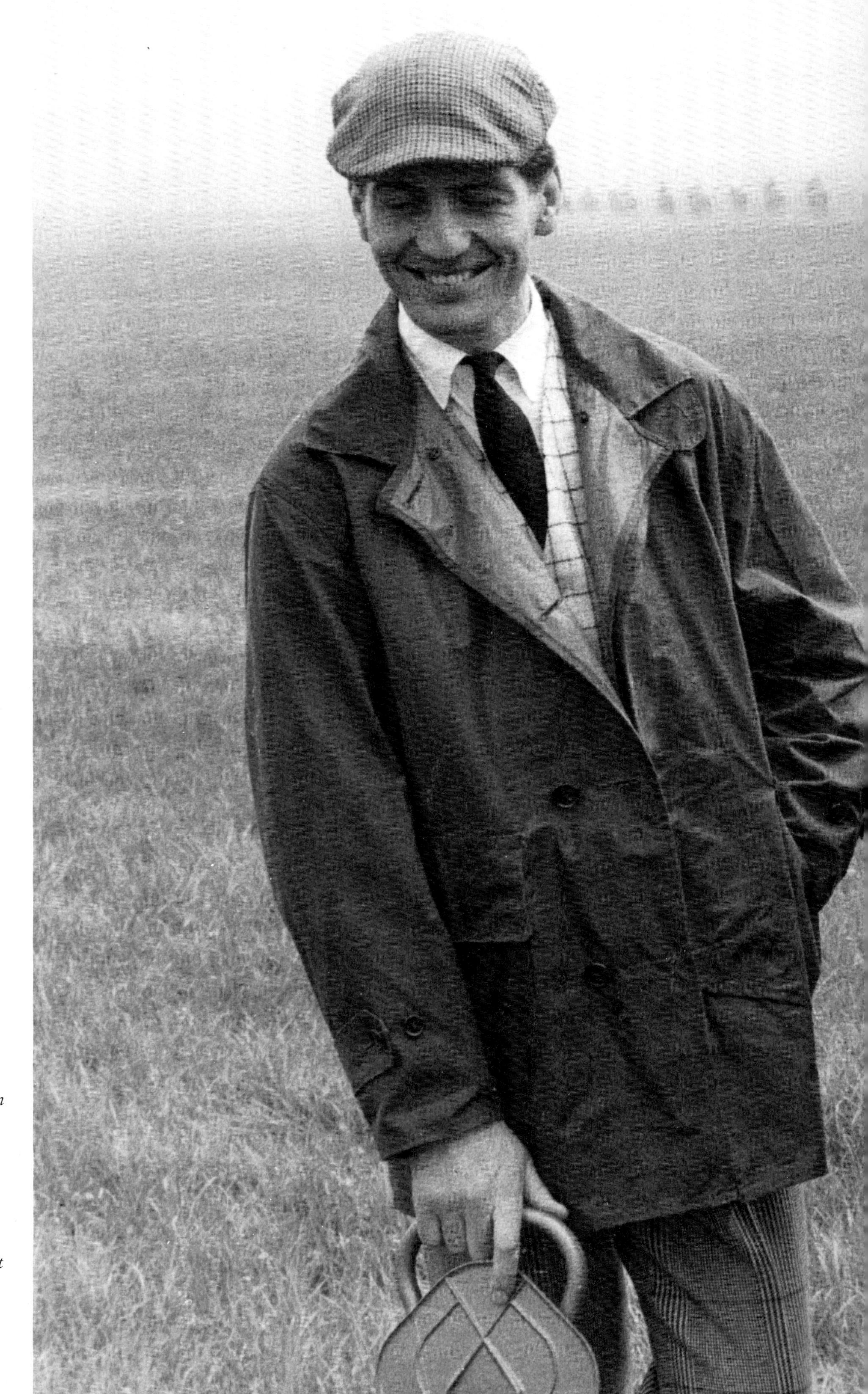

'A loud ha ha'
Country fashion for a Vogue editorial: Robin Tattersall (wearing Parkinson's trousers), Susan Abrahams and Pat Marshal, Newmarket Heath racecourse, 1956
OVERLEAF *Barbara Mullen in the Red Fort at Agra, India, 1956*

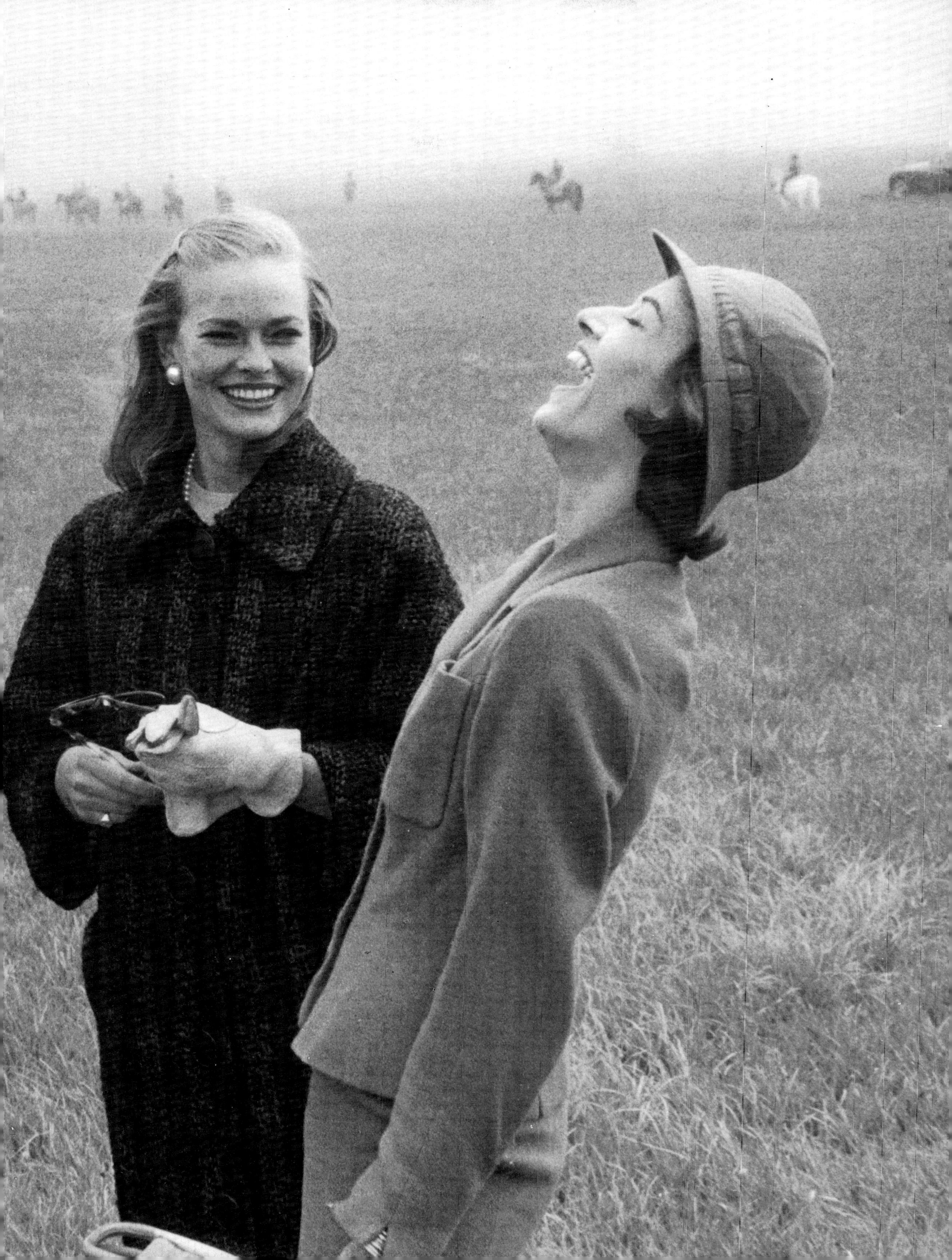

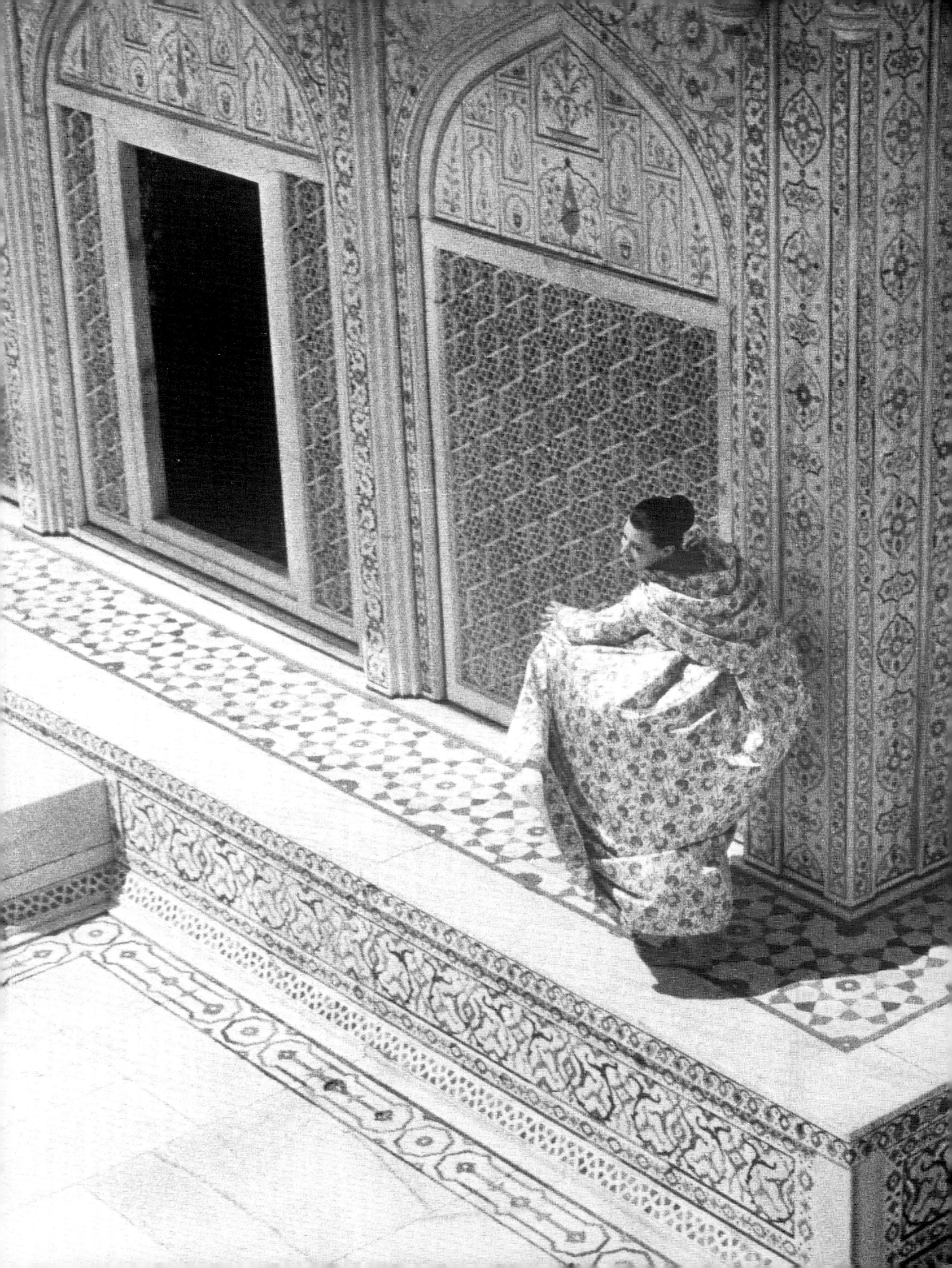

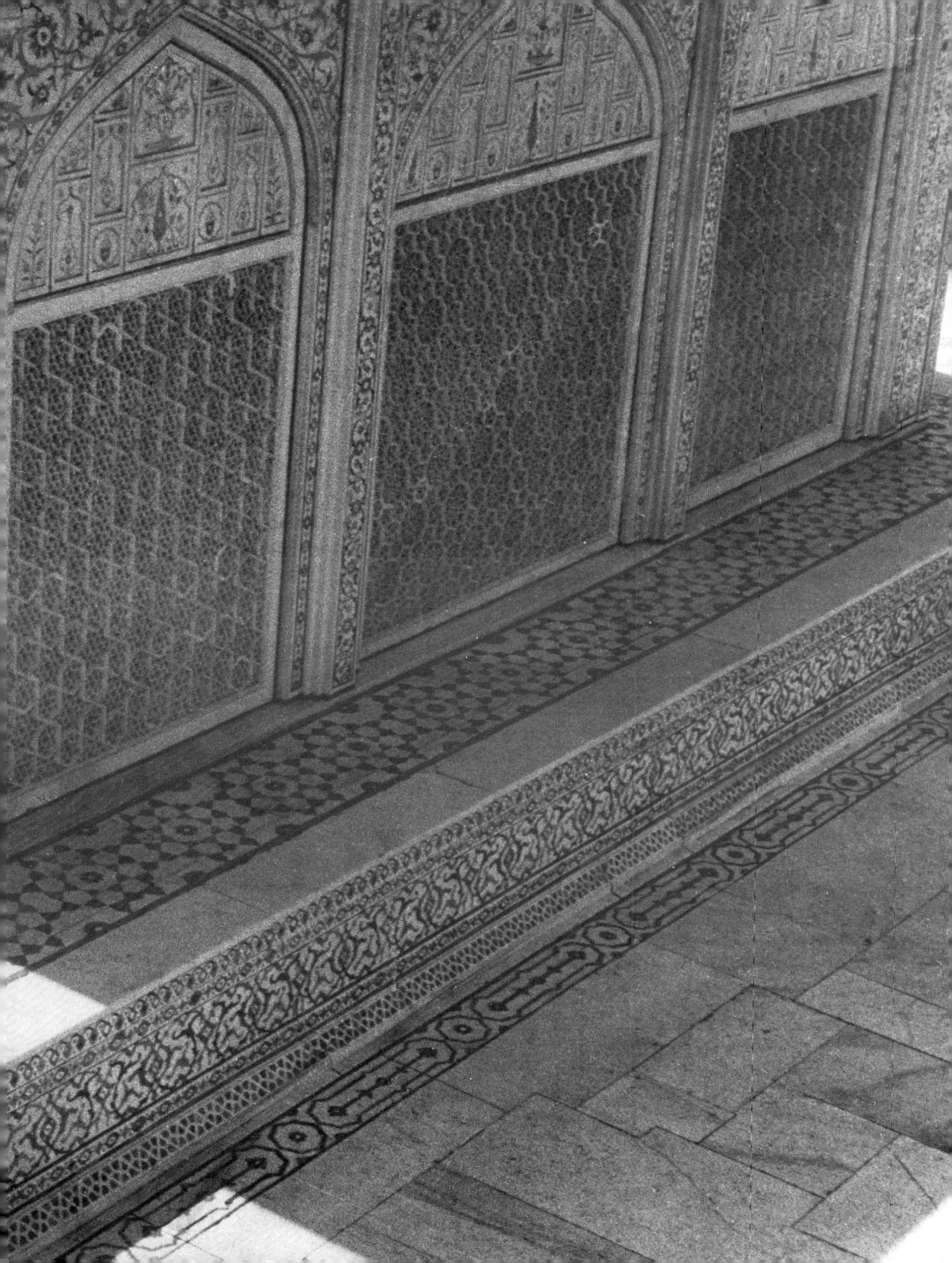

1960s

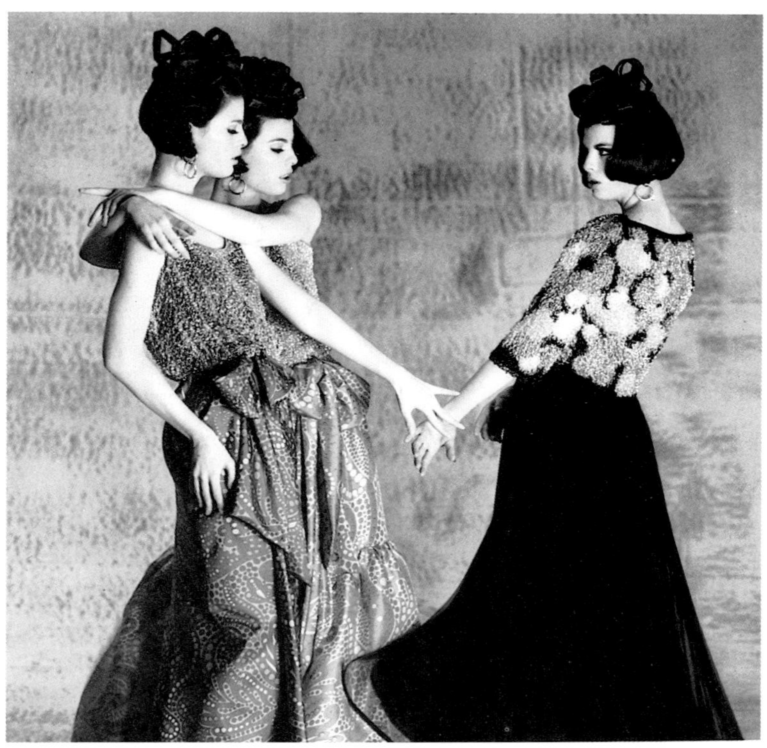

THE QUEEN HAS TRIPLETS

The British find the words 'Haute Couture' impossible to pronounce correctly without embarrassment (the Americans, perhaps, even harder – when someone asked Jean Patchett why she did not try to speak a little French when she was modelling at the Paris Collections of 1950, she replied: 'No way. It makes such a mess of your face'). Yet year after year it dictates the fashion contents of their glossy magazines, and never more so than after the 'dorm feast' of the Paris Collections. In the early sixties when working for Jocelyn Stevens's new *Queen* magazine, I covered seven of these biannual Collections in a row, a marathon worthy of inclusion in the Giscard d'Estaing book of records. If ever I took memorable pictures during those hectic Collections, it would have been because I insisted on seeing the clothes live – walked in, whirled and twirled in – and this meant I had to sit through the shows. Invariably they would start forty-five minutes late, a well planned delay – no models would emerge on the runway without ten minutes of slow handclap. Generally there were six shows a day, starting at 9.30 am, and one often watched a thousand dresses pass across one's dizzy vision, but I sat it out because my camera expected it of me.

I became aware that many of the couturiers would design the same dress in three or four different colourways of the same fabric. If they felt a particular look was important for their season they would send several girls out of the *cabine* (dressing room) into the crowded Salon in a consecutive rush of blue, green, pink, brown, etc., each with different accessories. It was a very effective ploy – often it brought the house down and punctuated the show with great applause – and my fashion editor would turn round and say, 'Quick, Parks, which do you prefer?' which solved nothing as in all honesty I would reply, 'All of them'.

I got to thinking about this, realizing that to photograph just one of that family of dresses was a disservice to the designers and really it was a witless solution to photograph three or four of the same dresses on different looking girls: 'Twins or triplets though . . .', and like the inveterate bird watcher I am, I reprogrammed my model search.

ABOVE *The Dee triplets in soft skirts and beaded tops by Lanvin, at the Paris Collections, 1964*
OPPOSITE *Katherine Pastrie in a one-piece swimsuit from Harvey Nichols, Tahiti, 1960*

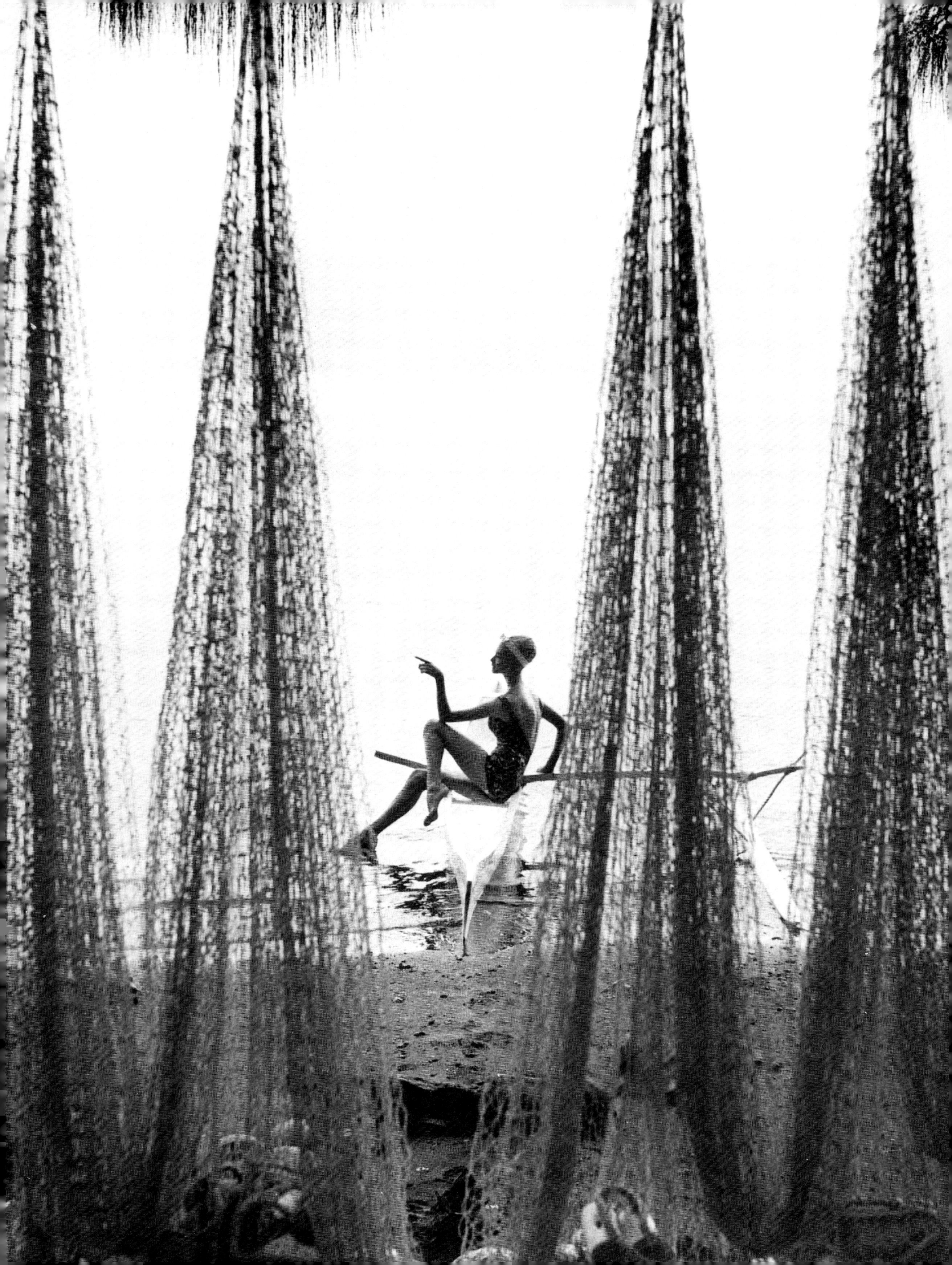

Some time later I was paying a visit to American *Vogue* to see my friend Polly Ferguson. As I stepped out of the lift on the 19th floor, three identical, pale skinned brunettes in line astern, trooped into the adjacent down elevator. Before I could comprehend that I had had a sighting of the rarist avis extant the lift doors slammed in my face and they had flown. It is on these occasions, is it not, that the next down elevator takes the longest 20 seconds to arrive?

By the time I got to the foyer of Grand Central Station hundreds of people were walking every which way. Fortunately I gambled correctly and headed in a panic towards Lexington Avenue and there they were – across the road, three arms upraised to hail a cab.

I was almost run over but I got there before they drove off. 'Excuse me, excuse me,' I yelled and pressed five dollars into the taxi driver's hand. 'Excuse me,' I repeated and got the girls out on the pavement. 'You were just in *Vogue*? Correct? Did you think of modelling? Yes?' They began to melt, which was fortunate for a lunchtime posse of interested gapers now surrounded us. 'I'm a photographer, Parkinson, but that's not important . . . how old are you?' (I was worried about cradle-snatching and that Mason-Dixon line problem.) 'Eighteen.' Thank God, I thought – and I was now beginning to comprehend my luck for they were very pretty and animated and slim. 'You have a mother? Might I call her? I have a plan. Her name?' 'Mrs Dee.'

Within half an hour I had spoken to Jocelyn Stevens in the *Queen* offices in London. He was a tremendous editor; the most impossible or improbable requests would receive the most enthusiastic reception. 'Remember we were worried about models for the French Collections?' I shouted across the Atlantic. 'Well I found them. I've found beautiful identical triplets in a *Vogue* elevator . . .' 'Fantastic! Are they still alive?' he yelled back in his screaming high crescendo. 'Will they travel to Paris? Get them, get them.'

That evening there followed a conversation with Mrs Dee. Everything was satisfactorily agreed until she threw a screwball: 'I don't think they can leave until a month from now, Mr Parkinson; you see two of them are finishing their semester at Hunter College.' Next day I was sitting in their tutor's office at Hunter. 'Well,' the lady said, looking over her heavy bifocals at me, the white slaver, 'it is most irregular to leave the course before it terminates but I suppose it's a rare opportunity for the girls to see Paris

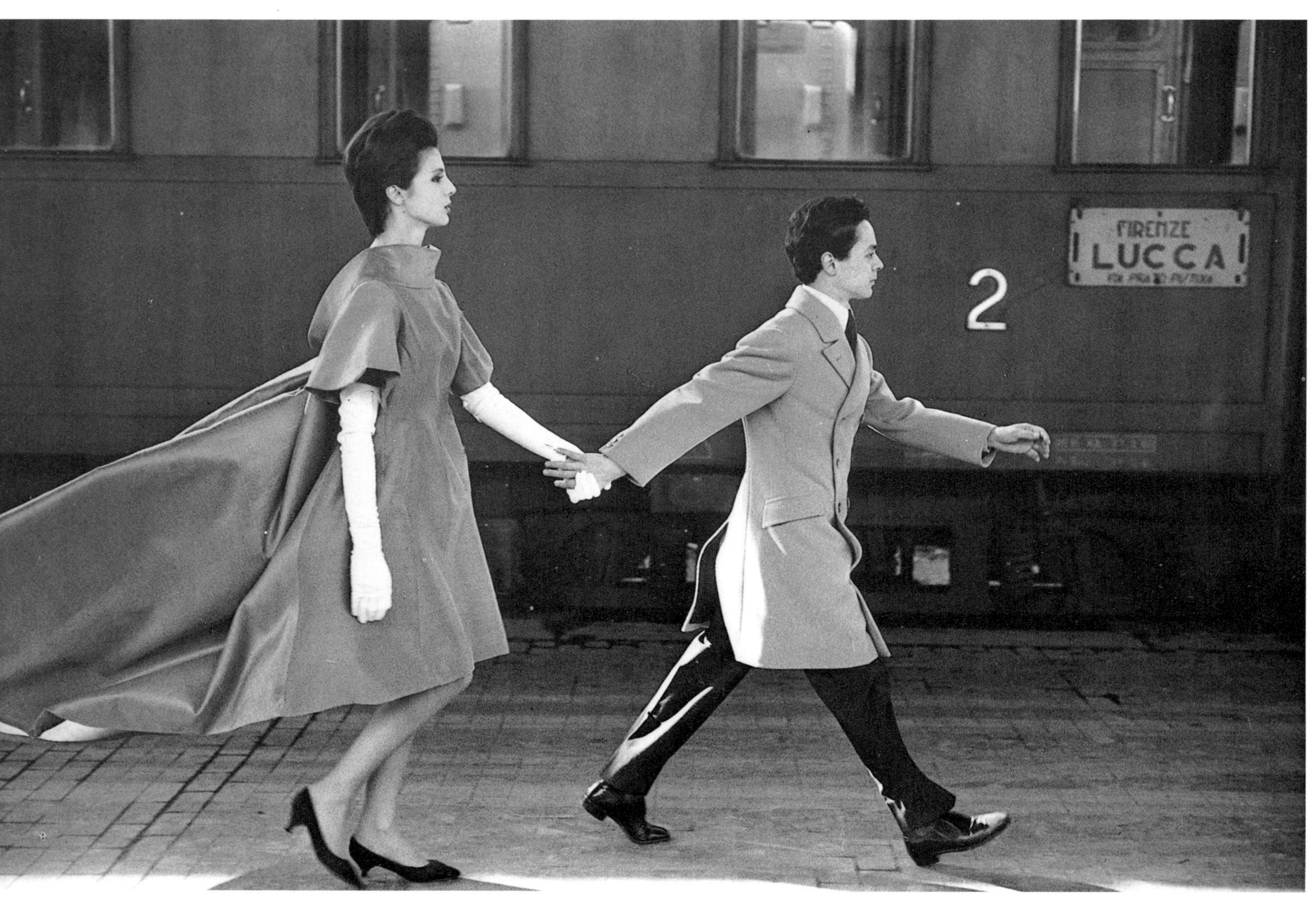

Capucci, the designer, with an evening dress creation of his own, Florence station, 1961

without any expenses – if Mrs Dee thinks it is a good idea, I cannot object.'

The girls were a sensation in Paris. The idea worked out beyond my wildest dreams and Jocelyn was over his private moon. The sisters were so alike that even after a dozen sittings I could not tell them apart – I found myself having to write their names on pieces of card in front of them on the floor.

Queen Elizabeth was about six months pregnant with Prince Edward at the time – a golden opportunity for Jocelyn to design a hilariously funny cover for the magazine; it carried a picture of the Dee girls with the heading 'Queen has triplets in Paris'.

There is an epilogue to this adventure, which was a nightmare at the time. I suppose with three girls it was almost bound to happen. After the first day's shoot, the two Hunter College Dees came to me and announced their sister was very homesick and would have to return to New York. I was dumbfounded. 'But you appeared to be so happy today and the photos are so good. Everybody is delighted with you and it would be most inconsiderate to the Editor to fly back now.' 'We are sorry, Mr Parks, but she is crying in her room and must return in the morning.' After ten minutes' grilling of the tearful sister my fears were confirmed: it was 'love'. 'I am sorry, you cannot leave.' I played the stern schoolmaster. 'You have promised to work for us for five or six days and that's what it's going to be.' More floods and wringing of hands ensued. 'Your boyfriend is being most unkind to you and very unbusinesslike to us. A bargain is a bargain both sides of the Atlantic.' 'If I get him on the telephone will you speak to him Mr Parks?' I said I would be pleased to do so and the operator was asked to try and find him.

We finally pinned him down at 2 am Paris time. 'I want you to send my girlfriend back right away; she never said she was going away for a week.' 'Listen here,' I interrupted him, 'she's in Paris working with her sisters, they can't go to Paris for much less than a week.' 'Where the hell is Paris then? Can't be far.' I quickly realized the weight of my adversary and there followed a transatlantic auction that went something like this. 'She can't stay a week. Send her back in two days.' 'No, five days.' 'All right then, three days.' 'Sorry, four days to complete the work.' I think we settled at three and a half; it was an embarrassing conversation but it dried the tears and all went happily to work on the morrow.

Coat and dress partnerships: featherweight raw silk dresses under slips of coats by Capucci, Florence, 1961

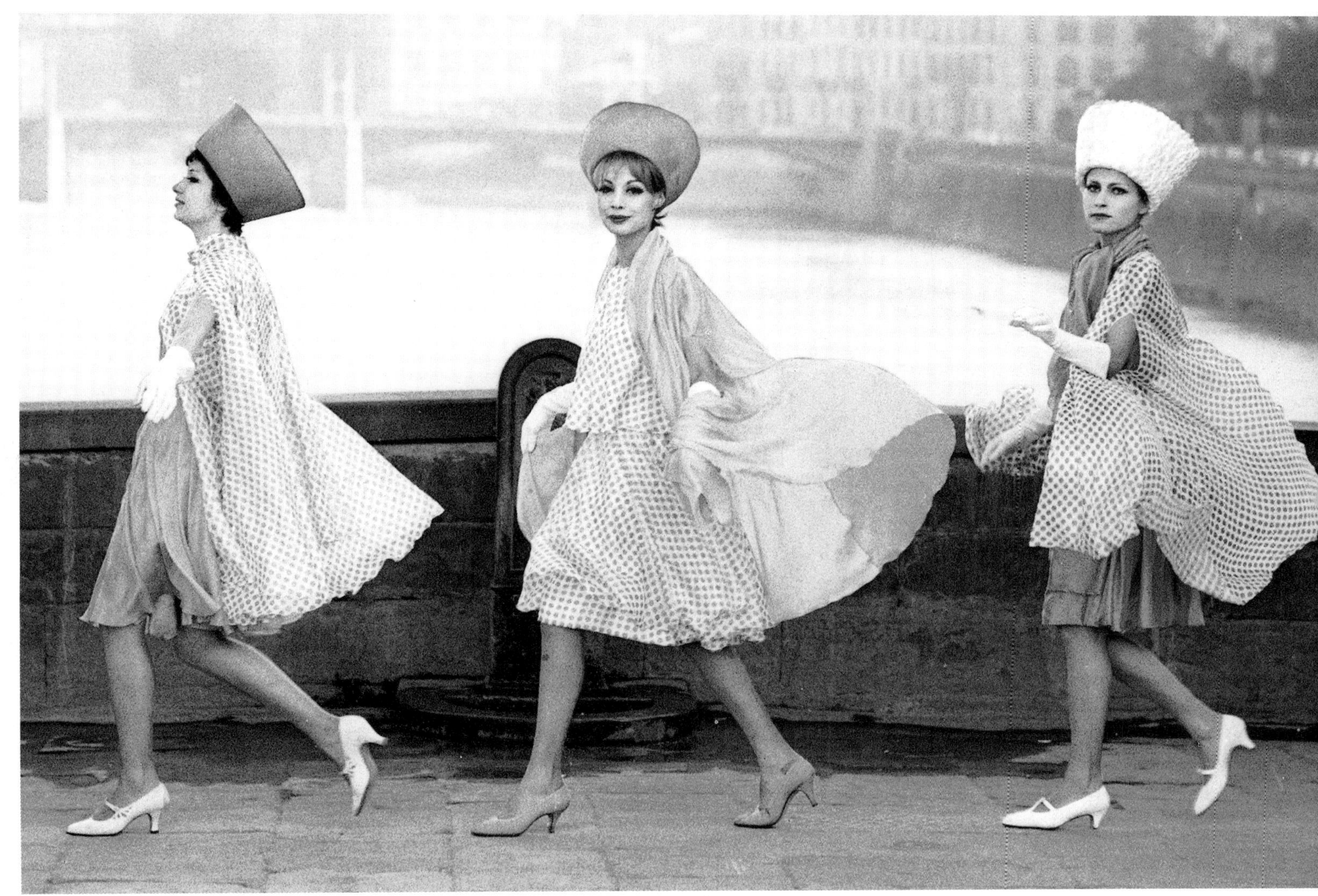

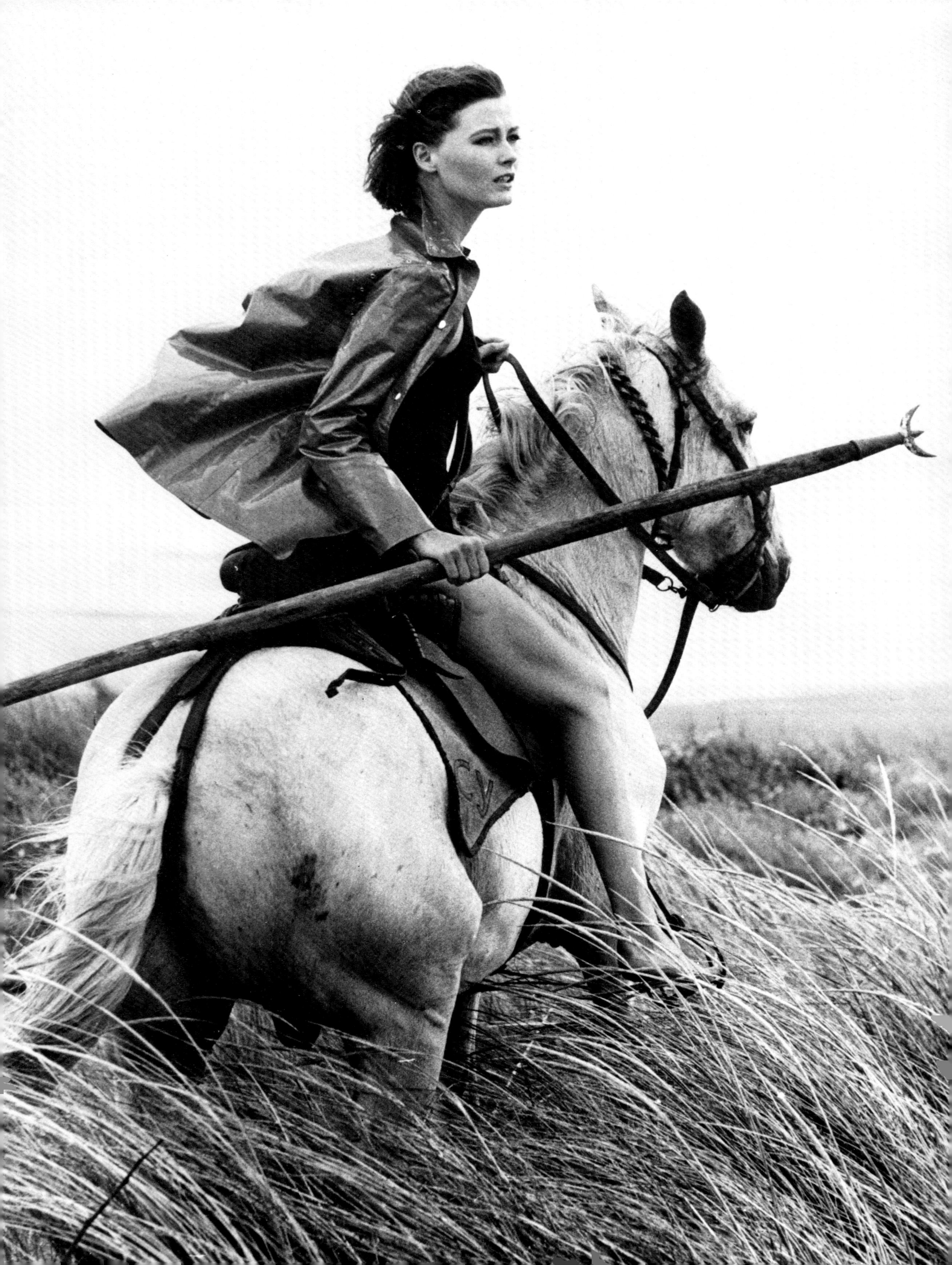

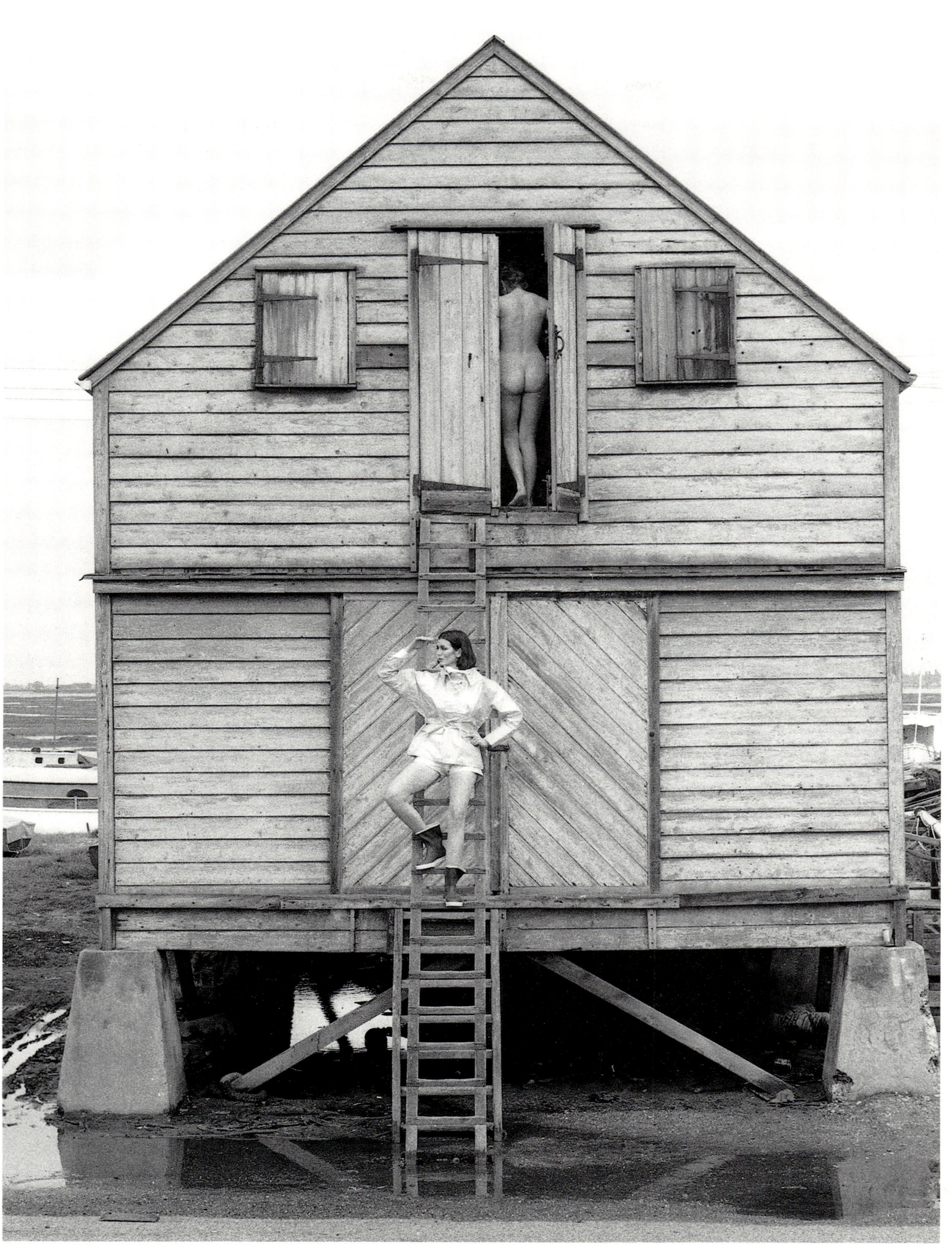

ABOVE *Carmen in a yellow oilskin smock from Captain O. M. Watts, 1961*
OPPOSITE *Maria Gudmannsdottir in a green PVC jacket by V de V, the Camargue, 1964*

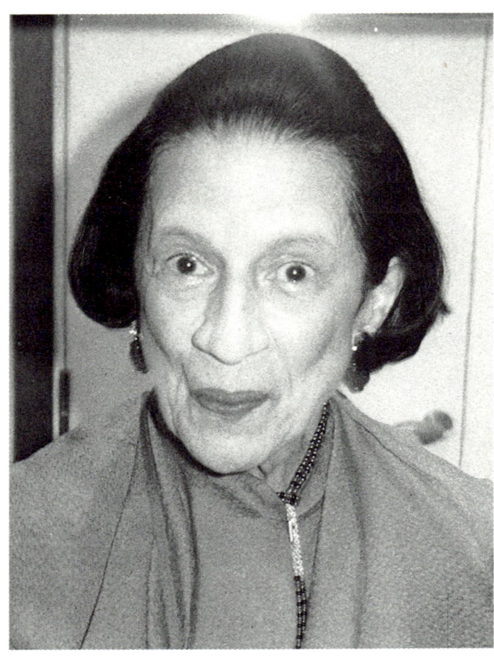

THE VREELAND FACTOR

Can it be true that beauty and style are strange bedfellows? I am thinking of a handful of people I have known who exuded style, but who were all far from beautiful. (Perhaps if you are just a little bit ugly, you are able to o'er leap the tag of beauty and grasp the unattainable style.) I am thinking of Gertrude Pidoux, Fashion Editor of British *Vogue* in the thirties, and Mrs James Rodney of *Harper's*; I am thinking of Edith Sitwell, Elsa Schiaparelli and Anna Piaggi. This brings us, down through the family tree of fashion, to the Empress of Style herself, Diana Vreeland: she was the Alpha and she will be the Omega. Nobody was anybody in fashion, in my generation, who had not worshipped at the shrine of Diana Vreeland.

Her looks are menacing and give no quarter. She is a totally black and white person living in an unrestrained circus tent, a cacophany of colour. She is an amalgam of bird and beast, some vulture that prefers its profile crossed with something dark and ominous from *Alice Through the Looking Glass*.

Her office on the famous nineteenth floor of the Graybar Building at 420 Lexington was the last cavity in a maze of corridors, but it is said that once upon a time a blind person emerging from the elevator had walked, with tapping stick, directly to it following the scent of the Floris burning oil which flickered as permanently as La Flamme Eternelle below the Etoile. The walls of this office had the appearance of a giant patchwork screen; swatches of fabric were cheek by jowl with a hundred different illustrations, photographs and drawings and love notes and phrases like 'success is infatuated with efficiency' and laudatory cables, all pinned higgledy piggledy.

Over ten years ago I was in New York working with American *Vogue* when I got a message to go and see Mrs Vreeland the following day at 4 pm. I sat there saturated in the fragrance of burning oil, admiring as always this immaculate person with the long black cigarette holder. 'Parkinson,' she announced, 'you know Tahiti.' 'Yes, Mrs Vreeland, I worked there for *Queen* magazine in the early sixties.' 'Exactly, wonderful pictures I remember. More Gauguin than Gauguin. I am sending you back.' 'Thank you.' 'I recall that you were quoted as saying that in every field there grazed a white horse.' 'Correct.' 'I am sending you back for two reasons, in the first instance with 200 pounds of gold and silver 'Dynel'. [False plastic hair very promotable at the time.] I am sending you with some illustrations of what I wish you to achieve. I wish you to select the finest Arab stallion that you can find in Tahiti, check with some veterinary, and caparison him in the manner of the Grand Epoch. I want to see an illustration, as this one here, where the horse's mane and tail are plaited to the ground. Use all the Dynel you want, you don't have to bring it back.' 'I understand, Mrs Vreeland.' 'Secondly, we are sending you to Tahiti with a plastic city.' 'A plastic city?' 'Yes, you hear me aright. You will enter upon people's lands, you will dig holes, you will run concrete and you will erect this fantastic city of shining screens and tones against the solid dragons' teeth of the mountain ranges.' 'Yes, Mrs Vreeland, I understand perfectly, but what about the law of trespass?' 'Don't bother me with incidentals. Choose the two girls you wish to take. You are leaving on Wednesday week.'

ABOVE *Diana Vreeland, 'Empress of Fashion', Editor of American Vogue from 1962–71*

I had a further discussion with a member of the Art Department about the plastic city and how it would look with its various panels, so I am fairly confident that it did exist somewhere outside the lady's imagination. Yet I was unreasonably relieved when I was told that the plastic city had been scrapped. 'Too large', someone announced, 'to get into the baggage hold of a 707. But Parkinson, don't you dare relax. She wants an alternative idea from you because you know the area so well.'

It so happened that a friend had been talking the previous night about kites – wonderful kites made and flown by the Art Seniors of Rhode Island University. Mrs Vreeland liked the idea very much indeed and told me to proceed. I called the University and an intelligent youth brought to New York a brilliant collection of photographs illustrating kites created during the last semester. I became very excited; all types of weird shapes were possible, and for a magazine that had so recently dumped an impressive plastic city, I did not consider the cost of, say, three, out of the way. I made my choice, gave the student a name to contact within Condé Nast for payment or if there were any problems, and flew off to Singapore and Hong Kong where I was to do a feature before going on to Tahiti. The fashion party with the girls arrived in Tahiti, bringing with them, as planned, 200 pounds of gold and silver Dynel, and two kites. 'Only two kites,' I enquired. 'Yes, Parks, only two. The Art Department got in on the act, and they thought the kites rather expensive, so they made a change in your choices. But they are very pleased and I know you will love them. Such a good idea of yours . . .' I began to smell a rat, but had no time to worry, as there was plenty to do to find the horse, and anyway there was no wind.

I soon found the veterinary: an imposing gentleman in an equally imposing office. 'I remember', I said, 'when I was here a few years back that there seemed to be a white horse grazing in every field à la Gauguin.' 'Well, you won't find any horses now.' 'No horses now?' 'No, I'm afraid not. The French are here now, and we have eaten them.' Failure of the first part was now staring me in the face. I became downcast and guilty, wondering how to justify the 200 pounds of Dynel. 'But wait a minute.' He brightened, 'There is a plantation owner up in the hills who has a few riding horses, and I believe a stallion.'

The stallion was brown, young, badly broken and very nervous. The owner, however, was rather intrigued at the idea of having his baby caparisoned. We set to work at dawn the next day, some eight elderly seamstresses with bodkins at the ready for the plaiting and anchoring of the Dynel to the rather flimsy harness arrangements. By noon we were doing better than expected. The owner of the animal had now been comforting it for some four hours and would allow no other person to hold its head. He assured me that all would be well as the dam was so intelligent. I did not share his confidence – a horse's eye is the barometer of the impending storm, and I did not like this white-rimmed stare. By three pm he was looking very good. At least 150 pounds of Dynel was on him, one way or another, and he did look very like one of the Vreeland illustrations. The model was dressed, made up, and ready, and she had told me, 'I don't mind horses.'

At about 3.15 the cameras loaded, and the bridle of this magnificent vision of super elegant horse was transferred from the hand of the owner to the well-manicured hand of the model. 'Let's go!' is all I said. I usually have a critical eye for detail but I do not know whether the animal took one step or two steps, or no steps at all. But it did take a monumental Bucephalean leap that they would have recognized as something special at Cape Canaveral. The model, I do remember, was for an instant also airborne but she returned to earth before the horse. The animal came down a little later, a four-point landing on four stiff parallel legs. Most of the Dynel continued earthwards, but some remained, together with an array of well-anchored orange blossom and hibiscus. The animal, now quite stationary, emitted an equestrian scream the like of which I had only ever heard at a disembowelling in the bull ring at the Feria in Seville. This terrible tocsin announced 'the shake'. It began at the horse's ears, passing down the neck, through the entire body and out of the tail. Not a vestige of seven hours of decoration remained. The horse quite quietly stood there surrounded with everything that it had so brilliantly rejected, and none of us could move. It then picked up its feet in a particular and tidy way and walked over to its master. The gentleman made a tiny bow to me, as the French do so well, and walked off with his horse. It was then I realized, looking down at my cameras, that I had not taken one single exposure. Later I did take a timid picture of a girl and a white pony, silken bow in mane and tail, to show Mrs Vreeland that I had tried.

Three days later it was the kites' turn on the island of Moorea. In order to change the models' clothes and their hair and make-up, we had taken a couple of rooms at a very pleasant primitive hotel. On that windy day the hotel was also the centre of a visiting party of American matrons, almost identically dressed Daughters of the Revolution. Just to make a show for them, we began to unpack the first kite right there in front of the gift shop.

The instructions were so easy to follow: spring clip A into link A, Pulley B into rope link B, and so on. For the kite to fly it had to be anchored to the mast which could then be cut out in the picture. The breeze was perfect; the forty ladies were all assembled awaiting the exciting moment of the launching of the kite. One could hear an undertone of 'They're from *Vogue*, New York, you know, it's bound to be beautiful.'

I must have said it again: 'Let's go!' Within ten seconds a hush fell upon the audience, a giggle stifled here and there, but a tremendous hush, the like of which I have seldom heard. I had pulled the three ropes that ran through the pulleys, the assistant had thrown his pale pink bundle into the air, and the breeze had done the rest: correctly anchored to the mast, and billowing out at some ten feet from the ground, was a ten foot male penis. The designers had not cheated us with just this simple object; pendulous below were the two testicles. Everything was undeniably lifelike and mobile. I do not know the opposite of 'Let's go', but I said it and the assistant and myself made a rush at this erection. We threw ropes away, grabbing at spring clips and speedily gathering up the offending spinnaker.

We did try out the other kite in a very private place, but it was identical and pale blue. The best comment came from my assistant: 'That one is for the cold weather.'

To telephone New York from Tahiti was not easy, and an arrangement was made that I would call each evening around sunset to find out how the pictures were looking that I had already forwarded. For obvious reasons I remember the gist of the conversations quite vividly. 'Hullo, Hullo.' (Plenty of that went on.) 'Can you hear me Parkinson? Mrs Vreeland wants to know how the horse shot is coming.' 'Sorry to tell her, not well at all.' 'You want me to tell her "not well at all"?' 'Yes, I do, not well at all.' 'What's the problem?' 'There are no horses now, the French ate them.' 'The French ate them? Shall I tell her that?' 'Well, what's the alternative? It's the truth.'

Then a few nights later: 'Hullo, Hullo, is that you Parkinson? Mrs Vreeland was enquiring about the kite pictures. When is she going to see something of the kites?' 'Never.' 'Did I hear you say never?' 'Yes, I guess never is the best word.' 'But what happened with the kites, Parkinson?' 'Well, I can't tell you over the telephone, but the kites are obscene.' 'What scene with the kites?' 'We have a problem with the kites – I will tell all when I return. We are as sorry as you are, but just tell her "No kites".' 'Well, I'll tell her, but she'll be very disappointed.'

So much goes wrong when you are working for a top magazine and you learn to roll with the punches through occasional horrendous confusion. But Mrs Vreeland was always in there punching for the impossible and the unattainable. When her ideas succeeded, and they often did work out well, they were triumphant. She gave the roar to get something not attempted before and there were no post mortems if they did not succeed. She knew that all her contributors would give their all for her, so failure was never discussed before or after the event.

There were elements within the *Vogue* hierarchy who questioned her expensive impracticalities, otherwise she would still be there today. Her 'LOOK' was never wrong, but it was her 'LOOK' and it threw the management and the advertising departments into chaos. She was inclined to illustrate a thousand dollar Oscar de la Renta skirt with a five dollar T shirt from Woolworths. She gave birth to a new breed of girl absolutely on her own. Not easy to classify, but certainly the girls had to be athletic, with strong limbs to shine with oil and long clean hair to stream out or shake in the wind. She had crushes on girls she had discovered through friends, or even hearsay, and she would fly them post-haste to her office from the remotest corners of the world.

Detractors laughed then as they laugh now, but never before or since has American *Vogue* commanded the respect that it assumed under her Editorship. Designers from all the capitals of fashion cherished her approval. Vendeuses, having peeked through the curtains during the showing of an important Collection, would run back to 'le maitre', 'Mrs Vreeland is clapping.' She gave birth to a generation, the very last generation to appreciate fashion and style – for it is clear to anyone in this ephemeral trade who is sufficiently unblinkered to see it, that we are presiding over the dying pangs of style – and she gave birth to an Amazon to illustrate it her way.

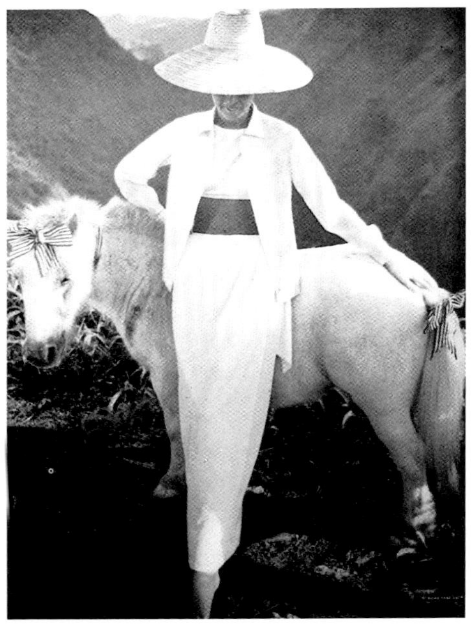

White jersey sarong wrap with shirt, Tahiti, 1965. (This is the photograph taken instead of the one Diana Vreeland really wanted – which would have featured a white stallion caparisoned in flowers and plastic hair.)
OPPOSITE *Swimsuit by Rose Marie Reid, Frenchman's Cove, Jamaica, 1960*

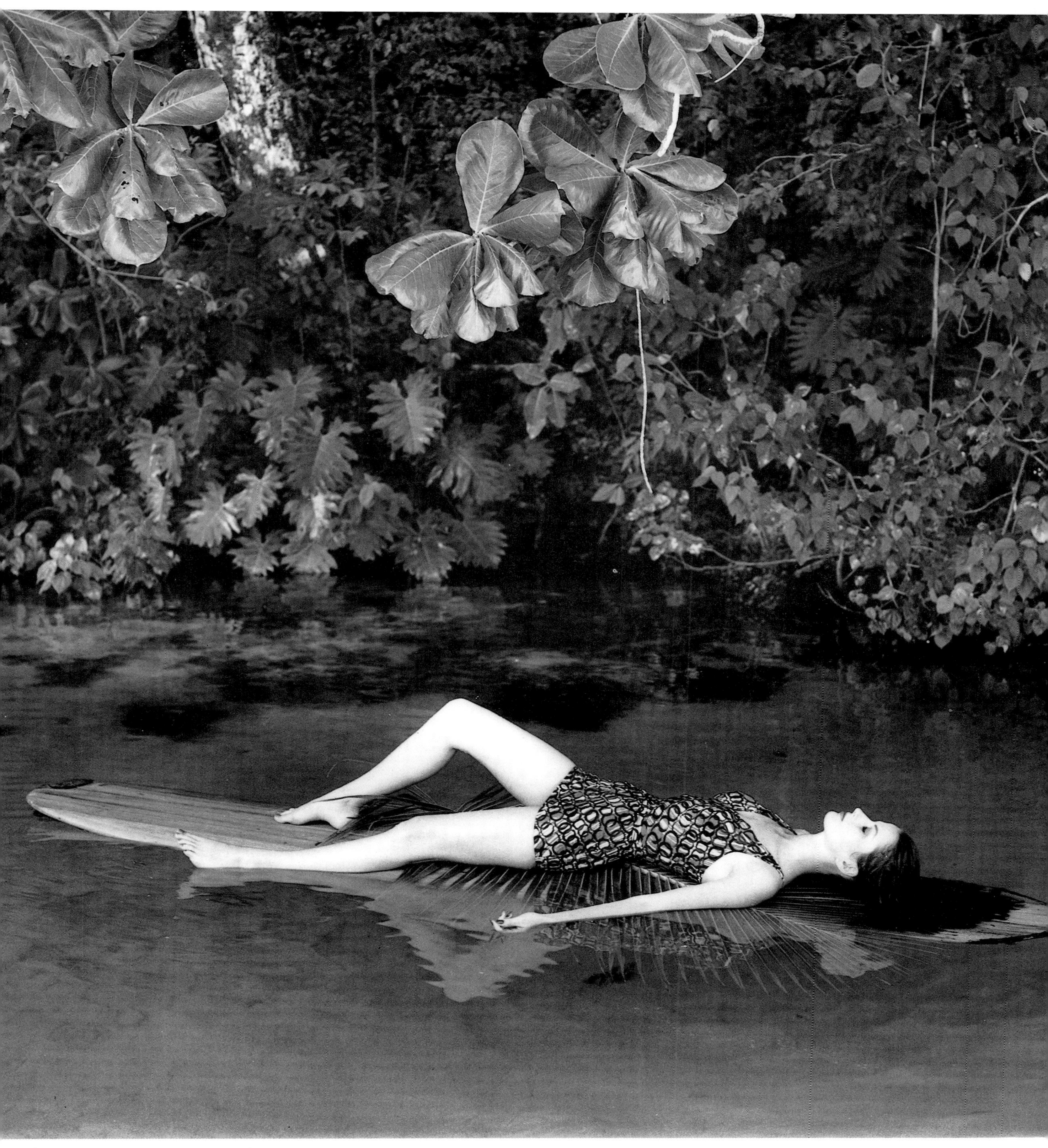

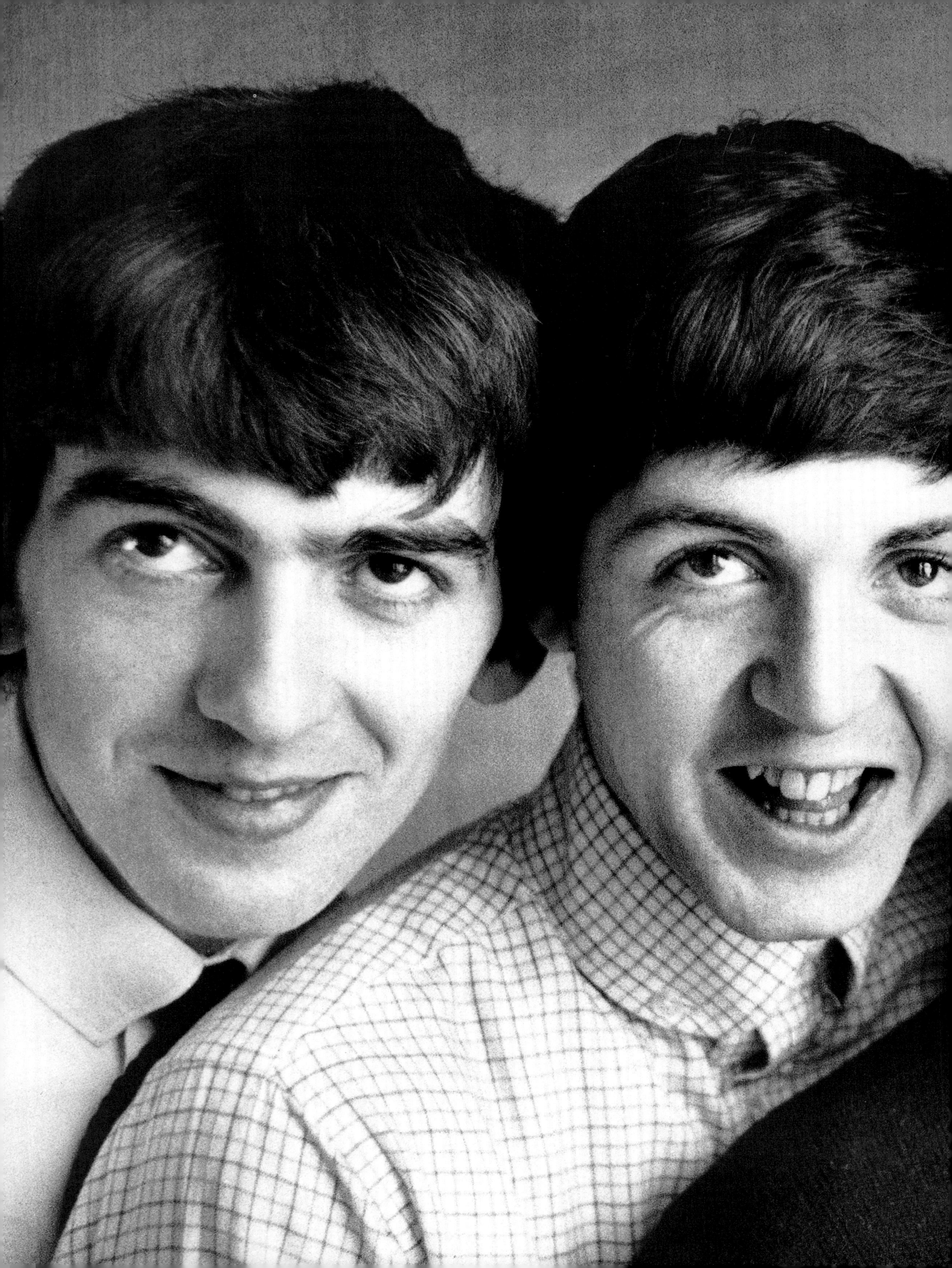

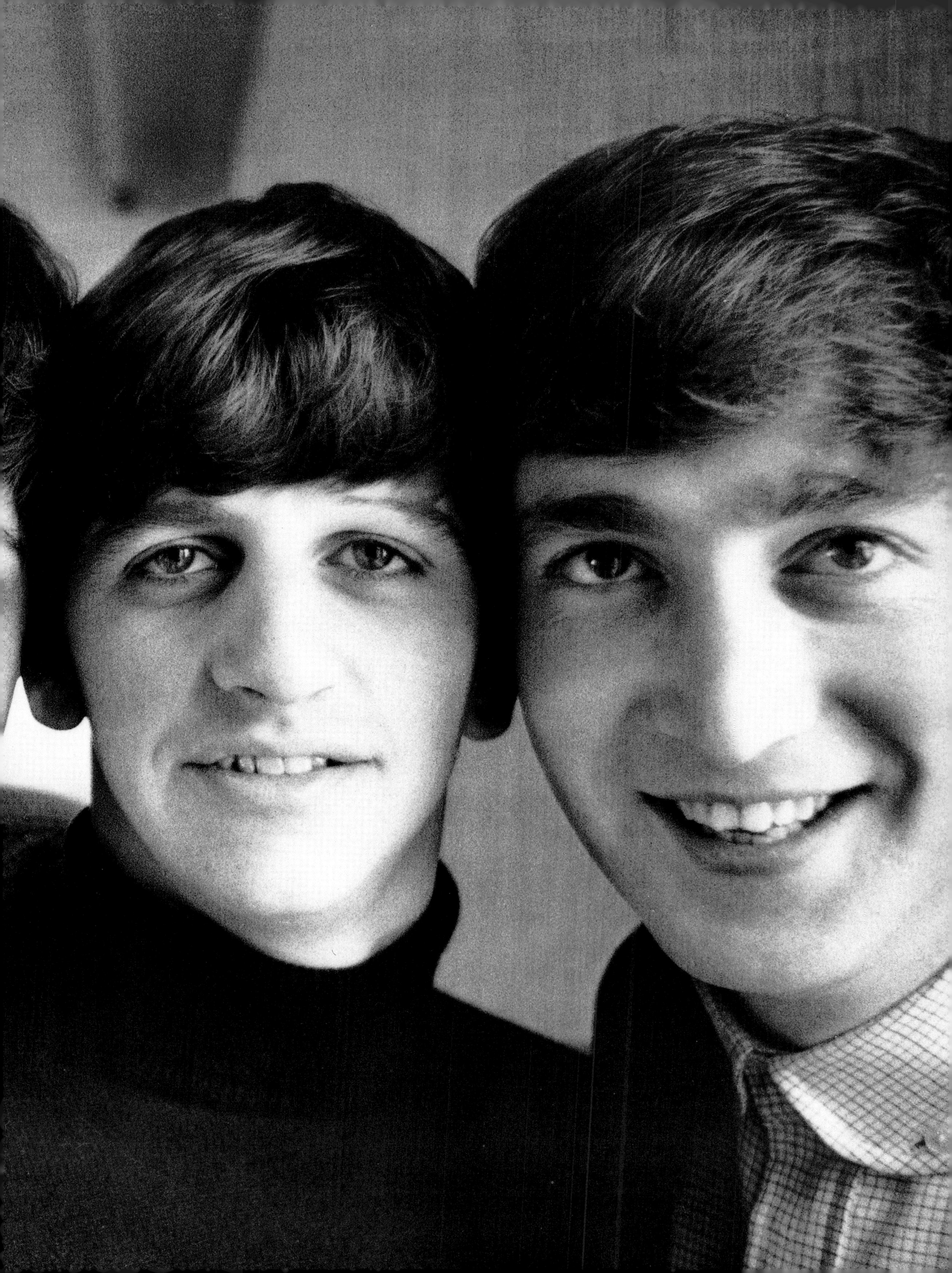

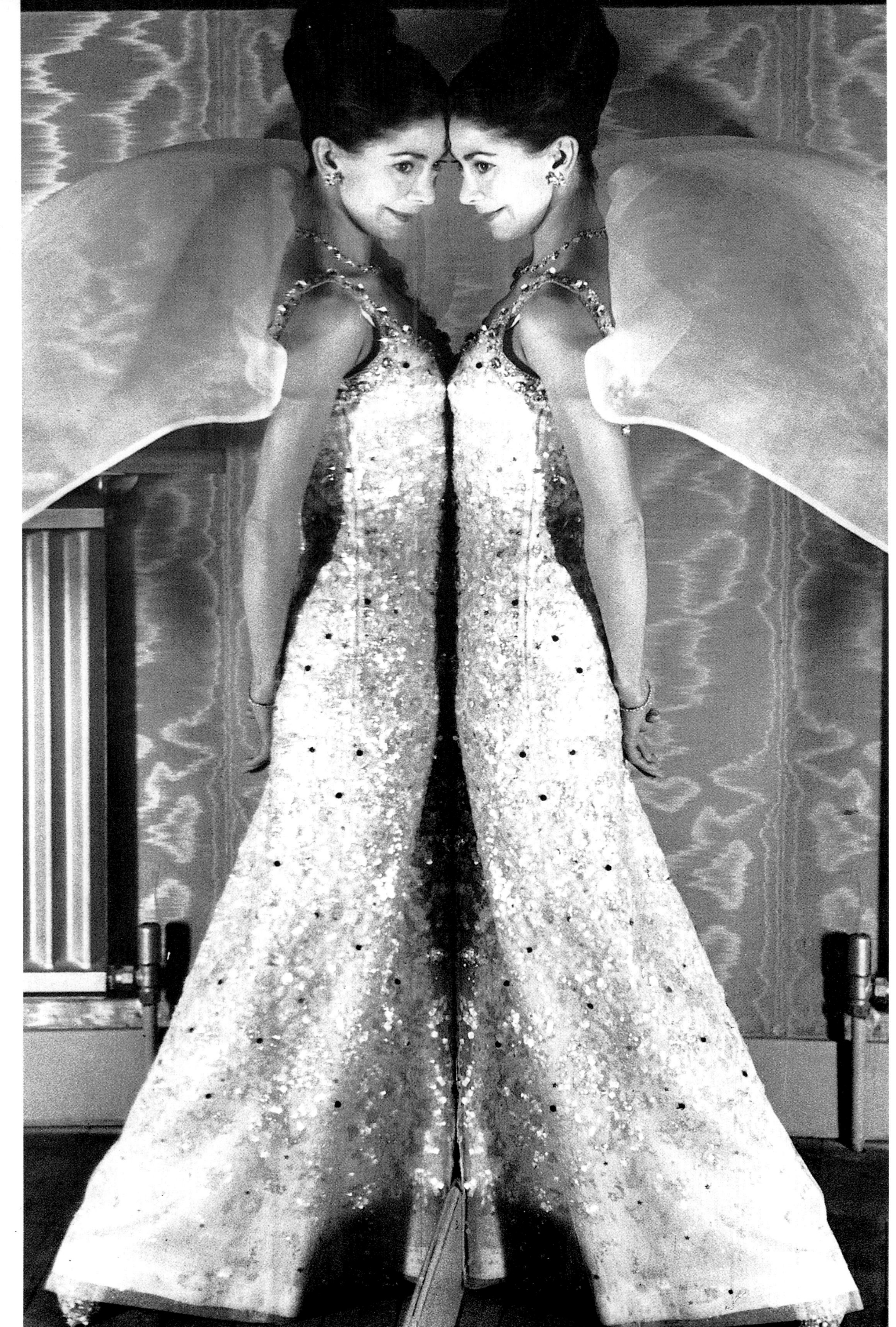

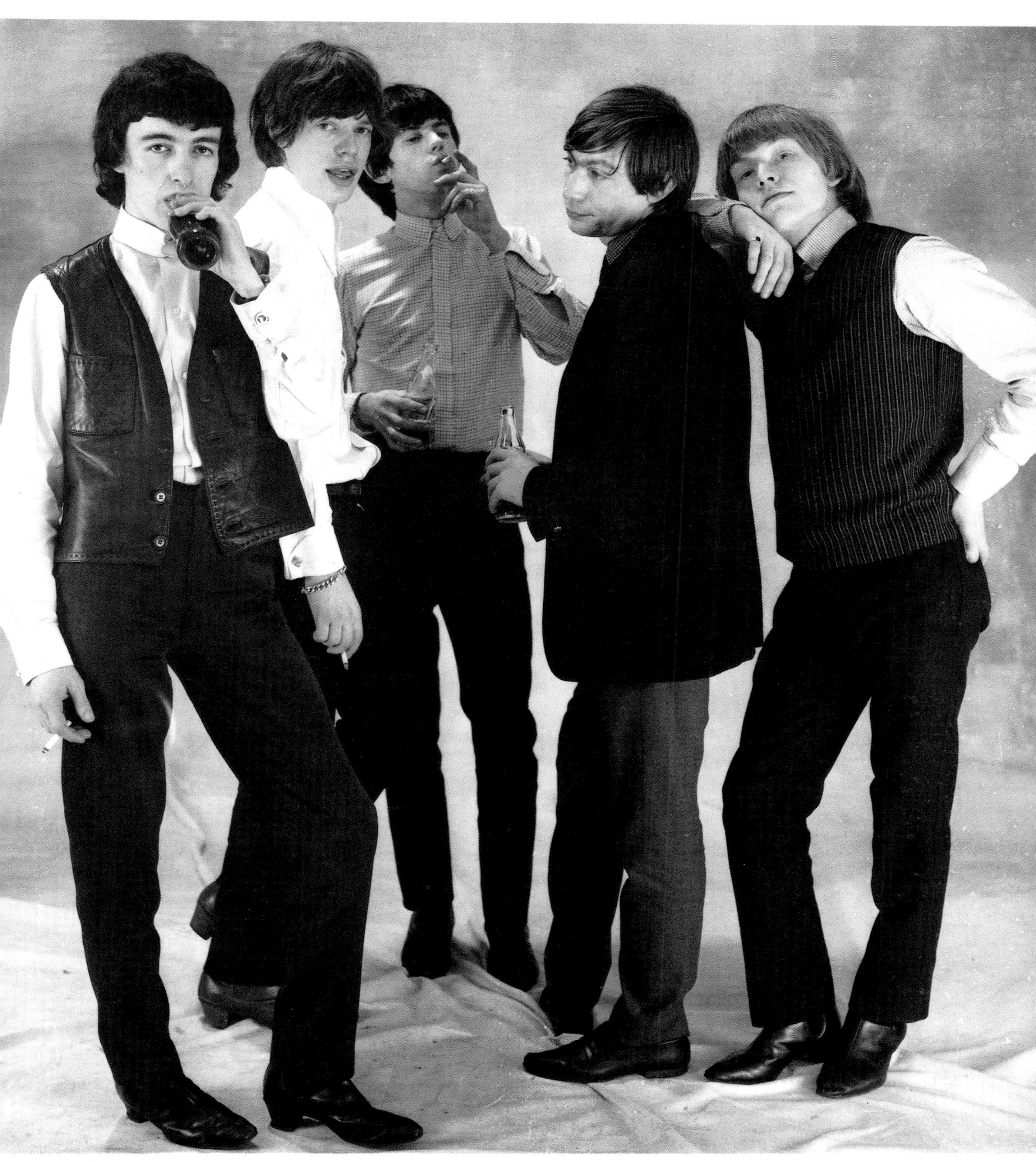

ABOVE *Bill Wyman, Mick Jagger, Keith Richard, Charlie Watts, Brian Jones – The Rolling Stones, 1964*
OPPOSITE *Dame Margot Fonteyn in a Dior dress, early 1960s*
PREVIOUS PAGES *George Harrison, Paul McCartney, Ringo Starr and John Lennon – The Beatles, 1964*

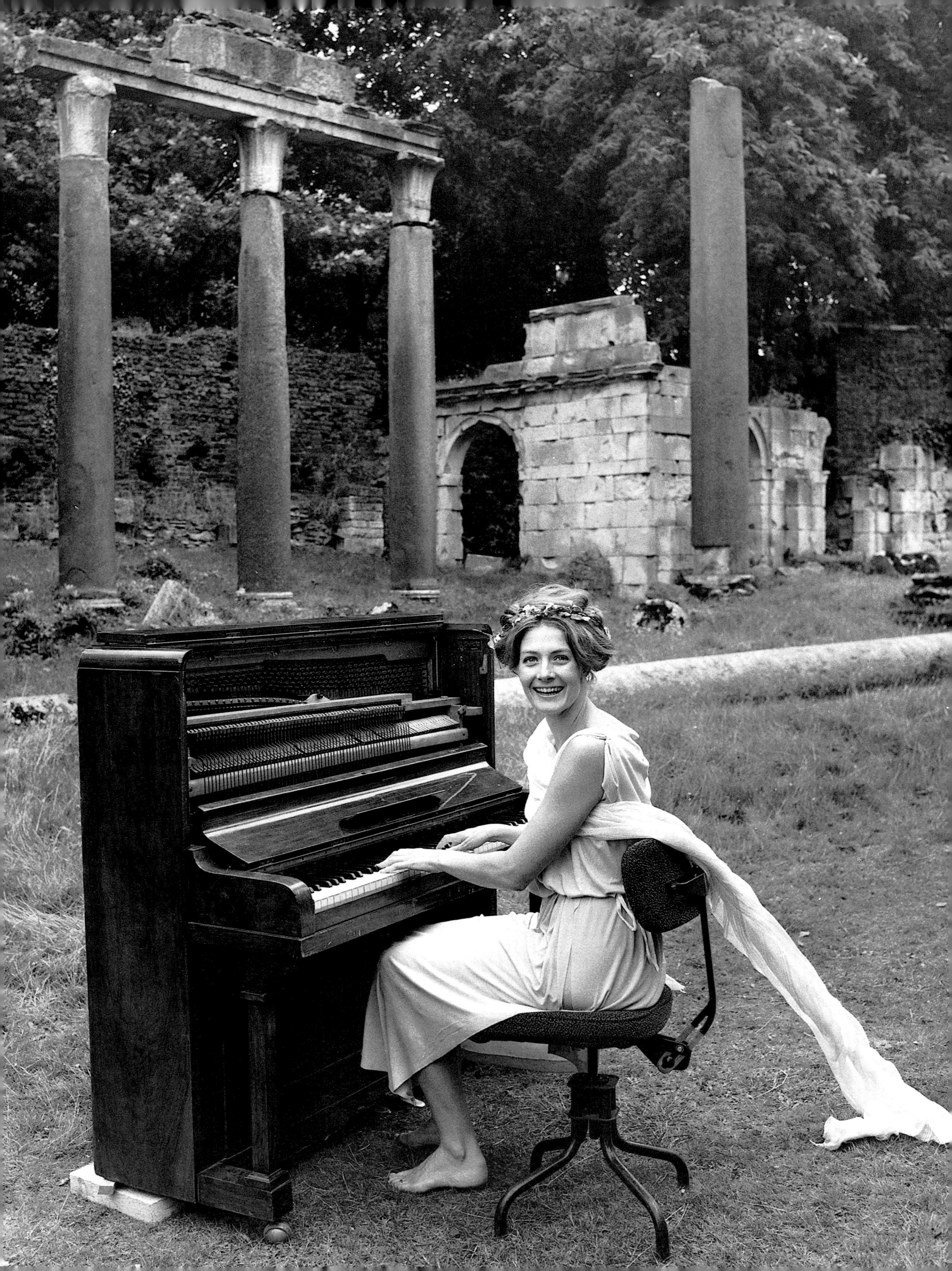

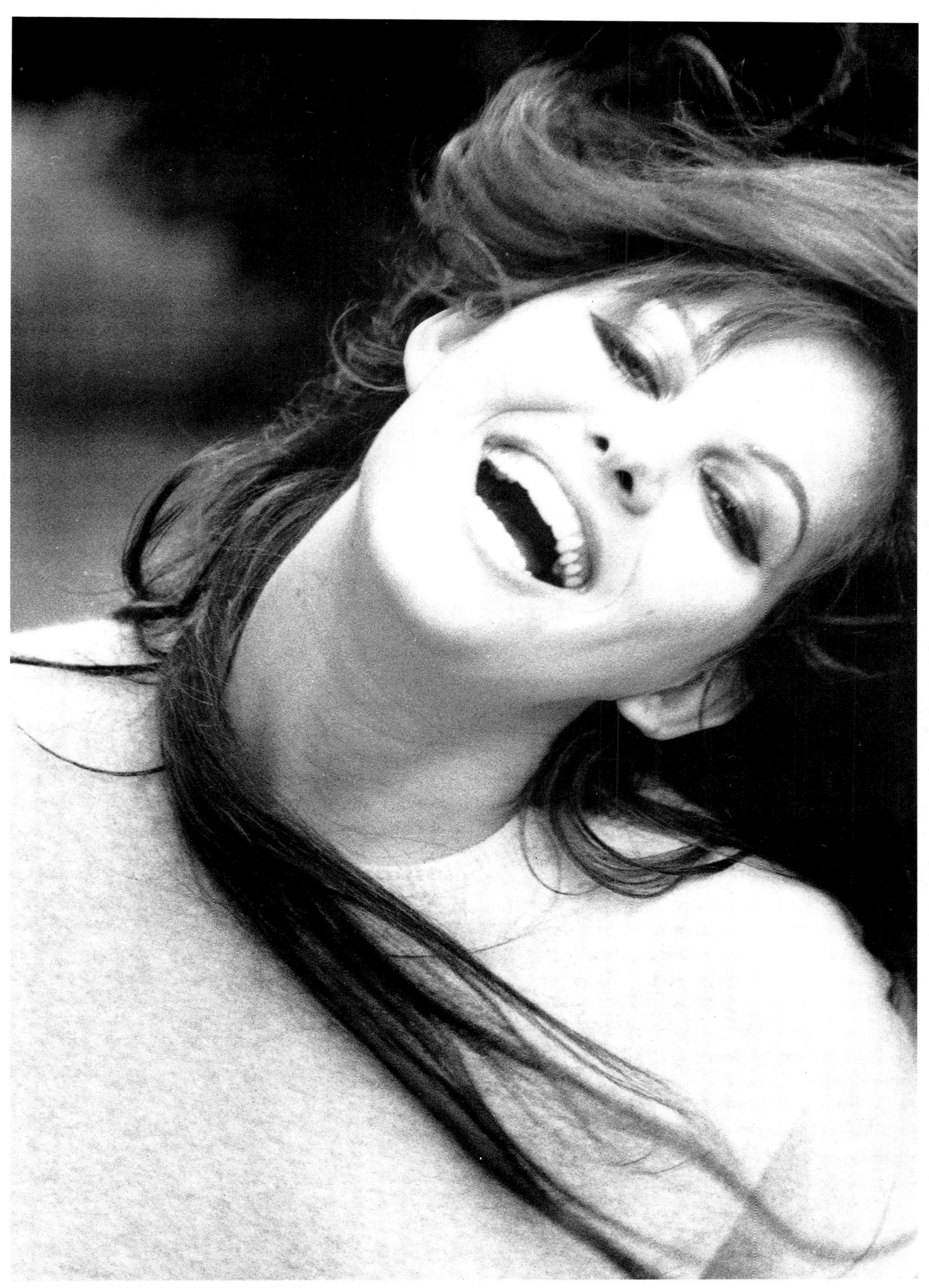

ABOVE *Claudia Cardinale, 1961*
OPPOSITE *Vanessa Redgrave rehearsing for Karel Riesz's film 'Isadora Duncan', 1969*

1970s

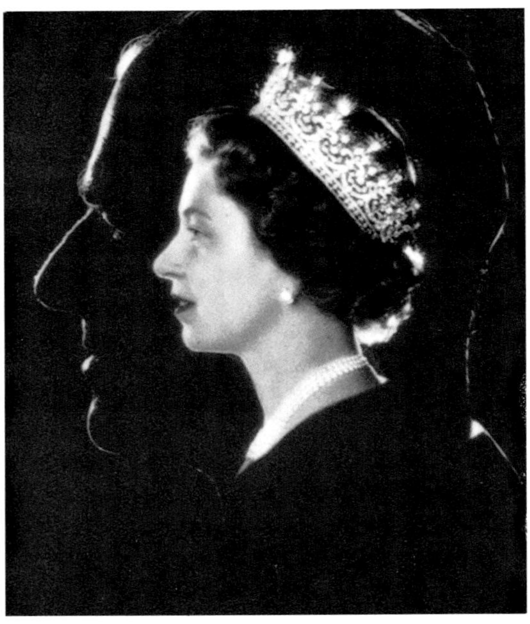

LOOK THIS WAY, YOUR MAJESTY

There are two groups of citizens, other than their close friends, who have the honour, and I say good fortune, to spend various periods of time with Royalty. The first is made up of Equerries, Private Secretaries, Pages, Press Officers, Ladies-in-Waiting and Footmen etc. They might freely be described as 'servants' in one way or another. Members of this group, I understand, certainly in the lower echelon, have to sign something akin to the Official Secrets Act, which makes absolutely certain they can never sit down and write the best seller which would at last take the lid off the goings-on at Buckingham or Kensington Palace.

Since I have met just about all the Royal Family, and my inherent overboard Royalism has only been accentuated by these meetings, my discretion must obviously continue, for I am from the other group. My group might perhaps come into the category of the 'tradesmen' like the dressmakers and the hatmakers and the shoemakers, and perhaps the jewellery cleaners, who spend various spells of time with them. But I must confess I feel particularly unprotected from the media who, after the publication of some new set of pictures, will ring my telephone incessantly. 'How do you get her to look so relaxed?' 'Why is she smiling? What did you say?' 'Do you like the lady?' 'Did you choose the dress?' 'Does she like the photographs? How many did she reject?' 'How many sittings does this portfolio represent?' 'Do you think that she gets on with her sister/mother/aunt/children?' 'Which of them all is your very favourite?' 'Have you ever eaten at their table?' 'What do they eat/drink for breakfast/lunch/tea/dinner?'

But it is rare to find an interview in which the Queen's dressmaker is quoted about her choice of clothes or hats or shoes. Does the Press ask them and they refuse to reveal anything? I have always tried to be polite, and to appear to come clean with the Press without telling them anything – not that there is anything much to tell. But a weekend at Balmoral *en famille* is a fascinating experience; it adds up to an enormous amount of real fun and rip-roaring, thigh-smacking hilarity and mirth, identical to any weekend with an upper, or even lower crust, family. That Royal Family of ours is just a family, forget the Royal bit. Of course, one maintains one's respectful distance (one remembers not to give the Queen a thump of joyful

Queen Elizabeth II and Prince Philip photographed for a postage stamp design, 1977

friendliness on the shoulder, or bite the Duke of Edinburgh in the calf), but the more you join in as a friend the more they relax.

Positively for the first time, but let us hope not for the last, I would like to recall here one of the most enjoyable afternoons that I spent at Buckingham Palace, photographing the Queen and Prince Philip for the Silver Jubilee stamp (certainly not, I should add here, my favourite stamp). It was in 1977 that the Post Office made me a proposition about this stamp and offered me a sum of money for doing it. I did not know whether to accept it or not, for I have never before or since charged any of the Royal Family for any of my many sittings.

The Post Office gentleman and the designer of the stamp and the printer showed me what they hoped to achieve and a day was suggested by the Palace. 'You will get Prince Philip first, for twenty minutes, and subsequently Her Majesty for the same amount of time. We will put the two pictures together. Please take the Queen with and without a crown.' I suggested that the designers should come along, as there was little or no chance of a retake!

As the great day approached, I realized with some alarm that the time set aside for the sitting was the rest period between the official luncheon at the Palace for the State Visit of Emperor Hirohito of Japan and the laying of a wreath on the Unknown Warrior's Tomb at Westminster Abbey.

I had chosen the White Drawing Room for the photography, a very handsome much-gilded room which overlooks the garden in the north east corner of the Palace. Prince Philip was in a very good and chatty mood. He arrived soon after three o'clock and we got him away in his twenty minutes. Then there was a gap. Her Majesty's Private Secretary appeared and announced, 'Mr Parkinson, the Queen will be down in five minutes, she will arrive through this door. Shall I introduce your colleagues or do you wish to handle that yourself?' 'Thank you, don't worry, I will do that myself,' I replied. It was surely the longest five minutes that I have ever endured and I could count my insistent heartbeats. Suddenly there was a frisson, and it was behind us. Quite silently a section of mirrored wall, one of a pair of William Kent occasional tables which supported a large vase containing a great flower decoration including a flush of six-foot delphiniums had, as one unit, turned in a small arc and the Queen had made her entrance. 'Mr Parkinson,' she said, 'you asked for crowns.' 'Thank you, Your Majesty, I would like to introduce ...' At this point I forgot everybody's name, including my assistant's and my own; we were well off balance with all the spinning around. I have a sneaking suspicion that the Royals rather enjoy entering from unexpected and unannounced doorways – Princess Anne has done it a couple of times – and it becomes a most disarming party game. You never know quite where they are coming from! The Secretary, viewing my plight, made the introductions after all. The Queen stood there smiling over a pile of crowns that she had very informally placed one upon the other in an old cardboard box. It was like the Tower of Pisa thrown up in some diamond dream.

We made a lot of progress photographically in the first ten minutes and I was hopeful of getting the lady away on time. At this point I became aware, again behind me, of a rush of air and a crescendo of hideous noise. The Queen started to shout, barely audible above the din, 'It's Charles, Mr Parkinson, in his helicopter; I keep asking him not to do this, but he enjoys landing so close – less far for him to walk, I suppose.' The plain background had blown over, the heavy velvet curtains were almost horizontal into the room, and as I fought with them I noticed that the magnificent flower decorations were taking even worse punishment. Mercifully the helicopter was soon down and the noise extinguished and on we went with a change of crowns and some adjustments to the windblown hair. Around about the half hour I was finished and made my bow. But the Queen did not seem to want to leave. 'Your Majesty, I have just been working on the Seychelles and I understand you are shortly to visit Mahé to give it its Independence.' 'Yes, that's right, what is it like?' 'Well, Ma'am, Government House, where you will be staying, is charming and the Governor so pleasant. There is a private cemetery in the grounds in which all the previous Governors are buried, including one who found it very convenient to change his nationality overnight from French to English.' 'Oh, dear, I hate haunted places, is it haunted?' 'Not to my knowledge, Ma'am, the Governor didn't mention that.' 'What is the Governor's name?' 'Sir Hugh Greatbatch, Ma'am.' 'What a wonderful name! Mr Parkinson, do you think we choose the names rather than the men to send to these places? . . . So, you think we will like it at Government House?' 'Yes, Ma'am, I'm sure you will but Sir Hugh is very worried.' 'Worried? About what?' 'Well, Ma'am, he confided in me that he has been having terrible trouble with the drains!' There are moments that one should have a camera, and one never does, and this, of course, was one of them. The Queen exploded into a roar, a peal, of laughter that some Pressmen are lucky enough just once in a while to catch. She has a glorious laugh, and I was fortunate not only to have experienced it so intimately, but also to have promoted it. I glanced out of the window, for London seemed to have become very quiet. The Mall was empty, no traffic was moving. A large posse of Household Cavalry was drawing up nearby, several landaus were empty and waiting, and I could see Prince Philip and the Emperor of Japan pacing slowly up and down. It was then that I remembered the wreath at Westminster Abbey. 'I must not detain you any longer, Your Majesty.' I held out my hand and made my bow again and this time she moved away towards the door that she should have come in by.

I trust that the following epilogue to this story will not be considered too prideful: just occasionally, when I am depressed and feel that I am a filthy rotten failure, I think back to that afternoon when half of London had been brought to a standstill, and every second that the Queen of England continued to chat to me the traffic got worse and so did the tempers of the drivers trying to get home.

I hope that is a permissible reminiscence.

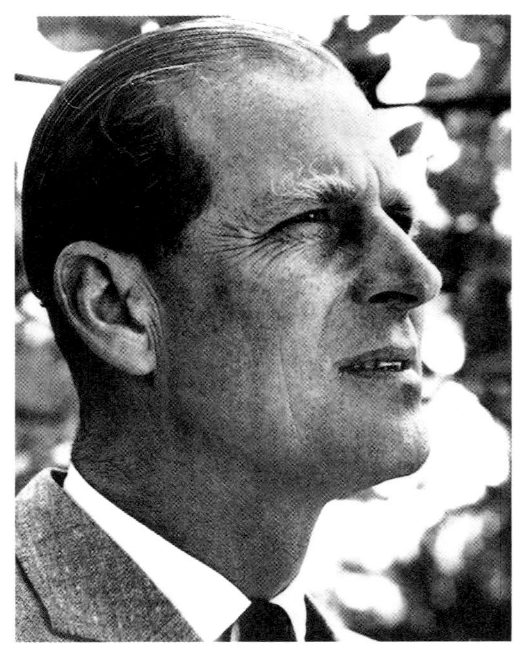

BRITANNIA RULES

One of the earlier occasions that I had had the honour of photographing a member of the Royal Family was when I was working for *Vogue* in the mid sixties.

A cable came into Tobago from New York. Tobago is a developing country so we have been waiting for our telephone for twenty years. 'You'll be much happier without it', is what they tell me at the telephone office. So the cable man rode nine and a half miles on his little motorbike over the bumpy roads to deliver it – and was rewarded with a dollar and a cold Guinness. From his countenance the message had to be read immediately; it went something like this: 'Britannia arrives Port of Spain dawn Wednesday please contact Press Secretary on board Richard Colville making mutually convenient sitting time for Prince Philip during two day Tobago visit at weekend.' A new picture of Prince Philip was required to be used in American *Vogue* and elsewhere on the West Coast of America for he was to visit Los Angeles after his Caribbean cruise on a fund-raising tour for charity.

From the roof of the Hilton I watched the pre-breakfast arrival of the Britannia. Once you have seen the ship it is easy to recognize its three high and equidistant masts from which three oversize and different standards are flown. I was able to contact Richard Colville on the telephone later and mercifully he had been fully alerted about the sitting. He suggested that a plan must be devised to get me into the Royal Security Area where the Royal party was taking its luncheon without making the vast Press Corps aware of the special privilege being accorded me. 'Tricky,' he added, 'but we will manage it. See you on the Docks in Tobago and we'll take it from there.'

OPPOSITE *Princess Anne riding in Windsor Great Park, 1969*
ABOVE *Prince Philip, Duke of Edinburgh, Tobago, 1966*

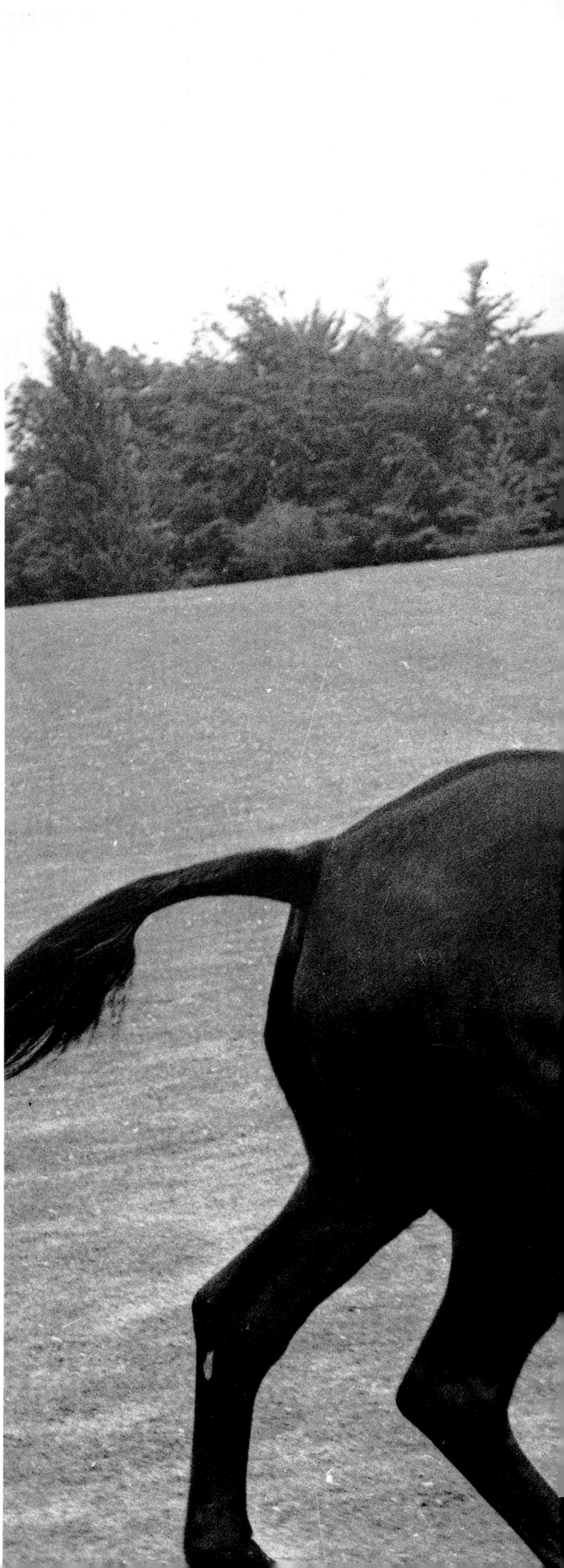

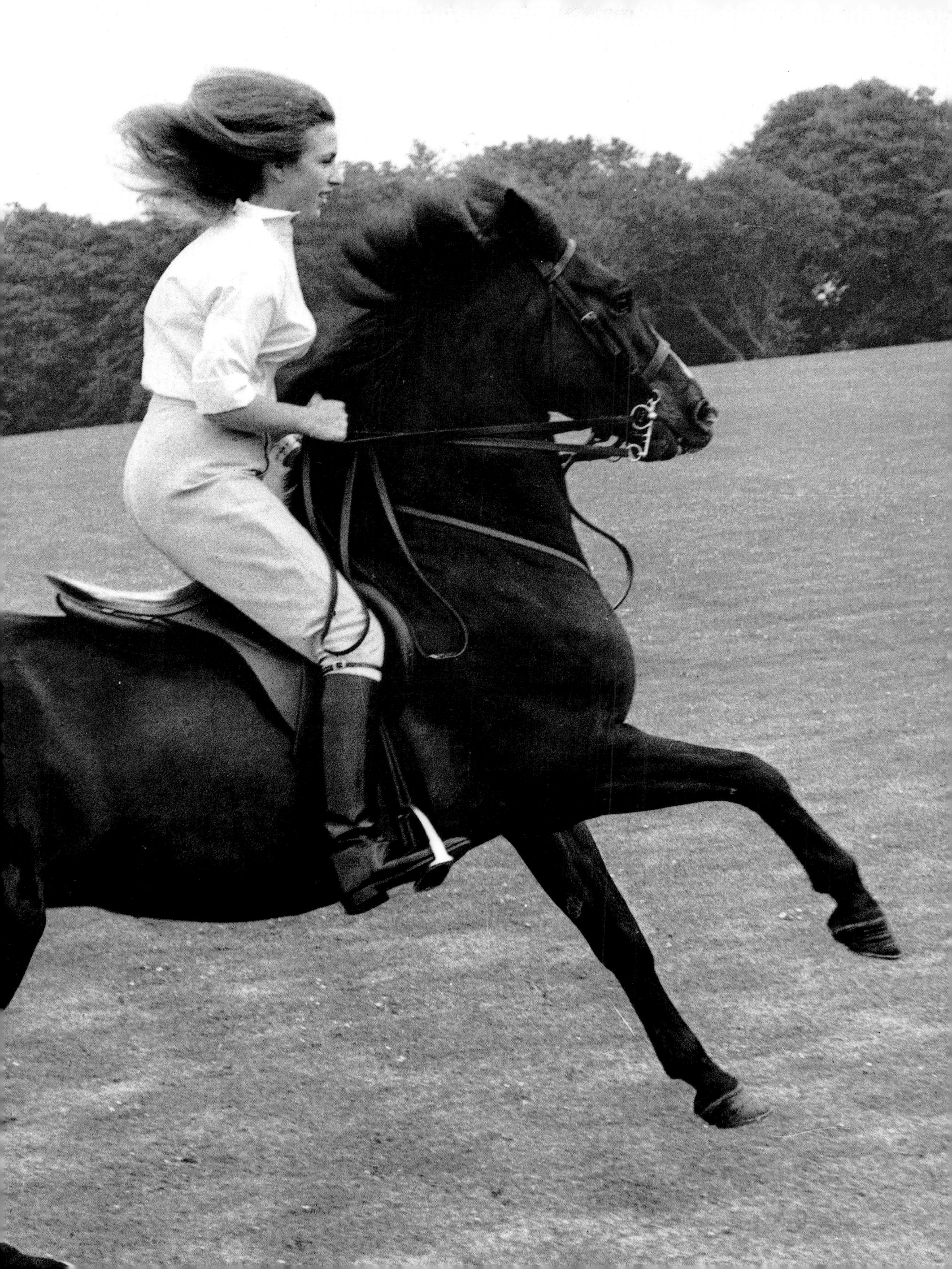

The Britannia anchored outside Scarborough harbour at 9 am, in a heavy swell. The Queen and Prince Philip came ashore in a suitably fine barge, the Queen looking pale against the acres of red, white and blue bunting which practically covered the landing area. Two moderately posh and overpolished open cars had been commandeered for the Tobago Royal Procession; sitting up in the second was Richard Colville. I pushed through the scatter of a crowd and walking alongside the car I introduced myself. 'Parkinson, get yourself to Crown Point Hotel Foyer with your cameras and your stringer at 11 am – merge into the curtains, and we will take care of the rest.' As I pushed my way back through the cheering crowds, I was repeating to myself, 'Merge into the curtains? Was that what he had said . . . me, a 6ft 5in merger?' Well orders is orders. So at 11 am on the dot, with two heavy camera cases, I was most effectively merged into some fairly unattractive brown, damp smelling drapes. (My stringer, Noel Norton, a Trinidad friend and photographer, had been advised where to meet me later.) Half-hidden there I observed, at first hand, a Royal Progress that must have been much in the manner of Elizabeth the First, except nobody was in ruffles or doublets or mounted on palfreys, and to be sure not a wimple was in sight. They came in reverse order of seniority in rather dull tropical suiting from Gieves and in frocks made in fabric from Liberty's. First came the Press Corps, chattering and sweaty in the unaccustomed heat, and a brigade of photographers, then the tour organizers, security men, and uniformed elements of the Trinidad and Tobago Police Force, then the Equerries and Ladies-in-Waiting, and finally, after a shortish gap, the Royal Couple. So complete was the effectiveness of my camouflage that for a moment I had an uncanny feeling that I might have overdone it. About half a minute after the Queen had passed, I became aware of an imposing male person standing quite still and looking straight to his front out to sea (this, I was soon to learn, was his wont). He started to speak with his lips pouting to the left to convey a message more clearly to me in the curtain. 'You are Mr Parkinson, correct? I am Surgeon Vice Admiral Sir Derek Steele-Perkins, medical officer to the Queen. Pick up your cameras and follow me at ten paces.' He then took off in the direction of the departing procession as if he was pacing some extensive quarter-deck. Seizing my sixty pounds of camera cases, I counted to ten and took off in his wake. My naval commander continued to look neither to right nor left. Then he lifted his right hand and was speaking again. 'Bend down and move along the building down that path, and when you arrive at the wall, jump it. I will meet you on the other side.'

With Herculean intent I succeeded in climbing the formidable wall at first attempt and, still clinging to my cameras, I jumped down on the other side into the arms of my good friend, the Superintendent of Tobago Police, John Grell. 'Parkinson,' he shouted, 'What the Hell are you doing? I arrest you here and now; the area that you have entered is of the highest security.' My mouth opened and shut and nothing came out. To my relief, I saw the Surgeon Vice Admiral approaching. 'It is quite all right,' he said to John Grell, 'I am looking after Mr Parkinson'. Superintendent Grell was not impressed: 'And who are you, might I ask?' he demanded from the Vice Admiral. But eventually he was satisfied and he handed over his prisoner to the plain clothes Admiral with the discreet crown on his buttonhole who continued his directions: 'Keep bending double behind this hedge and follow it down there for fifty yards; you will then be in the area where Her Majesty will be taking lunch. Richard Colville will meet you.'

It all worked perfectly. Richard Colville was waiting, and as the admiral arrived from another direction, Colville turned to him saying, 'Absolutely perfect, Derek, you managed to get Parkinson in right on the dot without any of the Press knowing. Have some refreshments, Parkinson, Prince Philip will be ready for you in ten minutes.' While I was munching on a sandwich the Admiral found Noel Norton and also managed to get him in without raising any suspicion.

I chose to meet Prince Philip under a small almond tree where I had placed a chair. The sunlight was particularly unglaring so I had forewarned Noel that I would be using the 35 mm Nikons. All were loaded and at the ready. So there we were, under this umbrella of a tree, the seated Prince and, at his feet on the grass, two acolytes. The charm, or otherwise, of this group must have caught the Queen's keen movie-making eye for she approached with whirring camera to get it all down. I was on my third or fourth roll of film, and with my free eye (you can only use one on a camera), I was watching the Monarch herself zooming in on the squatting Parkinson. In about twelve minutes I was reasonably happy that our mission had been successfully accomplished, and I stood up to leave. The Queen, still holding her camera, was now by Prince

Prince Andrew, 1978

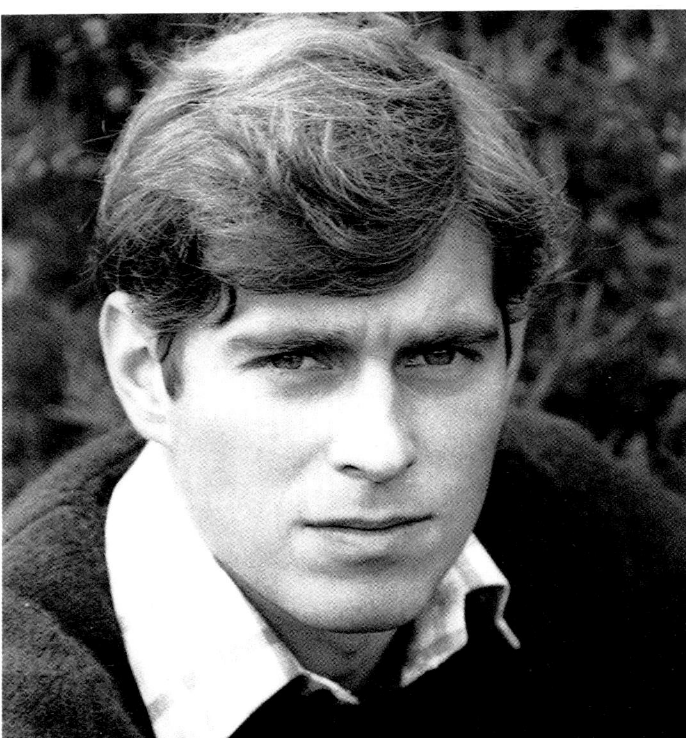

Philip's side; he turned to shake my hand, 'Thank you very much Mr Parkinson, history was made today.' 'Really, Sir, how was that?' 'Well, you are the first photographer who has ever trodden on me.' 'Oh Sir, I am very sorry, I was not aware that I had done so.' 'Mr Parkinson, lift your left foot.' And there, in the grass under my foot, was an exposed roll that Noel Norton in his nervous over-efficiency had dropped on the ground and forgotten. I shook the Prince's hand again and thanked him for being so observant, but it was the Queen's comment that I have been wondering about ever since . . . 'Oh Philip, did they break the plates?'

I shall probably end up in the Tower for giving my hypothetical explanation but here it is. I served my apprenticeship as an assistant to, and behind the camera of, Richard Speaight who by considerable coincidence photographed many times the Duke and Duchess of York and their daughters (the present Queen and Princess Margaret). Speaight used glass plates in those days. Time was often limited as it is still limited for Royal sittings. Because of the heavy unwieldy equipment of fifty years ago the success of the photography with slow film and lumbering lenses was very much in the lap of the gods. I remember Speaight once lifting eight or ten glass plates out of the hypo after processing and discovering that he had, perhaps as he had anticipated, not one single shot with everybody in the family group still. I remember he held his head in frustration. 'For goodness sake! I don't have even one sharp picture to take back for their approval. I'll have to telephone the Secretary for another opportunity. I'll have to tell him the plates have been dropped.' I imagined that a week later a Royal Nanny might be persuading Lady Elizabeth back into her party dress; and to her charge's queries about why the photograph had to be retaken, she might have replied: 'You have to pose again with Mummy and Daddy. The assistant dropped the plates.'

Princess Margaret, 1978

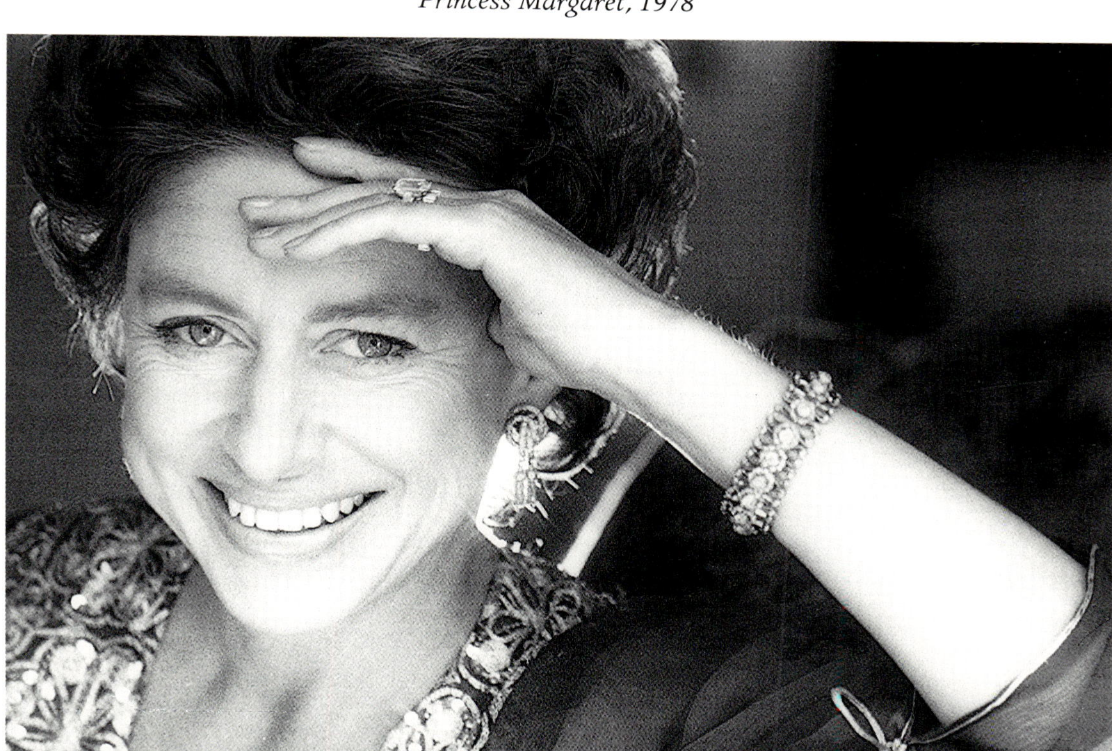

ROYAL BLUE TRINITY

Apart from the various photographs, formal and informal, which would be required for publication on 4 August to celebrate the Queen Mother's eightieth birthday in 1980, it seemed to me imperative that, if possible, this wonderful lady should be photographed with her two daughters. I proposed the idea and information was passed back to me that the three ladies would be available before lunch and after church one Sunday in June at the Royal Lodge, Windsor.

I had two or three weeks to think about this picture and plan it. I hazarded a guess that the three ladies would present themselves to my camera in *eau de nil* silk, pink shantung and a polka dot dress. It is always the fashion that dates an important portrait and frustrates its historic acceptance.

I was in New York and, with the help of the fabric editor of *Town and Country*, I bought a ten-metre remainder of a heavy royal blue satin. In London, ignorant of the invasion

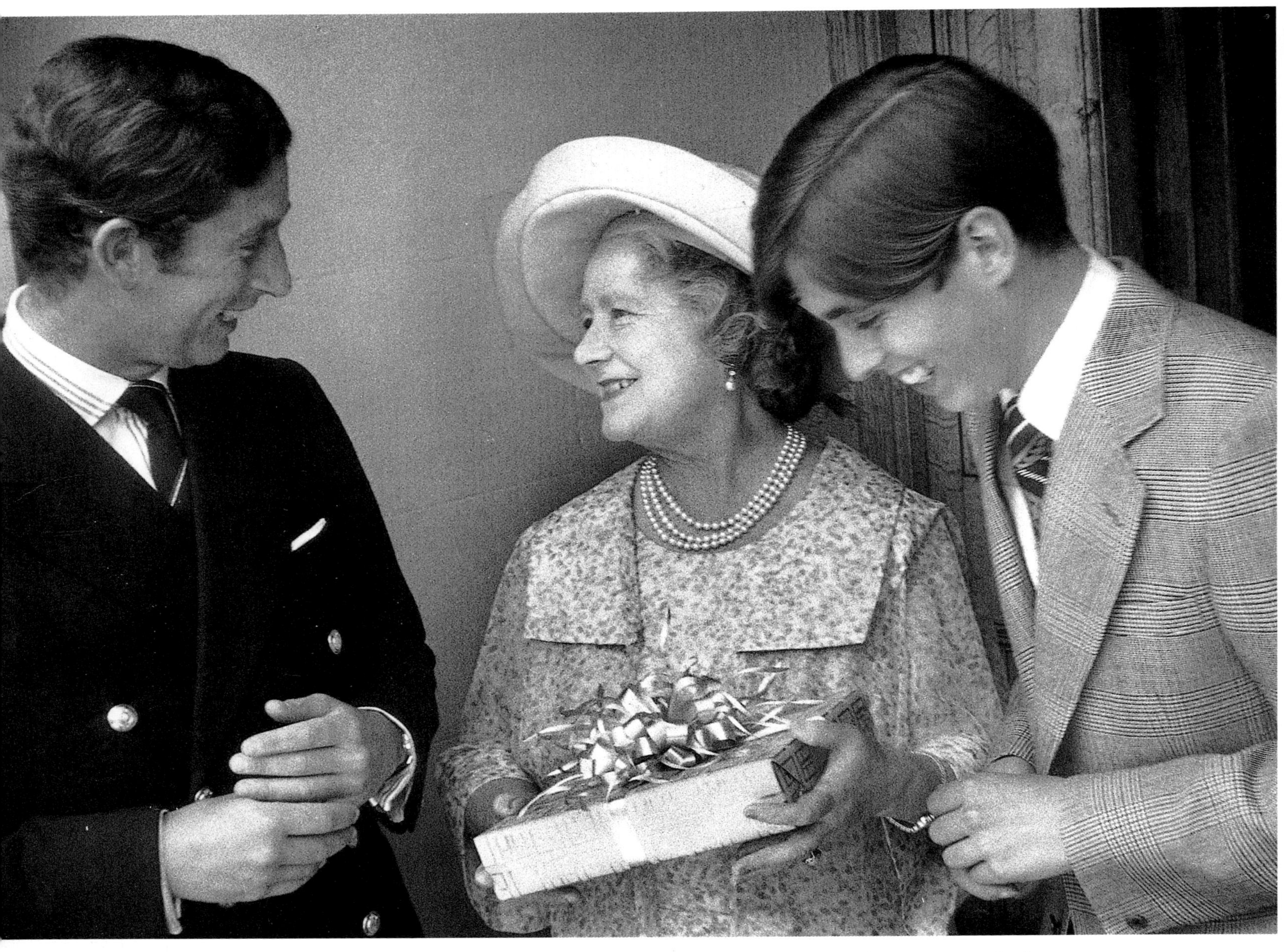

Queen Elizabeth The Queen Mother receiving presents from two grandsons, Prince Charles and Prince Andrew, on her seventy-fifth birthday at the Royal Lodge, Windsor, 1975

of the Iranian Embassy in Palace Gate by armed gunmen, I attempted to force my way into the nearby Royal College of Needlework through the police cordon, who were singularly unhelpful despite my protestations. I did eventually gain entrance and the needlework ladies were most considerate as they prepared to evacuate the building, and suggested something I should have thought of myself: 'Surely this is something that Hardy Amies could help you with – we only do the Royal embroidery here.'

I called Hardy who was on holiday in the country. 'Lovely idea, Parks,' he responded. 'Three capelets with one button at the back? We'd love to do it for you since you have brought the satin. Go and see Miss Lillian in the workroom in Savile Row.'

One week later I picked up three beautifully made abbreviated capes trimmed with tiny red piping, each on its own hanger in Hardy's elegant plastic bags emblazoned with the 'By appointment' Royal crest.

The historic noontime Sunday arrived and we were all set up, cameras at the ready, in the saloon of Royal Lodge, Windsor. The three plastic bags were ostentatiously arranged on an armchair that all had to pass to get to the location of the photography. My anticipation of what the ladies would be wearing for this group picture was, give or take a dot or two, absolutely correct. Everybody was in great heart and, unless my sensibilities were out of register, a good time seemed to be had by all. We worked away on the terrace outside the saloon without any comment on the different colours and styles of the ladies' dresses, and excellent pictures were taken.

I had telephoned Princess Margaret earlier as I believed she would be an ally in my plan and, on cue as we walked

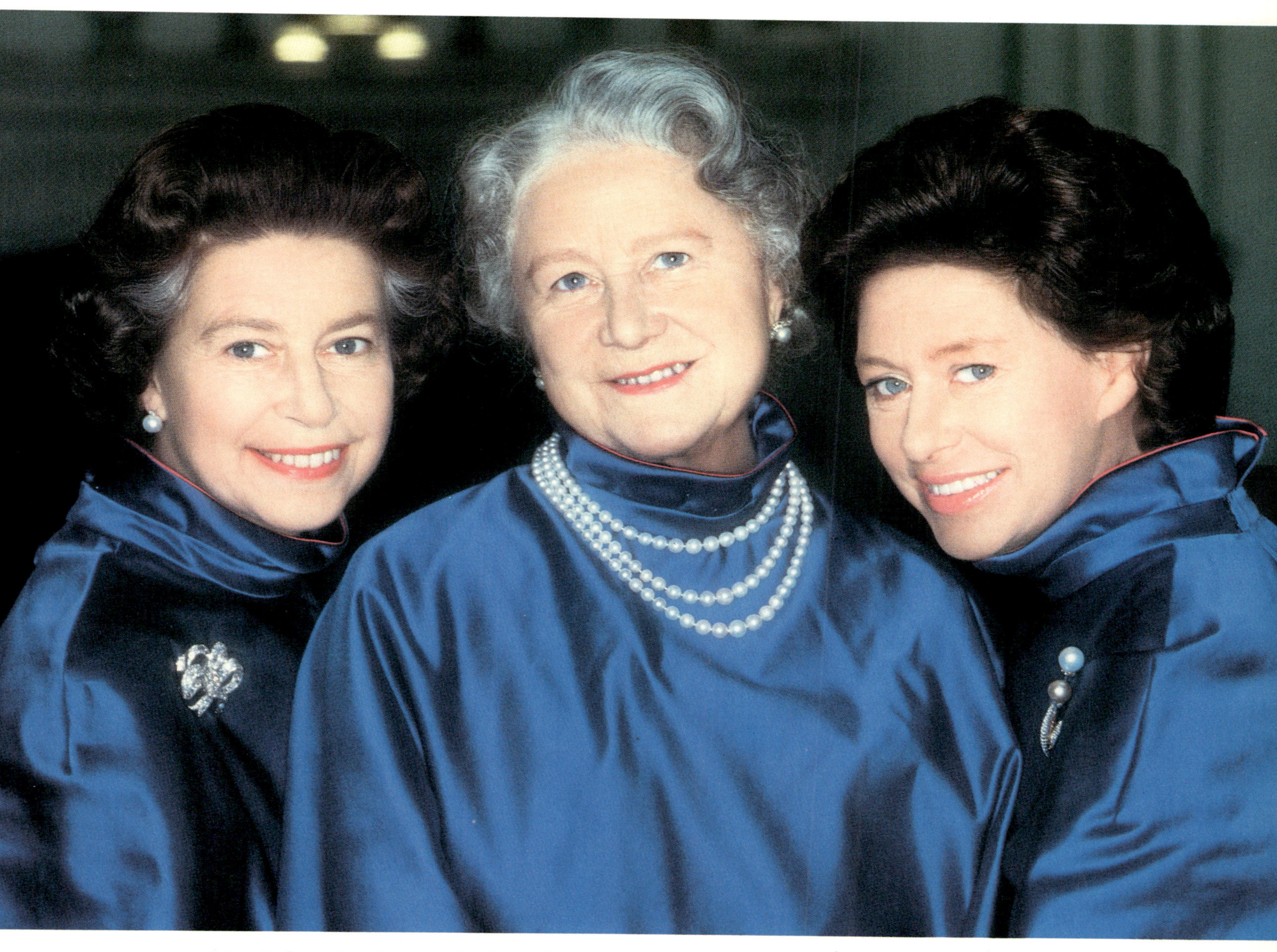

'Royal Blue Trinity' Queen Elizabeth The Queen Mother with her two daughters, Queen Elizabeth and Princess Margaret, an official eightieth birthday photograph, 1980

back into the saloon, she stopped by the capes and asked, 'And what are these, Parks?' 'Well, Ma'am, I asked Hardy Amies to make three Royal capelets which button up at the back, and if you are prepared to be photographed in them, I feel it may make a timeless, fashion-free picture which will ensure its place of importance in the future.' 'What a good idea,' she replied. 'Come on, let's try them on.' I am one quarter Italian – not enough to have picked up my camera and used it, as the paparazzi would have done with delight, as the three ladies buttoned each other into the capes. Just in case they felt unsure of my idea, I reassured them that the pictures could always be thrown out when I presented them for the Royal veto.

The Queen Mother felt particularly happy about her new garment, lifting her strings of famous pearls over the royal blue satin. 'How's that?' she said, turning to her younger daughter, 'You should take off your pearl brooch and pin it by your left shoulder if you are going to be on that side. All right, Mr Parkinson, here we go . . .'

During the sitting I was issuing instructions, trying to get the best picture – 'Ma'am a little this way. Ma'am come forward two inches. Ma'am chin up just a fraction to balance the picture' – when Princess Margaret really put me in my place: 'Listen, Parks, it's absolutely no use, you Ma'aming us like this, because we haven't the slightest idea who you're referring to – you see, we're all Ma'ams!' At which point everybody collapsed with laughter and the pictures were done.

'Goodbye, Mr Parkinson, thank you for everything. Don't leave your nice capes behind.' 'Your Majesty,' I replied to the Queen Mother, 'those capes will never leave here – you can always use them for gardening.'

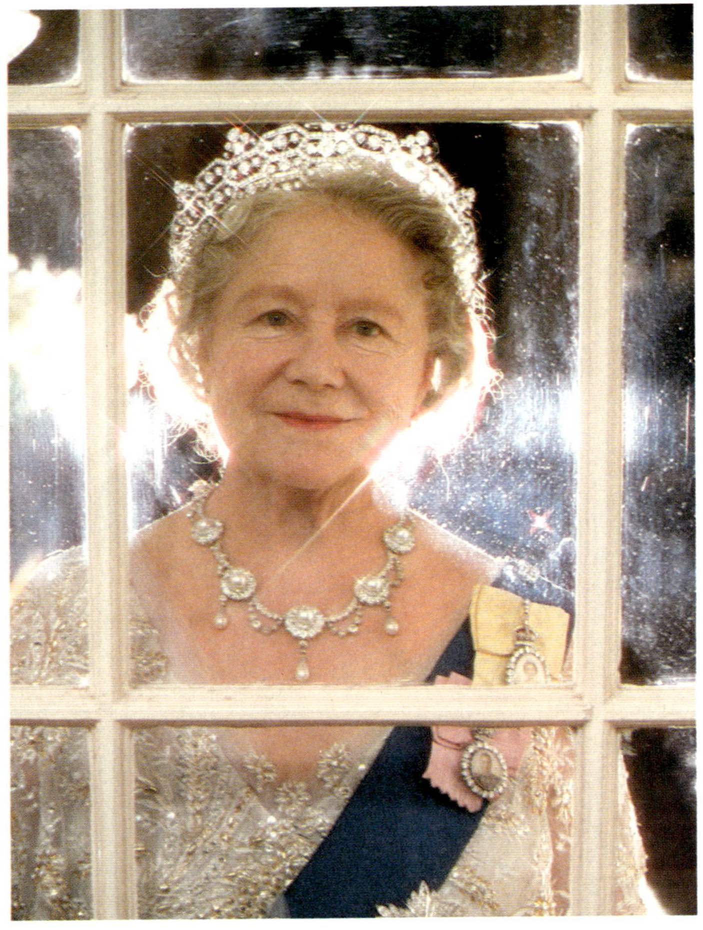

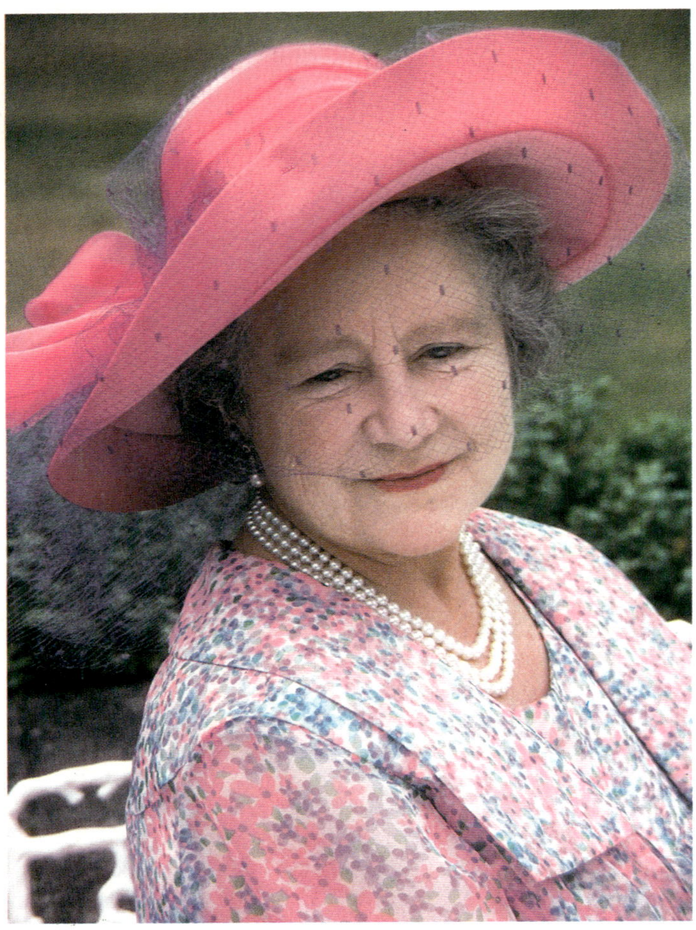

ABOVE LEFT AND RIGHT *Queen Elizabeth The Queen Mother, official eightieth birthday photographs, 1980*
LEFT *Queen Elizabeth The Queen Mother at the Royal Lodge, Windsor, an official seventy-fifth birthday photograph, 1975*

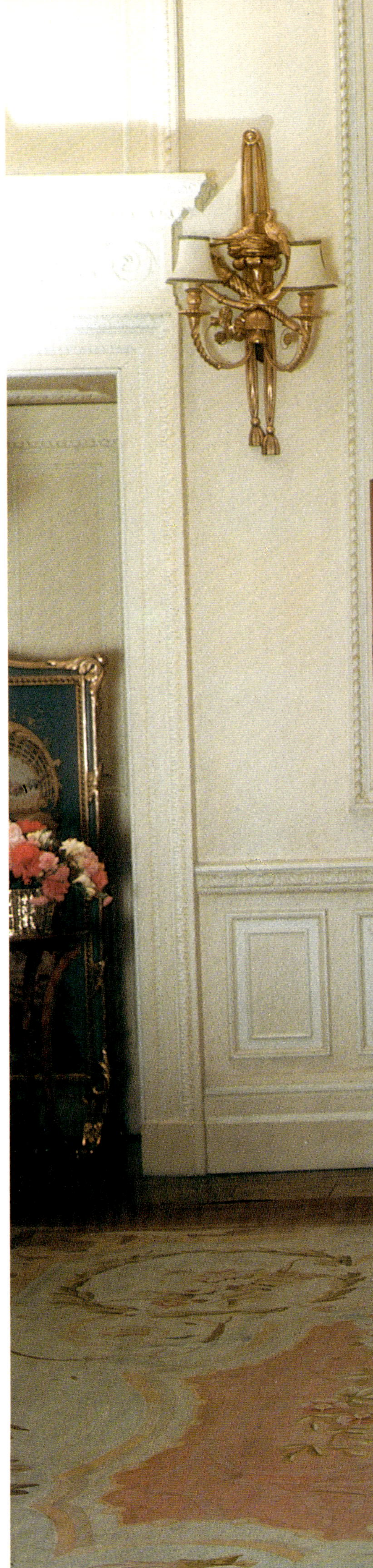

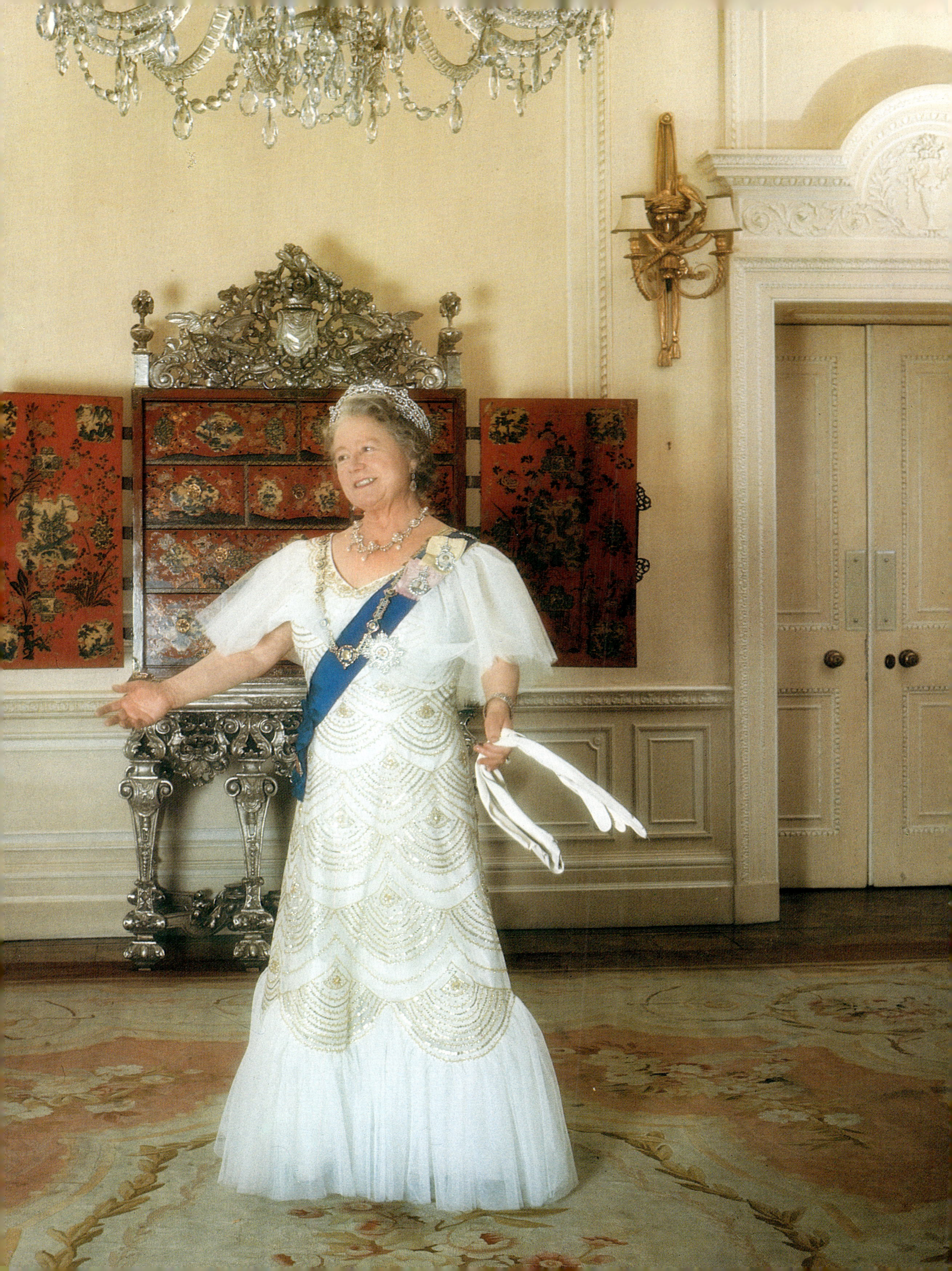

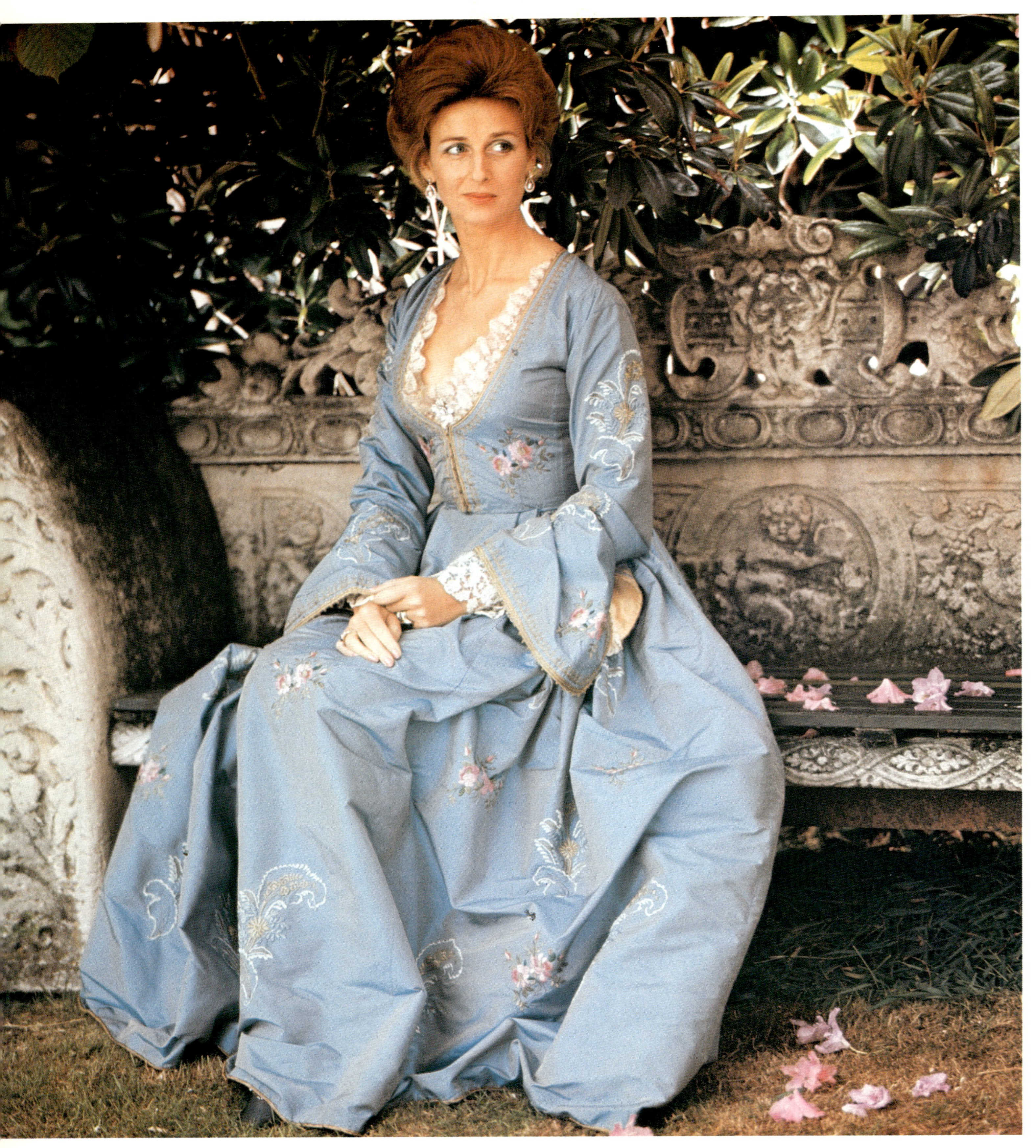

Princess Alexandra wearing an eighteenth-century dress once owned by her mother, Princess Marina, 1972

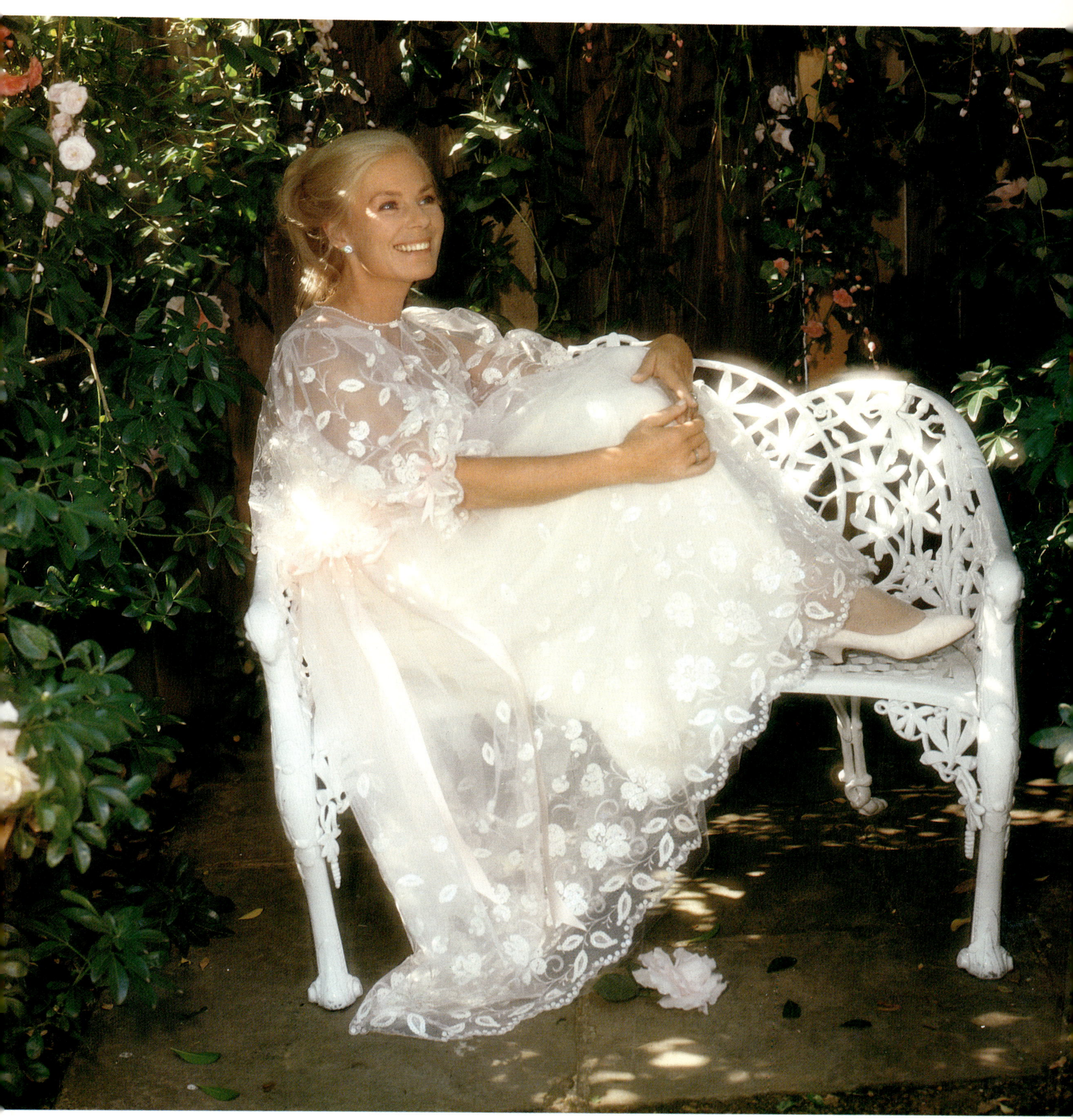

The Duchess of Kent wearing a dress designed by the Emanuels, 1982

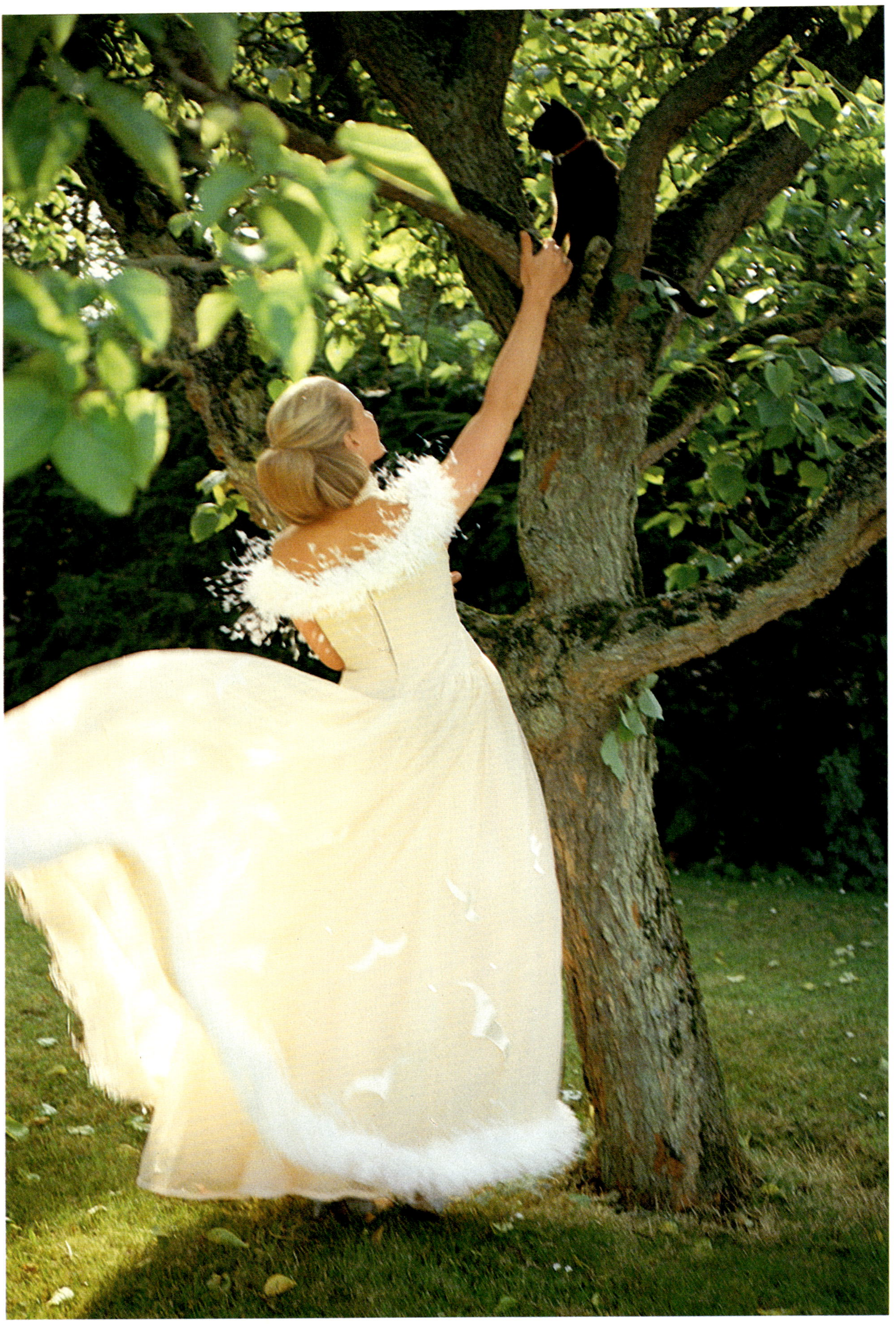

ABOVE *Princess Michael of Kent, 1981*
OPPOSITE *Princess Anne wearing a diamond tiara, necklace and earrings and her diamond and sapphire engagement ring, 1973*

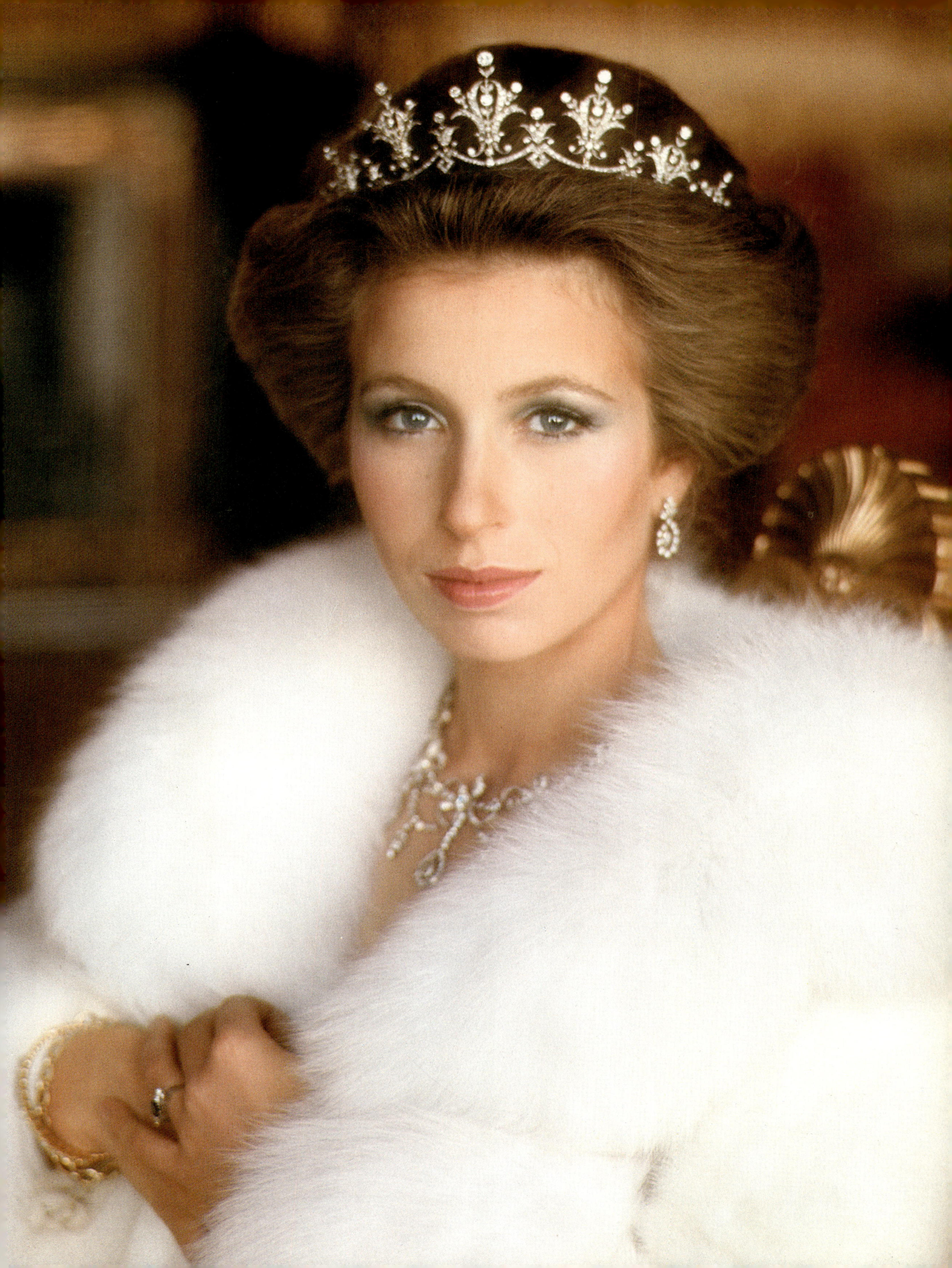

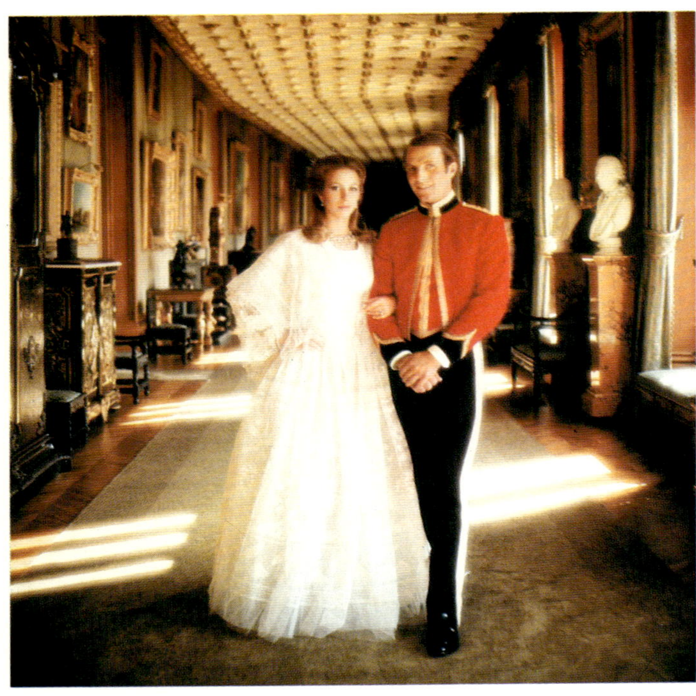

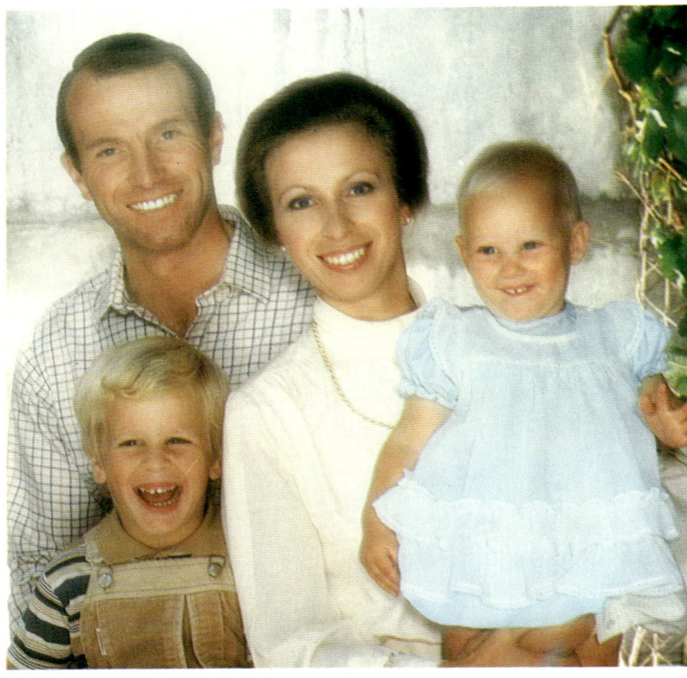

TOP *Princess Anne and Captain Mark Phillips in the Long Gallery, Windsor Castle, one of the official engagement photographs, 1973*
ABOVE *Princess Anne and Captain Mark Phillips with their two children, Peter and Zara, at Gatcombe Park, 1982*
RIGHT *Princess Anne's wedding group, 1973*

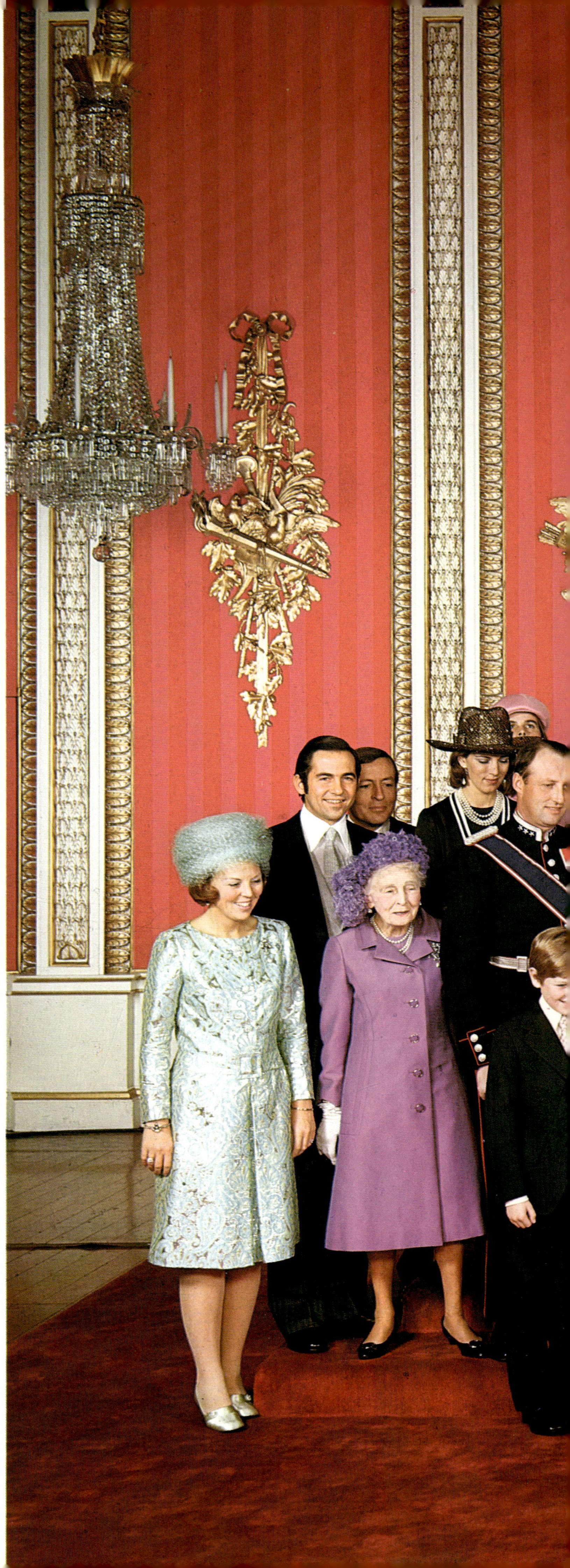

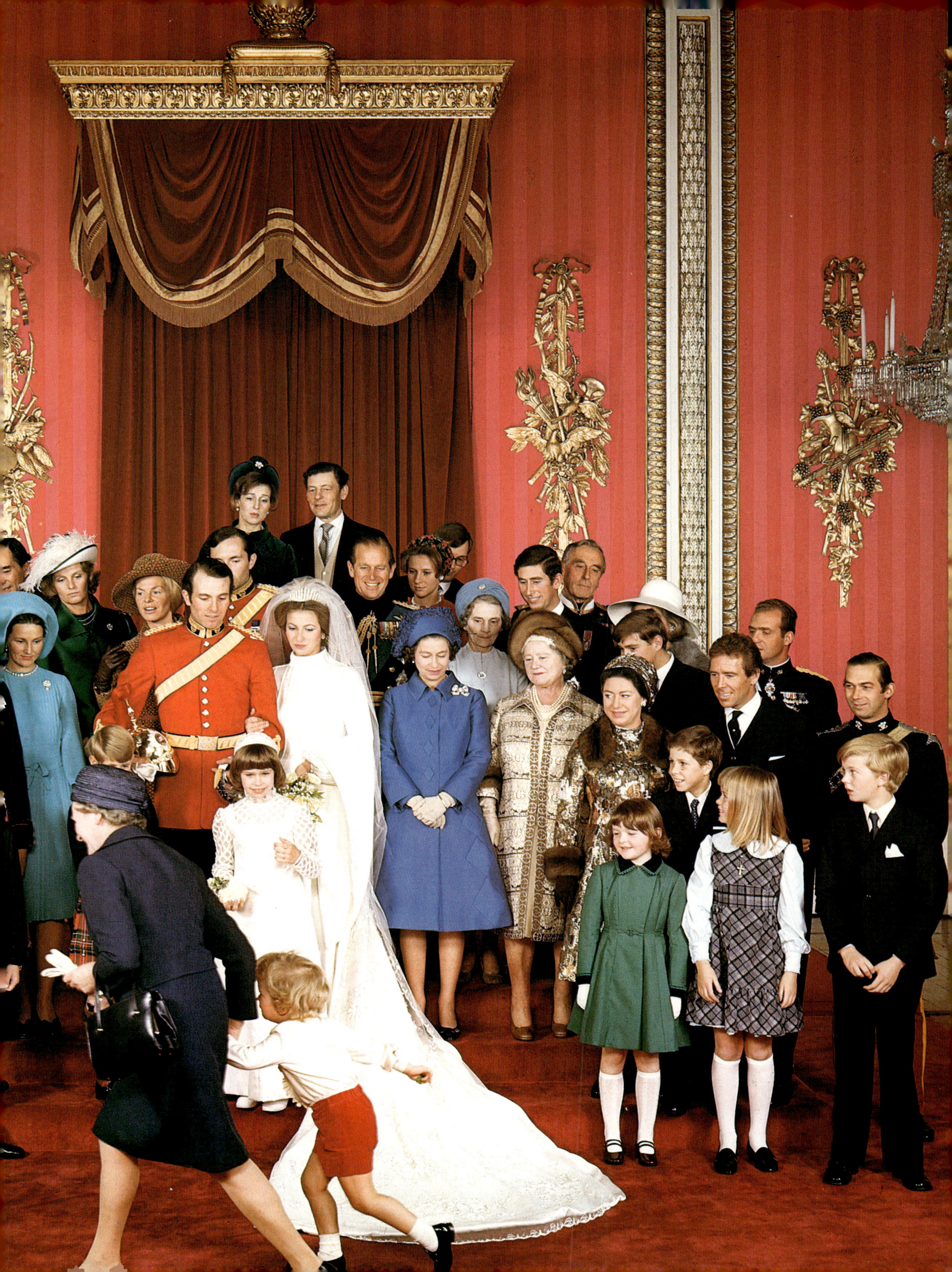

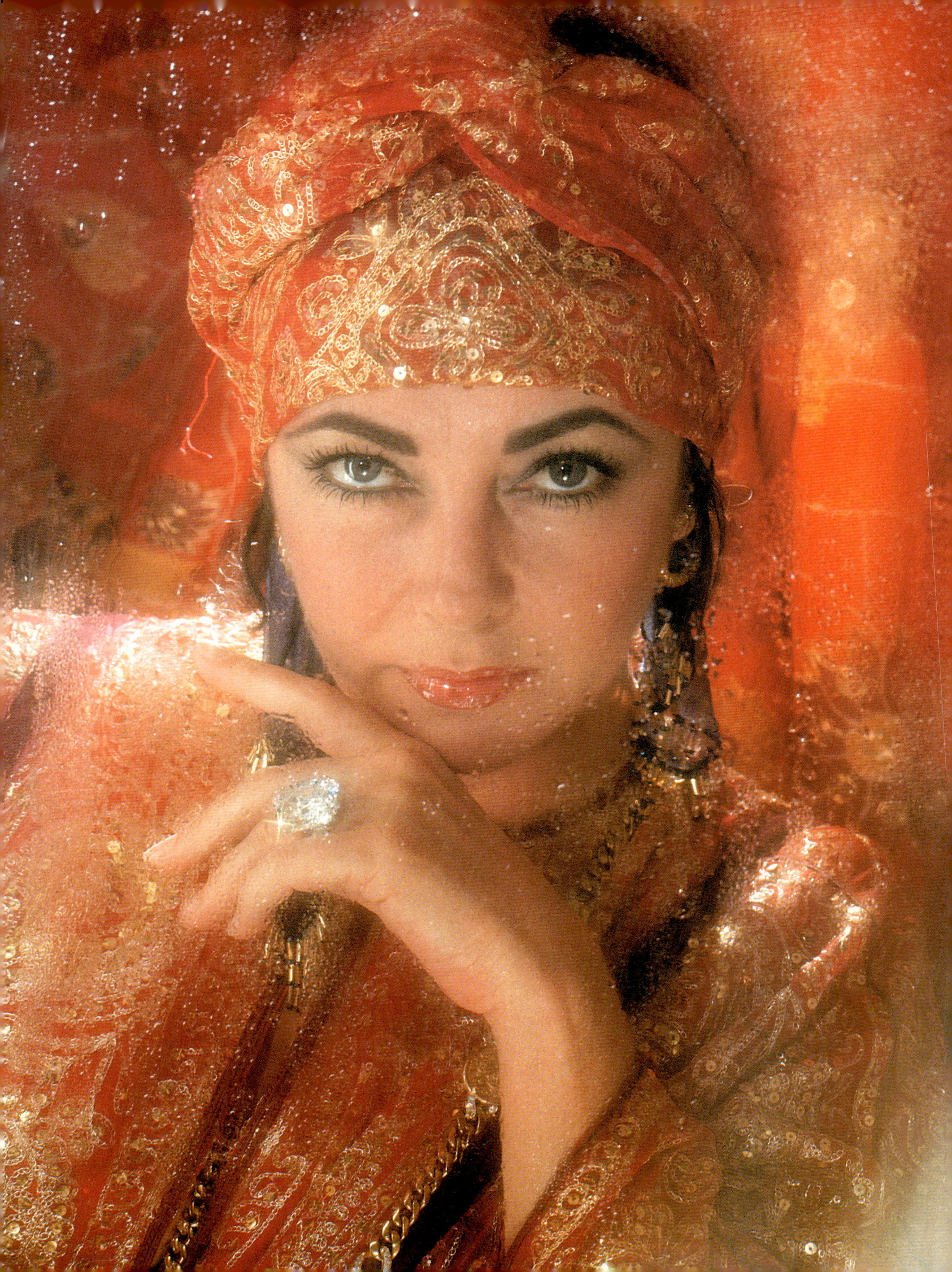

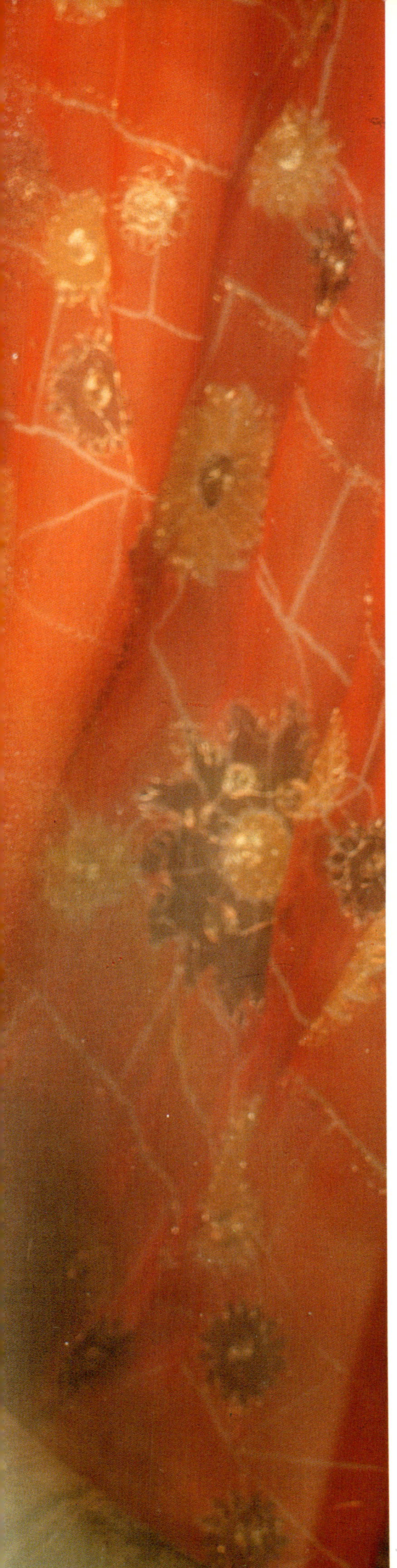

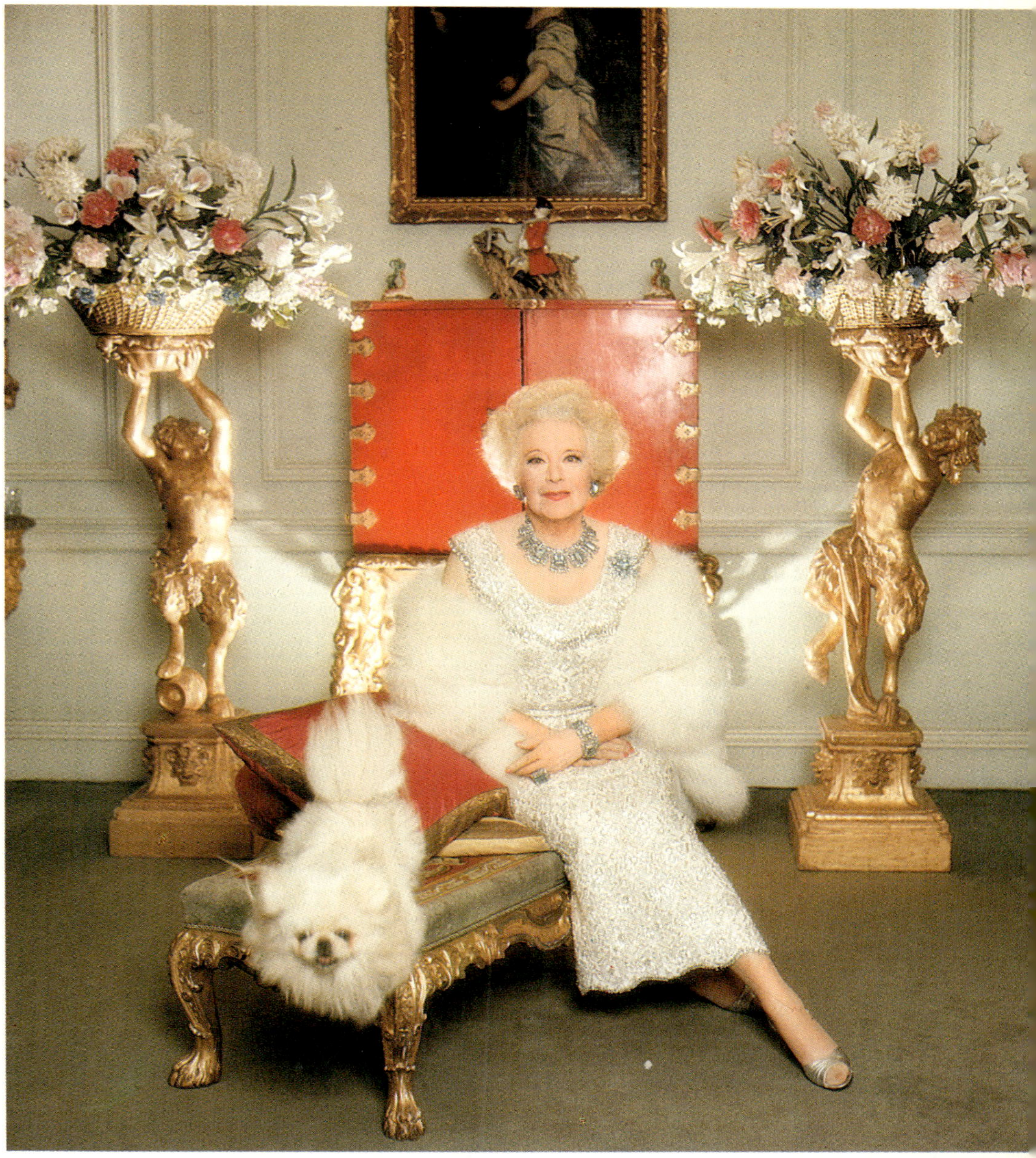

ABOVE *Barbara Cartland with Twi Twi, 1977*
LEFT *Elizabeth Taylor in Vienna during the filming of 'A Little Night Music', 1977*

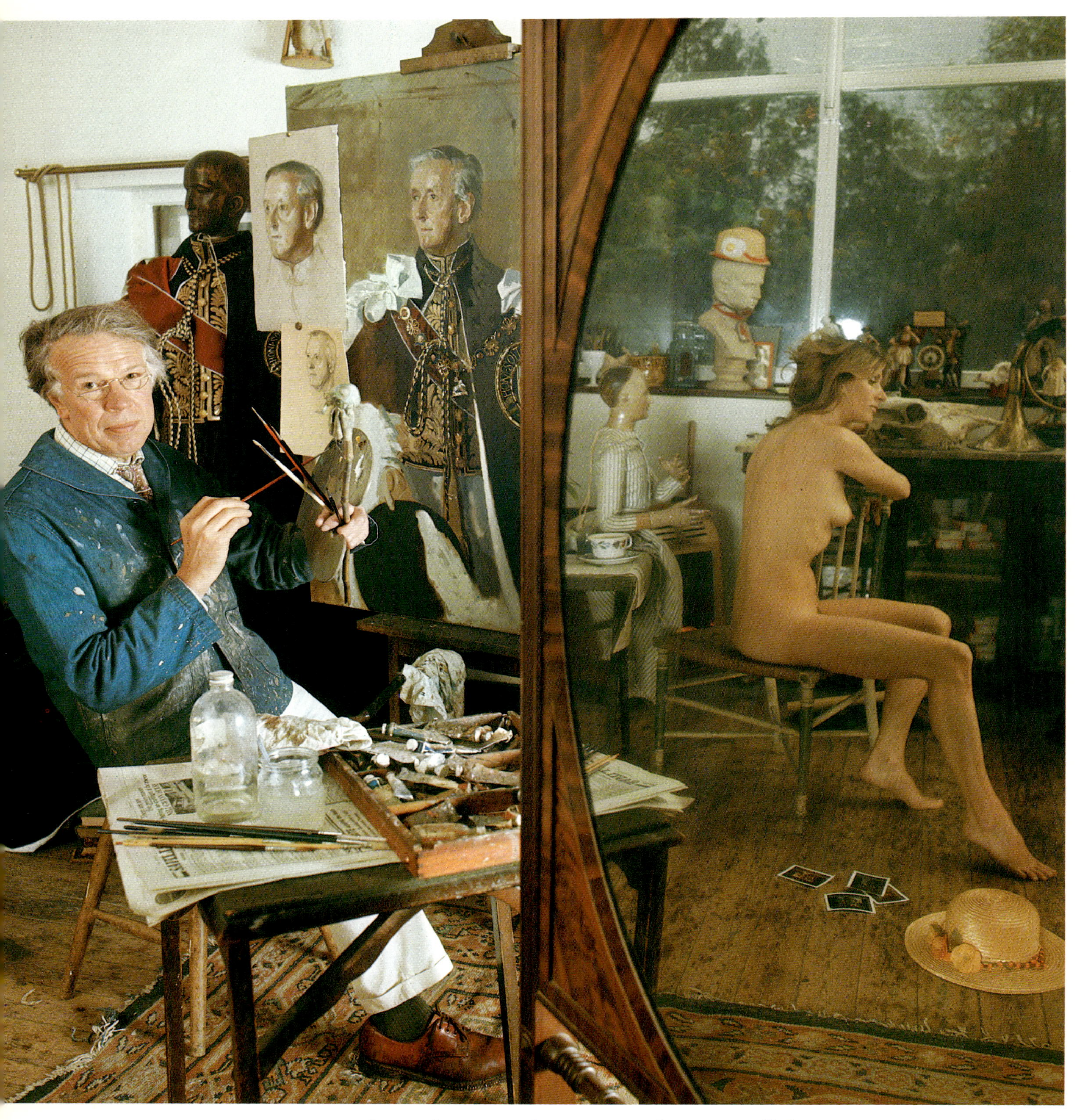

ABOVE *John Ward,* RA, *at work on a portrait of Viscount De l'Isle, 1975*
OPPOSITE *John Piper in his garden, 1976*

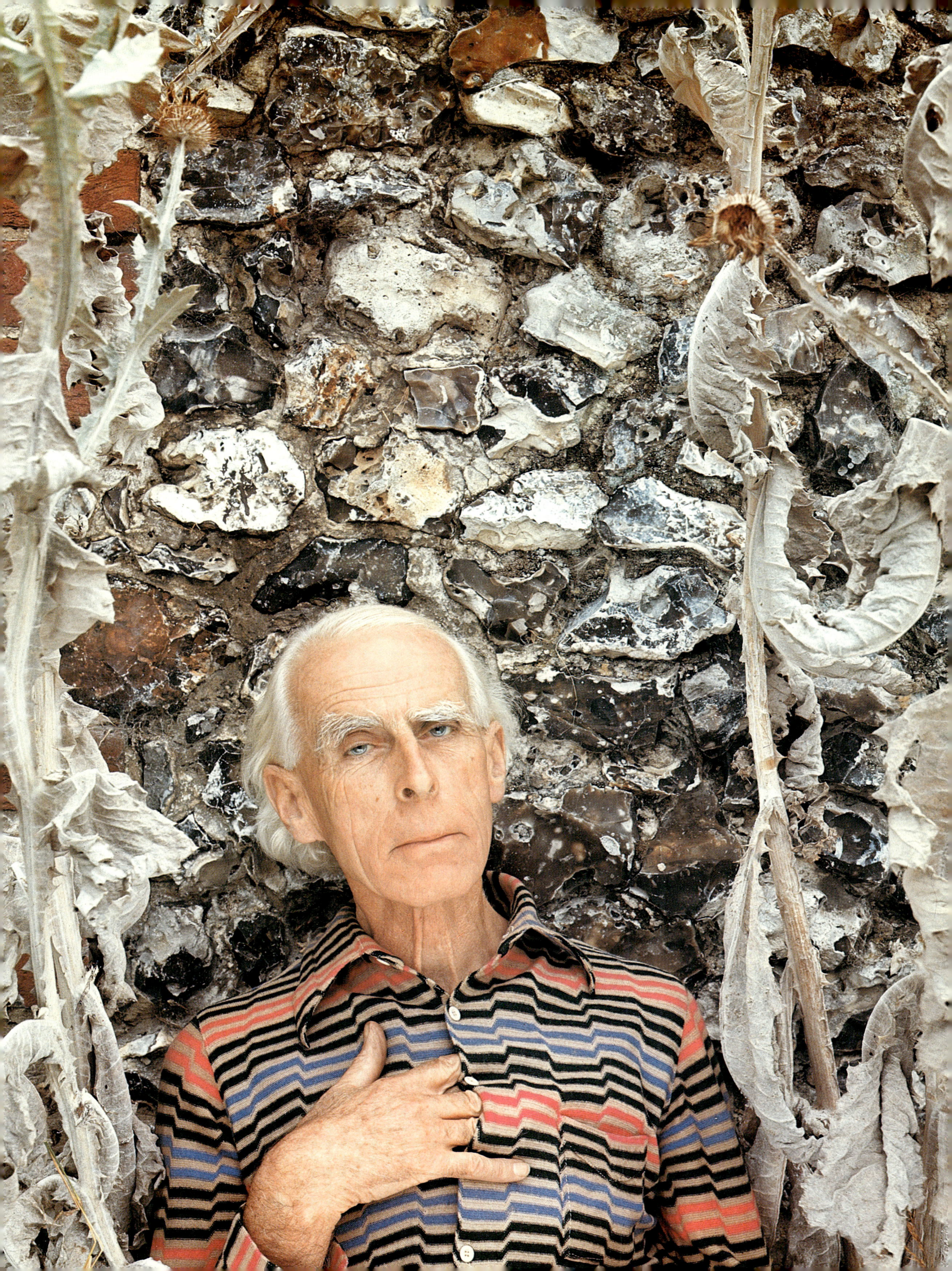

I was on the inaugural flight from London to the Seychelles in 1971 with a team from British *Vogue*, and we stepped out into a totally unspoilt and idyllic world where the entire population had come down to see the big bird land.

On one of the outer islands, Praslin, I discovered the longest, whitest beach that I have ever walked upon. I decided to use it as the background for a cheap black trouser suit that had to be photographed. We all hated the garment and christened it 'the dog'. Full of invention, Grace Coddington, the Fashion Editor, had stuck together about six pairs of different coloured 'flip-flops' which made excellent beach platform shoes and plonked a white cotton sou'wester-type hat on Plonya's head. I set up the camera, pulled a couple of Polaroids to get the correct exposure, as we all stood and waited. 'What shall we do with this dreadful garment?' I asked, 'It is a real dog if ever I saw one.' At the mention of the word 'dog', about 150 yards away a lone black Labrador appeared out of the seagrapes and headed towards the sea. Halfway across the beach he stopped and turned towards us. 'Don't move,' I whispered to Plonya, 'lift your arms to welcome him – something extraordinary is going to happen.' I held my breath as I watched the apparition on the ground glass of the camera come waddling towards the black figure with the white hat that he could now see. At the climactic moment, when the composition was impeccable, the divine handler who maintains that over-crowded kennel in the sky decided that a flea, dormant till this second, should awaken and bite the animal under the tail; discomforted, the dog stopped, and, standing as they do on three legs, turned to remove the nuisance. Click. 'Hold it.' Click. 'Hold it.' Click. There was time for only three exposures before he turned and disappeared.

I do not exaggerate when I say those three clicks sent electric shocks up my arm. All of us recognized that by some mysterious intervention we had taken a picture that could never be taken again.

Our next trip was to Bird Island where we were met by millions of Sooty Terns who have chosen this small island for nesting; each year they return and each year they have their young and leave. Hitchcock was right; birds by the million are most menacing, and terns scream when they are disturbed; and with their half-fledged young puddling about your feet in centuries of guano the mother birds dive bomb you in dozens. Plonya put on her usual energetic performance and we admired her for being so brave – no other girl could have managed it.

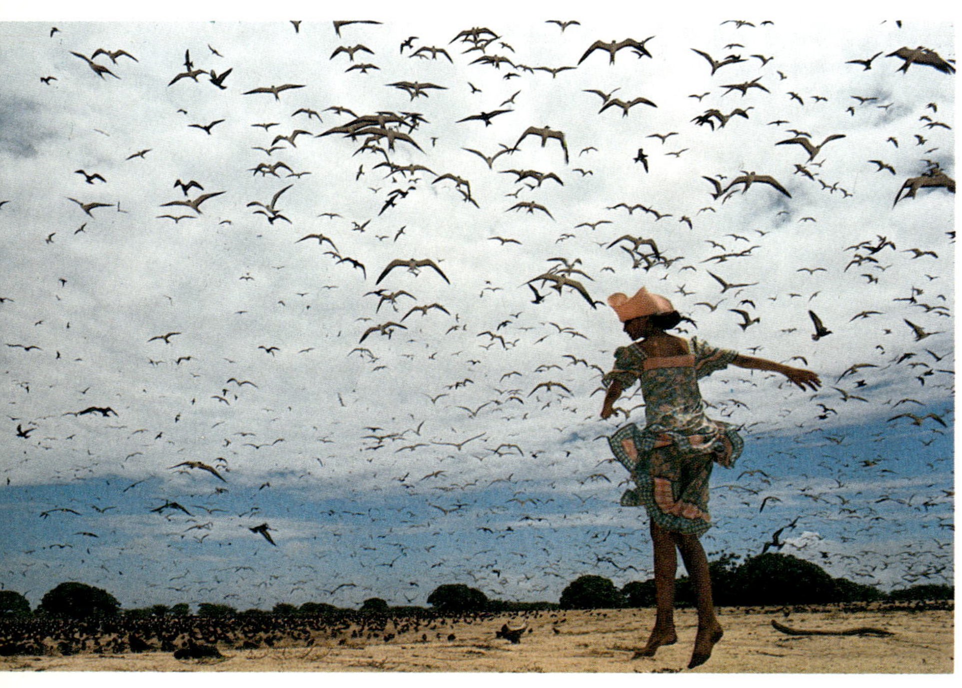

Apollonia van Ravenstein on Bird Island, Seychelles, 1971

RIGHT *'Dog Friday'. Apollonia van Ravenstein on Praslin Island, Seychelles, 1971*

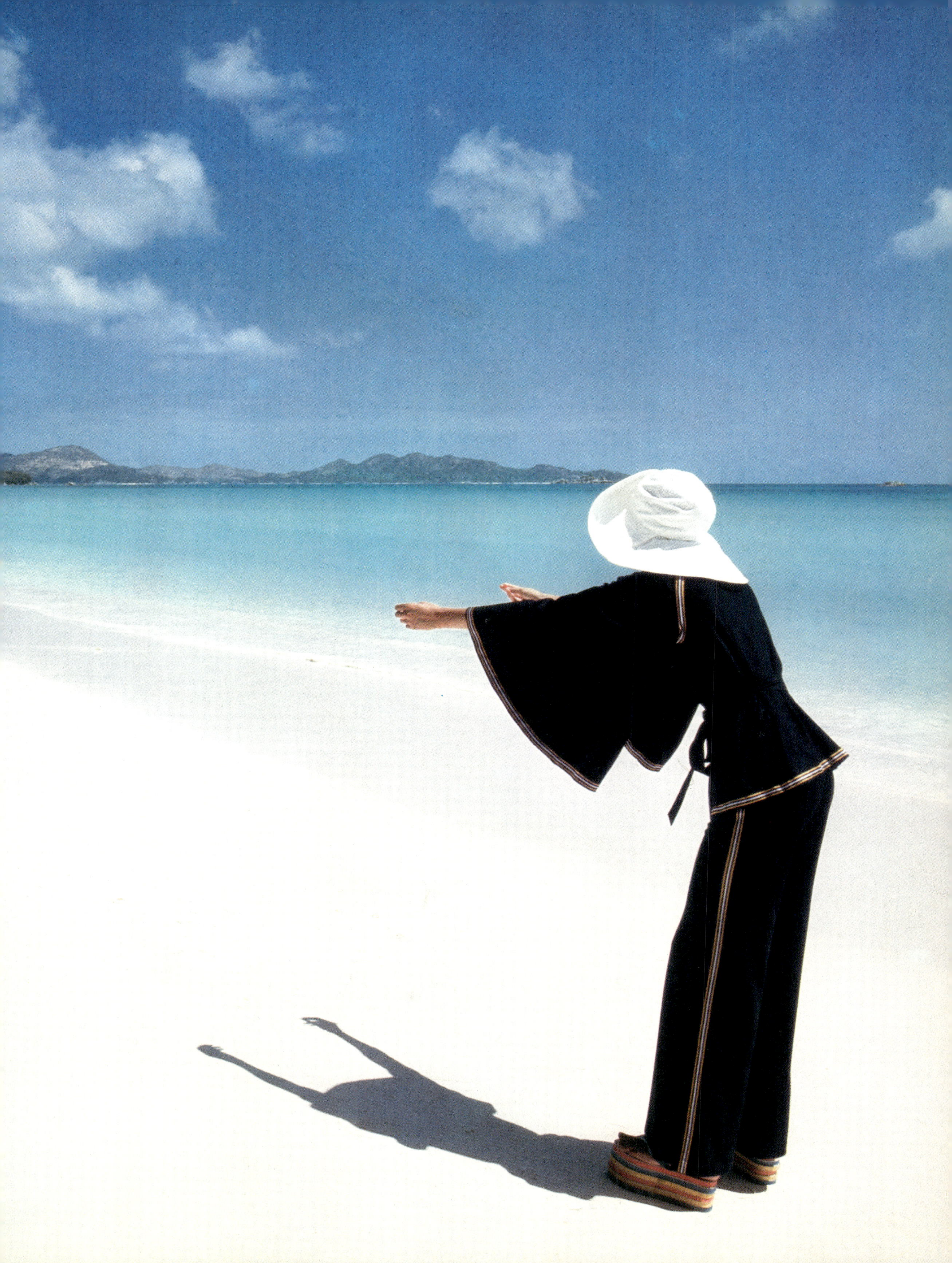

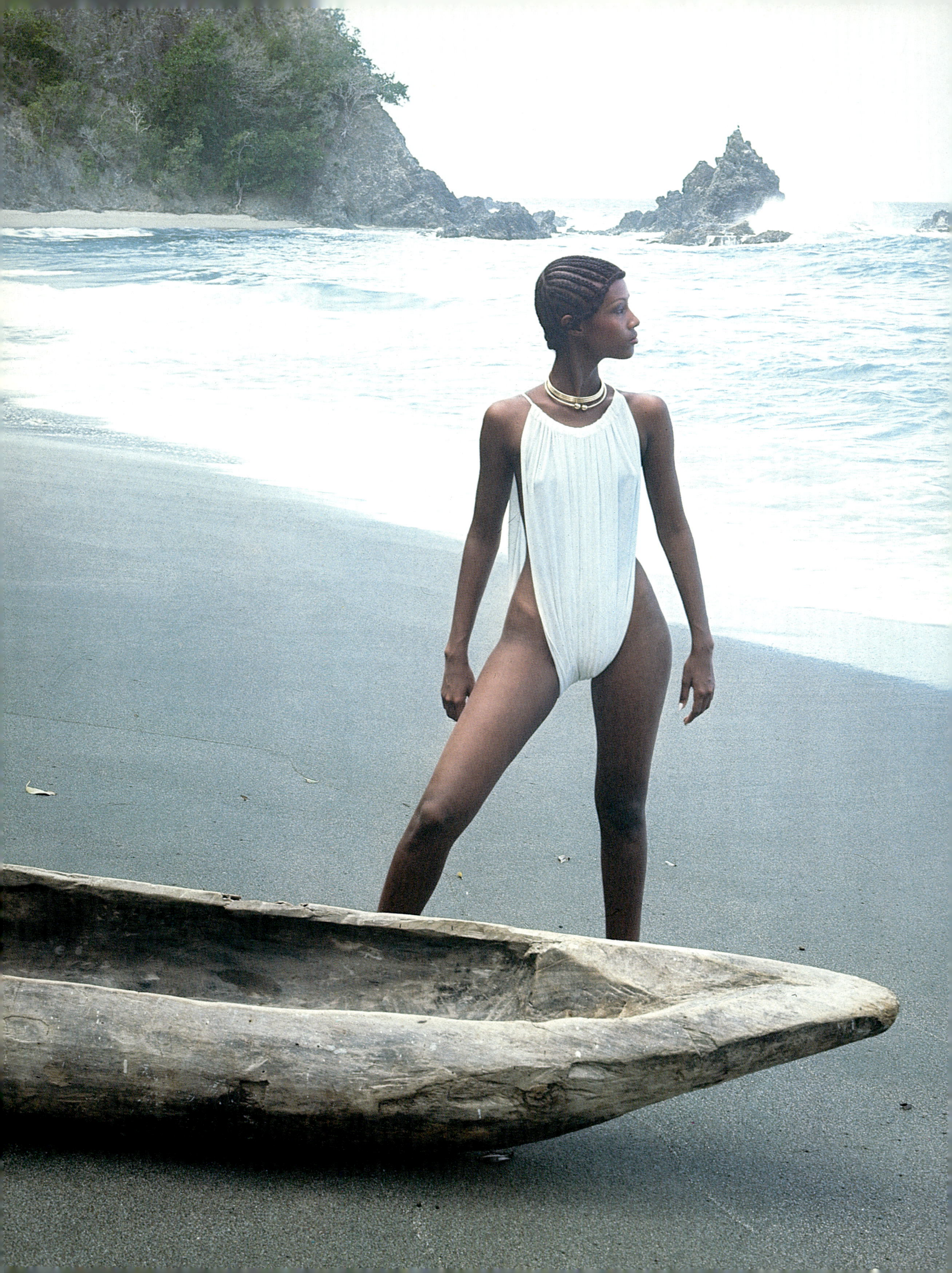

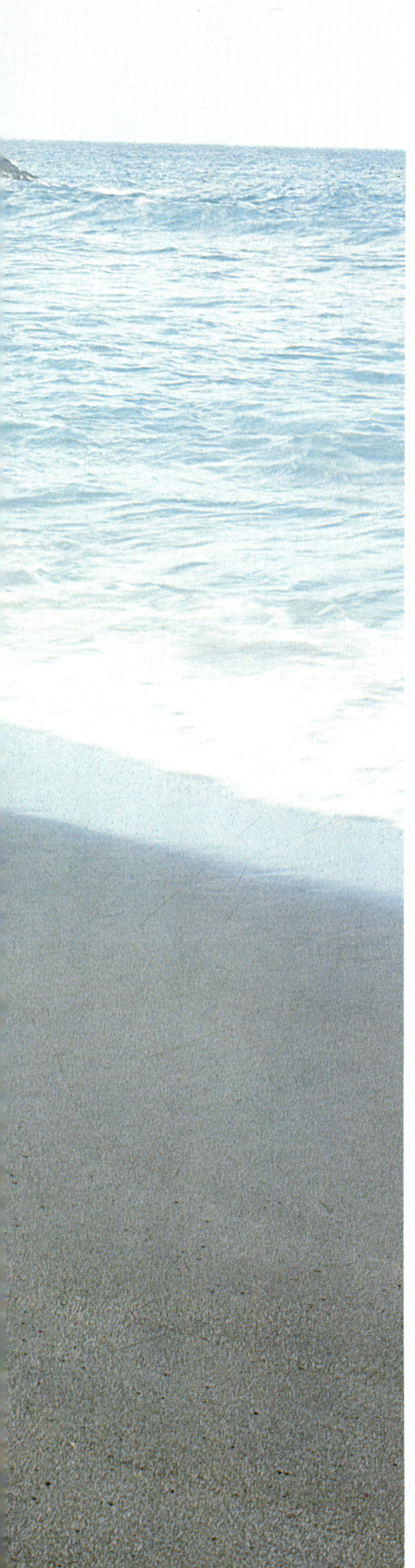

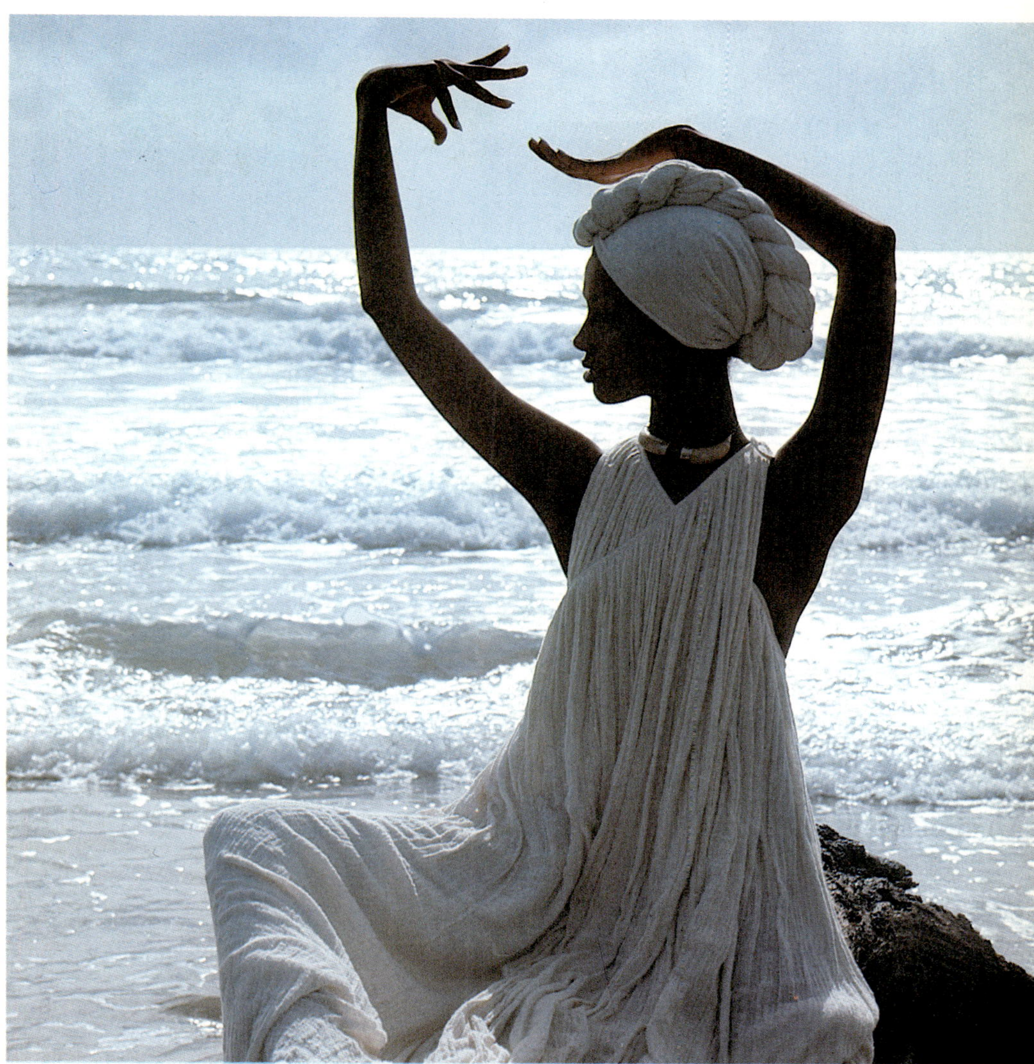

I was the first photographer that Iman worked with, and this was the first occasion that I photographed her. I had removed from my sitting room wall, where it is usually majestically suspended, an antique dugout canoe; I carried it to a nearby bay and placed it on the black sand and waited for Iman to change. We were to photograph a simple white one-piece swimsuit. It was totally modest by comparison with today's string bits that travel in a matchbox, but plead as I might Iman refused to put it on. The sun went in, the sun came out; she remained adamant, and I was desperate. For the first time in my life, and I doubt I shall ever do it again, I fell on my knees in the sand, my hands palm to palm. 'Iman, please put this suit on – or at least tell me your objection to it.' 'It is because of my mother,' she explained. 'She would realize that any man standing at the side during the photography would be able to see most of my body in profile.' Eventually she conceded and although I review the picture on the left with pride, I would enjoy it even more if the white fabric that passes over her pubic mound and between her legs had been equidistant instead of being proud to the left. I was aware of this imbalance at the time but was much too scared to run forward and adjust it, for that would have been the final straw.

LEFT *Iman in Shuji Tojo's loop of white Hurel jersey, King Peter's Bay, Tobago, 1976*
ABOVE *Iman wearing cheesecloth curtains from Mexicana, King Peter's Bay, Tobago, 1976*

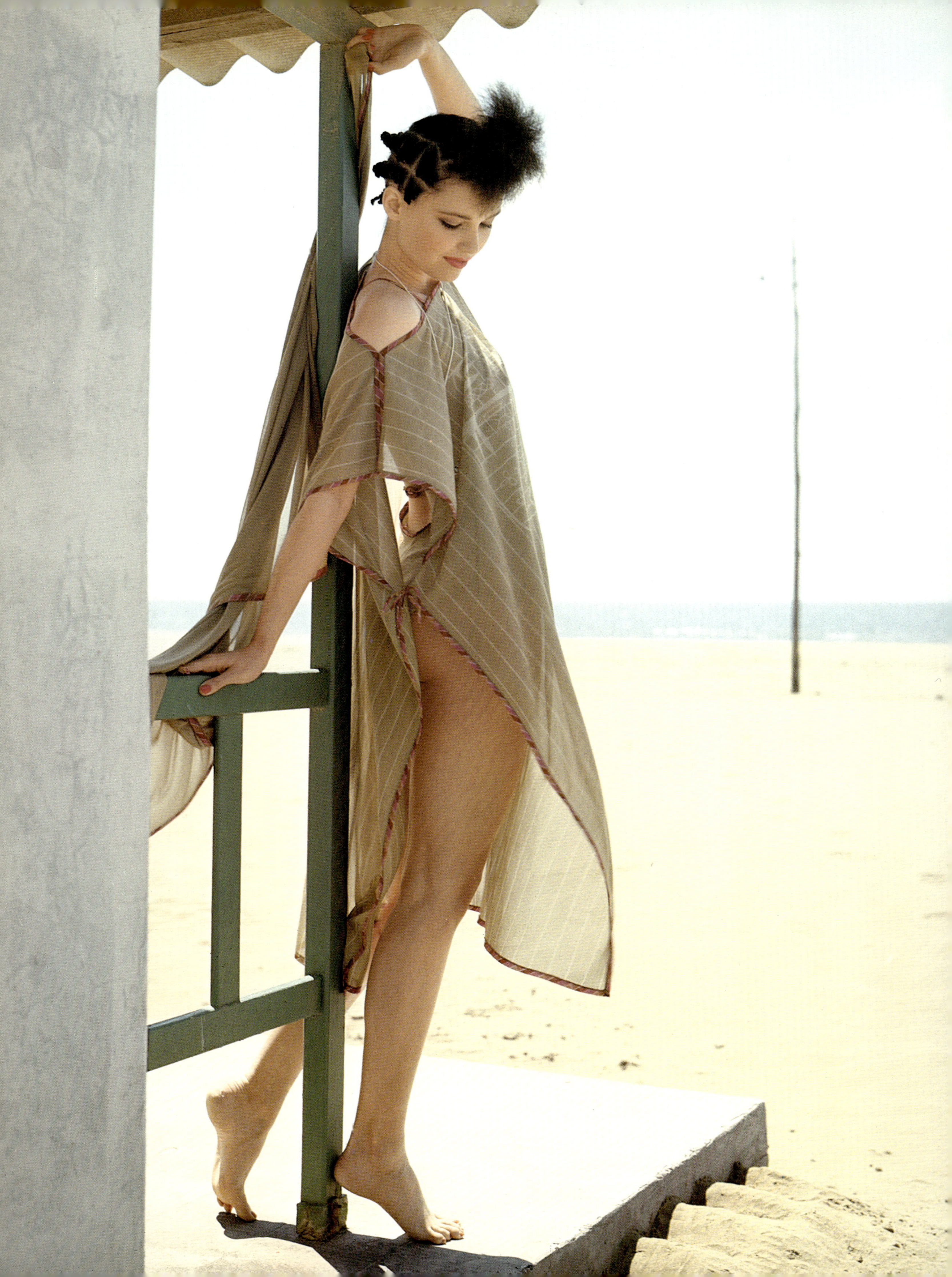

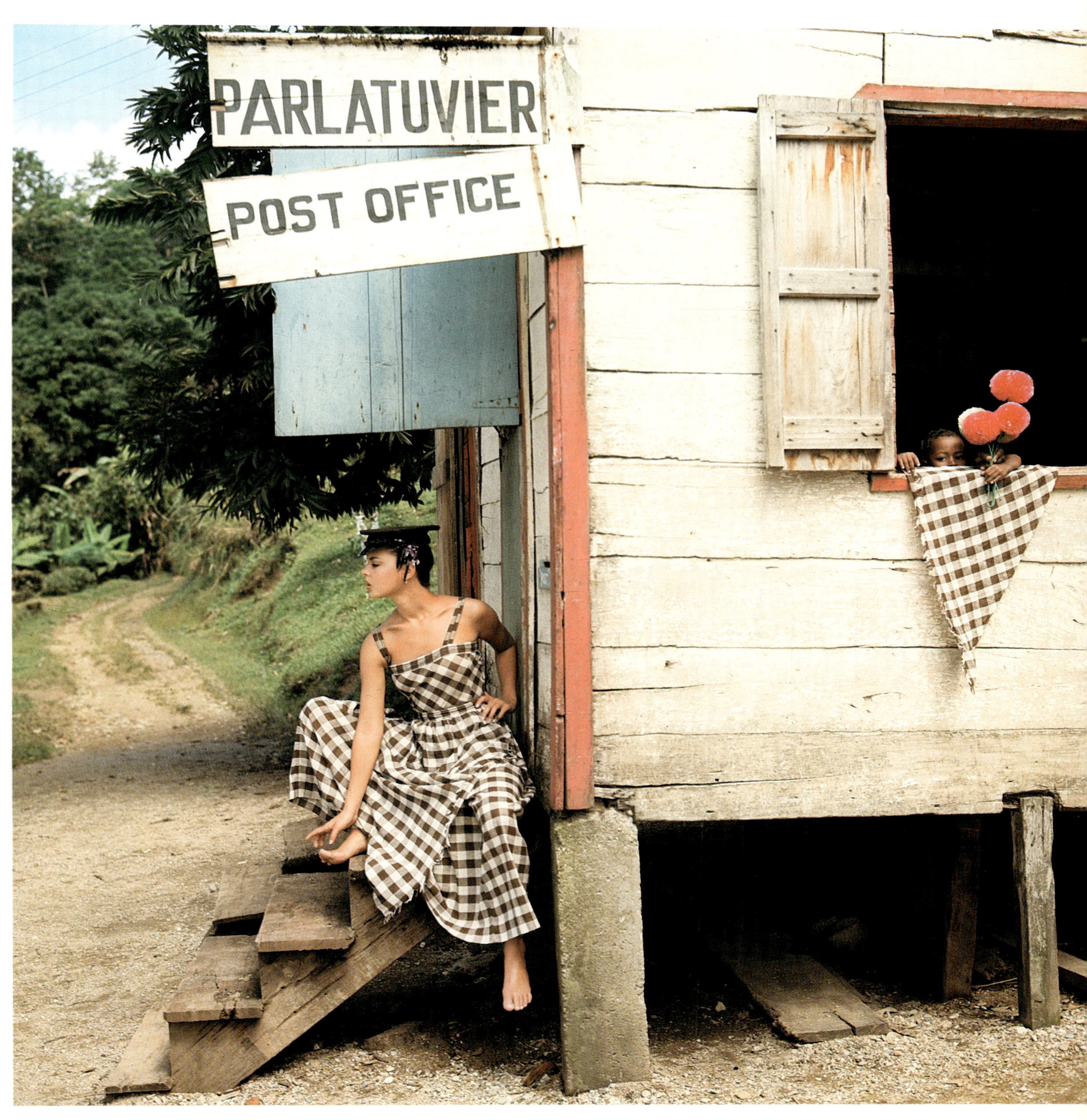

ABOVE *Lesley Branner in a cotton gingham dress by Laura Biagiotti, Tobago, 1977*
OPPOSITE *Beach dress by Giandonato, 1977*

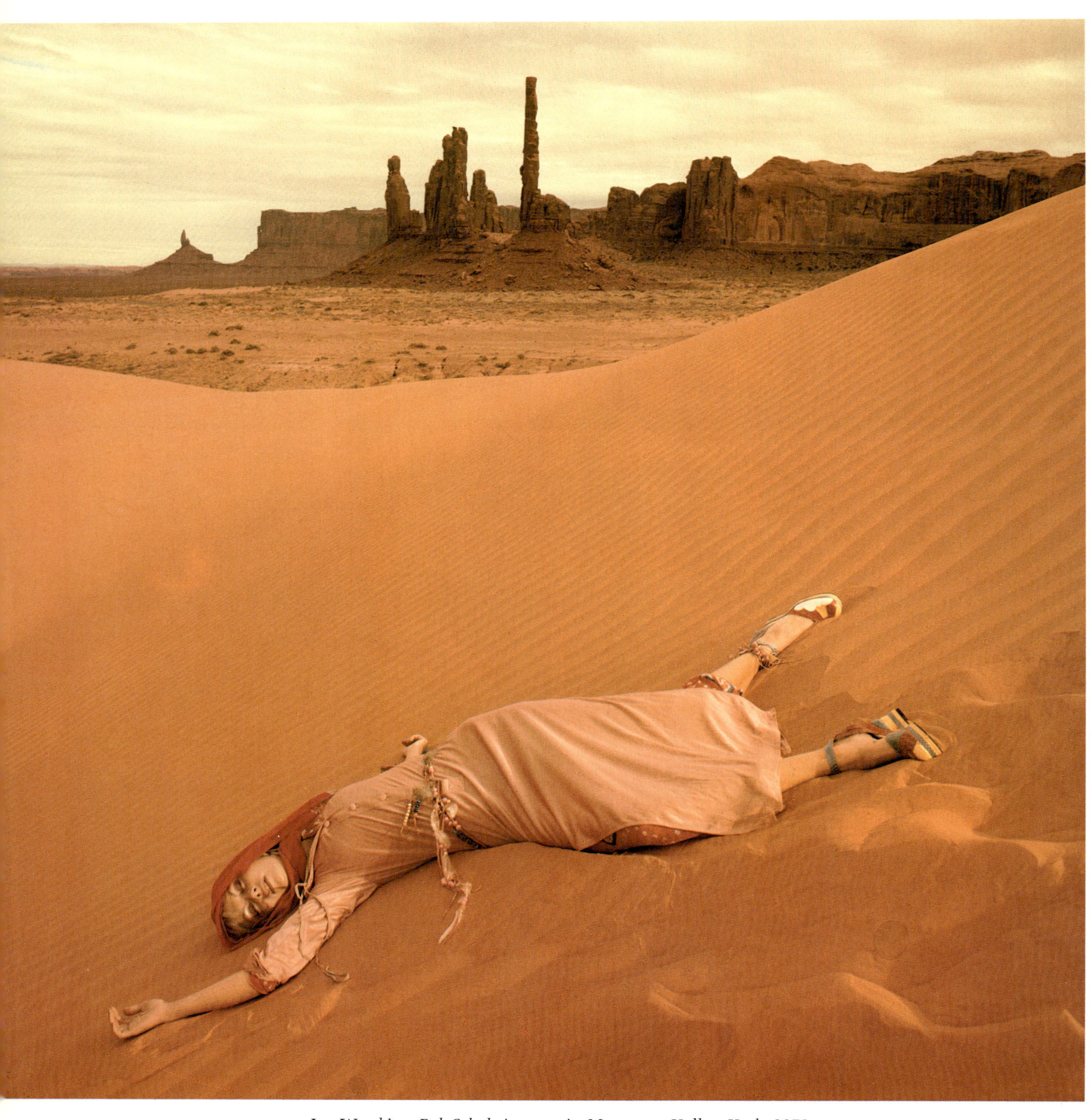

Jan Ward in a Bob Schulz jersey suit, Monument Valley, Utah, 1971

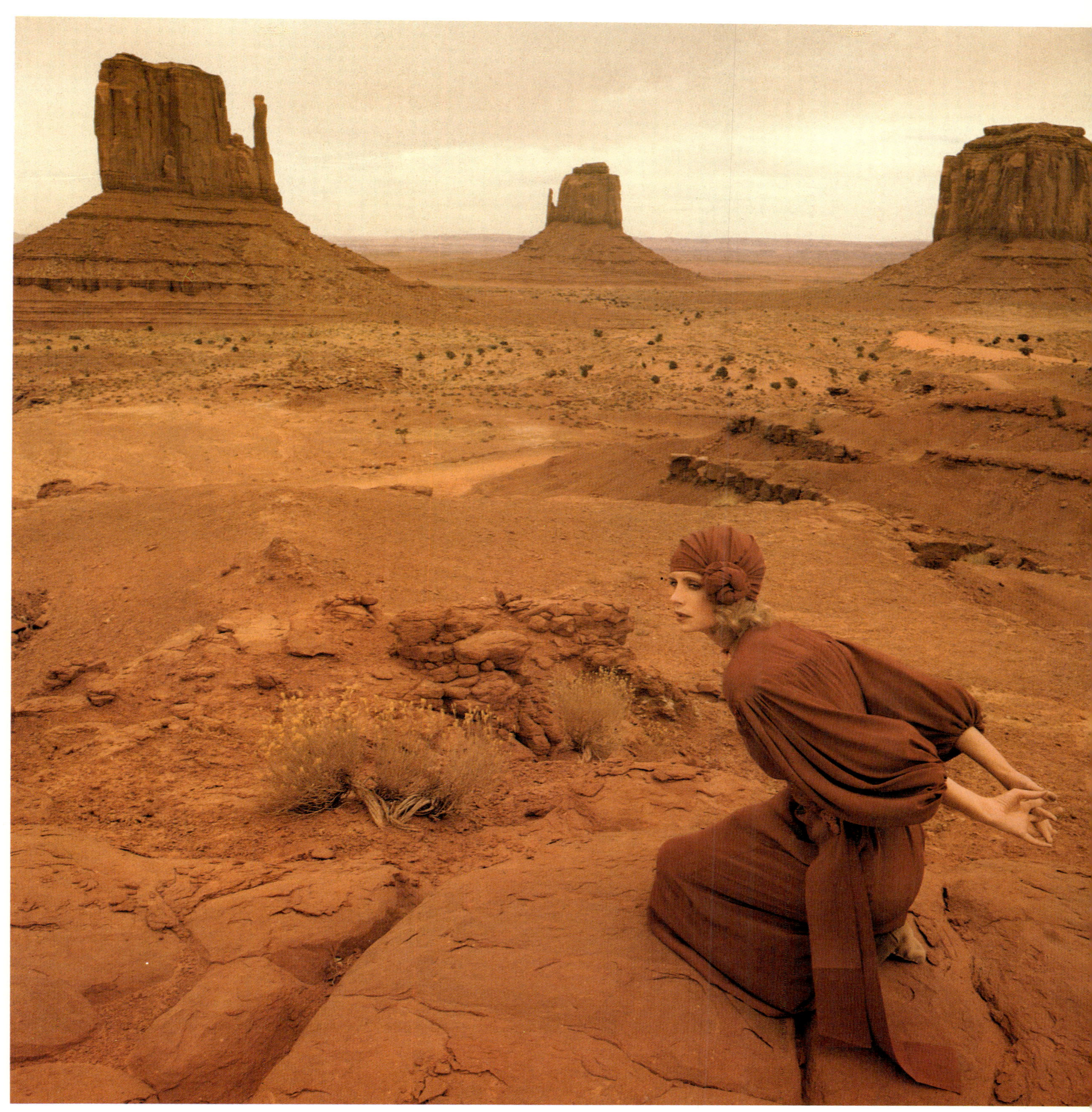

Jan Ward in a Jean Muir dress, Monument Valley, Utah, 1971

Andrea Holterhof, Hôtel Meurice, Paris, 1979

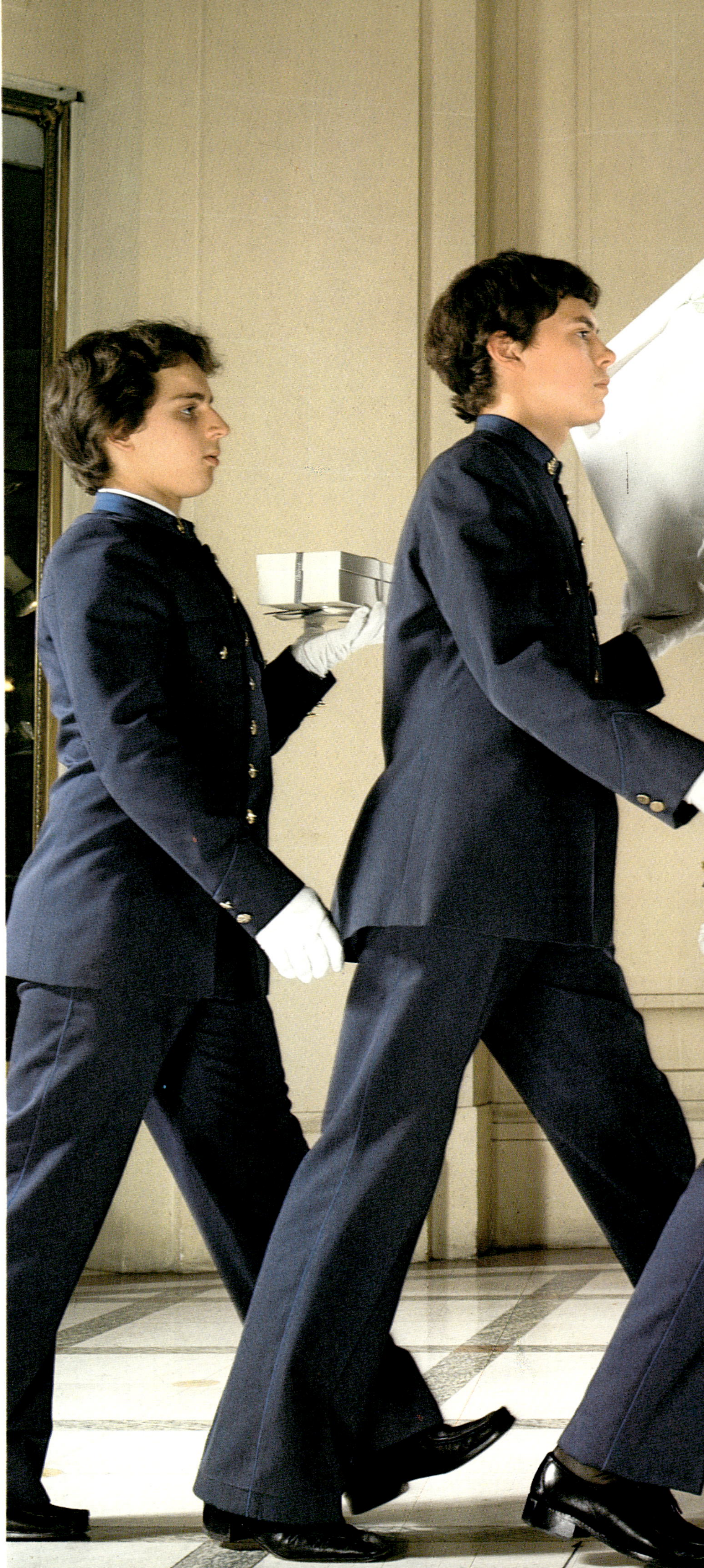

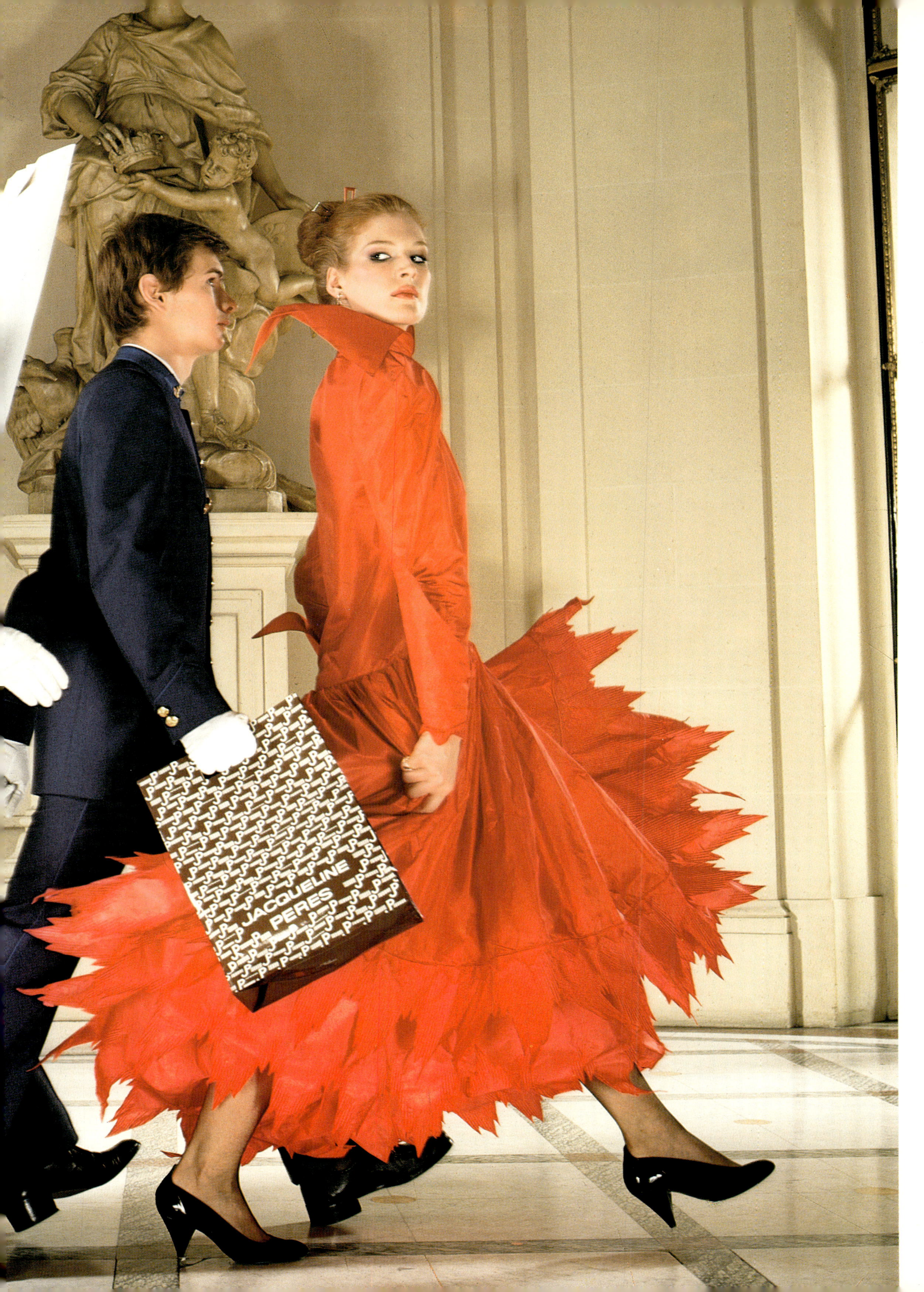
JACQUELINE
PERES

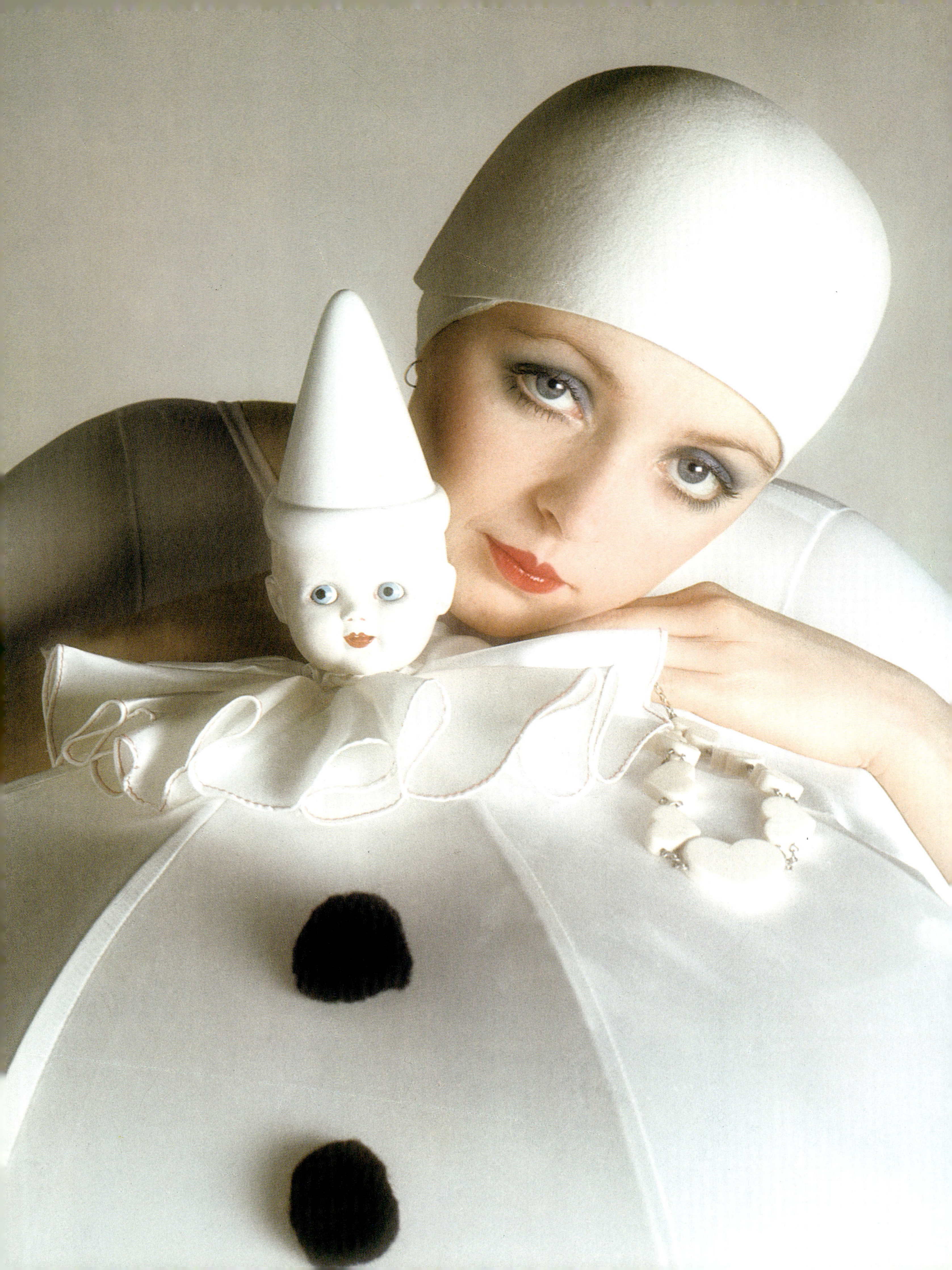

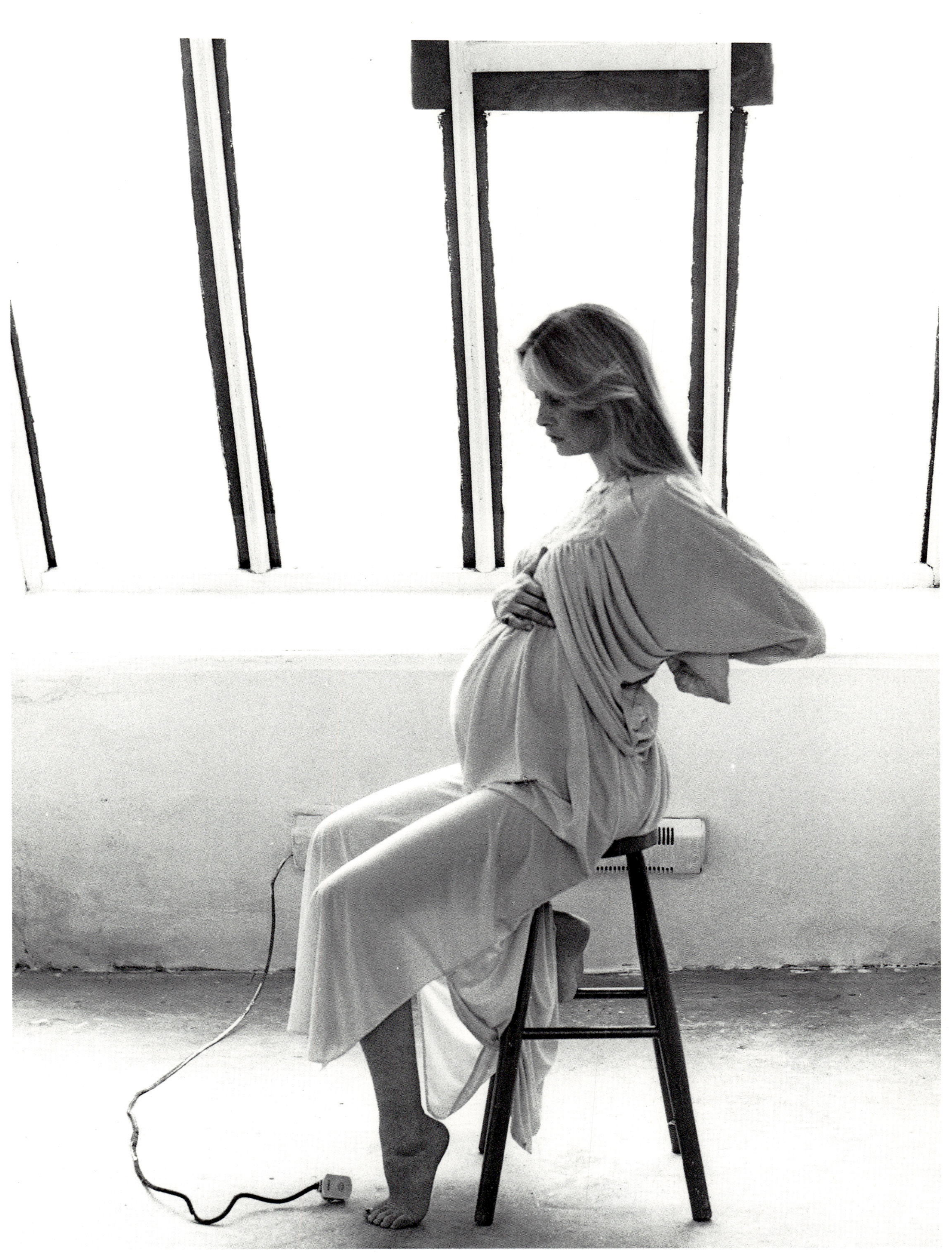

ABOVE *Twiggy expectant, 1978*
OPPOSITE *Linda Deganais modelling Dior make-up, 1973*

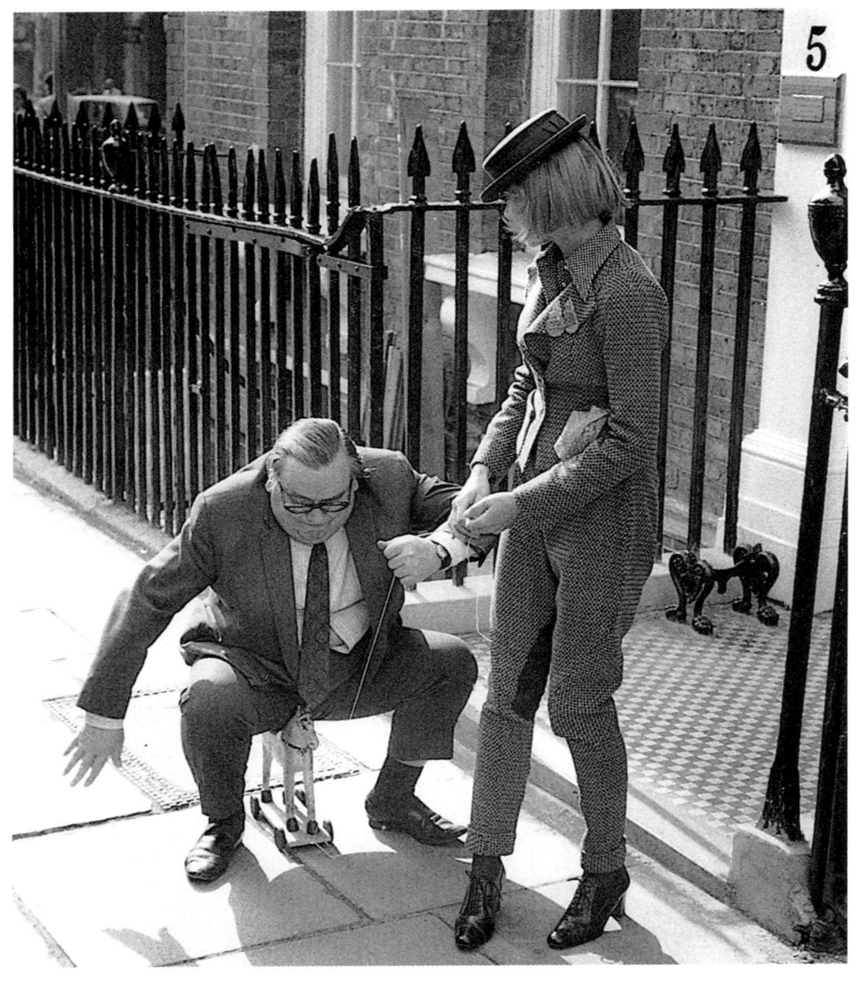

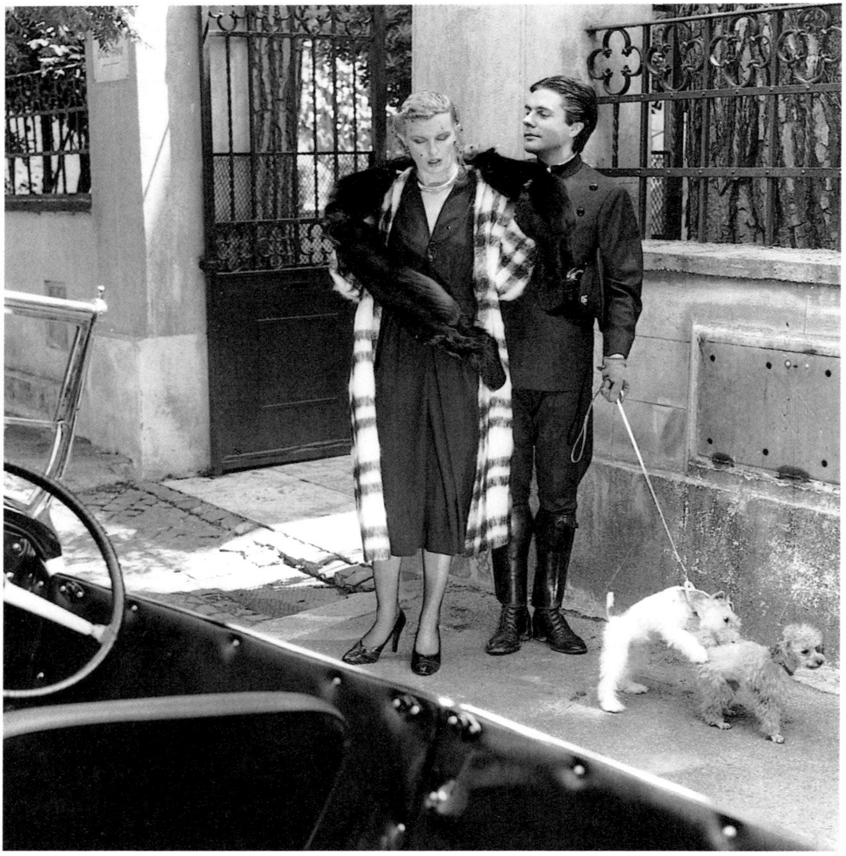

TOP LEFT *Christiana Steichen in Tuttanbankem tweed jodhpurs, Clifford Street, London 1972*
LEFT *The model wears clothes by Lancetti, the 'chauffeur' is Robert Pascall, Parkinson's assistant, Italy, 1978*
OPPOSITE *Unisex fashion, Milan racecourse, 1978*
OVERLEAF LEFT *Beverley Johnson in a dress by Roberto Capucci, Italy, 1977*
OVERLEAF RIGHT *Beverley Johnson in an outfit by Rafaello, Italy, 1977*

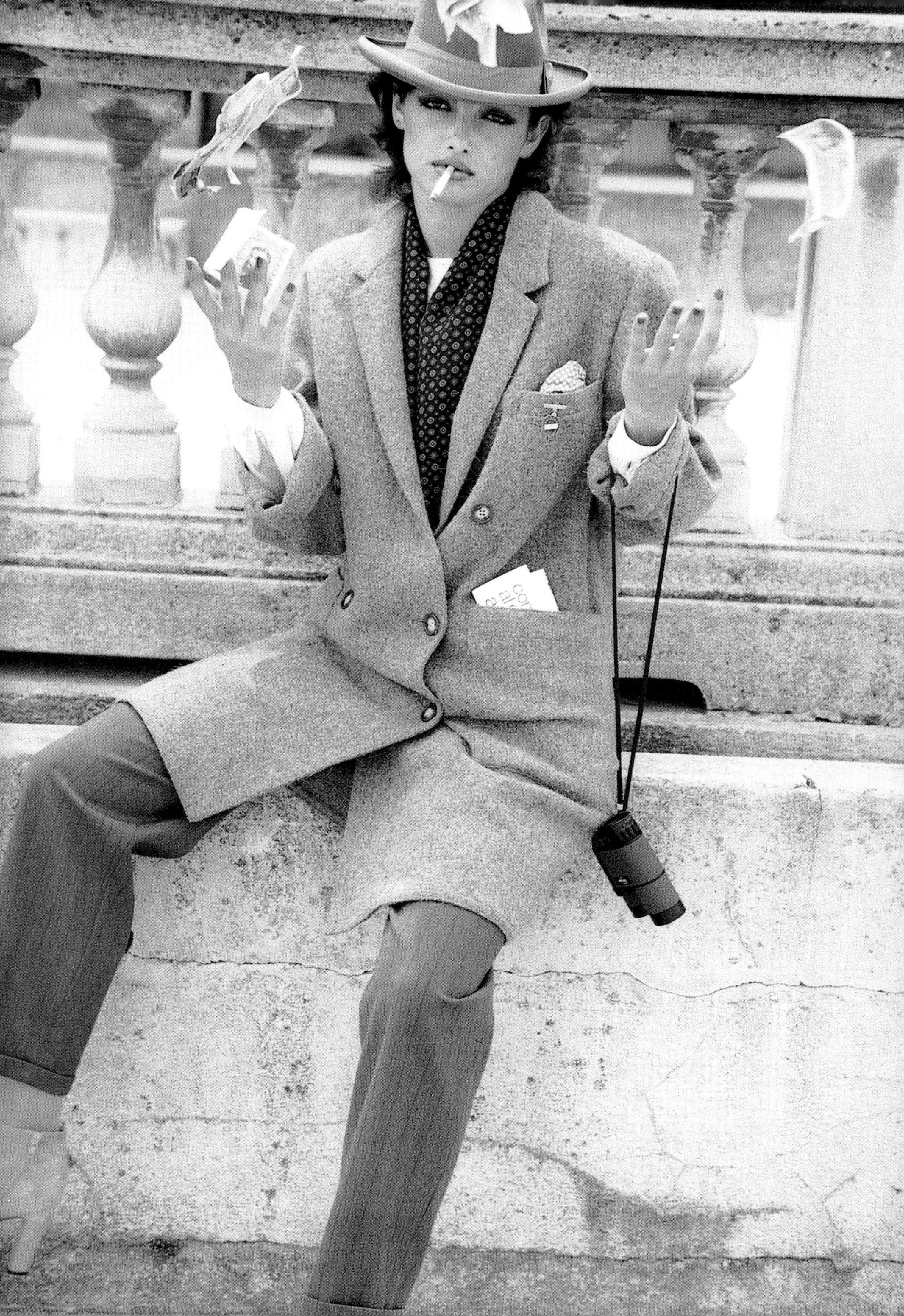

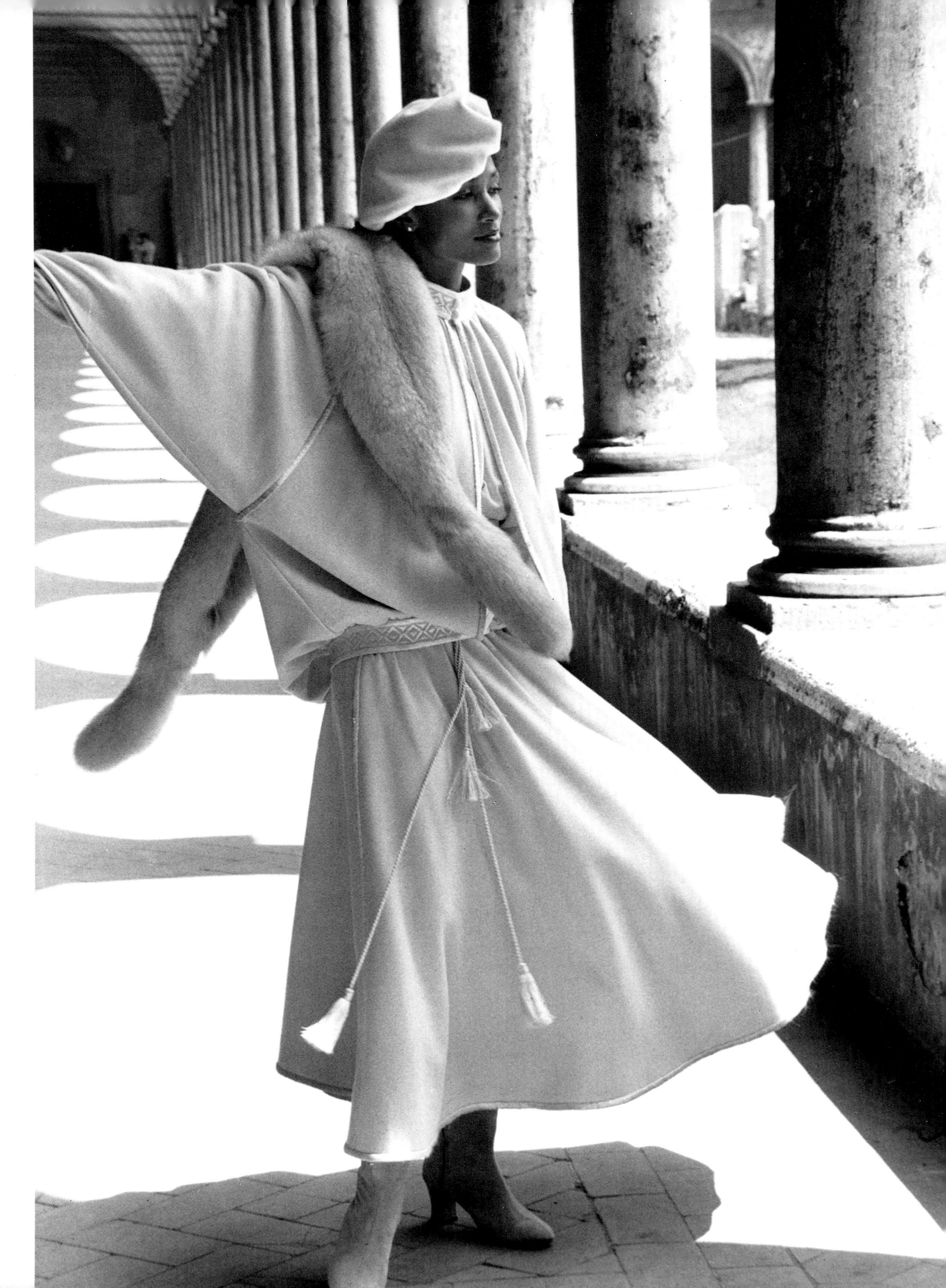

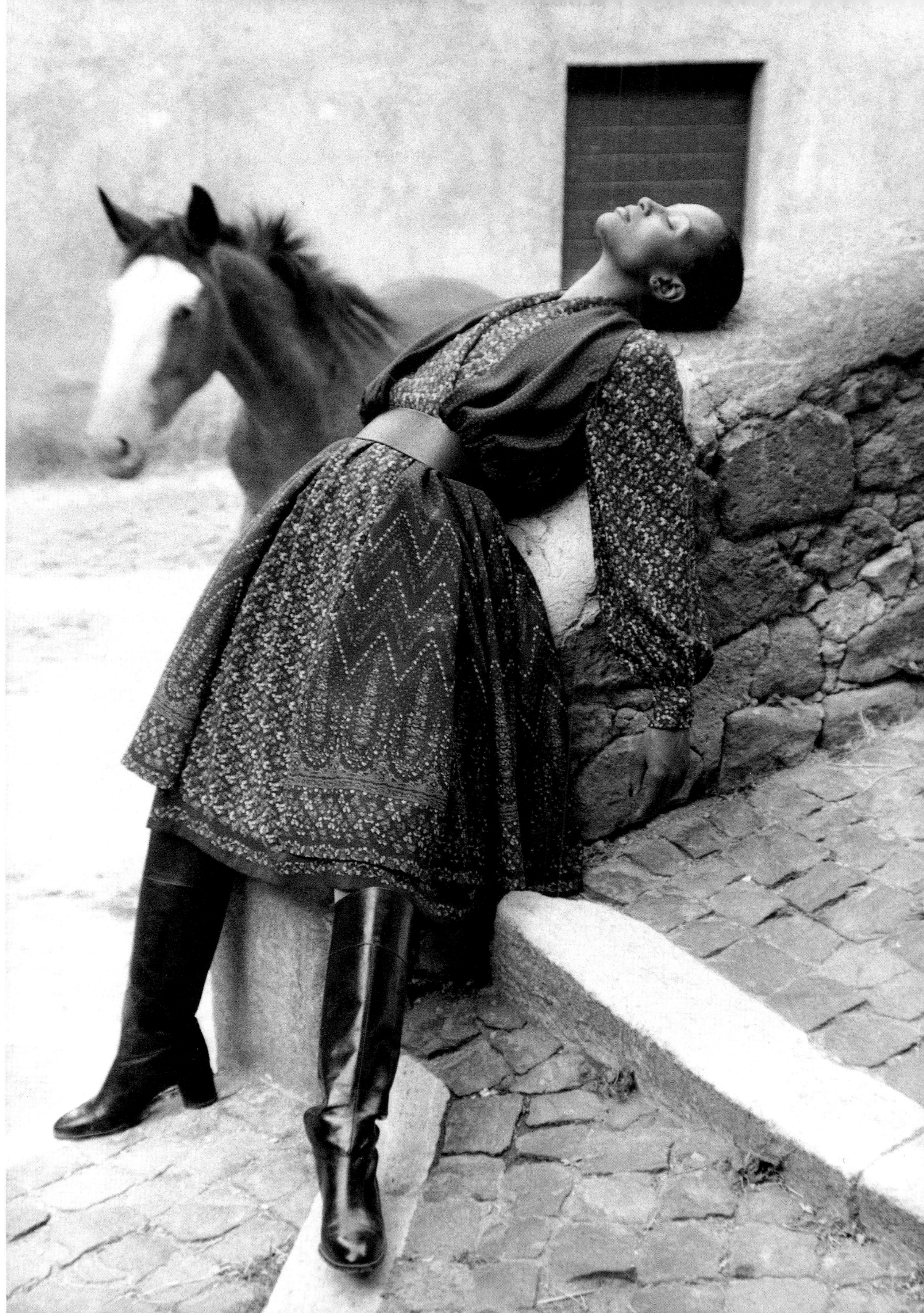

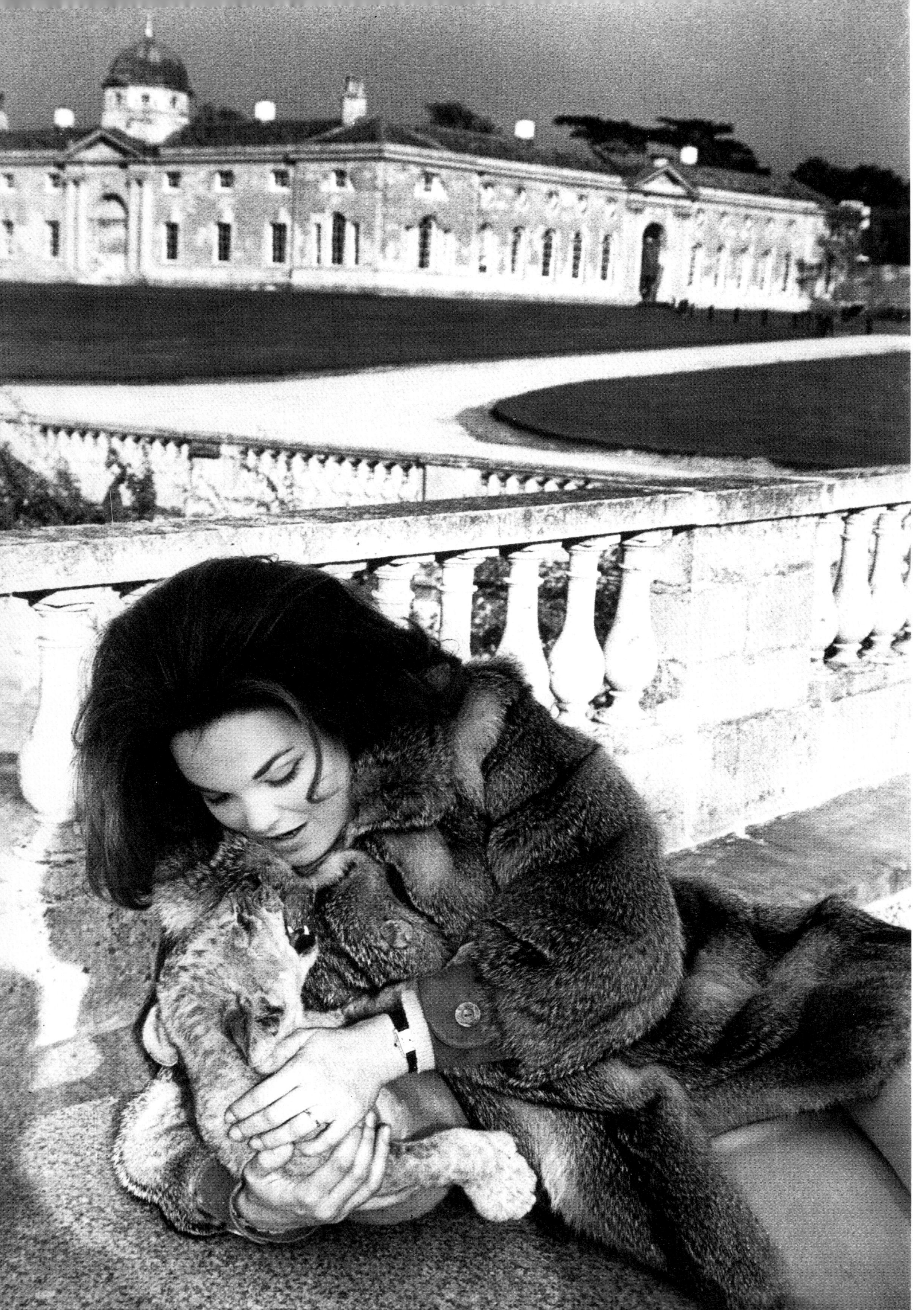

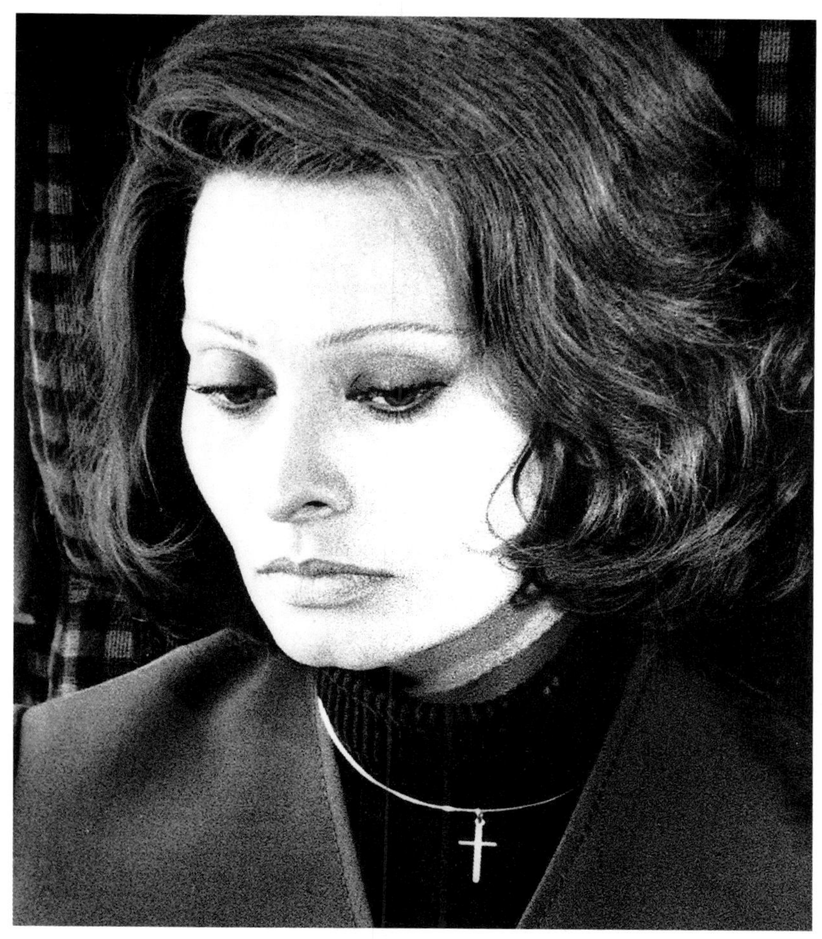

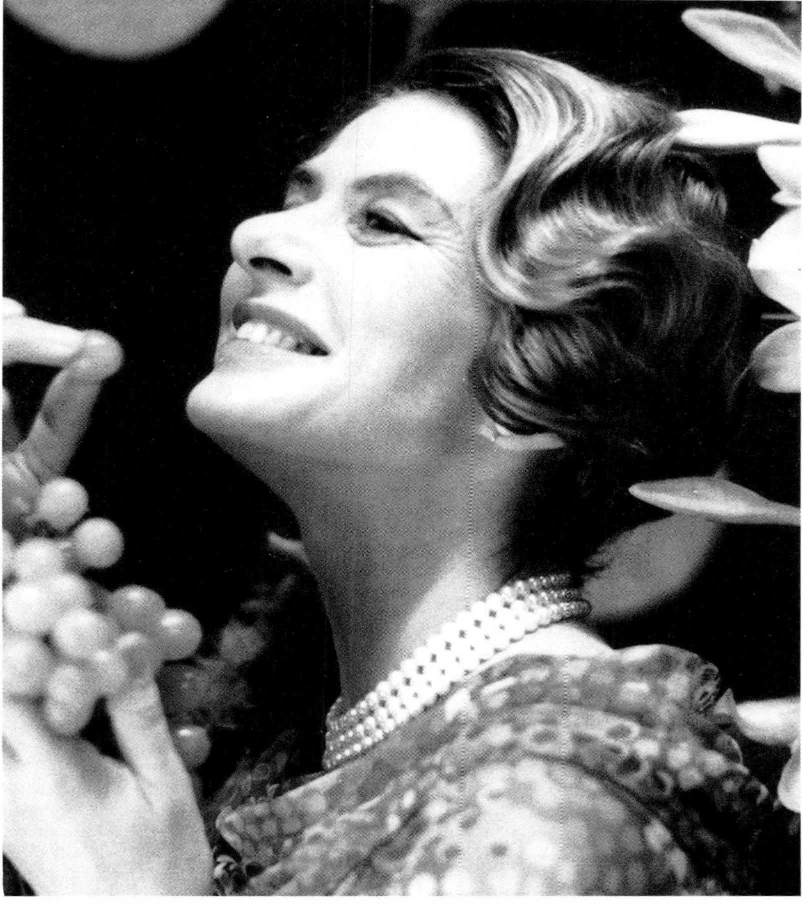

OPPOSITE *The Marchioness of Tavistock (Henrietta Tiarks) at Woburn Abbey. A Maxwell Croft fur coat advertisement, 1974*
TOP RIGHT *Sophia Loren, 1974*
RIGHT *Ingrid Bergman, dressed as she appeared in John Gielgud's production of Somerset Maugham's play, 'The Constant Wife', 1973*

1980s

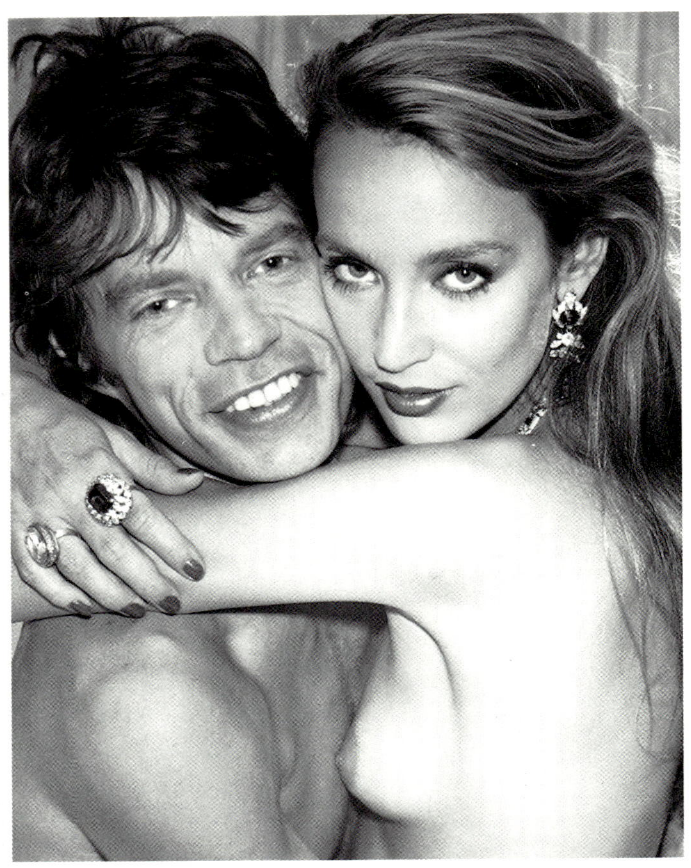

HARVEST TIME

In the mid seventies I found myself suddenly barred from working for Condé Nast because, on my own account and on behalf of other photographers, I had objected most strongly to their interpretation of the copyright law. After thirty years' association the severing blow was heavy, yet I look upon this historic occasion with considerable satisfaction, because unless you are cast upon the market place you are never able to assess your real value. Most photographers after they are sixty-five become half-maimed and blind to boot, shambling off to some distant darkroom to reprint, hopefully for resale, some of their more memorable pictures. Yet an American magazine called *Town and Country* scooped me up. Since then, Frank Zachary, its Editor-in-Chief, and Nancy Tuck Gardiner, its Special Projects Editor, have guided my camera to some of the world's most rewarding locations.

My first assignment for them was a twenty-page colour contribution in an issue that they were putting together on Britain in general and London in particular. From that first story, an entirely new creative instinct was unlocked in my Pandora's box camera. Suddenly a new breed of beautiful people came to be photographed, people who wore their own jewellery and their own St Laurent dresses and sat in their own drawing-rooms under family portraits. I was stunned by this new beginning, but my camera was more level-headed and photographs of the beautiful women of Sweden and Mexico and Jordan and Greece and Columbia and Barbados and California and Newport and New York proliferated.

I look forward to every new project that *Town and Country* propose with renewed enthusiasm, especially as the increasing circulation figures suggest that the readers, too, are enjoying the vision of the style and elegance that we are putting on the pages.

ABOVE *Mick Jagger and Jerry Hall, 1981*
OPPOSITE *Andrea Holterhof in a Chanel outfit, 1980*

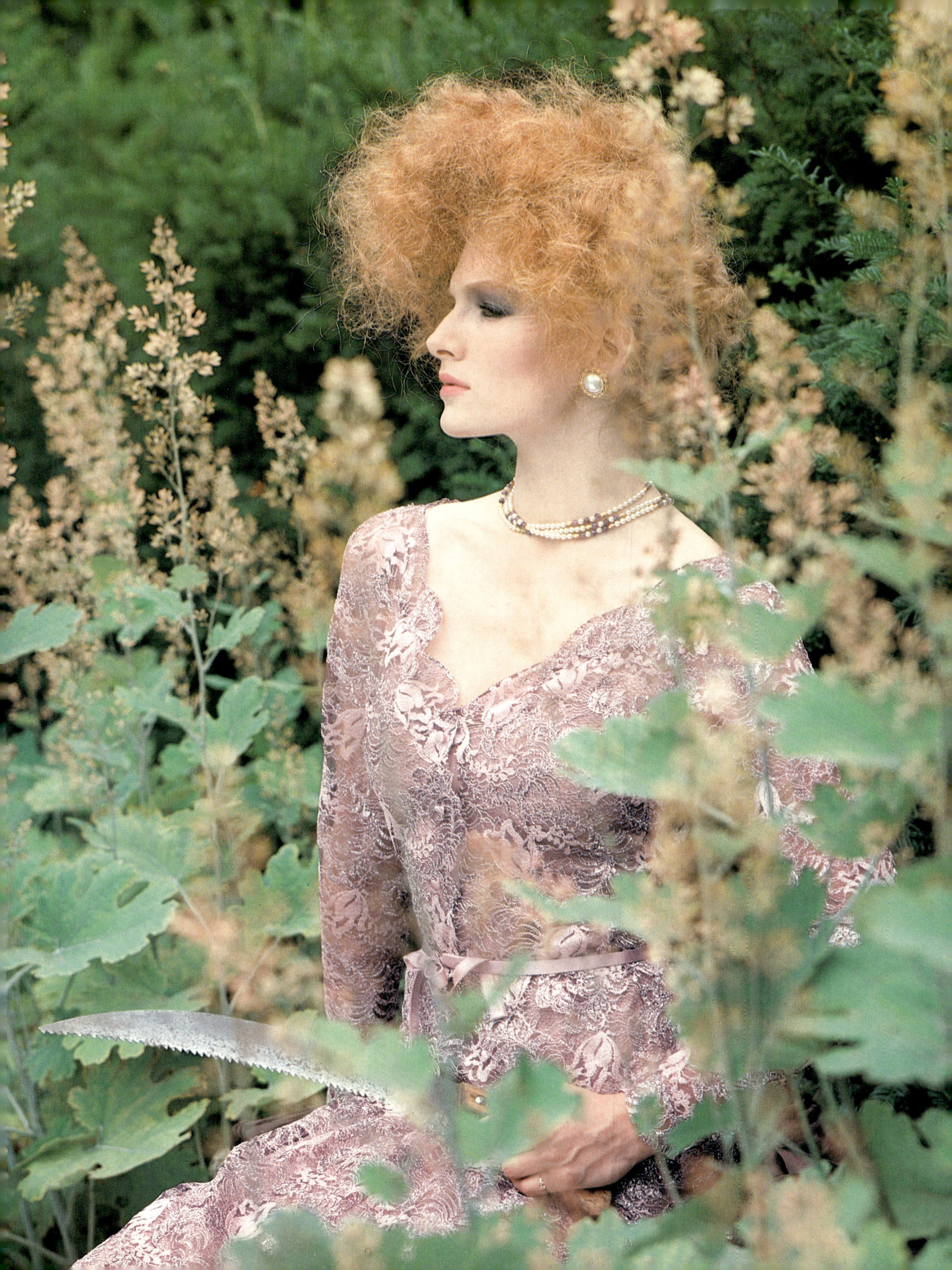

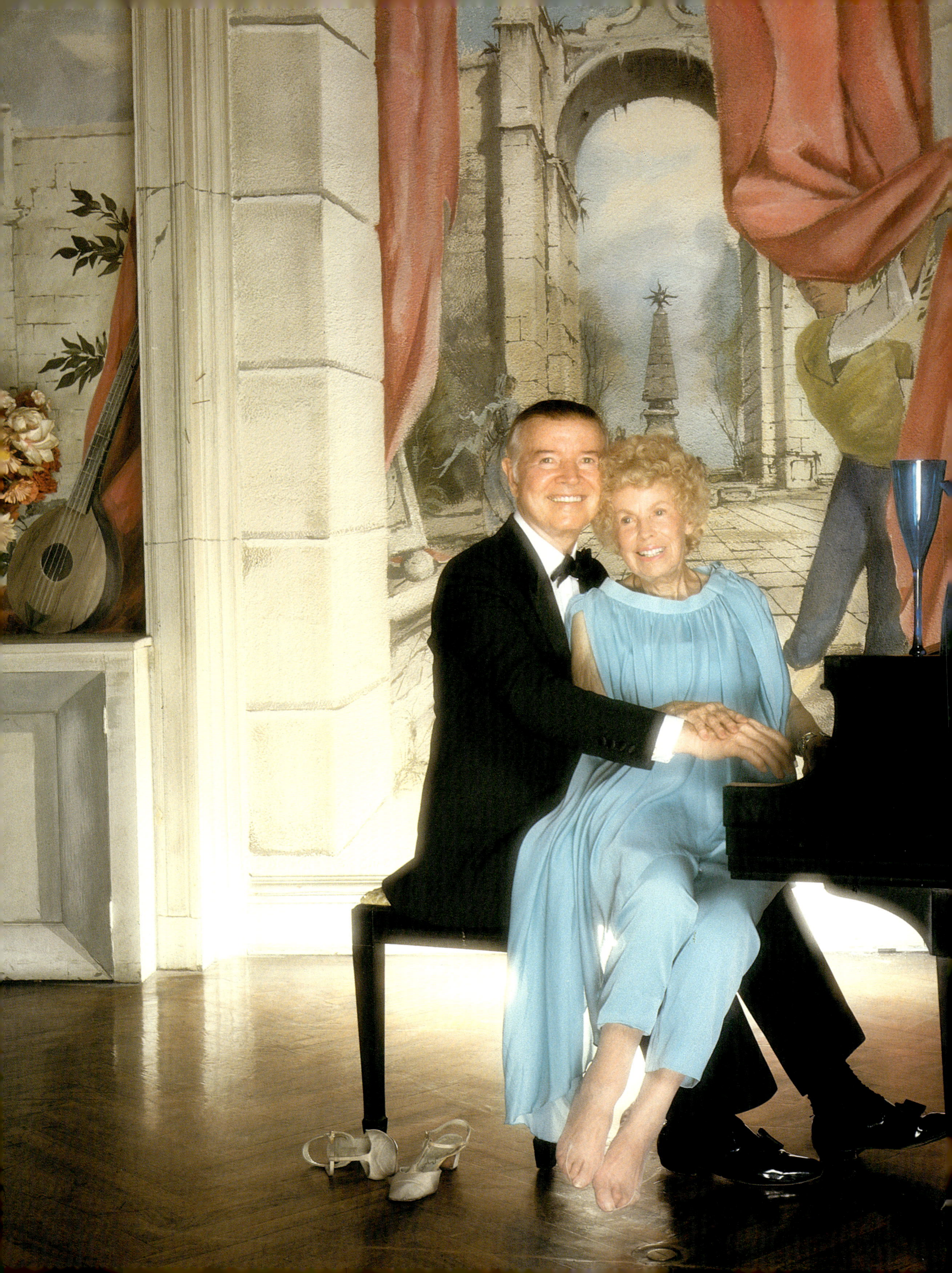

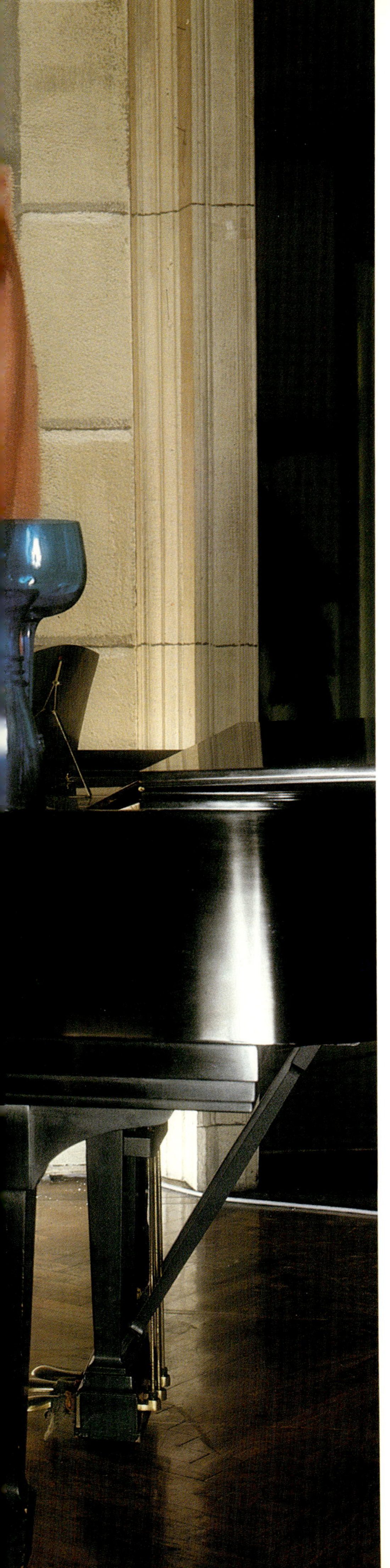

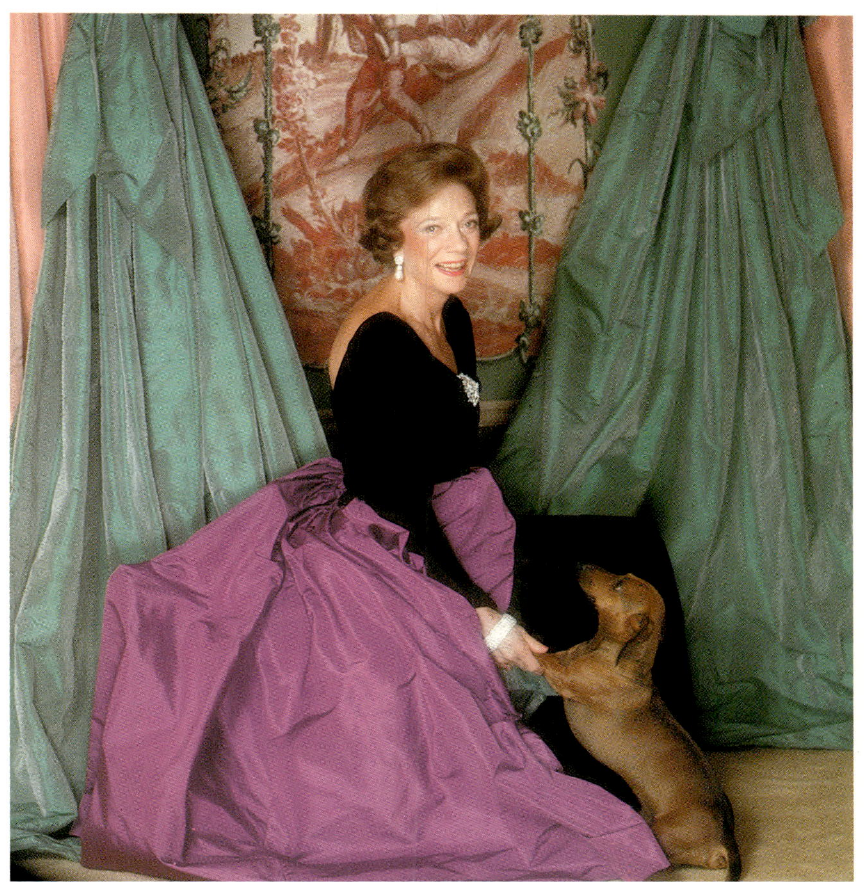

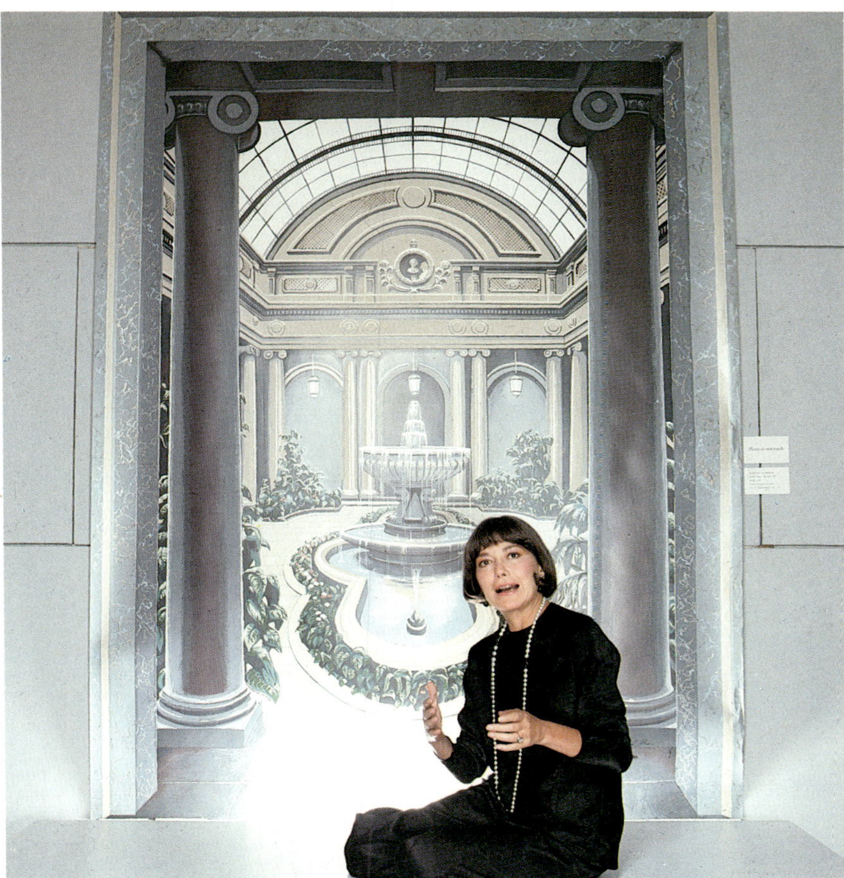

LEFT *Eugenia Sheppard, the columnist, with Earl Blackwell in his muralled ballroom, New York, 1981*
TOP *Mrs Brooke Astor with her dachshund, Frederick the Great 'Freddy', 1981*
ABOVE *Mrs Lisa Taylor, director of the Cooper Hewitt Museum, New York, in front of nineteenth-century trompe l'oeil wallpaper, 1981*

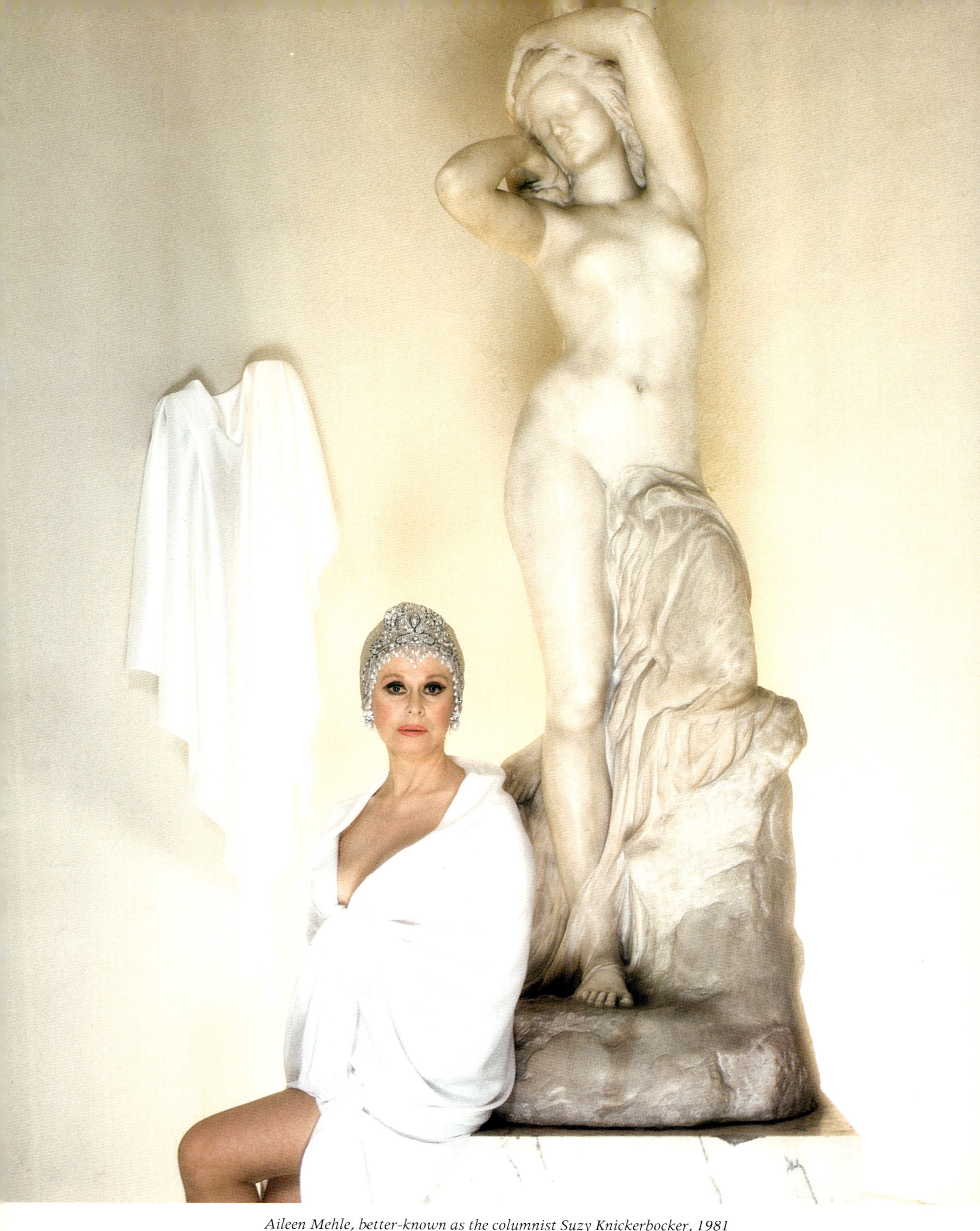

Aileen Mehle, better-known as the columnist Suzy Knickerbocker, 1981

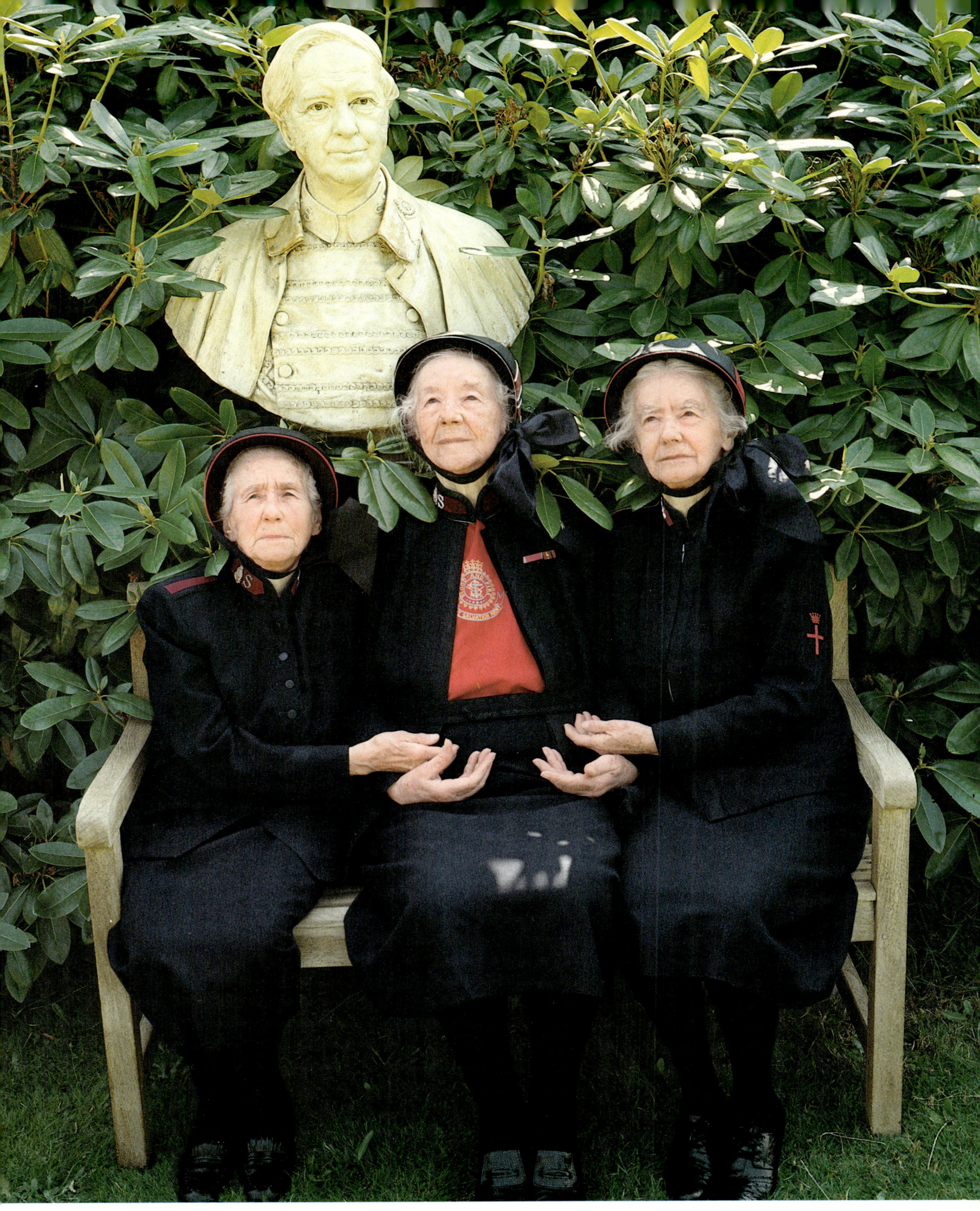

The granddaughters of the founder of the Salvation Army, Major Dora Booth, Lieutenant-Colonel Olive Booth and Commissioner Bramwell-Booth, with a statue of their father, Bramwell Booth, in the garden of their home in Finchampstead, Berkshire, 1981

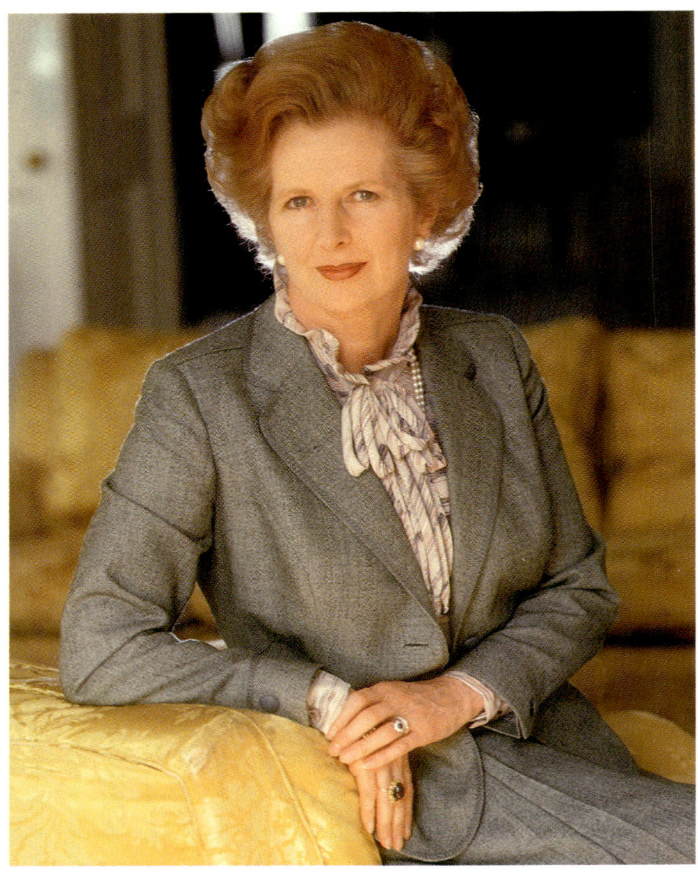

The Rt Hon. Mrs Margaret Thatcher MP, *1982*

Queen Noor of Jordan, King Hussein's American-born wife, 1981

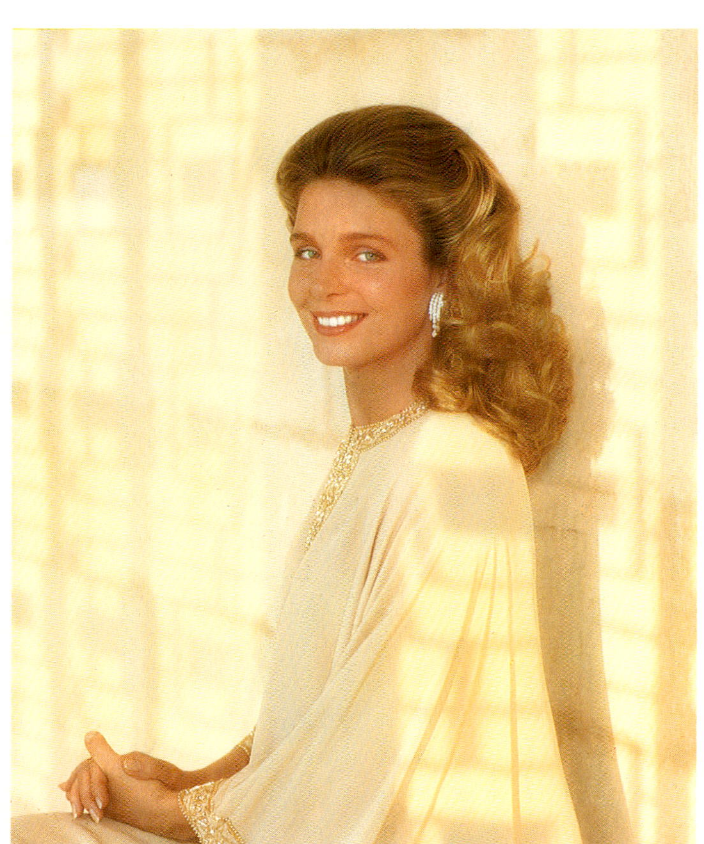

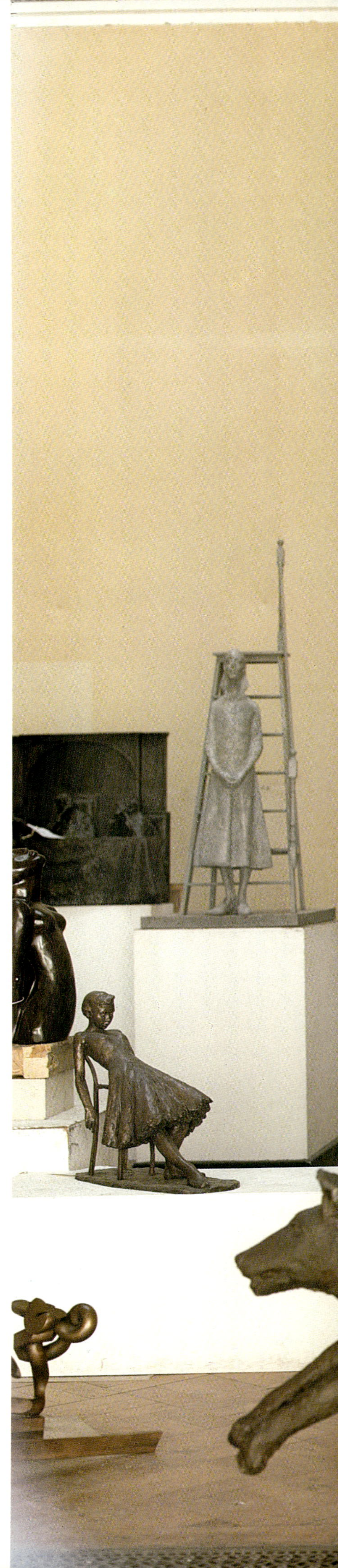

RIGHT *Sir Hugh Casson, President of the Royal Academy, at the Summer Show, 1982*

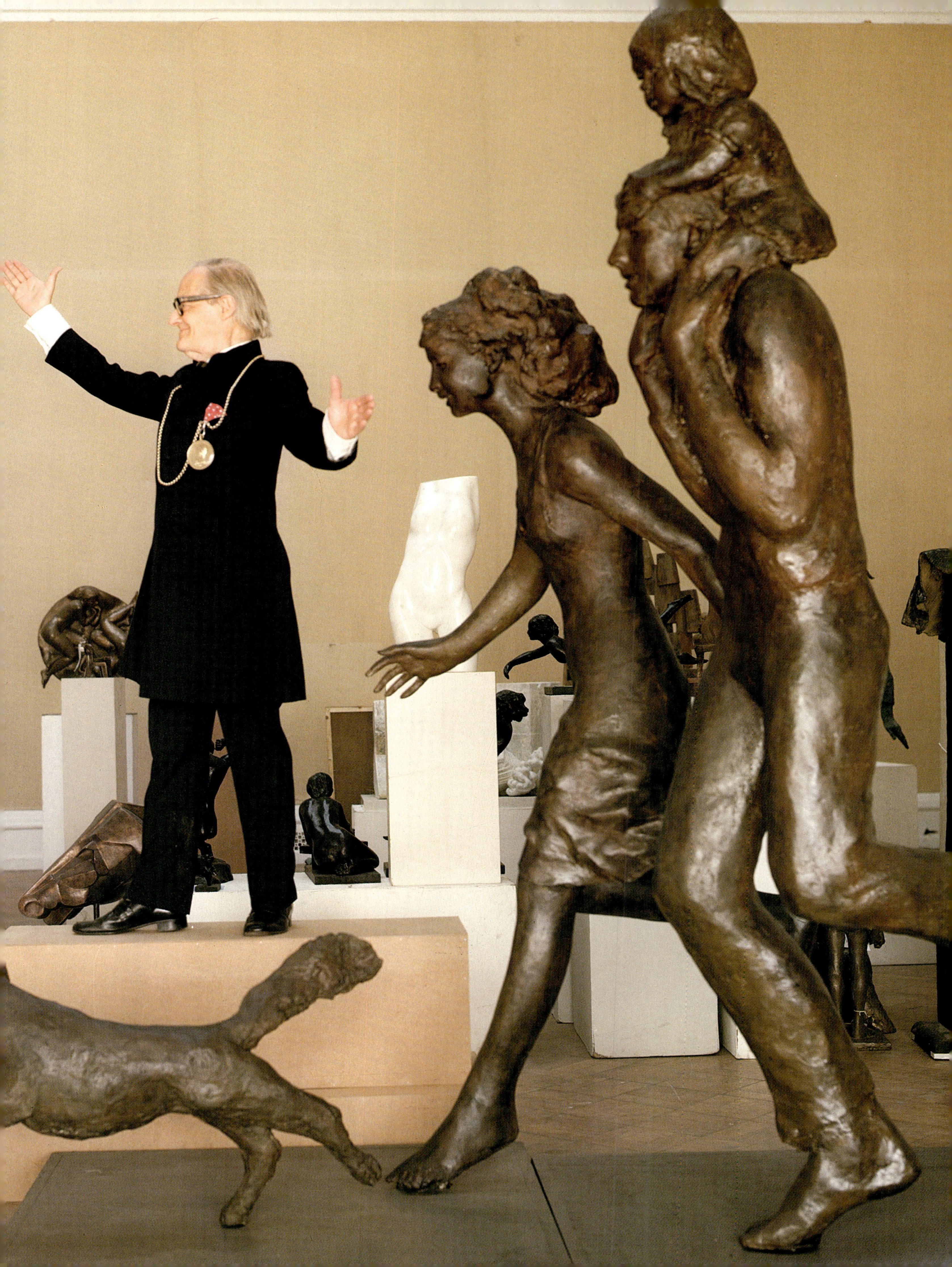

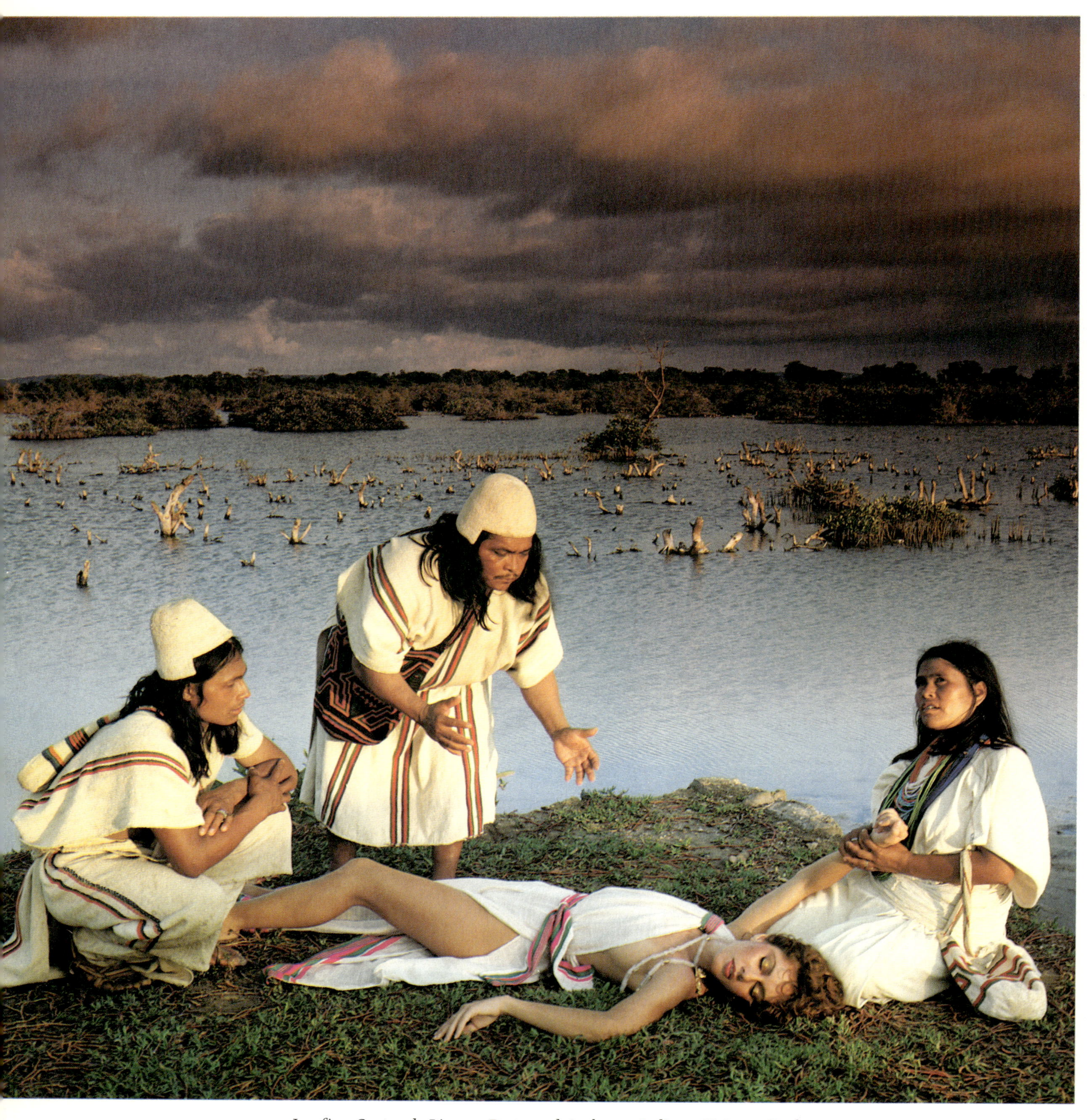

Josefina Castro de Linares Porto and Arthuaco Indians, Tairona Park near Santa Marta, Columbia, 1979

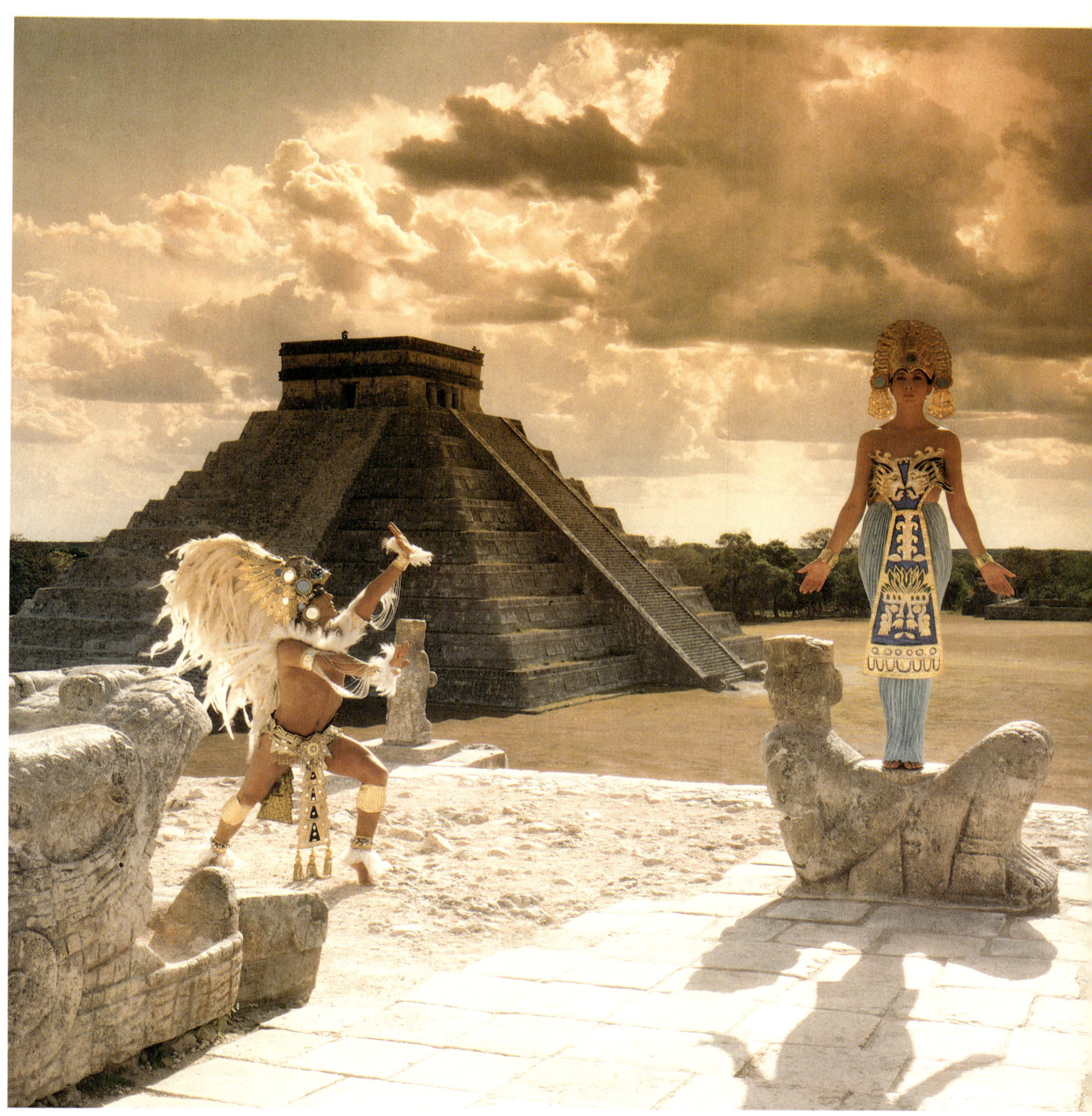

Jorge Tiller of the Ballet Folklorico de Mexico and Cecilia Fernandez de Steiglitz, Temple of Kukulkan at Chichen Itza in Yucatan, 1980

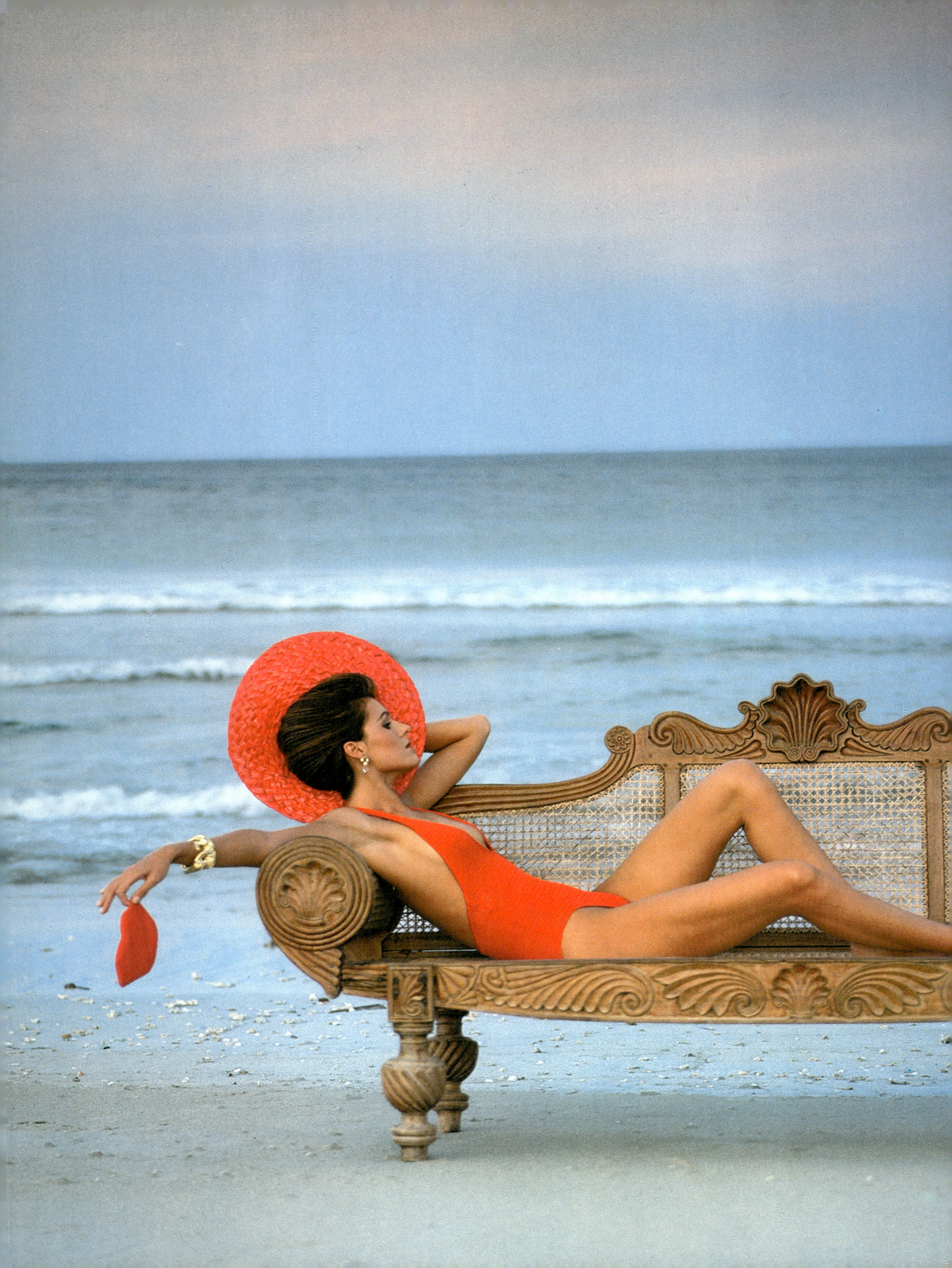

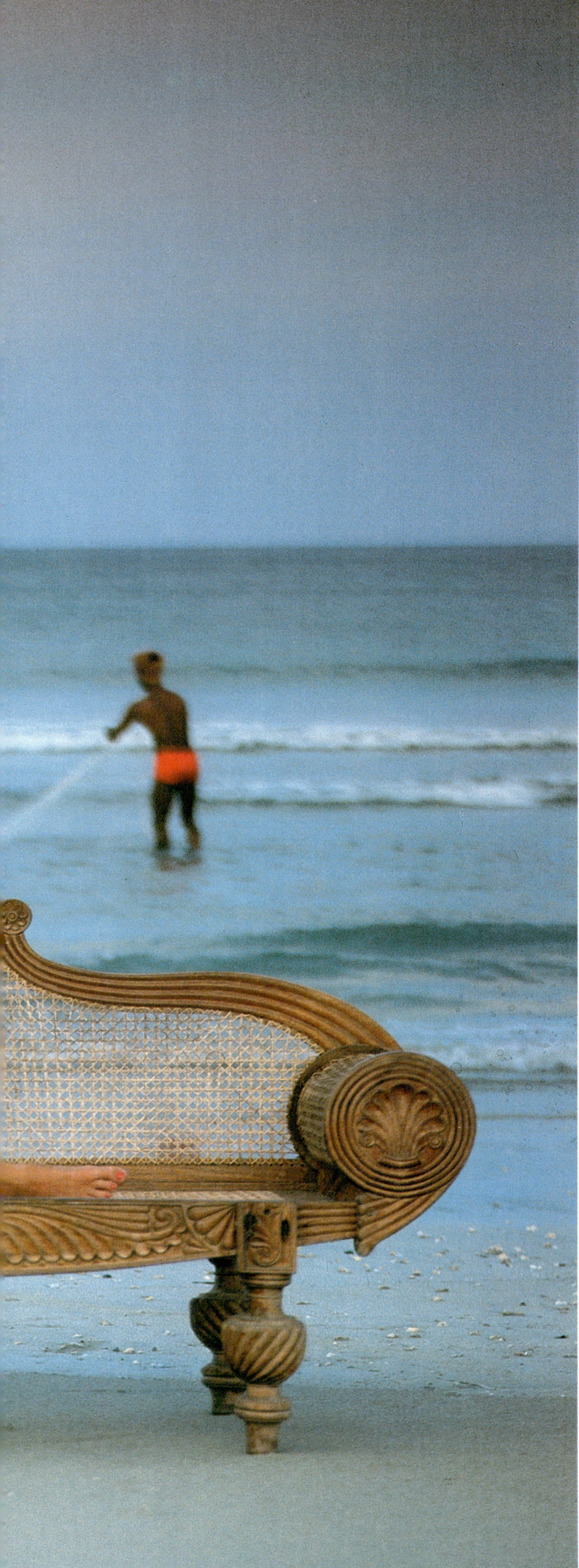

Count and Countess Crespi had a beautiful daughter – they called her Pilar. 'Parks, would you enjoy a trip around Sri Lanka and would you care to photograph Pilar Crespi there?' asked Nancy Gardiner of *Town and Country*, attempting to whip up my enthusiasm for a journey which I would have given my eye teeth to take – until I actually got there.

We were booked to stay at the Gallface, a handsome and antique seaside hotel, the flipside of the iced-water world of Hiltons and Holiday Inns. This famous colonial hotel thrives, with some justification, on the slogan 'At the Gallface, the Best is getting Better'. Needless to say, it sports a personable and eccentric new owner, and if it should be your first visit, comparison is not easy. We enjoyed our stay there for almost a week, drenched by mountainous seas and monsoon rains, then in desperation we moved north east to Trincomalee in our ultimately successful search for sunshine.

Sometimes Tourist Boards can be dubious and over-keen hosts. I am the most punctilious respecter of local traditions and religious practices, but on this occasion life was blighted by a guide who used the hourly admonition; 'Face the Buddha. Absolutely no photography whatsoever unless you face the Buddha'. The small omnipresent official would even find headless Buddhas, often used as cattle tethers, standing isolated in fields. Pilar was much too beautiful to photograph continually from the rear, so eventually we gave up the unequal struggle and abandoned the obsessive guide and Buddha country, heading for an elephant nursery near Nandi.

The more enlightened rural Sri Lankans are engaged in the preservation and nurturing of young elephants, an endangered species on the relatively small island continent. The Government has established a farm for baby elephants who would otherwise not survive in the jungle. Some are abandoned by their parents and others are brought in because they are found wandering sick or injured. Twice a day this small tame herd are taken down to an adjacent river to wash and cool off and frolic in their elephantine water sports.

I anticipated that this location might provide a good picture, and Pilar, being a courageous girl, never hesitated to pull on a swim-suit and jump down into the river with them. She was soon sitting and rolling with their enormous bulks. Even the smallest elephants weigh over a ton and are particularly heavy on their feet. Pilar was soon in hysterics, and I have an almost unprintable picture taken when a baby elephant sought to explore her nether regions with a trunk of unerring aim. Eventually she managed to beat off his persistent attentions with a broomstick.

We all have the happiest memories of Sri Lanka and its most decorative and friendly people, but nightmares still continue with that command: 'Face the Buddha'.

Pilar Crespi in a Krizia bathing suit, on the coral sands of Trincomalee, Sri Lanka, 1980

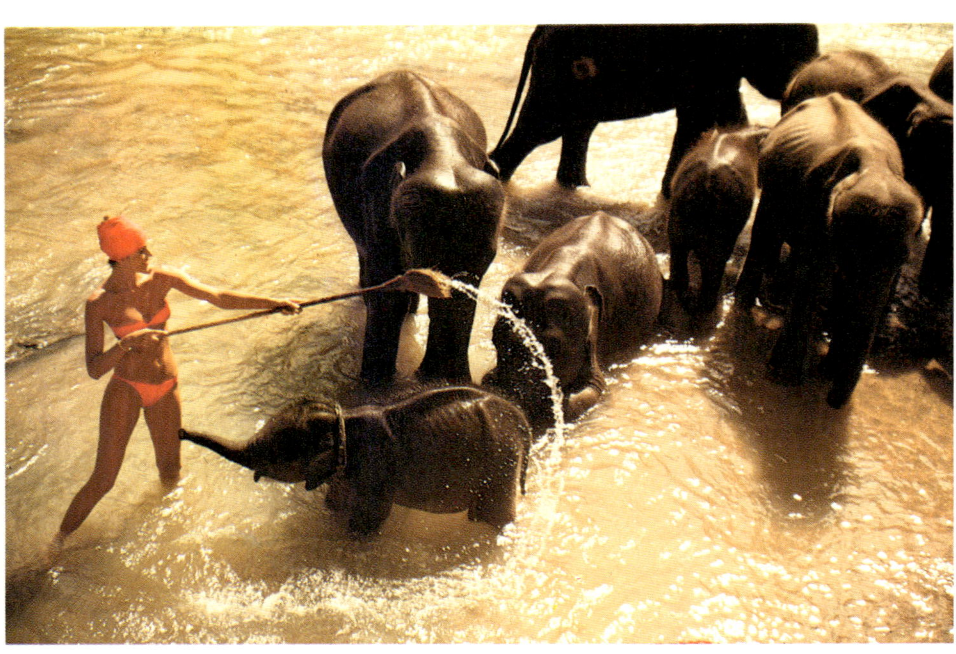

Pilar Crespi in a Norma Kamali bikini, elephant orphanage near Kegalle, Sri Lanka, 1980

RIGHT *Pilar Crespi in a Calvin Klein suit on the 1,840 steps of Mahintale leading to the burial place of Mahinda, son of the Indian Emperor Asoka, Sri Lanka, 1980*

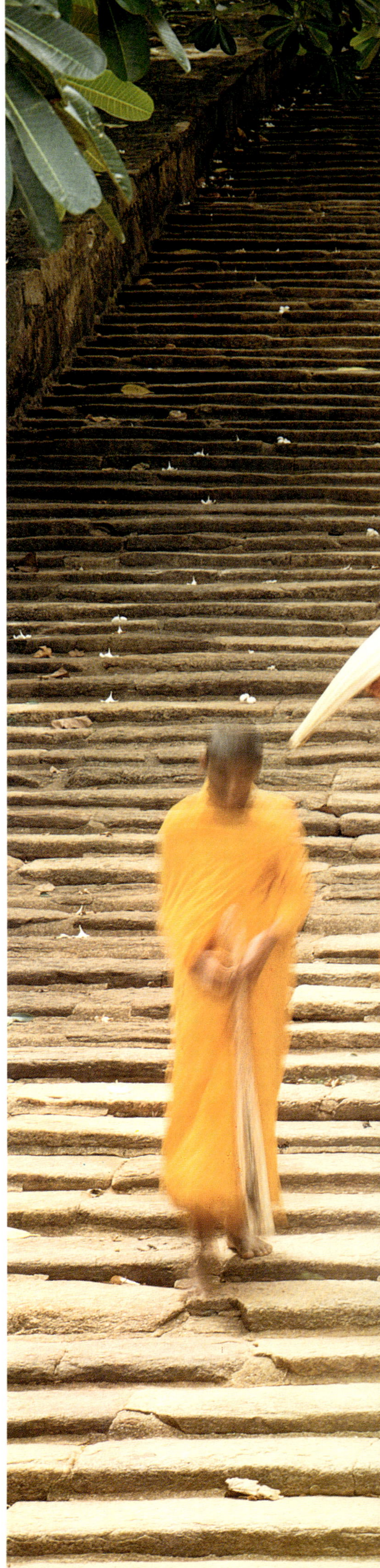

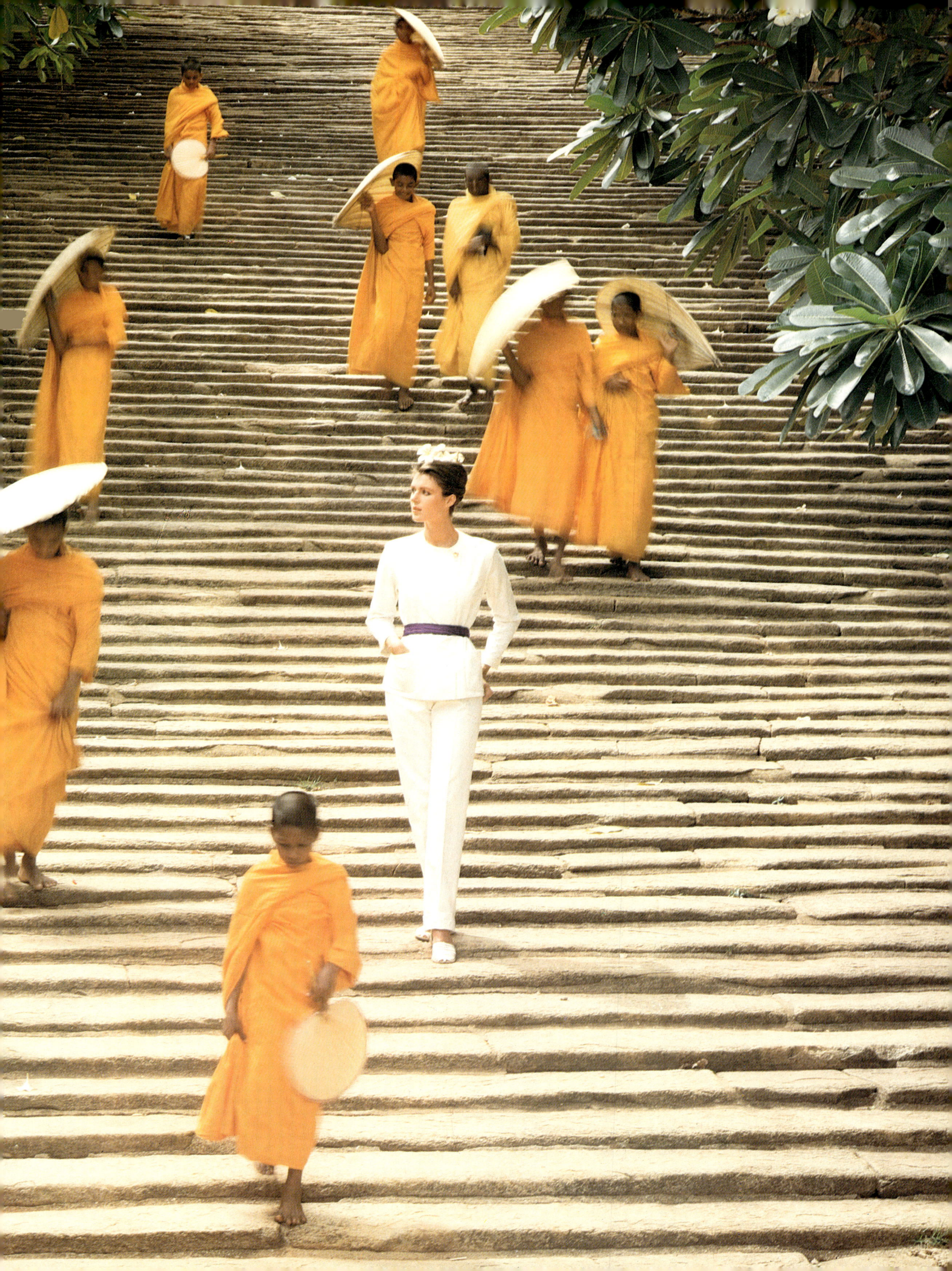

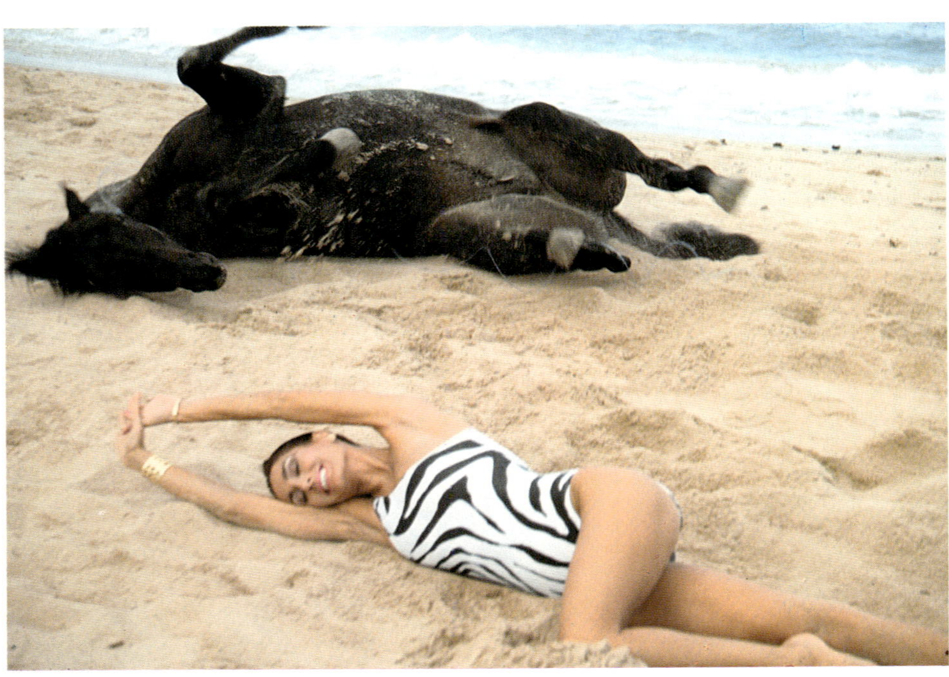

RIGHT AND ABOVE *Natividad Abascal Romero-Toro, the Duchess of Feria and Marchioness of Villa Alba, Barbados, 1982*

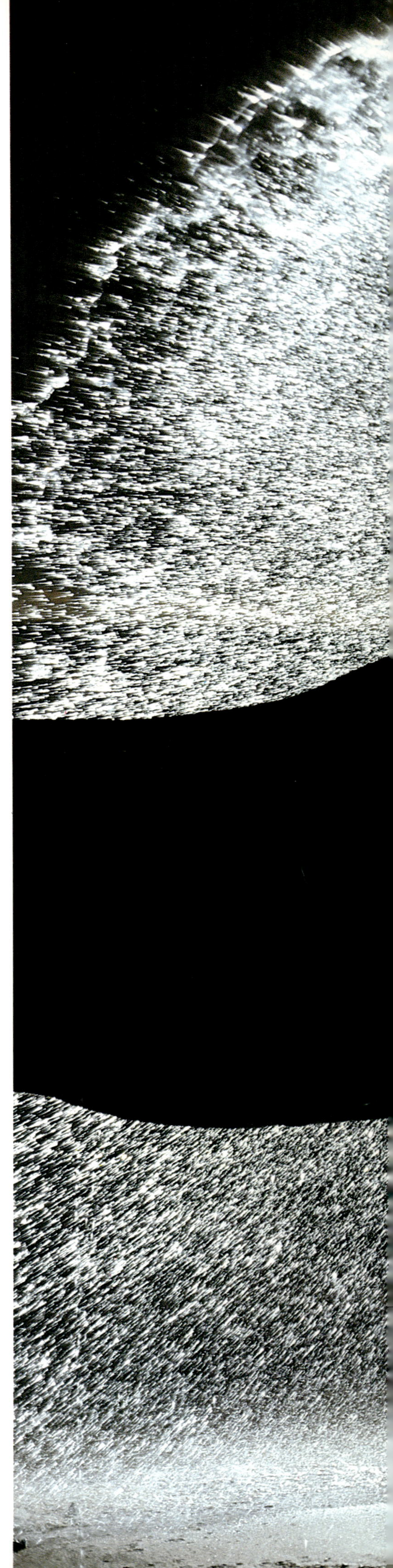

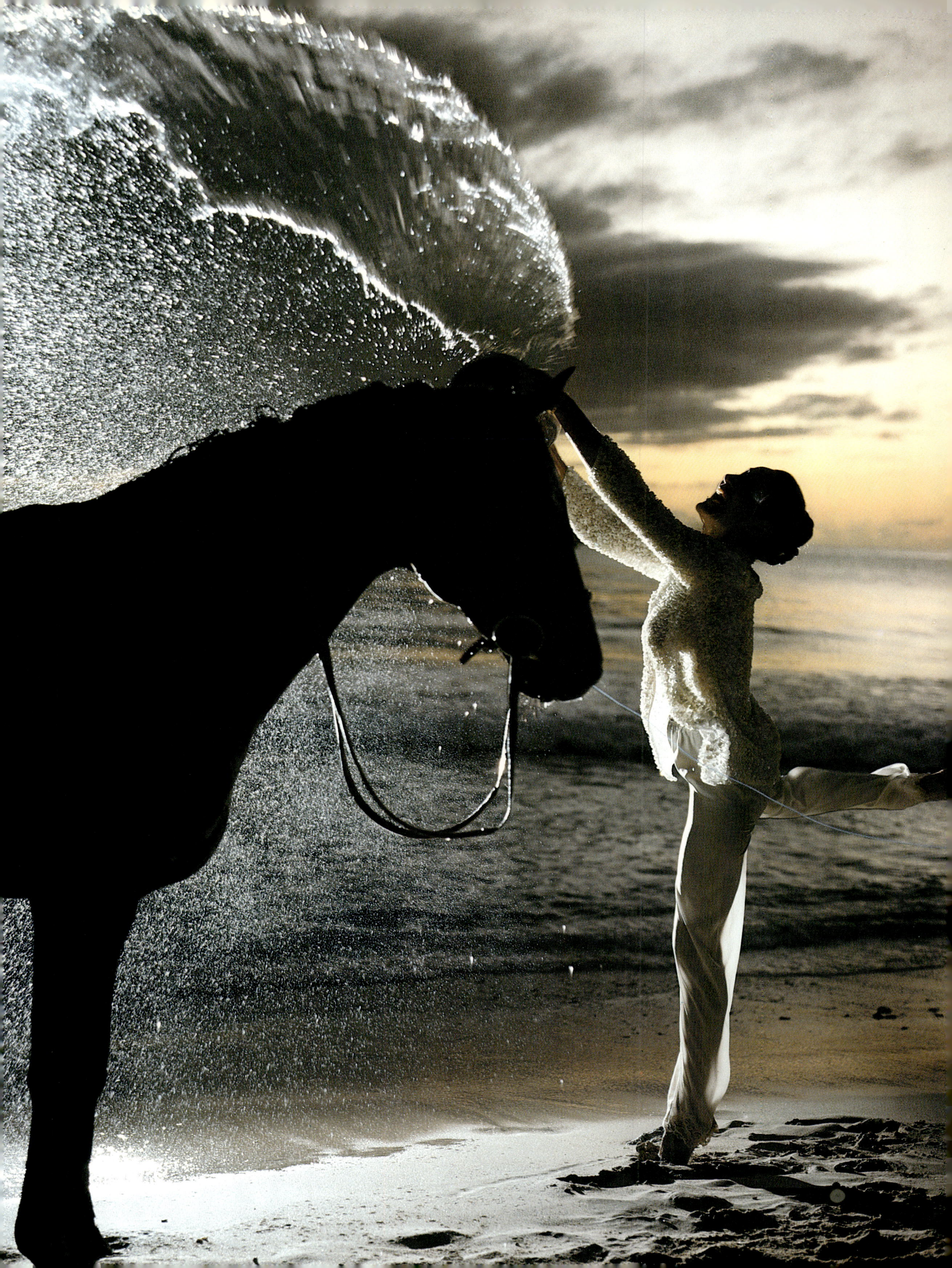

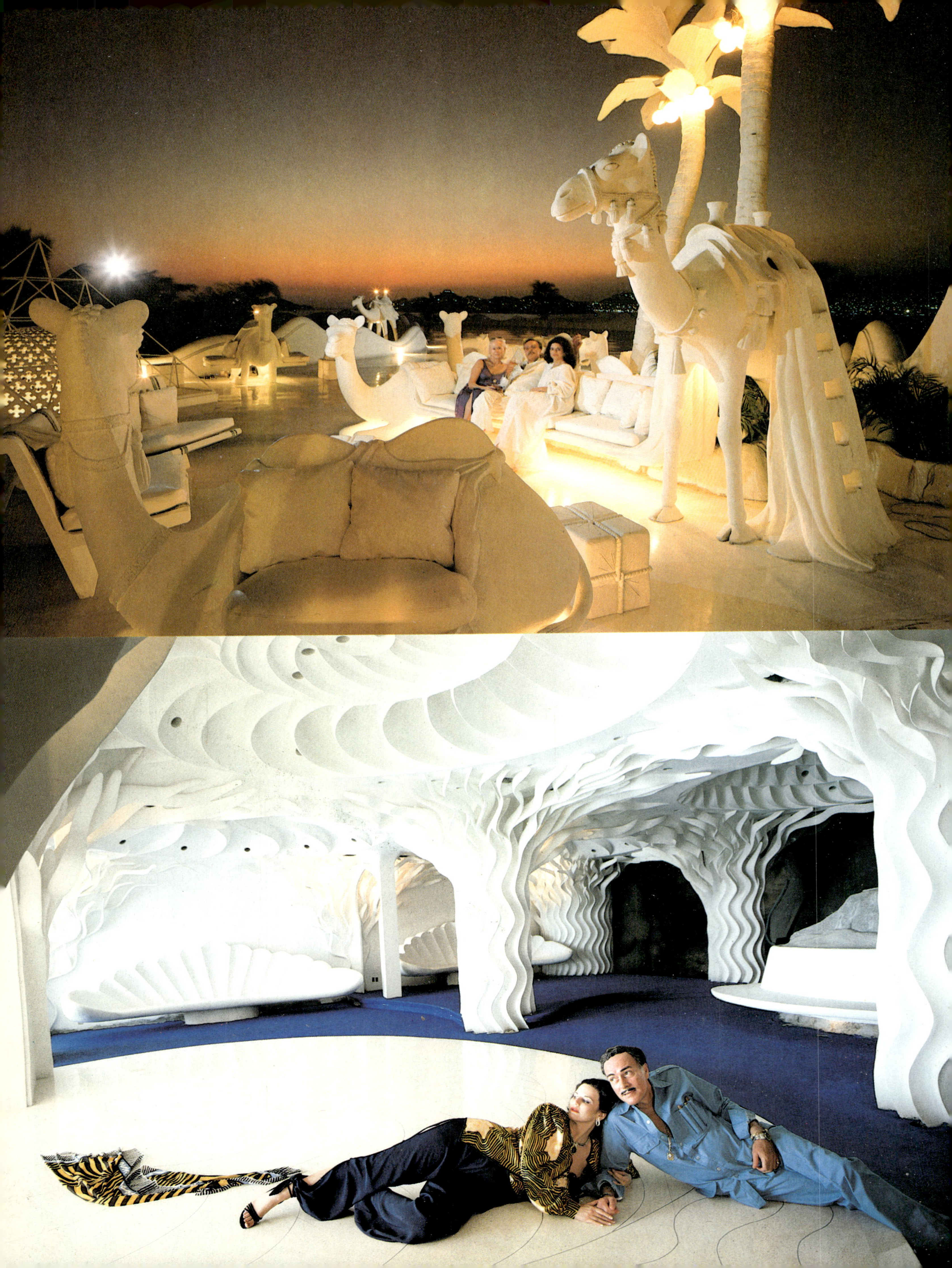

WHAT IS TASTE?

By proposing this question I have seized a tiger by the tail. I ask it here, as I have asked it many times before, never to receive a satisfactory answer. Perhaps there is no definition. An editor once described my approach to photography as walking perilously along the razor's edge between good and bad taste. I think she was about right, which is another demonstration of my quandary.

Did the Victorian age demonstrate better taste than the refinement of the eighteenth century? Is Las Vegas a total climax of bad taste, put together with such sure confidence that it all comes out the other end as good taste? Does a woman who always wears black have more taste than a sister dressed by Zandra Rhodes? Are designer jeans the bottom while Levis, from which they sprang, more refined? Are those new spectacles with side pieces that loop downwards before they make their wandering way to the ear in better taste than the straight side pieces we have known for centuries? Are the photographs of Helmut Newton who brilliantly portrays some of the world's most beautiful women naked in wheelchairs or martingales in better taste than those of Diane Arbus who had a penchant for cripples? Is kitsch better than Art Nouveau? Does Gaudí have better taste than the Adam brothers had? Is a Rolls Royce superior, as a demonstration of a person's taste, than a Lamborghini? Mozart or Vivaldi? Where can one possibly go for a decision?

I have constantly thought about the right and left, the up and down and the black and white of it all; I offer the flicker of a solution that almost satisfies me, but which will probably be discounted by everyone else. Taste, naturally, is a very personal thing, but again, every generation throws up some character who is described as an 'arbiter of taste', thus this arbiter makes decisions for whole sections of those who are too simple to recognize good or bad taste, which does not make it very personal. I have this idea that if something is perpetrated with enough persistence, enough confidence, and perhaps enough money, it becomes good taste. It may not be labelled as such right away but in time, if it is recognized by enough (so-called) arbiters, it can move in that direction.

Which takes me to the tiger; recently I was commissioned to travel to Acapulco in Mexico to photograph the coming-on-to-be-finished house of Ricky and Sandra di Portanova. The Baron will not discuss how many millions and millions this edifice will have cost upon completion, for naturally this is a tasteless topic, but he has, with his wife, put together a remarkable home of mammoth proportions. Asked why it was so large, Sandra said that she thought the measurements were in feet, and it turned out that they were in metres. During part of its construction an army of fifteen hundred artisans was employed.

'Poor you', was the concerted chorus from my acquaintances in New York and Mexico when they heard that *Town and Country* had asked me to point my cameras in the direction of 'Arabesque'. 'What will you do with it? It is absolutely ghastly.'

The Baron has surrounded himself with the minutiae of good taste. He has a rare collection of Fabergé boxes, he maintains a permanent suite at the Connaught, his shirts are from Turnbull & Asser, he is an excellent cook in the Italian manner. (He never quite knows when or where he might wish to cook, thus to avoid any embarrassment to his guests five kitchens have been designed in various parts of the house.) A chain smoker of his own brand of Havana cigars, he does not use an ashtray. He is a very sophisticated man with tasteful acquisitions too numerous to mention, so despite its many detractors I entered his new home with an open mind.

Two streams encouraged by gravity splatter through the house, they are named Ricky and Sandra. In a cool penumbric cave to Poseidon, stands a double life-size statue of the Sea King. For his pleasure the Baron can organize, at the push of a button, a vast cascade of water fifty yards wide by fifty feet in height – a most impressive and torrential eccentricity. The Baron has included, against the day thereof, an enormous night club of exceptional beauty which is decorated to represent a submarine palace with the walls and ceilings in the finest 'cement fondu' of the many convolutions of bisected shells and coral.

There are six self-contained suites for guests with two swimming pools. The hosts' private pool, which is but a few paces from their bed, is on the way to the size of a football pitch. Their dining room table is formed from an over life-size recumbent wooden camel.

The land did not give on to a beach, so one was dynamited. As in most houses built on the side of a hill, you enter by the roof. As you pass through twenty-foot high iron filligreed gates, unless you look to your right you will not see the most fantastic creation of all. Hidden behind a four-square simple Moorish tower is a totally white oasis in which a dozen or more white cement camels stand, kneel, and chew their cud in brilliantly arranged groups; from their saddles and paniers comfortable seating areas have been designed beneath a group of tall white cement palm trees with clusters of opaque glass coconuts to illuminate the fantasy. It is a breathtaking conception of all-pervading peace. The roof area stretches away as a wide flat river of milk meandering to the sunset. It is, in fact, marble but it looks and shines like liquid. The roof is large enough to accommodate three guest helicopters landing simultaneously.

So, what is taste?

'I have always wanted to build my sort of house', the Baron Ricky is talking, 'and I have done it. I really don't care if people like it or not or if they criticize it; it is my house, it is not theirs. You are the first person to sleep here, Parks, and I am delighted that you were comfortable. It is possible that I will never live here, but that is not

OPPOSITE *Baron Ricky and Sandra di Portanova (above, with Nancy Holmes) in their villa 'Arabesque' overlooking Acapulco, Mexico, 1981*

important. I have designed it and something has been achieved that I wished to do.' He repeated again, 'It is my house.' He flicks the ash from his endless cigar to the left, to the right and even behind him. He talks very fast, almost without a breath, using the ash flicking as punctuation and emphasis, while Sandra sighs as her whitest of furniture becomes spattered. 'Tell us, Parks, what it is like sleeping here? Any mosquitoes? Is it cool? Did you enjoy the pools in the early morning? Isn't it a good idea that they are all the same depth of five feet? Plenty deep enough. Did the servants bring you a good breakfast? Excellent.

'I worry that there are a few flies around this house. What are we going to do about them? I foresaw that they would arrive sooner or later . . . the workmen do not bury their rubbish, so much food has been left about.' Sandra nodded, 'Ricky, they will all be gone soon and then we will get rid of the flies.' I was delighted by this conversation about the common housefly in this most palatial of all dwellings and interjected my own pet topic. 'You are quite right, Ricky, anybody who has studied the private life of the fly cannot tolerate them around their homes', but then as a diversion I added, 'One can have a lot of fun destroying them with a good swatter.' The Baron's countenance livened visibly. 'How very interesting. You appreciate fly swats, Parks? I have dozens of them – It is a great sport with a well-balanced swatter. You see, for instant destruction the fly should bounce, it's all to do with wrist work like cricket . . . you can cut one through the slips or to leg or even return one over the bowler's head . . . I love the game. Tomorrow when I come back', he went on enthusiastically, 'I will bring you one of my favourites. I have a pair like Purdeys and I will make you a present of one, you'll see – beautifully balanced.' 'Thank you, thank you,' I said, 'I would really appreciate that.' Ricky continued, 'I had an idea when in London this summer to have Aspreys build me a pair of silver swatters using my favourite design as a model – good idea don't you think? So if you enjoy the one I'll bring tomorrow I could let you have one in silver. Perhaps we could weave our initials into the killing whisk like tennis rackets, NP for you and RP for me. Remind me, Sandra, when we're in London.'

You can gather by the way I write about the man that I like him. Sandra is talented, efficient and immensely likeable too, so the sum total of what they have created together has a style and quality and is the amalgam of their enthusiasm and taste. It is an incomprehensible barn of a place, one span of an arch that frames Acapulco across the bay is 25 yards at the base, but there is nothing ghastly about their house. People who have not entered it spell ghastly E.N.V.Y. From the photographs that I show here it is clear that I loved it and them, but perhaps as the creator himself has announced, 'I will probably never want to live there'.

We are no nearer in our definition of good taste, or whether this amazing house has a modicum, of it. Could it be that Baron Ricky di Portanova has walked, as I delight to walk, along the razor's edge that separates the good from the bad? Since it is recorded that this is my habit, then as a self-ordained arbiter I submit that Ricky and Sandra have made the perilous journey with consummate success.

OPPOSITE *The Hon. Edward Richard Lambton, son of Viscount Lambton, as Adam, 1967*

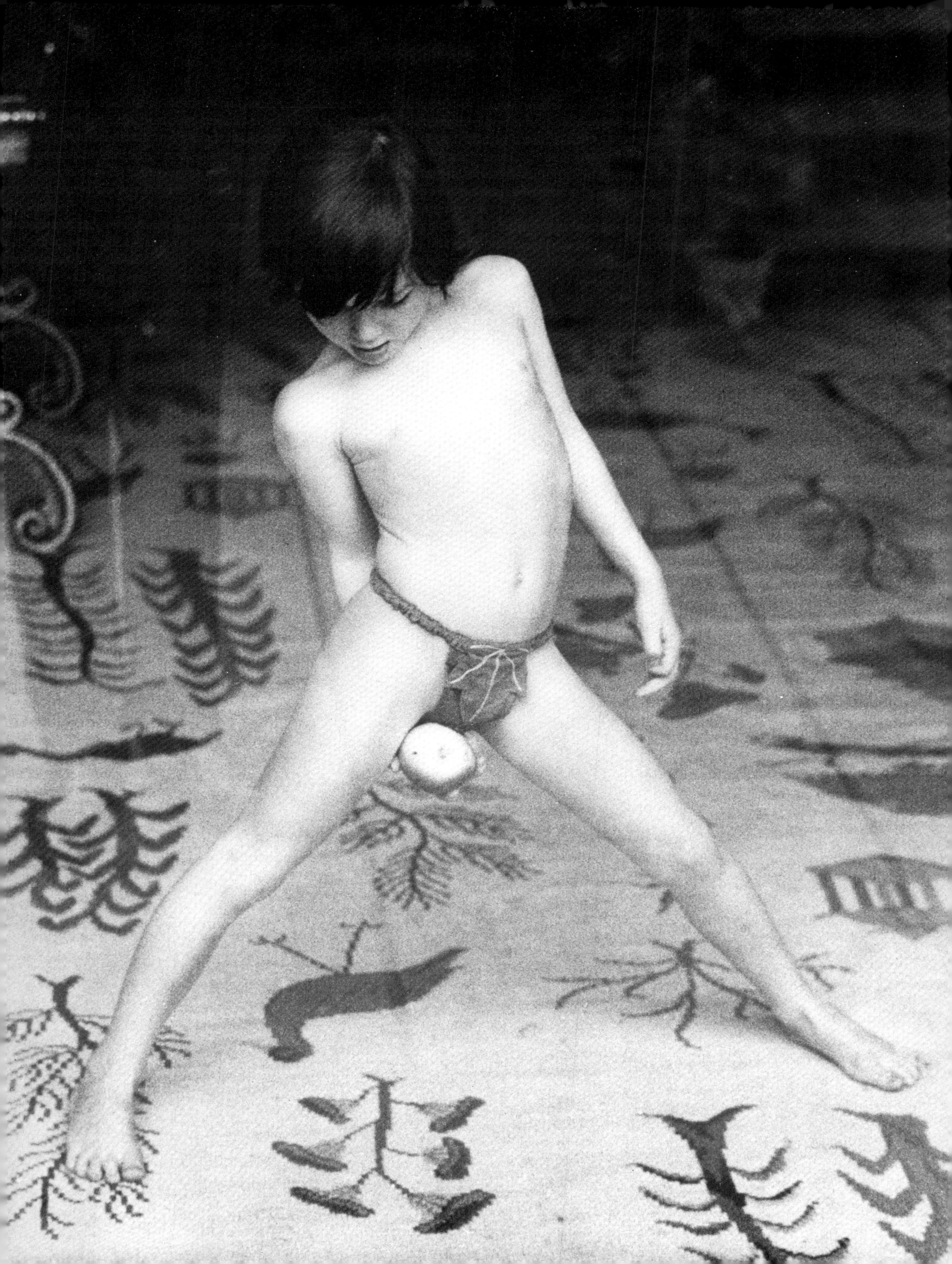

TOP GIRLS

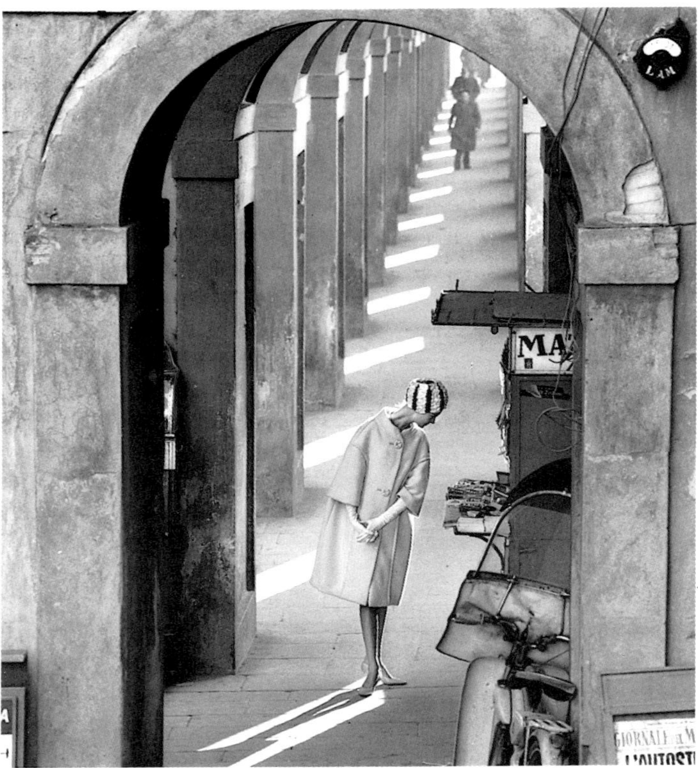

NENA

Everyone who gets into the fashion trade knows that half the best models in the world come from Sweden. Tall, cool, slim, usually blonde with long legs and beautiful hands – if they don't come from Germany they come from Sweden.

We were working in Stockholm in the late fifties when we needed one of just this kind of Swedish girl. 'I have managed to find out,' I told the Fashion Editor, 'the name and location of one of the smartest girls' schools in Stockholm, and I'm going to wait outside when the senior girls leave this evening.'

It was my lucky day: a shapeless beanstalk blonde who stood head and shoulders above her raincoated friends stepped out from the school. That hollow phrase, used a hundred times, was heard again: 'I'm a photographer; *Vogue* is doing a feature here in Sweden . . . have you ever thought of doing any photographic work?' Nena stood still and unbelieving and, as always happens, the parental warning about talking to strange men on the street came welling forward in her reply. 'Don't worry,' I attempted to reassure her, 'we are perfectly *bona fide*. Why not come to the Grand Hotel about this time tomorrow evening with a friend and ask for the Editor from *Vogue* magazine?'

Nena von Schlebrugge was not particularly athletic, like Carmen or Plonya, but she was very cool, calm and ice-smouldering. I have a passion for tall gangling blondes, and as Maurice Chevalier reminded us, ducklings soon grow into elegant swans. Nena did just that. I watched her develop in my camera and long before she was twenty she had become a great star in New York.

She had a mother who was a superb cook, and a German father. I never discovered who smoked more, Nena or her mother – the intake of both was phenomenal. Nena hardly had the frame to absorb all that nicotine, but she is still alive and well and, if my information is correct, married to a professor of political history and living in a lighthouse.

The sixties were her special time, but she never quite became a flower person in the Haight Ashbury of San Francisco or the Chelsea of Mary Quant. She hovered like some half-filled helium balloon between the two until she made her most decisive statement by upping and marrying Tim Leary. By that time she had moved away from my flagging influence. She was an exceptionally beautiful girl and however you lit her always looked wonderful. I do not think many with her innate elegance will appear again – with or without cigarettes.

ABOVE *Nena in a tweed coat by Galitane, Florence, 1961*

OPPOSITE *Nena in a dress by Susan Small and casual coat with pale beige coney fur lining, 1958*

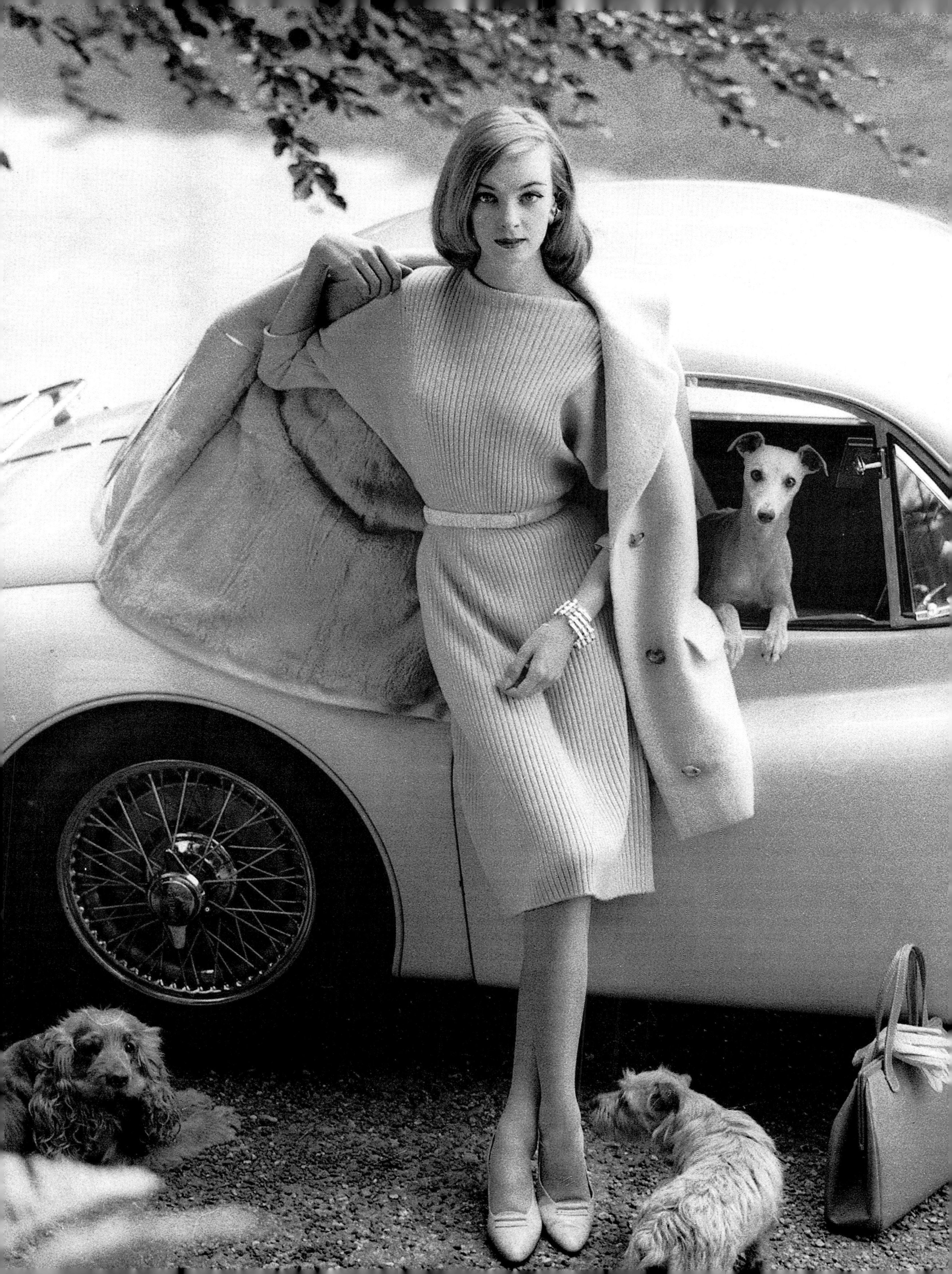

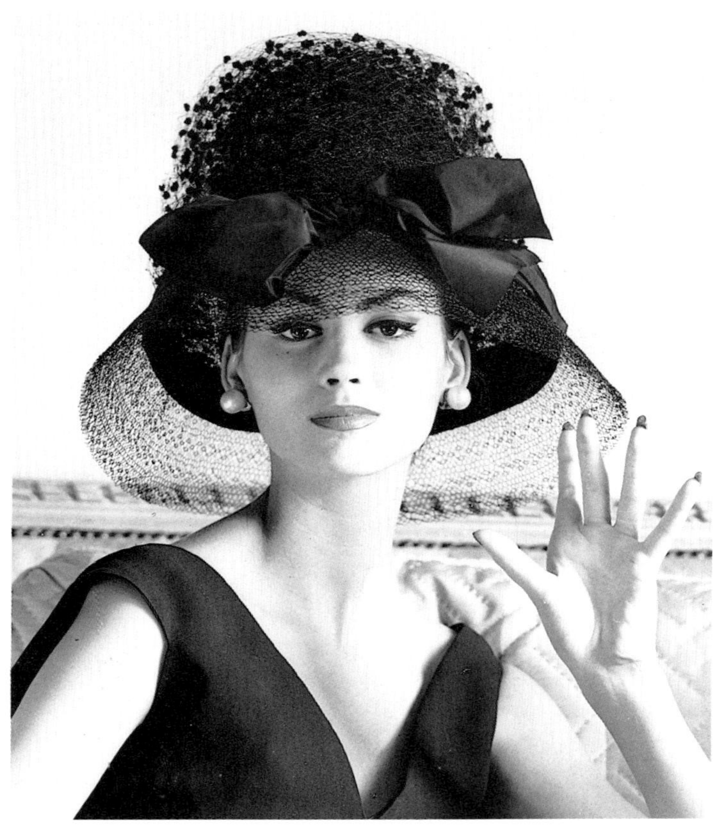

PASTRIE

Katherine Pastrie was French, but what is of greater interest is that few girls of that nationality make good photographic models. There have only been a handful – Bettina (famous with Aly Khan and Jacques Fath,) Sophie Malgat, Regine and the incomparable Maxine de la Falaise. French girls usually come a little small for the camera, whereas there are dozens of fashion house runway models who are beautifully French. Most haute couture designers prefer to make their frocks on French girls because they are more the shape of the majority of their clientele.

Pastrie was as French as *tarte aux pommes* or *crème brûleé*. She made a point of letting everybody know it. In the early days of our work together, she could be decidedly temperamental, but mercifully as time passed she became more mellow. (There is a wine analogy here.)

I cannot remember how she first stood before my camera in the early sixties, but suddenly she was there every week. Jocelyn Stevens was beside himself in admiration for her, which was not unjustified, and for the *Queen* magazine he alternated his passions between blonde Celia Hammond and brunette Pastrie. When a trip to Tahiti was being organized he shouted, 'Take Pastrie, Parks – every glance a Gauguin!' The Fashion Editor, Annie Trehearne, and I were to travel from London to Paris and were then to meet Pastrie there at 10.30 pm for the midnight take-off. By 11.30 pm there was still no sign of Pastrie and in those days there was only one plane a week to Tahiti, it used propellors and took for ever. We telephoned Pastrie at home, just in case. She was in bed with her husband on the other side of Paris – she had thought the trip was tomorrow. She had a handsome husband, a year-old baby boy, and a fast car which rushed them to the airport ten minutes before departure. As the tractor pushed us away from the terminal, there was the forlorn husband having a waving gesture lovingly returned by Pastrie with her left hand, while her right was being fondled by another gentleman in the next seat.

The energy and interest that she showed to men she could concentrate and apply to a camera, and we did exceptional pictures together. She was, and is still, a beautiful woman, brilliant at wooing the camera lens with her darting blackcurrant eyes and devastating pout.

Any gentleman who wishes to meet Pastrie today must have lunch with her. She married a Mr Bubb and, together with her son and a dedicated French staff, they run a first-class bistro within a pig's trotter of Smithfield Market in London. On the corner of Faringdon Road you will see the sign 'Bubbs'. Pastrie in her proper French manner sits at 'le comptoir'. Nothing has changed. She still has wonderful legs, and her face is still full of beauty. The blush we once applied to her cheeks artificially arrives every day with a sip or two of Beaujolais. Bon Appetit!

ABOVE *Pastrie in a black tulle, satin and veiling hat by Bernard Devaux, 1960*
OPPOSITE *Pastrie in a Jaeger deep lilac chiffon bikini, Tahiti, 1960*

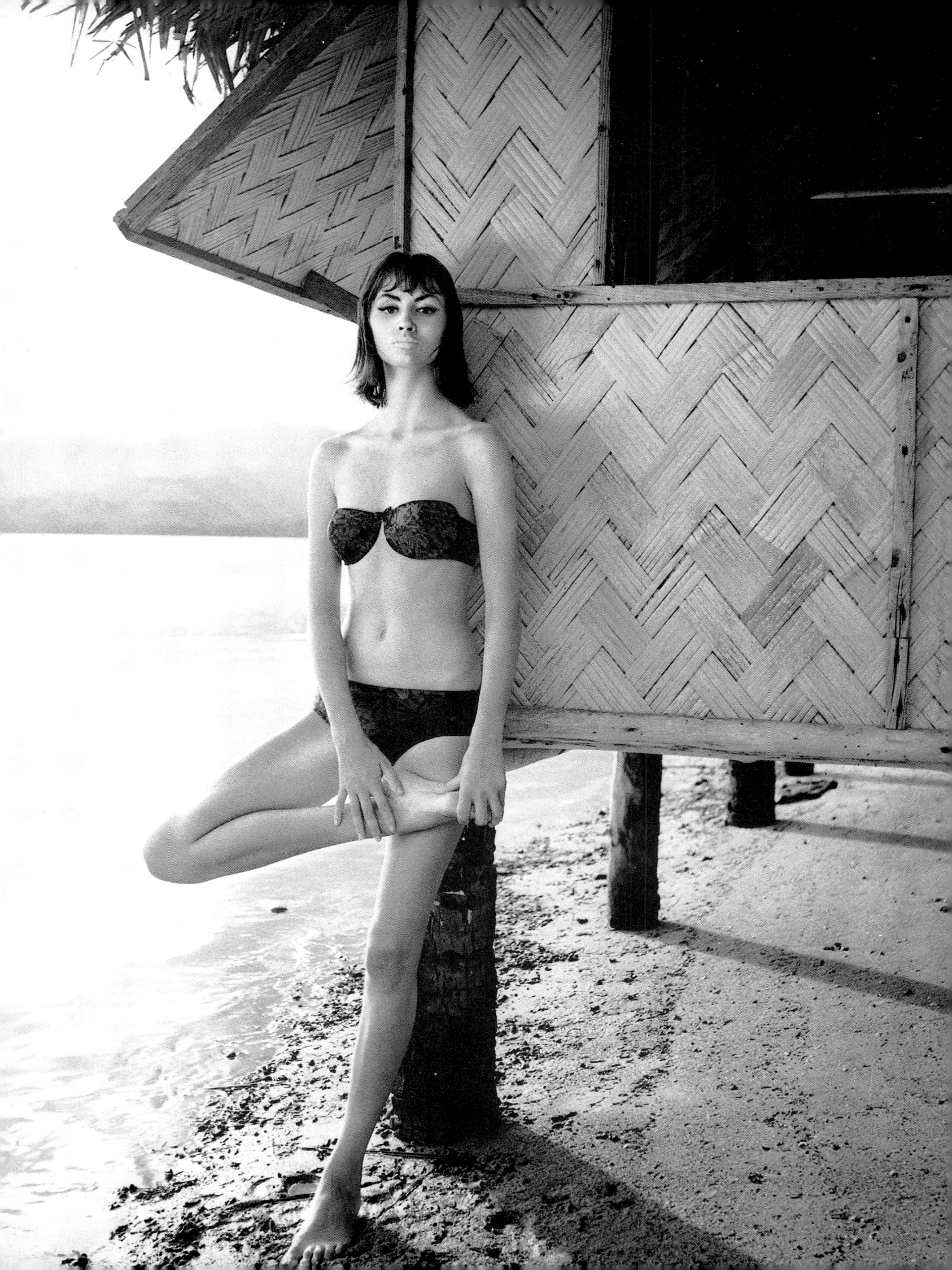

CELIA

In the late fifties I found it very difficult to discover new models, and only by ringing up the agencies and asking them to parade *all* their girls were we ever able to find new talent with some future.

One day in 1959 I rang Lucie Clayton and asked her to put on a 'cattle market' as we would unglamorously call them. 'But I have told you, Parks, we don't have anyone that you would like.' 'Never mind,' I replied, 'I'll be there 3 pm Wednesday.'

Upstairs thirty rather nervous young girls were sitting around like wallflowers. According to Parkinson's Law I started from the left, most methodically, 'Name? measurements? interests – can you ride? swim? etc.'; these latter questions were to make conversation so I could watch how their faces worked and how they reacted to me. An hour later I was downstairs drinking tea in the office. 'There you are, Parks, not much there as we told you.' 'What do you mean?' I asked with some excitement. 'You have a star up there.' 'Like who?' 'Celia Hammond,' I said. 'But Parks, you can't be serious, she looks Burmese or something.' 'That's the whole point and I'll book her for all day on Wednesday for *Queen* magazine.'

That day's shoot produced a cover and several inside pages from a girl who had never been photographed before. Jocelyn Stevens, Editor of *Queen* magazine, went crazy about her pictures, putting her under exclusive contract for a year; with that contract behind her she became an international star, and a great favourite of Diana Vreeland's.

I used Celia on every possible occasion. She was very punctual and hard working; she had a sweet mother and father (who was a tea taster) and she would emerge from their little semi-detached in Hampstead each day to go to work on the Tube. When I first found her she wore a neat fitted royal-blue woollen coat with velvet collar and cuffs. Within a few months she was in black leather and seemed to have a different illustrious man in tow every few months. If you detect a note of jealousy you are probably correct – she was a gorgeous girl, an absolute peach.

She had one fearful fault to which I would continually object. She loved animals – not only animals but small birds and beetles – far in excess of human beings. On one occasion driving down a motorway to a photographic location, inadvertently, as can happen, I hit a small bird. Celia let out a scream that could have been heard in the next county and, seizing my neck in her strong hands, she attempted to strangle me at 60 mph: 'Stop, you murderer, pull over, stop!' Great tears were coursing down her cheeks as she jumped out before the car had come to a halt on the hard shoulder. The next thing I knew she was charging back down the motorway looking for the corpse. A number of bewildered motorists took evasive action and managed not to run her over while she ran helter-skelter through their onrush. A couple of minutes later, she was back, sobbing her heart out and cherishing in her cupped hands a bloodstained six ounces of partly-plucked bird.

The day's work had to be abandoned for her face and eyes were so scarred with tears and redness that photography was out of the question. I drove her back to London, the wretched corpse on her lap, in silence punctuated only by the occasional sob.

Our first photographic trip abroad was to Jerez de la Frontera, something to do with sherry surely. After three or four days working there peaceably with great success, the manager of the hotel sought me out and with some concern announced: 'The night porter has told me, and I suppose it is none of my business, but the young lady you are working with leaves the hotel each night about eleven and does not return until after midnight. It is not an excursion that should be encouraged on her own.' So with consummate tact I enquired of Celia about her nocturnal wanderings. 'You're not very observant, are you, Parks? Haven't you noticed that the dogs and cats in this town are all starving? Well, before the butchers' shops shut I sneak out before dinner and buy a holdall full of best steak, and then when the whole hotel is asleep I sneak out again and walk all over town feeding the dogs and cats.'

I don't think Celia has ever lived in any of her apartments, houses or country cottages without sharing her abode with at least ten cats. It was inevitable that she would become a leading force in the attempts to ban whaling, to ban seal culling and to prohibit the wearing of animal fur coats. I suppose I got used to it, but for many years when she arrived in the morning to work as a model she would enter and enquire: 'Tell me, Parks, do I smell of cats this morning?' 'Well, now you come to ask me, yes!' 'Oh, dear, I must do something about that, but recently they've all had some awful complaint with their bowels.'

Celia Hammond, 1964

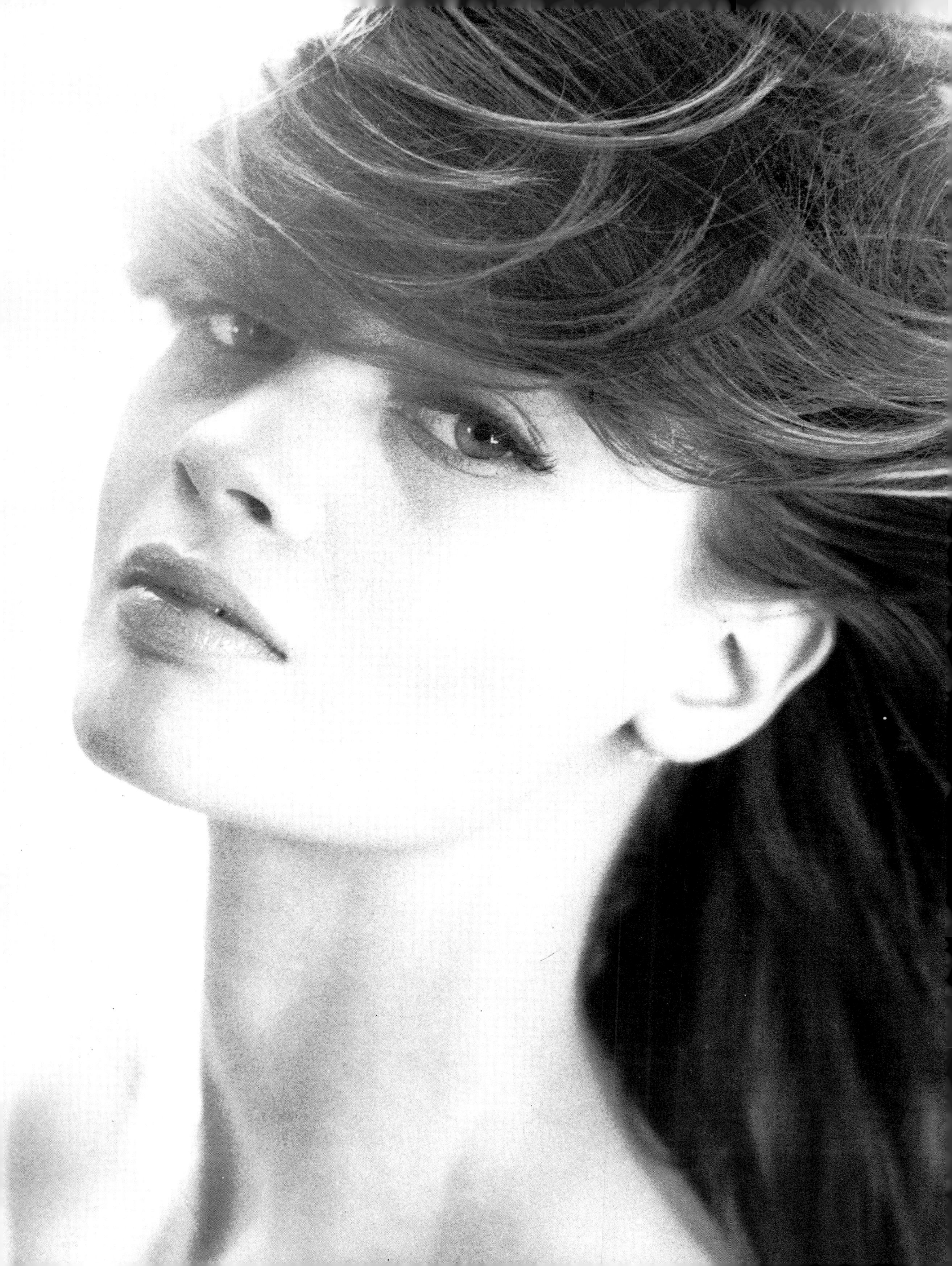

DOLORES

Dolores Wettach was of Polish extraction and I would give a free copy of this book to include Art Kane's picture of her in woolly stockings, elbows on knees, looking gloomily away, as one of my own. It is a great picture by a great photographer of a great model who started life as a nurse.

I took her on a trip to Peru and we lost her very smartly to a poor man's Conquistador and subsequently we never knew where she was at any given time. But when we did get together the pictures were excellent.

Wettach was a clear cut example of the move-on type of American and we were often amazed to see her sitting there in time for our departure at the airport. But when she could give us these photographs we were helpless to complain.

I should commiserate with the photographers who have followed me, for the girls who have followed the likes of Wettach and Carmen and Pastrie and Plonya are strangely lacking in the different 'look' that a model should have. If a girl looks like a model then she's not for my lens. Paradoxical as it may seem, I was always looking for the unusual undiscovered loner. Wettach was exactly that – a lovely girl, but never alone.

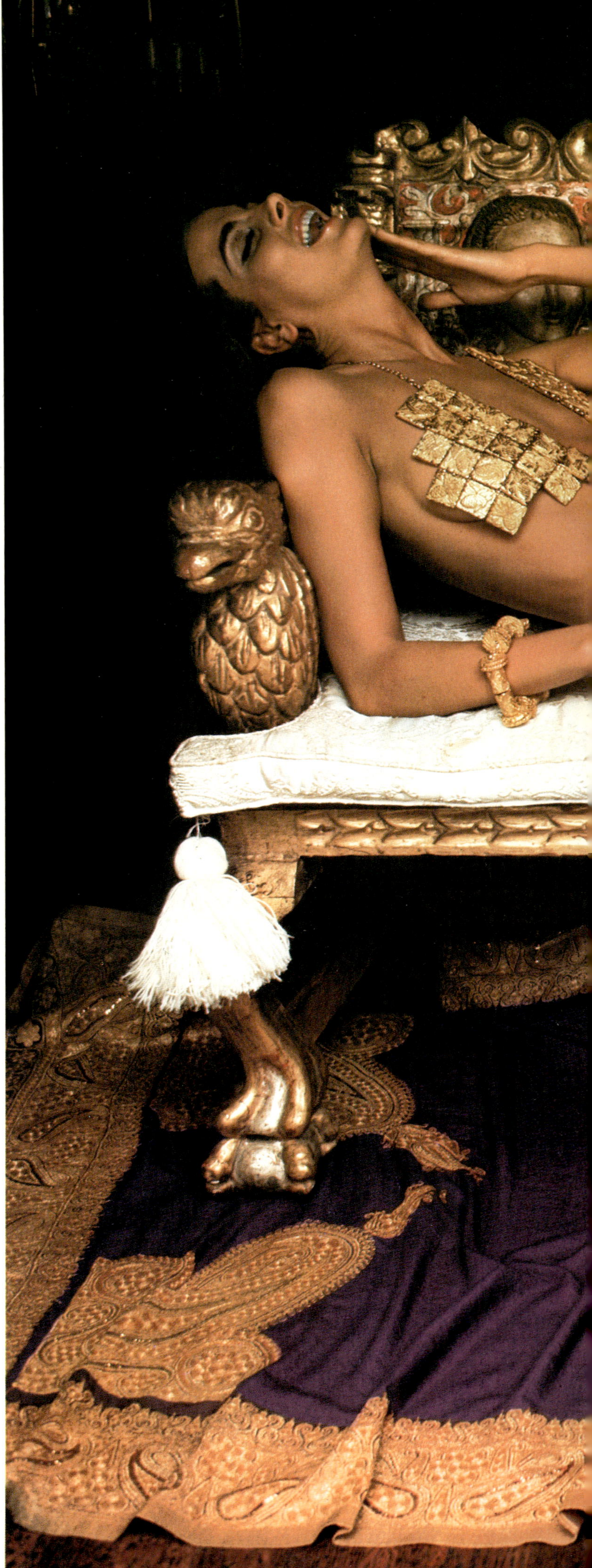

'Inca Metrics'. Dolores near Cuzco, Peru, 1965

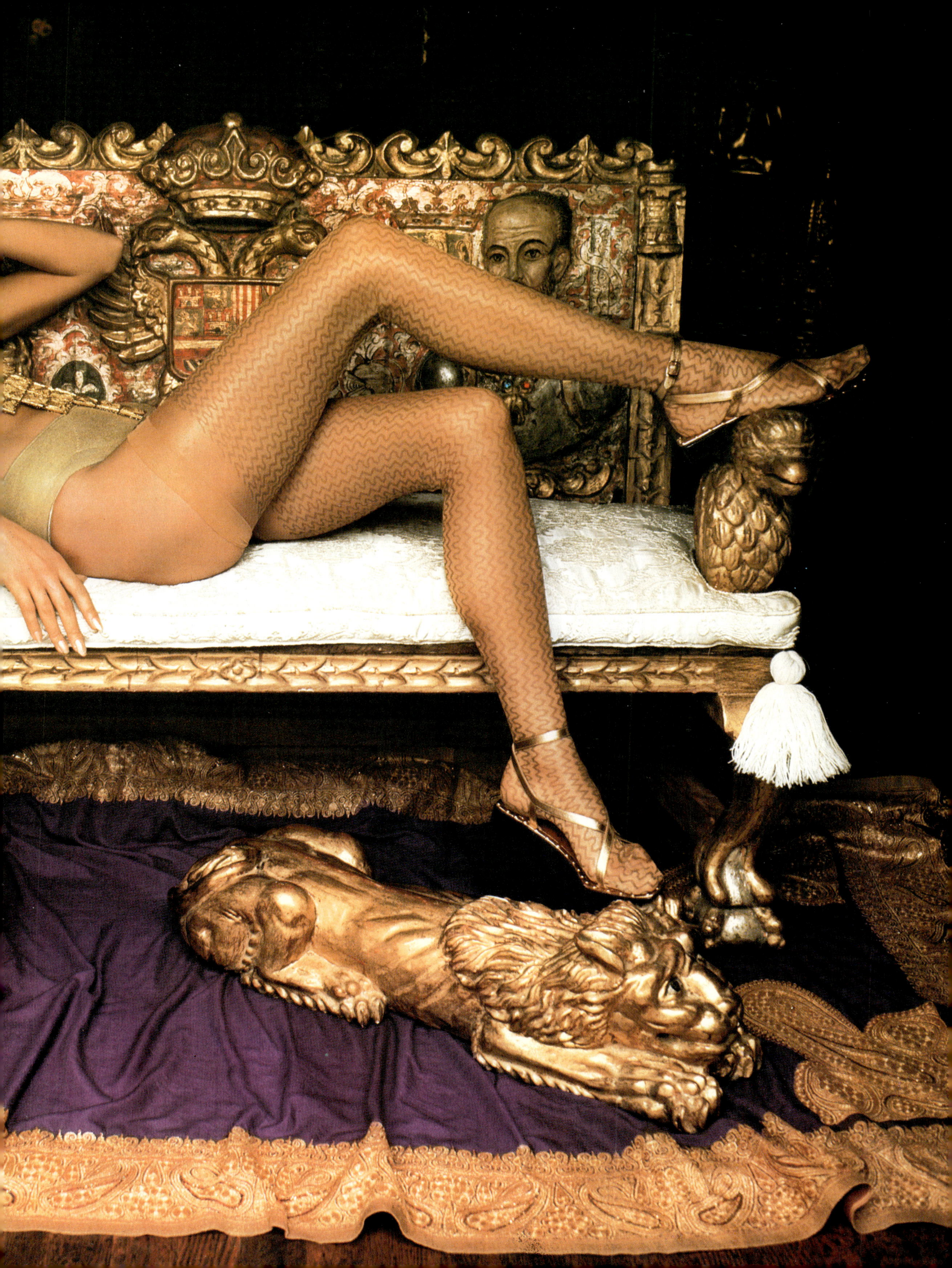

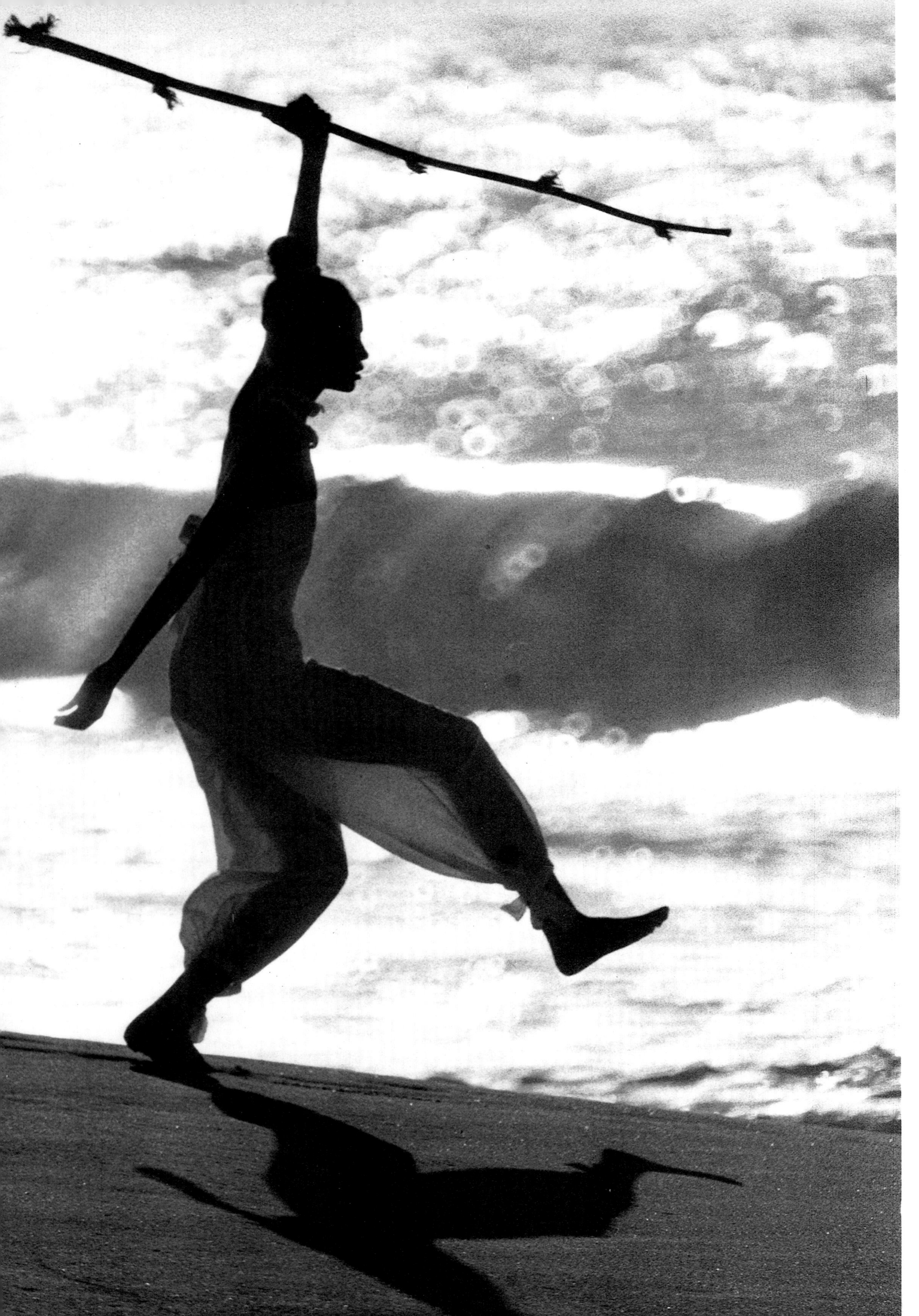

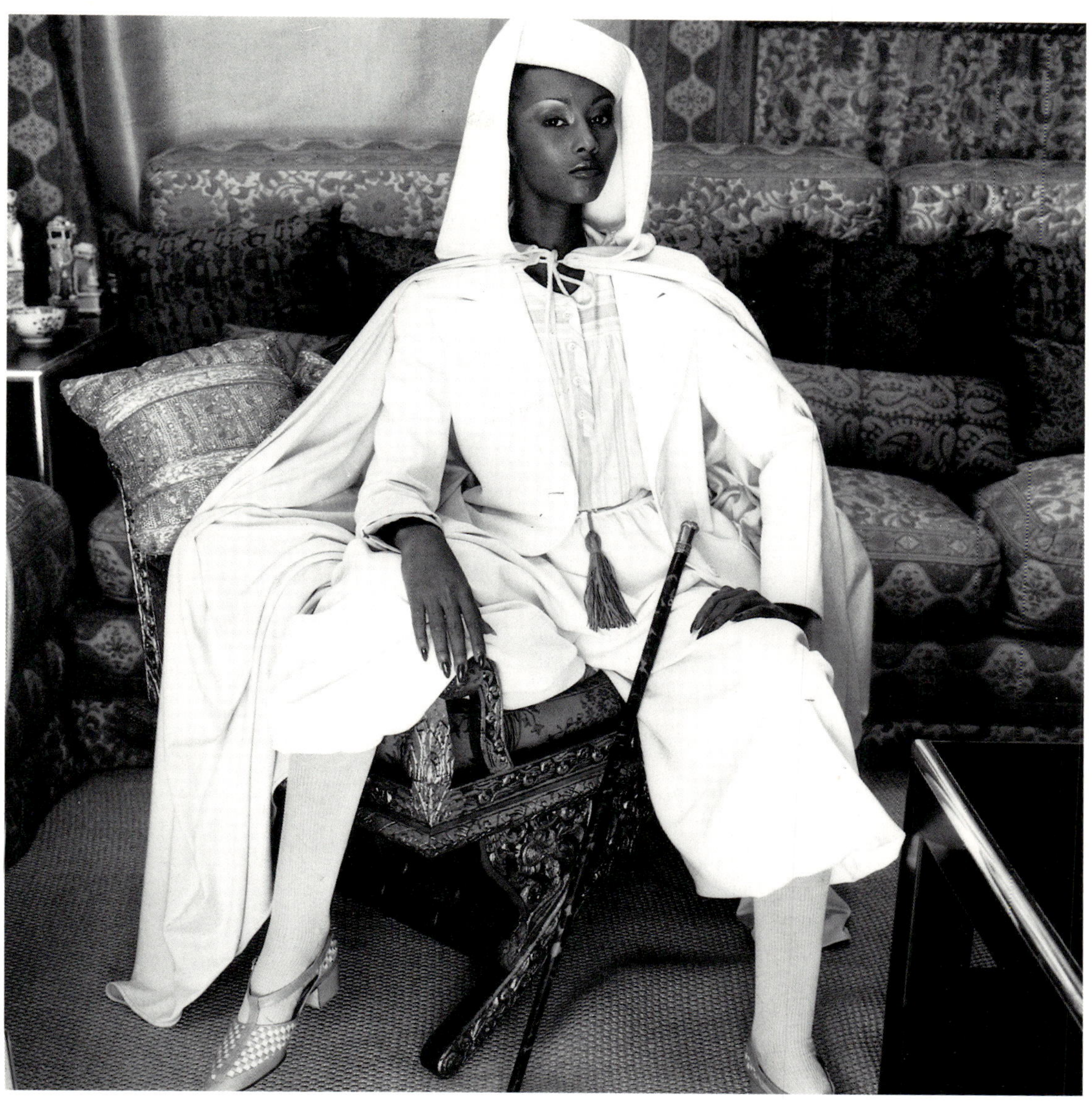

IMAN

Iman Abdul Majid is the world's most beautiful black woman. Quite simply this Somali leopard reigns supreme among the long-legged, long-necked girls so generously stained by the sun. She was born in Mogadishu in 1957 to a diplomat for Somalia to the Middle East states, and a gynaecologist. She was married, as is often required in her country, when she was fourteen or fifteen, but she does not talk about that anymore. She is now married to a Mr Haywood, a 6 foot 9 inch basketball player for the Washington Bullets, and has a daughter named Zulekha (though she is known as Zuzu).

Iman was eighteen when she was first presented to my camera and has continued to enrich it from time to time since then. She was nervous and unsure of herself (and me) as a young girl, and in consequence was not easy to direct on the first occasion that I photographed her, on King Peter's Bay, Tobago (see page 145). Iman and I have subsequently often laughed hysterically about the sitting; she can now confess that she was very worried about working for me because I was white, and I can now admit that it was the only time I have ever had to go down on my knees in front of a model.

ABOVE *Iman, 1977*
OPPOSITE *Iman in ivory cheesecloth by Krizia, King Peter's Bay, Tobago, 1976*

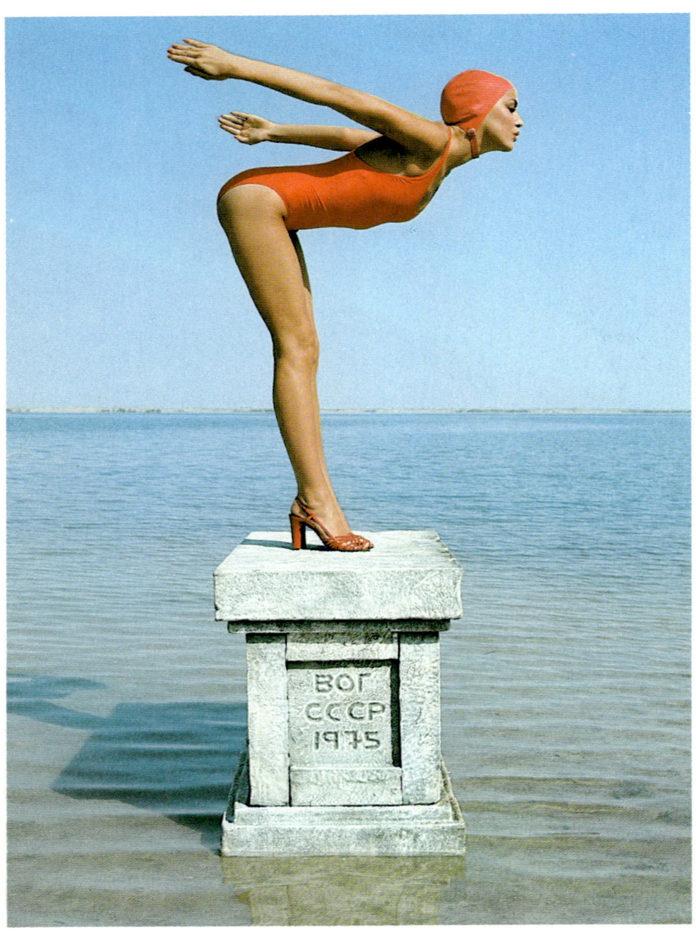

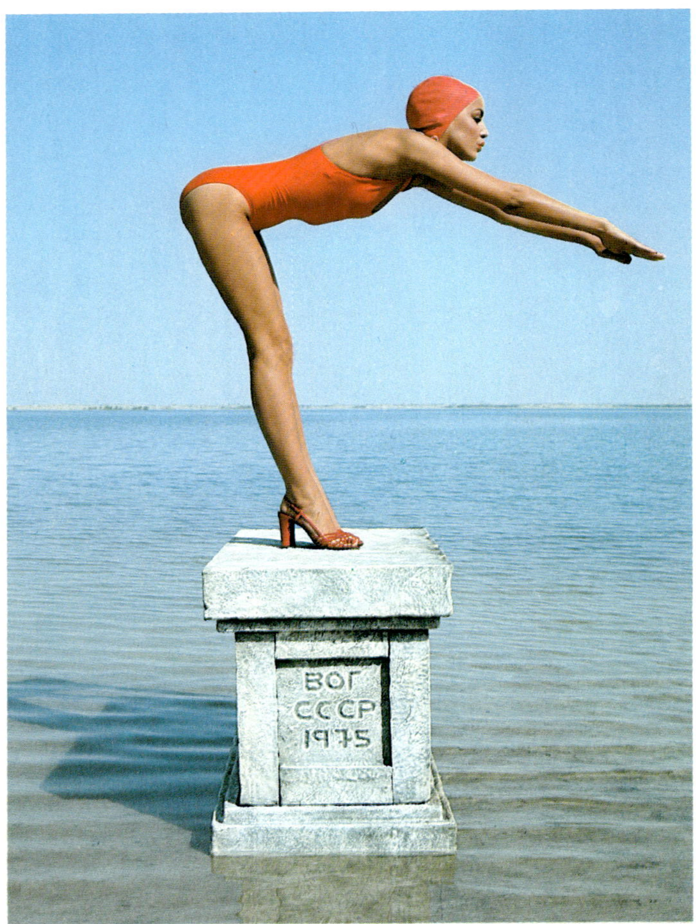

JERRY HALL

I have never been able to decide which came first in the chicken-and-egg analogy, my fascination with long-legged, good looking girls or with the breeding of thoroughbred racehorses. I would be quite well off today if I had concentrated on photographing the former rather than trying to breed the latter. But my passion for both remains. In movement I find it difficult to tell them apart.

Because, just sometimes, an ordinarily bred inexpensive horse can turn up and outrun the half million dollar stars, I have become interested in the breeding of the star models. How do they come about? Jerry Faye Hall, by truck driver out of compiler of medical records, has four sisters and a twin. Farming is in the blood. One sister is a vet and Jerry has invested some of her money subsequently in a Texas ranch that breeds quarter horses.

Our first job together was for British *Vogue* in 1975 in Jamaica. Aware of her rustic background, I assumed that she would be at home on a horse. 'Jerry,' I inquired the first night we settled into the Jamaica Inn, 'how are you with horses? – because I have found a pretty grey filly in a riding stable by Negril beach, and I thought that our first shot tomorrow might be in the blue sea, in the blue Gina Fratini ball dress on the grey horse'. 'Parks', she replied in her Texan drawl, 'I was born on a horse. My sister and I have broken horses for a living. I have yet to meet a horse I can't ride.' So next day I was able to reassure the stern lady proprietor of the livery stable that our girl was an expert horsewoman.

I briefed Jerry: 'Start here on the left and trot along the edge of the water. As soon as you reach that pole on the sand turn round and repeat the process.'

'Let's go,' I ordered. From walk through canter to gallop took exactly two seconds and my own terror was reflected in Jerry's face as she dashed away down the beach across my line of sight. The horse turned right, jumped a couple of gulleys and stopped dead in front of a barbed wire fence as Jerry flew over its head like some blue ballistic missile. When we got to her, hanging motionless as laundry might on a calm day, she was quietly moaning for her back was badly scratched. The horse owner was not far behind. 'That damn girl of yours has never been on a horse before in her life,' she snorted. To our relief Jerry opened her great blue eyes and said, 'That goddamn horse of yours has never been taught the way we ride in Texas.'

ABOVE AND OPPOSITE *Jerry Hall, Russia, 1975*
OVERLEAF *Jerry Hall with Antonio, fashion artist, Ocho Rios, Jamaica, 1975*

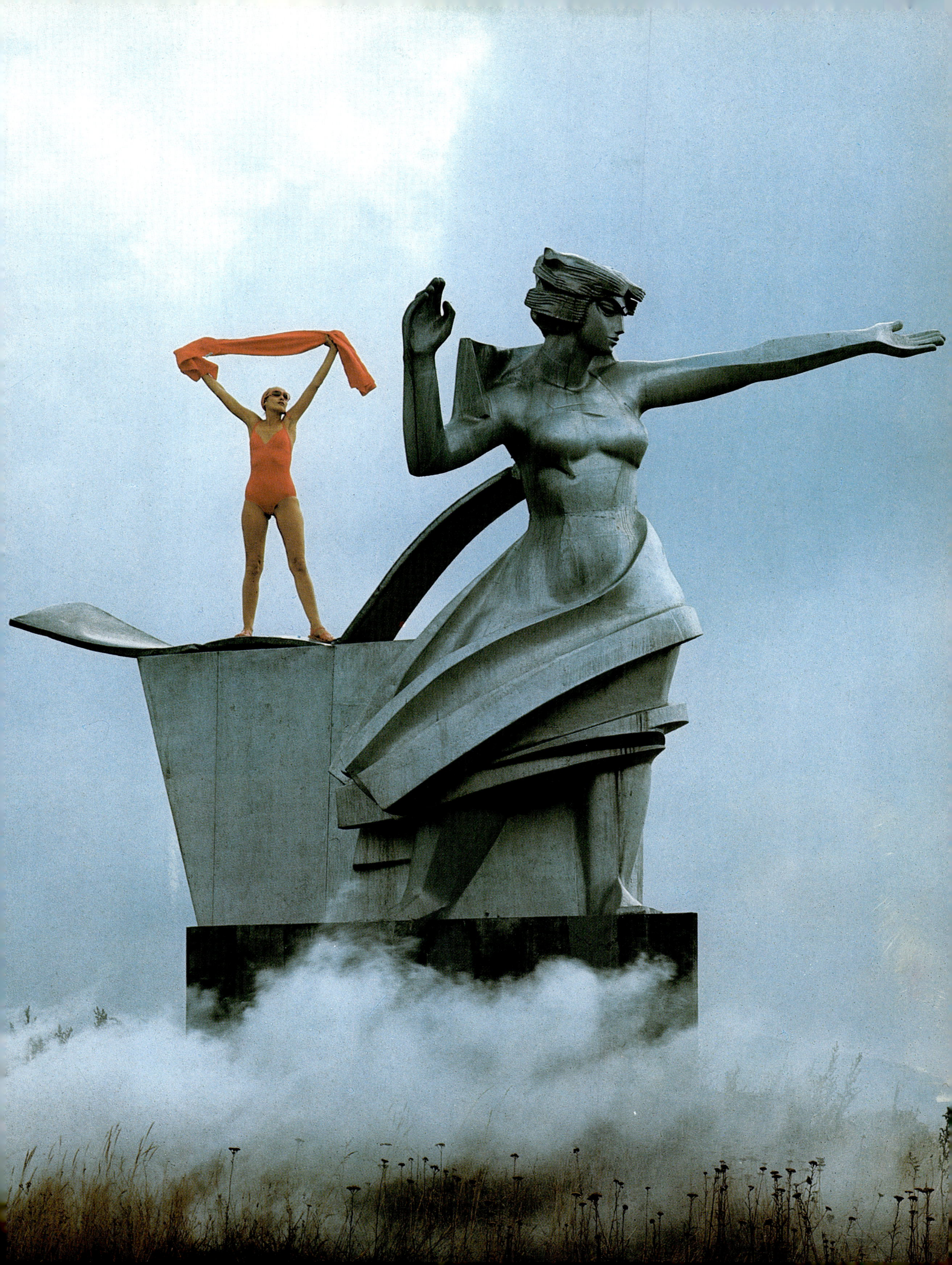

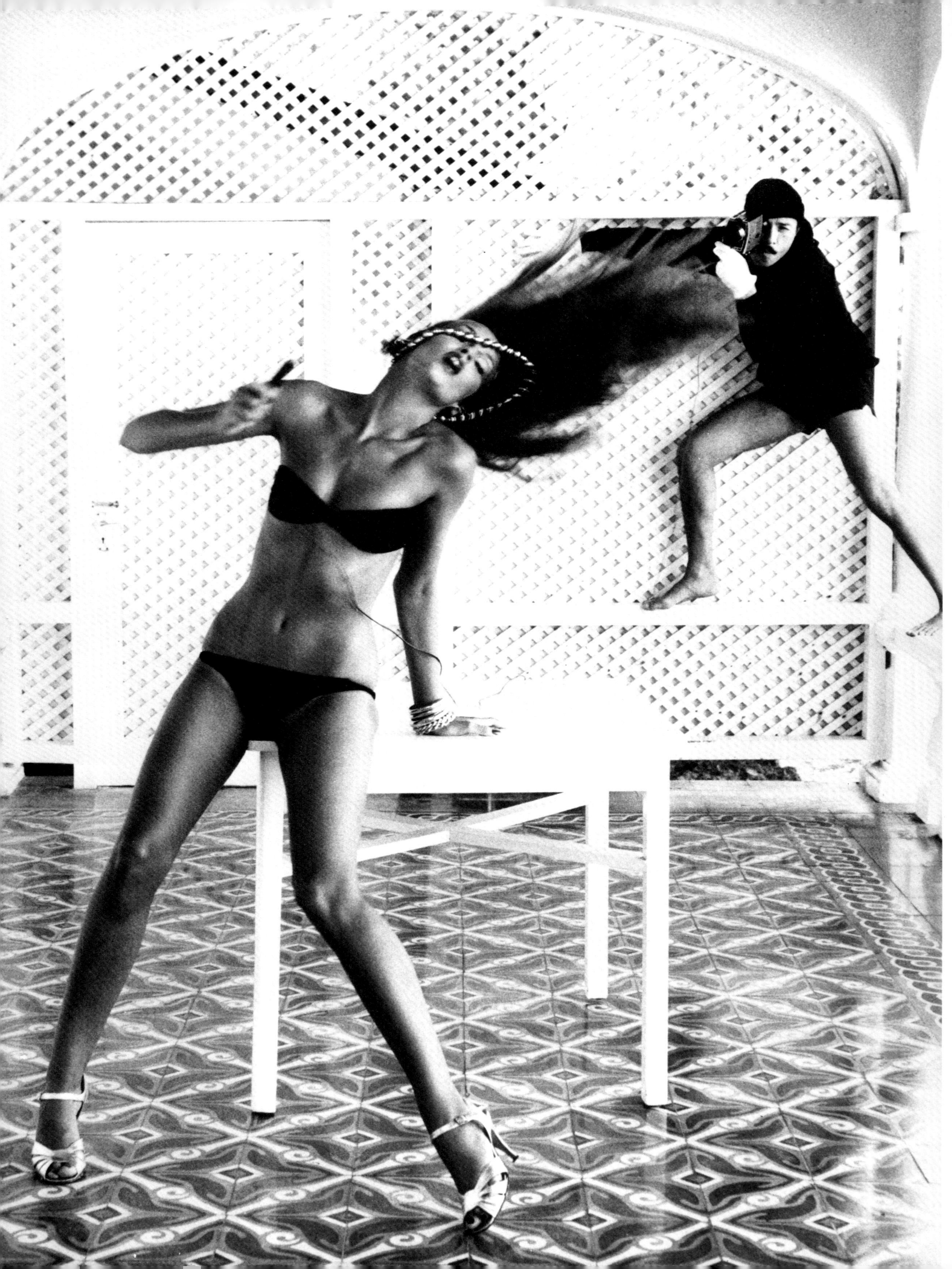

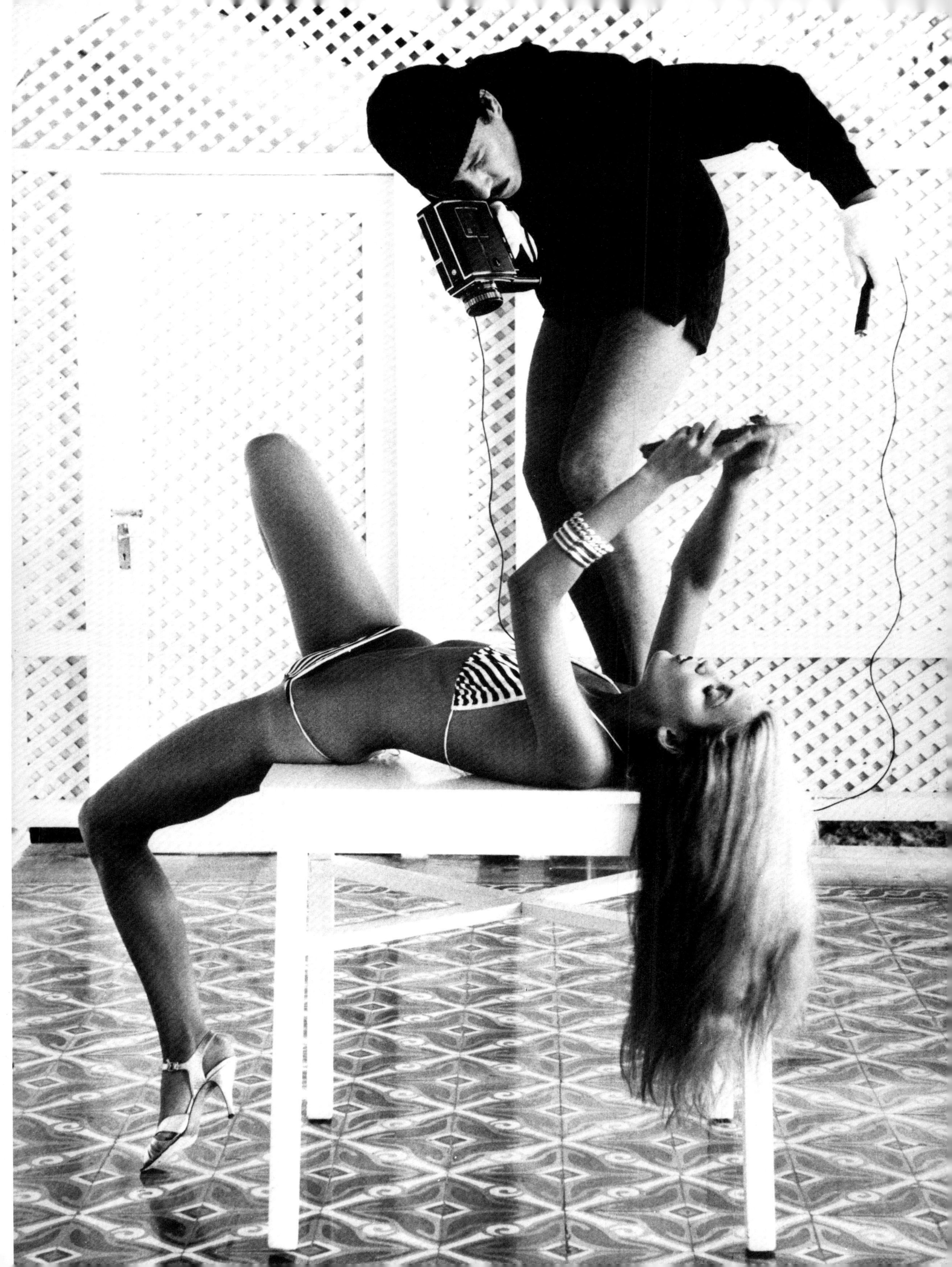

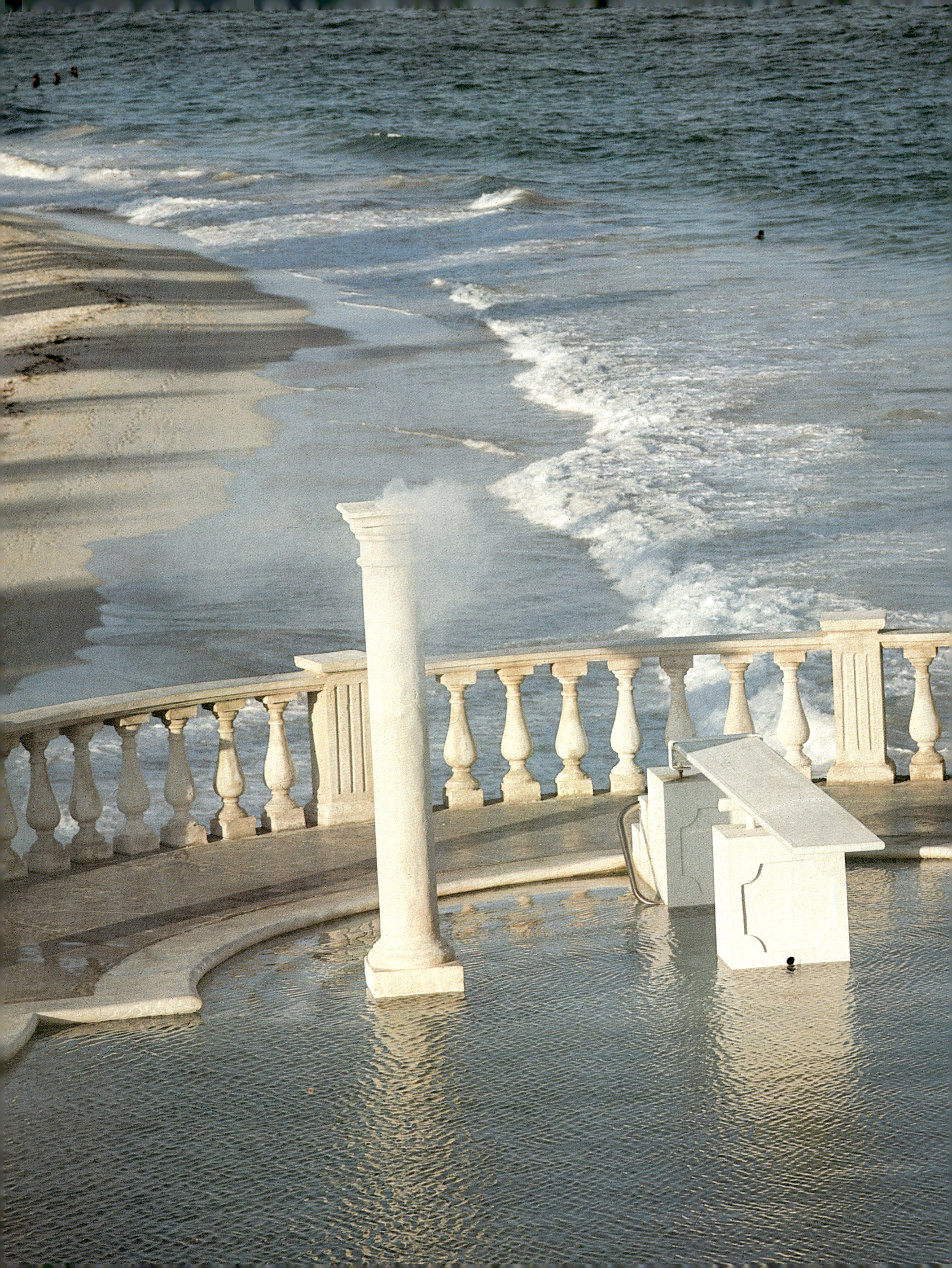

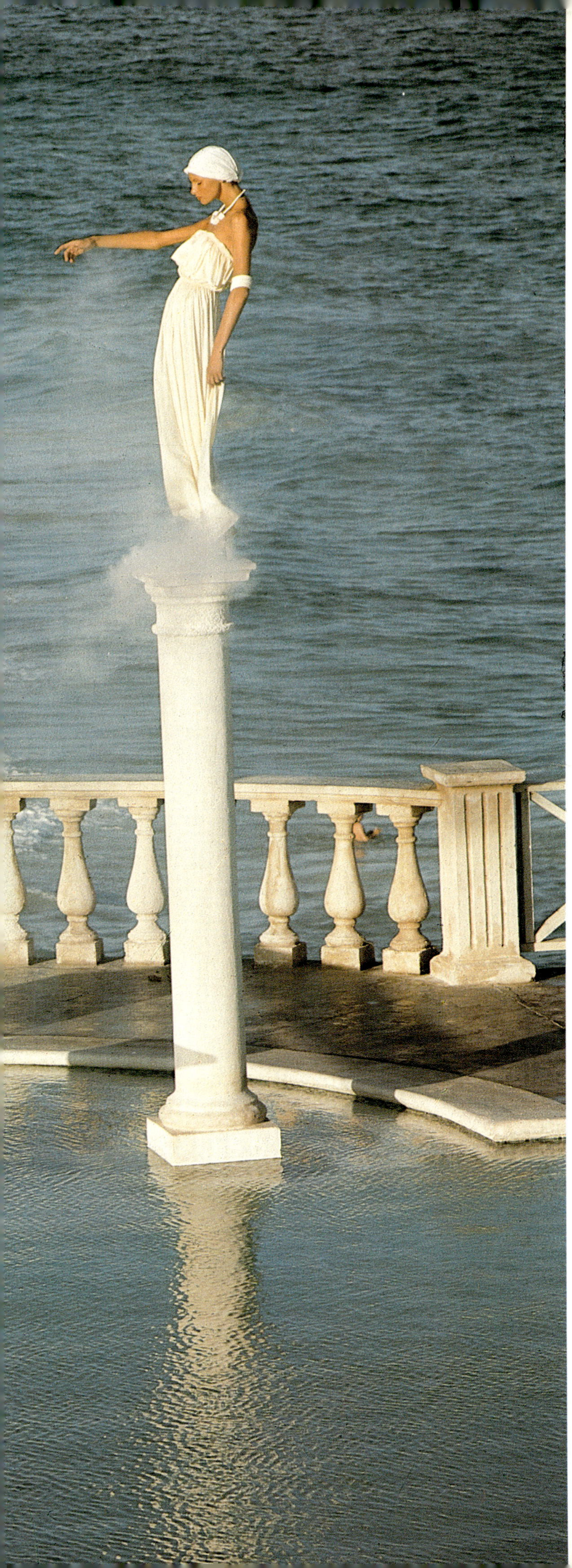

PLONYA

The maddest, the funniest, the hardest working model who ever earned a fortune was Apollonia van Ravenstein, or Plonya as she is known to half of us, Apples to the rest. She is still hard at it and looks wonderful at thirty-five. I give a private round of applause to this intrepid and fearless girl for she has given me two or three of the best ten pictures I will ever take. One of these was taken in the Seychelles, and is on page 143.

Plonya's courage and her willingness to try anything were scarcely better shown than on a trip made by a British *Vogue* team to Barbados. I had chosen to work at the Crane Beach Hotel which is on the east coast above the sea and has a particularly attractive pool layout. 'My dear Plonya,' I said gazing upwards, 'would you stand on top of that column if I get a ladder?' 'Why not?' she replied. 'What's so special about that column?' To get a better view of the sea beyond I had fixed my camera just below the hotel roof. We got two ladders and, just for the heck of it, decided to use up the smoke bombs we usually travel with.

Nobody who inspects the Crane Beach picture can believe that it is a straight photograph without tricks. 'Look,' they say, 'that model is not up there, it's too small and dangerous for her to stand, and the smoke is the giveaway – the smoke is used to cover the join where the two pictures have been put together.'

I wish now to announce publicly that it is, thanks to Plonya's spirit, a one-shot snap. Plonya was up the ladder in a trice and standing on the capital; my assistant followed her up with a smoke bomb and a cigarette lighter. Meanwhile someone else climbed up the second column with another smoke bomb. 'Light up,' I ordered. 'O.K. Get down the ladder and run with it out of shot.' They only had to do it three or four times and we had the picture.

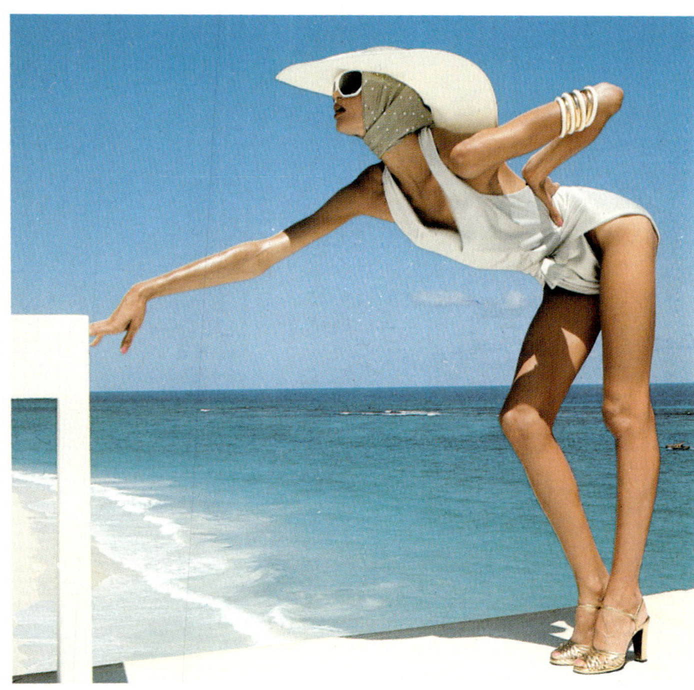

LEFT AND ABOVE *Apollonia van Ravenstein at the Crane Beach Hotel, Barbados, 1973*

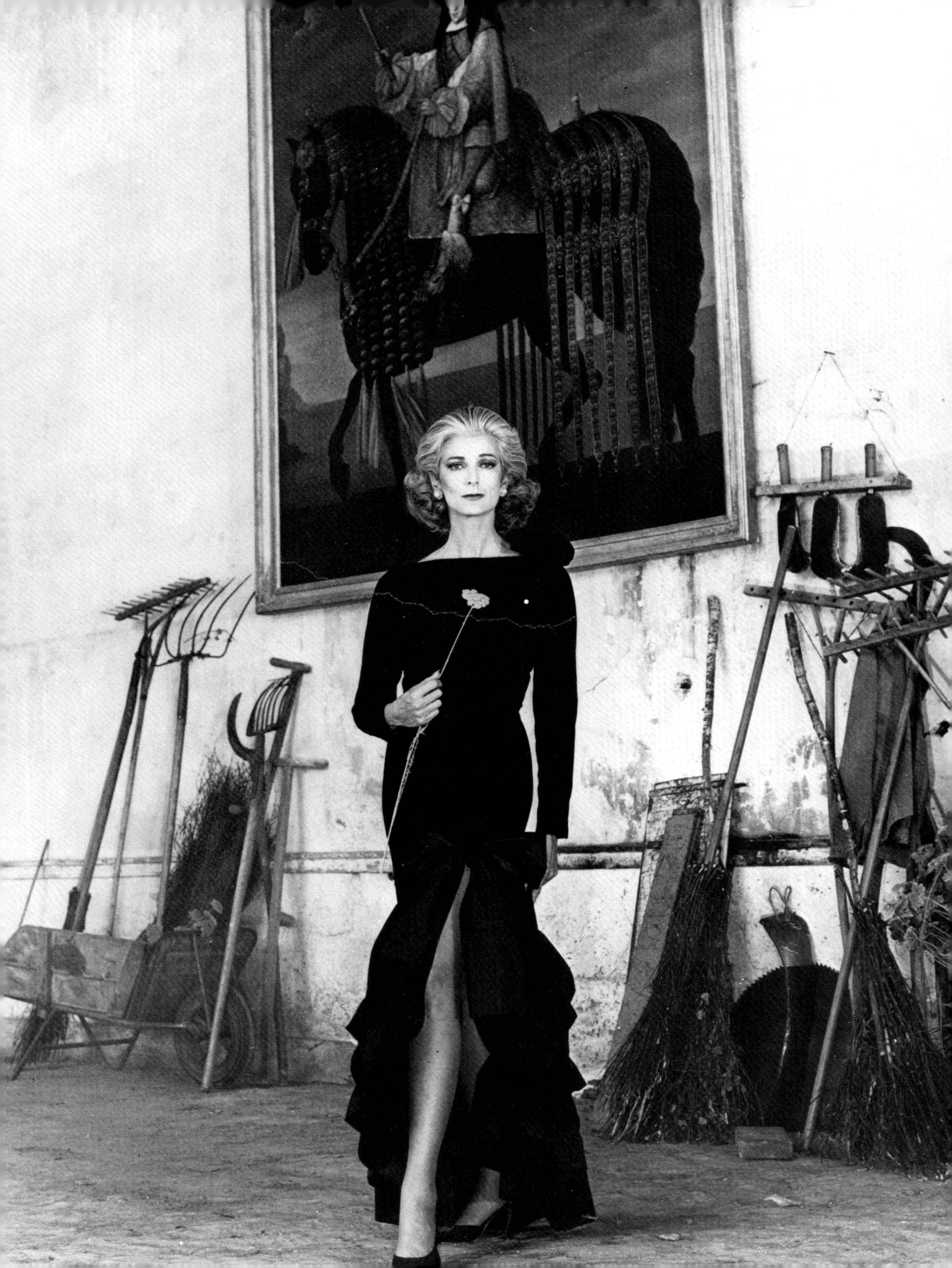

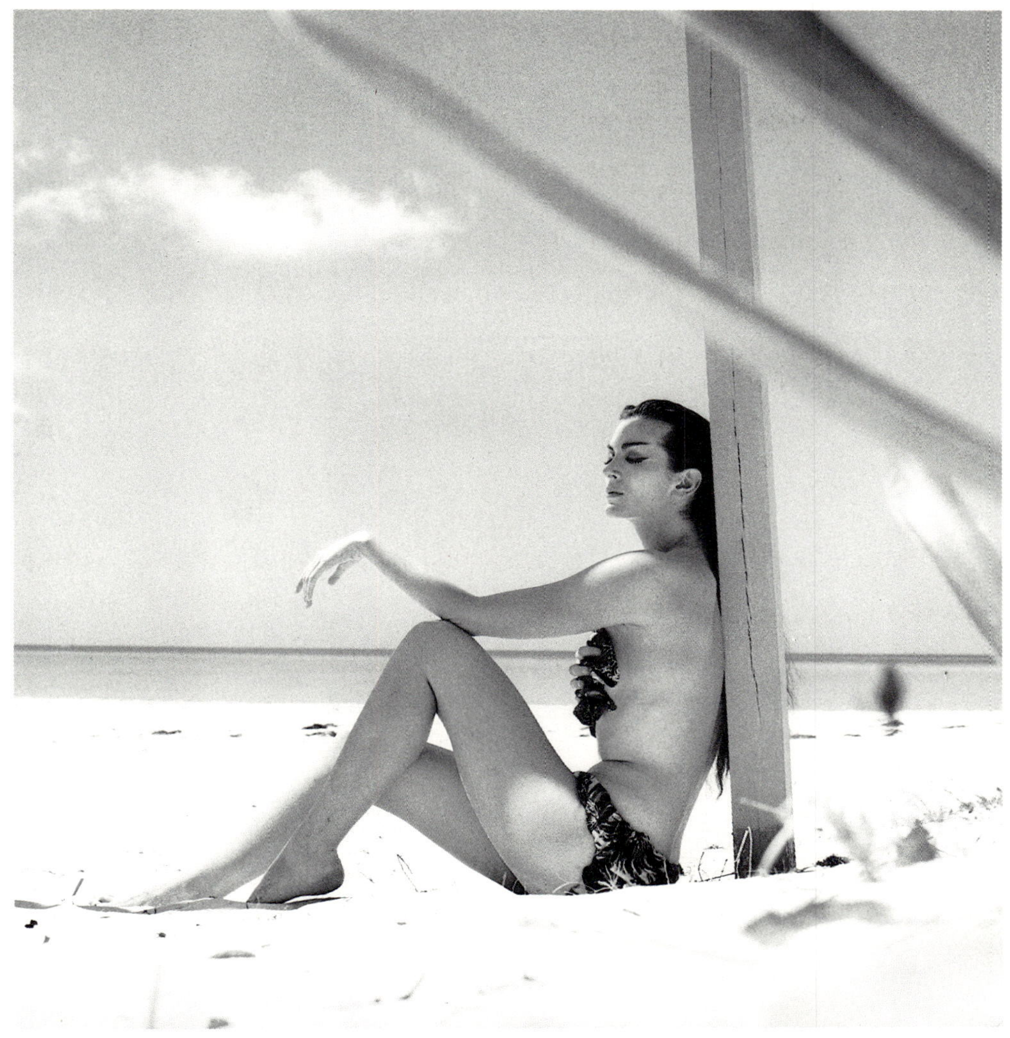

CARMEN

Carmen Dell'Orefice stroke Miles stroke Heimann stroke Kaplan, who has had three husbands and more hot dinner boyfriends than one cares to count later, is still known as just plain Carmen – though the plain has nothing whatsoever to do with her appearance.

When Carmen was thirteen, Mrs Landshoff found her on a Manhattan bus and scooped her up for a photographic session which achieved seven pages and a cover from the first day's shoot. The most famous of the first Carmen photographs were taken by Cecil Beaton, published in American *Vogue* in 1945 and again in *The Art and Technique of Colour Photography* in 1951. I was a latecomer to join the reverential Carmen queue with my camera. Together we did a lot of work for various *Vogues* in the early fifties.

Carmen is no longer a model – if she ever was – but is today the Empress answer to all those dressed-up teenager nymphets who find themselves zipped into Yves St Laurent ballgowns by fashion editors who are in mourning for their own brief youths. She has never forgotten that she inhabits a three score and ten leasehold body that requires constant maintenance, and she works at it relentlessly with massage, swimming and gymnastics. She is now fifty-two and holds every card in the pack.

If the Princess of Wales is a double Princess – larger than life, full of shy feminine charms, patently capable and potently Royal – then by this yardstick Carmen is a double female, hilariously funny but wise, electrically charged with the ability to reject the absurdity of the rat race circuit, always ready to lift those expressive, recently-European eyes to question the pompous or over-sycophantic. Carmen has been my best friend for over thirty years.

She was born to a timid and adorable Italian violinist and a powerful Hungarian. Her mother must have had a premonition that hers was no ordinary child. In 1945 Carmen had potential and promise but in the intervening years she has acquired an inimitable elegant maturity which I hope I have captured on these pages.

ABOVE *Carmen, Bahamas, 1959*
OPPOSITE *Carmen wearing a Chanel dress, 1980*

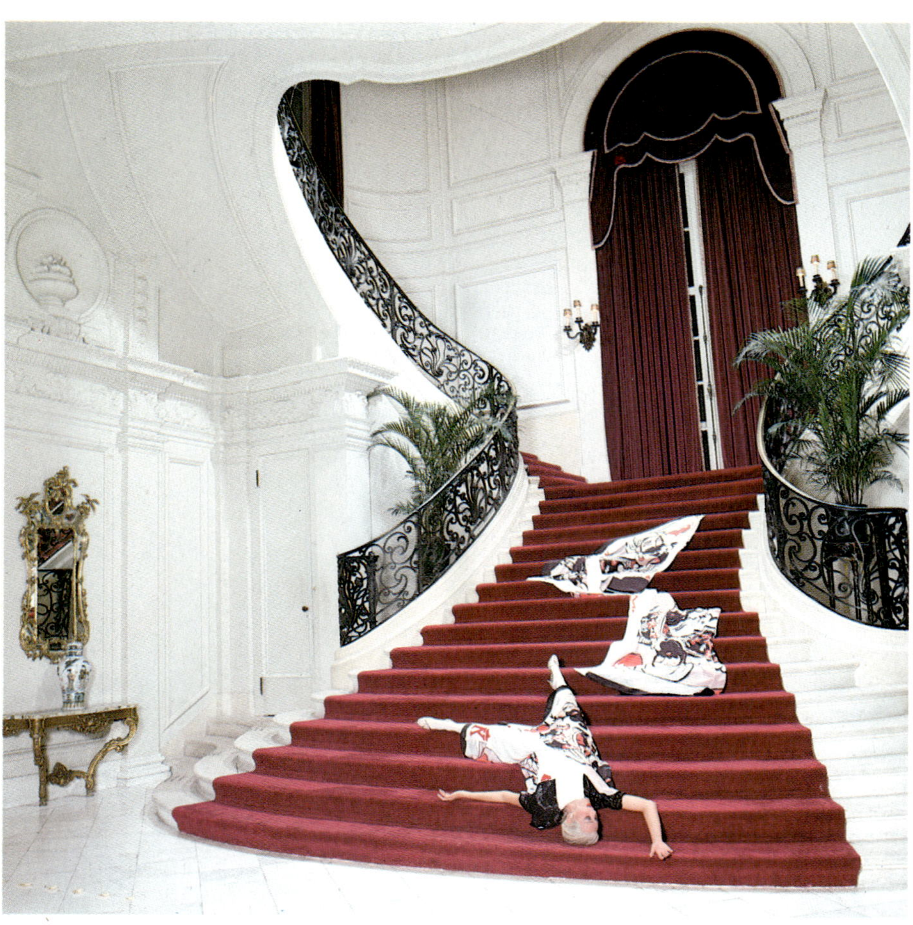

Carmen in a hand-painted dress by Michaele Vollbracht, Newport, R. I., 1981
RIGHT *Carmen in a dress by Dmitri Kritsas, with a mink coat by Maximilian, the Hearst Mansion, San Simeon, 1981*

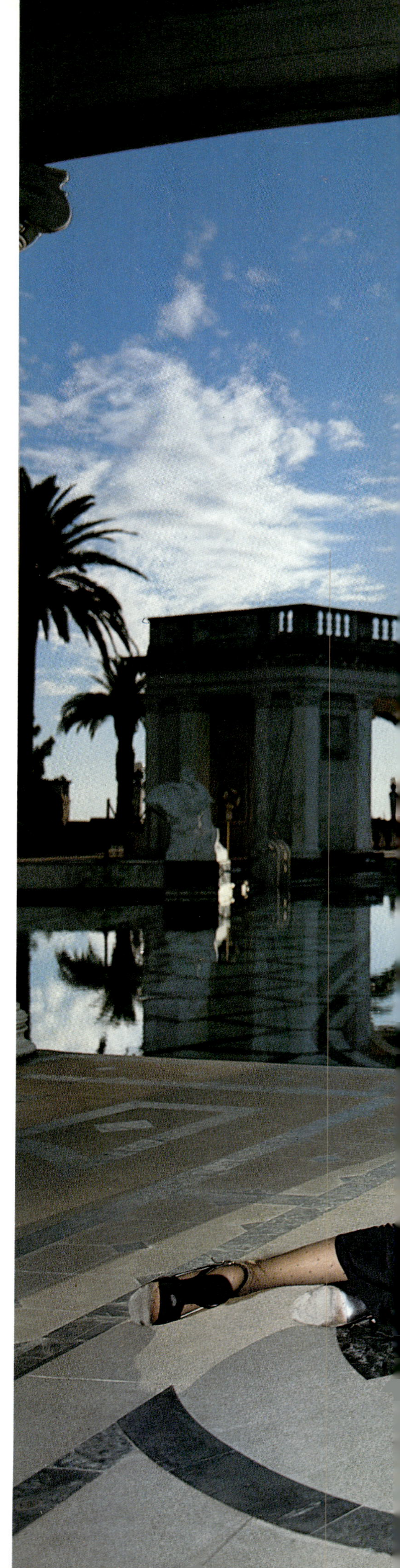

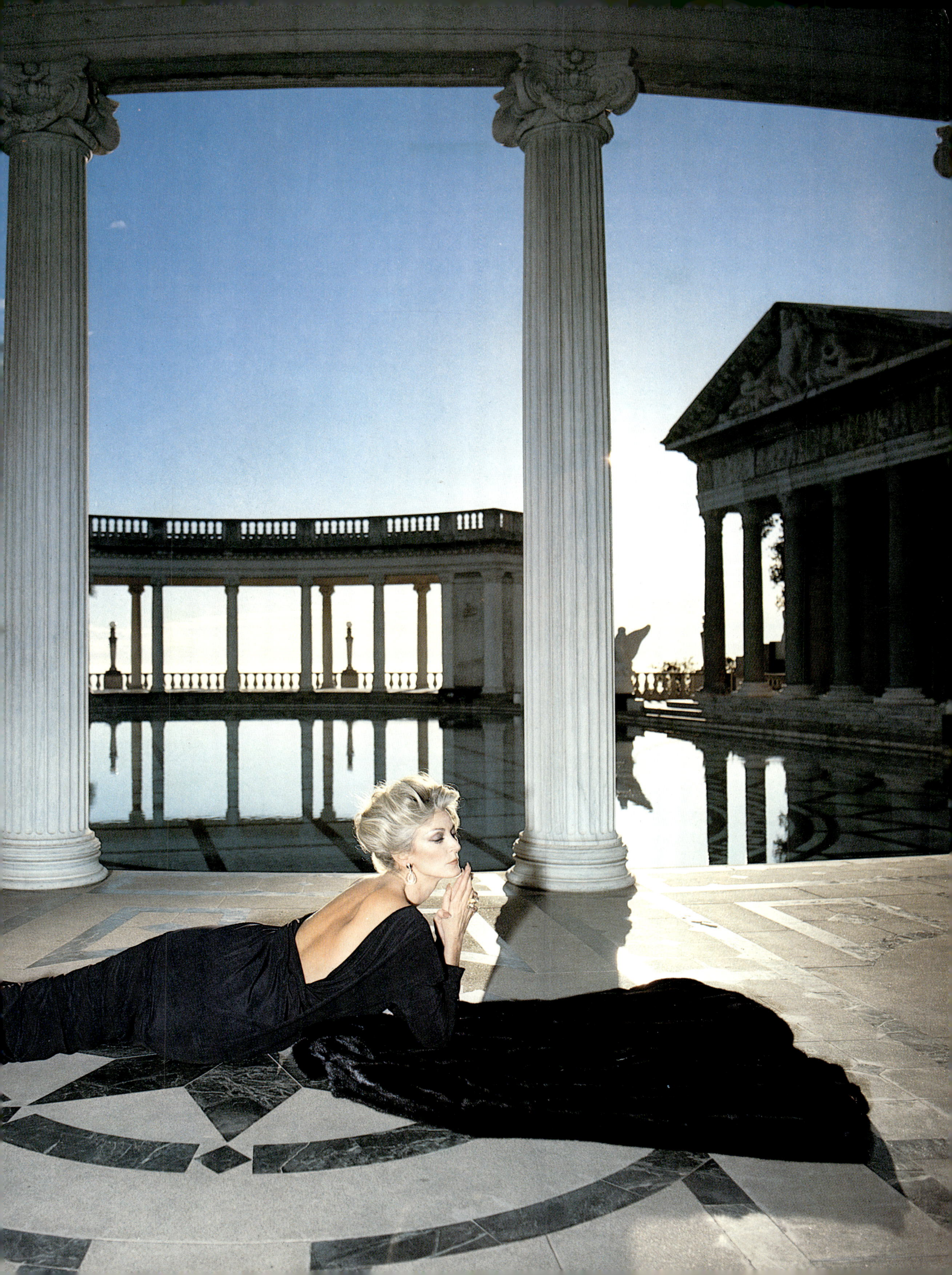